... if this item is overdue.
... ...le or telepho...
...his item type.

... when the library is

LIFE ROLES, VALUES, AND CAREERS

LIFE ROLES, VALUES, AND CAREERS

International Findings of the Work Importance Study

Edited by
Donald E. Super and Branimir Šverko
with assistance from
Charles M. Super

Jossey-Bass Publishers • San Francisco

Substantial discounts on bulk quantities of Jossey-Bass books are available to corporations, professional associations, and other organizations. For details and discount information, contact the special sales department at Jossey-Bass Inc., Publishers. (415) 433-1740; Fax (415) 433-0499.

For international orders, please contact your local Simon & Schuster International Office.

Library of Congress Cataloging-in-Publication Data

Life roles, values, and careers : international findings of the Work Importance Study / edited by Donald E. Super and Branimir Šverko with assistance from Charles M. Super. — 1st ed.

cm — (The Jossey-Bass social and behavioral science series)

Includes bibliographical references and index.

ISBN 0-7879-0100-8

1. Career development—Cross-cultural studies. 2. Work—Cross-cultural studies. 3. Sex role—Cross-cultural studies. 4. Social values—Cross-cultural studies. 5. Vocational guidance—Cross-cultural studies. I. Super, Donald E. (Donald Edwin), date.

HF5549.5.C35L54   1995

306.3'6—dc20   95-5488

                                                                       CIP

FIRST EDITION

HB Printing   10 9 8 7 6 5 4 3 2 1

070029830

Contents

List of Tables and Figures

Tables

Figures

Preface

This book addresses questions that are important to anthropologists, counselors, educators, psychologists, and sociologists, even to political scientists and politicians, from both national and cross-national perspectives. How we have addressed the questions, and the answers we propose, will be of interest to all who are concerned with how individuals in specific cultural and national contexts view work as part of their lives and with how these views influence their lives, their families, their communities, and ultimately their countries. To provide a glimpse of the content of this book, we list some of the questions here.

Do the same values exist, in the same hierarchical order, in traditionally capitalist and socialist countries? in Western and Eastern countries? in diverse ethnic and linguistic groups in the same country? And are life roles invariant across these social realms? Is the relative importance that women attach to their roles as homemakers and workers different in areas of long industrial tradition and in old agricultural but recently industrialized regions?

Are there any between-country distinctions *within* particular value domains? Is it possible to identify similar spiritual or religious values in countries with a recent communist past and those that have retained Roman Catholic traditions or are largely Protestant?

The objective of the international organizers of the Work Importance Study (WIS) was to examine work in the context of other, specific, major life roles, not just in contrast with leisure. In their original meeting, which I convoked at Wolfson College, Cambridge, England, in 1979, the organizers recognized that the current interest in the interrelationships of dual-career marriages, family formation and child rearing, citizenship, leisure, and education makes it imperative to identify specific roles, not just work and leisure.

A second objective was to develop instruments and insights useful in career counseling and in human resource development in business, industry, and government agencies. Career counseling once meant, and still means in some circles and some countries, vocational counseling. Similarly, human resource development has generally meant developing people to meet the employment needs of organizations. But since the 1950s, and later in some countries, counseling for also careers has come to mean not only counseling for occupational choice but also counseling for how people plan to use their lives, with attention to the variety of outlets provided (or denied) at work, in the home and family, in community activities, in leisure, and in study, for attaining goals within those roles and as activities that some people enjoy in and of themselves. Thus, counseling for human resource development has come to mean helping youths and adults of both genders to develop as competent and adaptable people for changing combinations of life roles, to be useful not only to an organization but to changing organizations, changing social conditions, and changing selves.

The instruments that the WIS identified as needed for counseling and for human resource development are measures of values and of the importance of the various life roles, called, for reasons made clear in Chapter Four, *role salience*. There were no existing measures of the salience of the major life roles. And as for values, the WIS organizers judged that work done on values in recent decades made it possible to develop not only a state-of-the-art instrument but also one that would be a truly cross-national measure that also would reflect the indigenous characteristics of each participating country, as described in Chapter Four and some of the national chapters that follow.

Although most of the WIS participants worked collectively and independently, using agreed-upon methods for cross-national development, the last two or three groups to join the project, either through a desire to catch up with the others or through the kind of communication failure that happens too easily in international work, merely adapted the existing instruments by using U.S. versions as models. The evidence suggests that no distortions resulted, but some unique values may have been missed in some countries or some roles may not have been well defined for that culture: the basic work had been European, North American, and Australian.

One distinguishing feature of the WIS methods is our emphasis on objective measurement and psychometrics. Survey techniques and interviews common in earlier work often relied heavily on one or two questions per variable studied. The WIS relied on psychometrically refined and treated inventories, pretested with enough items to provide scores that are internally consistent.

A final difference between the WIS and some other major studies is that we have not limited our subjects to "captive" subjects or to workers in one corporation, multinational although it might be. Like a few other projects, the WIS has sought the cooperation of subjects working in diverse representative settings as well as occupations, and of students in more or less representative secondary and higher education institutions: samples of convenience but well chosen. Not all of us were able to do this equally well. Our samples do vary, for in democracies, in decentralized systems, and in a world that lives with the pressures of time and money, researchers typically have little control over educational or industrial institutions. They must rely on goodwill, which is powerless against institutional constraints. Institutional and governmental policies sometimes change in ways helpful to research, at other times in ways that impede or prevent it. Nevertheless, the breadth of samples in the WIS is one of its strengths.

An overview of the contents of this lengthy book will help readers who want more than the table of contents offers but less than scanning chapters provides. Chapters One to Three are basic, theoretical, and oriented to the relevant scholarly literature; they deal with work, other roles, and values. Chapter Four presents the WIS history, greatly abbreviated.

In Part Two, Chapters Five through Fifteen are reports of the projects as conducted, and of their results, in each of the eleven member countries by the national teams, governmental and nongovernmental, many of them independent scholars.

Appendix A (the Values Scale) and Appendix B (the Salience Inventory) provide comprehensive presentations of the descriptive statistics for each of the national samples (except Israel, where the data became available too late), as well as for some of their pooled characteristics; the national chapters often refer the reader to the appendixes.

In Part Three, Chapters Sixteen through Twenty-five deal with studies of special cross-national or, in some cases, national topics of special interest. Here scholars in two or more countries have shared data with a colleague to examine some question of importance in special detail; some of the questions were proposed in WIS working conferences and some were identified independently. Again, the chapters refer frequently to the presentations of pooled data in the appendixes. Cross-national analyses of values by Šverko and by Trentini and associates are good examples of how these data can be used. Some assumptions, methods, and even conclusions in these chapters do not fully agree: the reader too must think and may derive from them important new insights or hypotheses.

In the final substantive chapter, which constitutes Part Four, the two senior coeditors of this book attempt a synthesis. This and the editing of individual chapters have not been easy tasks; in fact, the collaborative planning for common interests and methods does not guarantee uniformity in presentation, nor indeed in the reporting of some details. Nevertheless, we are pleased with the textured coherence, the sense of theme and variation, in the results we are able to bring together here—as well, we must comment, with the human process of this cross-national collaboration.

Acknowledgments are due especially to the national project directors who, all bilingual if not multilingual, worked creatively and harmoniously during the various stages of planning, execution, and reporting: except for that of the first Canadian leader, D. Stuart Conger, then of the Canadian

Employment and Immigration Commission, their names appear in Chapters Five through Fifteen. Two other national project directors played special roles in these efforts from the inception of the project: Professor José Ferreira-Marques of the University of Lisbon helped to plan the 1978 Munich symposium from which the project stemmed and has been an active leader and contributor since. Professor Branimir Šverko of the University of Zagreb joined the WIS at its first official meeting. He was referred to the project by Mr. Dragun Tarbuk of the Croatian Employment Service in response to a request for help in recruiting a leader from what was then Yugoslavia. Like other key people in the WIS, both Šverko and Ferreira-Marques could work not only in English, our agreed-upon language, but also in several other languages important in our cross-cultural work. Dr. Janice Lokan of the Australian Council for Educational Research in Hawthorn, Victoria, and Professors Rita Claes and Pol Coetsier of the University of Ghent, in Belgium, brought to our project valuable expertise in the techniques and management of large-scale research.

Unable to participate in the WIS because of his assumption of the duties of rector at the University of Lausanne, Professor Jean-Blaise Dupont has been a quiet but real source of support throughout, even lending his chalet high above Lake Geneva to Šverko, Ferreira-Marques, and me in January 1990 for a quiet week-long editorial retreat.

During its twelve-year history the WIS has been headquartered in several places because I moved during my "retirement": first at the National Institute for Careers Education and Counselling and Wolfson College of Cambridge University, England, with partial early funding from the European Research Office of the U.S. Army; then in the Department of Psychology at the University of Florida; and since then in the Department of Psychology at Armstrong State College, Savannah, Georgia, and in the Departments of Counseling at the University of Georgia and at the University of North Carolina at Greensboro. The tangible and intangible support of these institutions and their representatives has been invaluable.

Finally, two spouses, Olga Ferreira-Marques and Anne-Margaret "Peg" Super, were especially supportive as hosts at many of our meetings. Olga Ferreira-Marques, like her husband, is multilingual and at home in several countries. And my late wife, "multi-aural" and "multi-optical" if not multilingual, was my constant companion, host, resident critic, and source of encouragement; her presence in this final stage of the project is greatly missed.

The central thread of the tapestry that is this volume is the observation that the various roles each contain distinctive challenges and distinctive opportunities for the fulfillment of values. The roles, and a person's ability to fulfill them, shift with development, with age and stage. The Work Importance Study spans the last phase of my own career development. The process of career can be told as science, as this volume aims to do, or it can be told as narrative or life history, as we close this preface. In either case it is developmental. The roles shift. The focus of life shifts. The challenges and rewards, the sources and uses of energy—all these are altered. Because the WIS book was not finished, I invited my son, a developmental psychologist, to become the third editor as the work—indeed my life's work—neared completion. This too is a study in the importance of work.

Savannah, Georgia   Donald E. Super
September 1993

About the Editors

Donald E. Super, professor emeritus of psychology and education at Teachers College, Columbia University, died in June 1994. He had been active in completing this volume as international coordinator of the Work Importance Study, based in the Department of Psychology at the University of Florida. He was also actively affiliated with the University of Georgia and Armstrong State College (in Savannah, Georgia) and served as consultant to various government agencies, corporations, and educational institutions. Professor Super served as a consulting editor for several American, British, and international psychological journals, and he was the author or coauthor of such books as *Appraising Vocational Fitness, The Psychology of Careers, Computer-Assisted Counseling, Measuring Vocational Maturity,* and *Career Development in Britain.* He wrote or coauthored several widely used psychological tests for vocational counseling and personnel selection. He was an honorary fellow of the National Institute for Careers Education and Counselling in Cambridge, England, and was its director for three years while a fellow of Wolfson College, Cambridge University. Professor Super had served as president of several international and American organizations in the fields of psychology and education. In 1983, he received the American Psychological Association's Award for Distinguished Scientific Contributions to Applications of Psychology, and he received a Doctor of Science degree from Oxford University.

Branimir Šverko is professor of psychology at the University of Zagreb, Croatia, where he teaches work and organizational psychology. He was born in 1938 and obtained his doctoral degree in psychology in 1973 at the University of Zagreb. In 1975 he was the recipient of the Fulbright-Hays Fellowship Award and spent a year as a senior research scholar at the University of Illinois at Urbana–Champaign. He holds the chair for industrial psychology and ergonomics in the Psychology Department of the University of Zagreb. Professor Šverko is the author of more than seventy journal articles, monographs, and research reports. His research interests range from human performance and ability assessment to work motivation and job satisfaction. He has been the recipient of the Yugoslav Psychological Association Award for Outstanding Contribution in Psychology and the Croatian Psychological Society Award for Outstanding Research.

Charles M. Super is professor of human development and family studies at Pennsylvania State University. He is also an associate in practice at the Child, Adult, and Family Psychological Center in State College, Pennsylvania. He was previously at Harvard University and the Judge Baker Children's Center in Boston, Massachusetts. He has carried out research on child development and family life in the Netherlands, Kenya, Zambia, Guatemala, Colombia, Haiti, and Bangladesh, as well as in the United States. His writings have been published in psychological, anthropological, and medical journals, as well as in numerous volumes on child development. He is the editor of *The Role of Culture in Developmental Disorder* and coeditor (with Sara Harkness) of *Parents' Cultural Belief Systems: Sociocultural Origins and Developmental Consequences.* Professor Charles Super has served as consultant or committee member for the Social Science Research Council (U.S.), WHO, UNESCO, and UNICEF.

List of Contributors

Massimo Bellotto
Università degli Studi di Padova
Padova, Italy

Maria Cristina Bolla
Sintagma
Milan, Italy

Catherine Casserly
Occupational and Career Information
Human Resources Development Canada
Ottawa/Hull, Canada

Rita Claes
Department of Personnel Management, Work and Organizational
    Psychology
University of Ghent
Ghent, Flanders, Belgium

Pol Coetsier
Department of Personnel Management, Work and Organizational
    Psychology
University of Ghent
Ghent, Flanders, Belgium

J. Ferreira-Marques
Faculty of Psychology and Education
University of Lisbon
Lisbon, Portugal

George Fitzsimmons
Department of Educational Psychology
University of Alberta
Edmonton, Alberta, Canada

David J. Gouws
South Africa

Andrew S. Harvey
St. Mary's University
Halifax, Canada

Elzbieta M. Hornowska
Institute of Psychology
Adam Mickiewicz University
Poznań, Poland

Željko Jerneić
Department of Psychology
University of Zagreb
Zagreb, Croatia

Edgar Krau
Department of Psychology
Tel Aviv University
Tel Aviv, Israel

Alija Kulenović
Department of Psychology
University of Zagreb
Zagreb, Croatia

Ronelle Langley
University of Pretoria
Pretoria, South Africa

Janice J. Lokan
Australian Council for Educational Research
Camberwell, Victoria, Australia

Donald Macnab
PsiCan Consulting Ltd.
Edmonton, Alberta, Canada

Grace Martin
Psychology Department
Armstrong State College
Savannah, Georgia

Toshiki Mikawa
Department of Psychology
Otemon-Gaknin University
Osaka, Japan

Antonino Miragliotta
University of Palermo
Palermo, Italy

M. J. Miranda
Faculty of Psychology and Education
University of Lisbon
Lisbon, Portugal

Giovanni Battista Muzio
Sintagma
Milan, Italy

Nobuo Nakanishi
Faculty of Human Sciences
Osaka University
Suita, Osaka, Japan

Andres Nazario, Jr.
University of Florida
Gainesville, Florida

Dorothy D. Nevill
Department of Psychology
University of Florida
Gainesville, Florida

Wladislaw J. Paluchowski
Institute of Psychology
Adam Mickiewicz University
Poznań, Poland

Marisa Sangiorgi
Sintagma
Milan, Italy

Meredith Shears
Careers Centre
Swinburne University
Hawthorn, Victoria, Australia

Giovanni Sprini
Department of Psychology
University of Palermo
Palermo, Italy

Giancarlo Trentini
University of Venice
Venice, Italy

Vlasta Vizek-Vidović
Department of Psychology
University of Zagreb
Zagreb, Croatia

LIFE ROLES,
VALUES,
AND CAREERS

PART ONE

Introduction

Part One of this volume presents the background for the Work Importance Study. Chapter One reviews the current state of understanding of the human aspects of work from the worker's perspective, that is, about the meaning of work. Chapter Two summarizes a diverse body of theory on the roles people take throughout their lives, ideas that are not often put together for the use of what in Europe are called *work psychologists* and, in North America, *industrial/organizational psychologists* or *vocational psychologists*, depending on whether their primary focus is on organizations and the people in them or on the people who may move into and out of the organized labor force. Understanding multiple roles is essential to understanding people, not only at work but also at play, at school or university, or in the home. Chapter Three deals with the more familiar topic of values, but it seeks to place values within the more general schema of personality. Finally, Chapter Four introduces the Work Importance Study directly, describing its origins, objectives, design, and procedures.

How well the Work Importance Study was able at the outset to select the critical issues in the current state of knowledge of roles, values, and the meaning of work set ultimate constraints on the success of the project, as is always the case in major scientific undertakings. The interested reader may profit from examining the relationship of the state of knowledge, as reviewed here in Part One, to the project as it finally evolved as the Work Importance Study.

ONE

Studies of the Meaning of Work: Approaches, Models, and Some of the Findings

Branimir Šverko
Vlasta Vizek-Vidović

The issues concerning the meaning of work for an individual are often discussed in different contexts, from social sciences to politics, art, and religion. Yet the definitions of the meaning-of-work concept usually remain unclear and ambiguous. Basically, the concept refers to the set of general beliefs about work held by an individual, who acquires them through interaction with the social environment. It is generally assumed that the beliefs are related to the person's career orientation and behavior in the work situation, including job performance, turnover, absenteeism, and job satisfaction. Therefore beliefs about work have received continuing attention from researchers of both vocational and organizational behavior.

Three main approaches mark the study of the meaning of work in social sciences. Some researchers have attempted to capture the meaning of work for individuals by studying their work values or goals that they try to attain through their work. Another line of research has focused on the examination of the importance of work in people's lives, using such concepts as work involvement and work salience. And the third approach has tried to analyze the effects of work alienation, a hypothetical state arising from the lack of opportunities for self-fulfillment in work. This chapter discusses the three approaches and presents findings after a short overview of the meaning of work in the past and today.

The Meaning of Work in the Past and at Present

Because beliefs about work do not belong to the category of innate predisposition but stem from everyday experience, they are largely determined by sociocultural factors. In other words, great differences in the meaning of work are observable across different societies and cultures, as well as in different historical periods. In Western civilization the meaning assigned to work has been mainly shaped within the framework of the Judeo-Christian religious tradition.

According to Tilgher (1930/1962), the ancient Greeks regarded work as a curse or necessary evil reserved only for slaves and the poor and believed that the aristocratic elite should avoid it. Later on, mainly under the influence of religious indoctrination, such negative attitudes toward work gradually changed. Although the Hebrews also viewed work as a painful necessity, they added the notion that it was a punishment for original sin. Early Christians followed the Jewish tradition but also developed a concept of work as a means of redemption. They attached no intrinsic value to work: it served only to fulfill noble ends. With the advent of Catholicism, new and positive aspects of work were stressed: work was good for the moral and spiritual integrity of people, whereas leisure and idleness brought about all kinds of weaknesses and evils. The Reformation was the period of the greatest glorification of work. Martin Luther preached that to work hard and devoutly was the best way to serve God. To him, a job was a "calling," and he regarded work as a path to salvation. John Calvin developed the ideas further: work became a religious obligation and the highest virtue. According to Calvin, all human beings, without exception, must work, but they must not enjoy the products of their effort. The teachings of Luther and Calvin soon became widely accepted, giving rise to a moral code known as the Protestant ethic. The ideas of Protestant theologians underlay the nineteenth-century cult of work, which regarded all pleasure and idleness with disapproval: to them the goal of work was perfection in a person's occupation. The spirit of this age led Max Weber (1922) to formulate his famous and controversial thesis about the causal relationship between the Protestant work ethic and the growth of capitalism.

A general belief about the centrality of the work role in the lives of most people prevails in contemporary Western societies. The notion is supported by assumptions about the multiplicity of functions or meanings of work for an individual. According to various authors (e.g., Friedman & Havighurst, 1954; Morse & Weiss, 1955; Steers & Porter, 1979), work has four distinct functions. First, work has an economic function: people work in order to earn a living, for themselves and their dependents. Second, work has an important social function: it enables people to interact, meet, and be with one another. In fact, many employed people spend more time interacting with colleagues at work than with friends or members of their families. Third, work is a source of social status and prestige: people's positions in society depend largely on what they do at work. Fourth, work has an important psychological function in terms of its intrinsic meaning for an individual: it is an essential source of identity, self-esteem, and self-fulfillment. If we accept the view that all four functions to a greater or lesser extent determine the significance of work in the life of every individual, we have reason to accept an expanded thesis about the central role of work in the life of an individual.

However, the validity of this assumption may not be universal; it may not apply to all people. Doubts spring partly from the widespread notion that the jobs performed by a large part of the working population are not creative. The technological rationalization of human work has been accompanied both by the fragmentation or division of labor and by the increasing complexity and bureaucratization of organizations. As a result, work has become—for at least part of the working population—a monotonous, repetitive, and seemingly meaningless routine. Some people see such work as debasing, which seriously jeopardizes its meaning and psychological function at a time when improved living standards and better education have led to increasing aspirations for more stimulating jobs.

The rise in the general educational level has had yet another consequence: it has weakened religious indoctrination, which in some countries attaches great value to hard work and thus supports a general orientation to work. Since roughly the mid-1970s these countries have much debated "the crisis of the work ethic," one symptom of which, so the argument goes, is the value system of young people, who seem increasingly to prefer leisure to work. Such debates have stimulated interest in empirical research on the meaning and importance of work.

Work Values: What Do People Seek in Their Jobs?

Values are organized sets of general beliefs, opinions, and attitudes about what is preferable, right, or simply good in life. The dynamic approach to values assumes that they form a certain organization of a person's needs, desires, and goals, hierarchically structured according to their relative importance and priorities. Because such organization helps individuals in their orientation, decision making, and integration of activities, values can be conceived of as specific priority criteria that direct human behavior.

Values are hypothetical constructs, helpful in the analysis of human behavior, but they cannot be observed directly. They become recognizable only by analyzing the goals that a person considers important and strives to attain in life. Therefore, we operationally define values as general and relatively stable goals that an individual tries to attain. And we use the term *work values* to describe the general and relatively stable goals that people try to reach through work.

People try to attain a variety of goals or values in their work, including economic security and material rewards, social interaction, social status, and self-fulfillment. Researchers have attempted to gain insight into the relative importance of values and their hierarchical organization by examining individual preferences for different aspects of work content and context. What do people seek in their jobs? Which values dominate their work lives? Do they seek self-fulfillment and intrinsic job satisfaction or only economic rewards and material security? The answers are significant not only from the theoretical point of view but also for their important implications for the strategies of work organization.

Most studies in the field have tried to compare the relative importance of the so-called intrinsic values, those concerning job content and work itself, with the so-called extrinsic values of the work context, such as physical conditions at the workplace, salary, and prestige. For several reasons the results thus far provide no unanimous and definitive answers and no common priorities to the goals that people strive to realize through their work.

The first reason for the lack of definitive results is methodological, and it concerns difficulties that arise from the use of self-report measures in the study of values. The differences in the formulations of the questions that appear in different instruments can influence the value hierarchies. Furthermore, the subjects' reports about what is important to them (declared values) do not necessarily correspond to the value priorities that actually influence their behavior (operative values). Sometimes people are not aware of their values, and sometimes they are simply not honest, trying to gain social approval by hiding their true motives.

The second reason concerns the dynamic nature of values. Although values are usually operationalized as relatively stable goals, situational as well as personal factors can significantly affect their position in the prevailing hierarchy. Changes in the labor market, social policy, and educational or promotional opportunities can influence people to redefine their goals, as can internal changes connected with the maturation process or psychophysical health and the feeling of well-being.

Finally, generalizations of value hierarchies are difficult because of the great differences between individuals and between groups. For example, one variable clearly found to have a significant moderating effect on value ratings is occupational level. It has been consistently shown (Centers, 1948; Fridlander, 1965; Centers & Bugental, 1966; Fein, 1977) that subjects at higher occupational levels express a greater degree of orientation to self-fulfillment, whereas subjects at lower occupational levels are more often extrinsically oriented, stressing the importance of material rewards and security.

Work Involvement and Work Salience: Two Approaches to the Study of Work Importance

Insight into work values helps researchers to understand the qualitative aspect of the meaning of work for an individual. The analysis of work values reveals why people work or what they seek in their jobs, but it says little about the quantitative side: the *importance* of work in the life of an individual. To get a closer look at the quantitative aspects of meaning of work, researchers have generated such concepts as work (or job) involvement and work salience.

Work Involvement

In their extensive 1977 review of research on job involvement, Rabinowitz and Hall pointed out that although work involvement has been described in about a dozen different terms, researchers have taken two distinct approaches: one describes work involvement as a component of self-image and the other describes it as a performance–self-esteem contingency.

In one of the first studies dealing with the concept of work involvement, Lodahl and Kejner (1965) offered both definitions as equally valid. One definition, which says that work involvement "is the degree to which a person is identified psychologically with his work, or the importance of work in his total self-image," (p. 24) belongs to the first category. Later on, the authors offered another definition, which identifies work involvement "as the degree to which a person's performance affects his self-esteem" (p. 25). The second definition seems to more closely capture the idea of intrinsic motivation. Lawler and Hall (1970), who relied on the first approach, established the existence of work involvement as an independent factor, different from intrinsic work motivation and job satisfaction. They defined this construct as "the degree to which the job situation is central to the person and his identity," or as "psychological identification with one's work" (pp. 310–311).

On the other hand, the definition of work involvement as a performance–self-esteem contingency contains a certain similarity to an earlier attempt to study work importance by analyzing a person's "central life interests" (Dubin, 1956), which would define work involvement as the degree to which a person's work represents his or her central life interest. According to Dubin, work-involved people see work as a significant part of life, and events at their jobs strongly affect their other activities. For people who are not work-involved, central life interests lie elsewhere—their identities and self-images do not depend upon excellence of performance or success at work.

In psychological terms the concept of work involvement is an attitude. Saleh (1981) pointed out that work involvement can be described as a self-involving attitude, with the term *self* implying two things: that the construct does not refer to a group but to an individual, and that it deals with a central attitude, essential for a person's self-concept or self-image.

Several attitude scales have been developed to measure the construct of work involvement. The best known is by Lodahl and Kejner (1965): it has been used in its original or adapted version by other researchers in a number of studies. In its final psychometrically refined version, the scale consists of twenty Likert-type items with four categories of response. Adequate internal consistency coefficients have been obtained, but the hypothesized factorial unidimensionality of the scale has not been confirmed. Comparing the factorial structure across two samples (nurses and engineers), Lodahl and Kejner (1965) remarked that work involvement is a multidimensional variable, with at least three dimensions.

In an attempt to clarify and redefine the construct of work involvement, Kanungo (1979, 1981, 1982) provided an insightful critique of Lodahl and Kejner's scale. He asserted that the difficulties in measuring work involvement originate from ambiguity and confusion in the definition of the concept and noted several conceptual problems in the existing literature.

First, the definition makes no clear distinction between involvement in a particular job and involvement in work in general. Lodahl and Kejner's scale contains items that refer to both aspects of the concept. Whereas the item "I'm late for work pretty often" describes behavior connected mostly with a particular job (job involvement), the item "I would probably keep working even if I didn't need money" reflects a general attitude toward work (work involvement). Kanungo (1982) assumed that these are two different dimensions and went on to prove it by using factor analysis. The difference between the two aspects of involvement may be rooted in their genesis: job involvement is seen as relating to the degree of actual need satisfaction provided by the particular job, whereas work involvement is believed to reflect the centrality of work in a person's life, which is mainly a function of cultural conditioning, or socialization.

The second problem arises from the inadequate distinction between work involvement and intrinsic motivation. Thus in Lodahl and Kejner's scale the item "I live, eat, and breathe my job" refers clearly to involvement, whereas the item "Sometimes I'd like to kick myself for the mistakes I make in my work" refers more to performance–self-esteem contingencies, relevant to intrinsic motivation. Kanungo disputed the popular belief that job involvement is primarily a function of the possibility that a job can satisfy a person's intrinsic needs and argued that job involvement depends upon the person's perception of the job's possibilities to satisfy all needs, both intrinsic and extrinsic. Therefore, Kanungo asserted, the definition of job involvement should not be limited to the domain of intrinsic motivation, which Lawler and Hall (1970) also supported.

Whereas job involvement is often wrongly identified with intrinsic motivation, work involvement is sometimes confused with the Protestant work ethic. Some authors have tended to tie work involvement closely to the Protestant ethic (Dubin, 1956; Lodahl & Kejner, 1965) or to the corresponding middle-class norms (Blood & Hulin, 1967). The socialization of values inherent in the Protestant ethic may bring about strong work involvement, but it is quite certain that different socialization processes, supported by norms other than those of Protestantism, can also result in an orientation to work as a central life interest.

Some authors have not distinguished work involvement as a psychological state, with its sources or antecedents, from its effects or consequences. To illustrate this, Kanungo (1979) cited the following items from Saleh and Hosek's scale (1976): "What opportunity do you have to perform your work as you like?" (source); "I try to avoid extra duties and responsibilities" (effect); and "The most important things I do are concerned with my work" (work involvement as a state).

Finally, it is not quite clear whether job involvement is predominantly a cognitive or an affective state. In Lodahl and Kejner's scale (1965), the following item refers to affective response: "The major satisfaction in my life comes from my job." Another item depicts work involvement as a cognitive state: "The most important things that happen to me involve my work." Kanungo (1982) assumed that work involvement is primarily a cognitive state of the person's psychological identification with work, whereas affective as well as behavioral reactions are consequences of this state.

Kanungo's analysis of the work involvement construct (1982) aroused considerable interest and served as a starting point for further research. Although his contribution to the explanation of the construct is unquestionable, we must warn against the excessively restrictive character of his notion of work involvement as solely cognitive. Excluding the affective and behavioral components of work involvement necessarily means a more limited pool of involvement indicators that may be used as instrument items. The result may be a decreased level of instrument reliability, predictive validity, and predictability. Saal (1981) found that the total score of Lodahl and Kejner's scale, as compared with a partial score based only on cognitive items, shows correlation profiles similar to those of other variables, but the sizes of the correlation coefficient differ significantly: partial scores have lower correlations with other variables, a difference that was greater in situations in which the small number of items lowered the reliability. In fact, attitude theory presumes that each attitude is a multidimensional construct consisting of three distinct components: cognitive, affective, and conative. If we have agreed to regard work involvement as an attitude, there is no reason that we should not consider all three components. Saleh (1981) has adopted this view. The authors of the WIS project also adopted this view in our conceptualization of work salience.

Studies dealing with work involvement have proceeded in three main directions. The first group of researchers views work involvement as an individual variable and examines its relationship with various characteristics, such as age, sex, social and economic status, education, job tenure, marital status, value orientation, and numerous personality traits. The second group of studies views work involvement as a situational variable and examines its relationship with such variables as job characteristics relevant for intrinsic motivation, supervisory behavior, social climate at work, participation in decision making, and position within organizational hierarchy. The third group of researchers analyzes the consequences of work involvement, such as job satisfaction and job performance. In concluding their excellent review of the studies dealing with work involvement, Rabinowitz and Hall (1977, p. 284) summarized the description of a job-involved person as someone who

- Is a believer in the Protestant work ethic
- Is an older person
- Has internal (versus external) locus of control
- Has strong growth needs
- Has a stimulating job (high autonomy, variety, task identity, and feedback)
- Participates in decision making on matters that affect her or him
- Is satisfied with the job
- Has a history of success
- Is less likely than other people to leave the organization

Of course, this portrait of a job-involved person should be regarded only as a summary of empirically confirmed *correlates* of job involvement, without direct implications for causal relations. Because most of the studies reviewed here are cross-sectional, it is not possible to determine whether a certain variable is a cause or a consequence of work involvement—perhaps a third, moderating variable is causing them to covary. More longitudinal research is needed to get a better insight into the dynamics of the involvement process, as well as an understanding of the causal relationship between observed variables.

Work Salience

The studies dealing with work involvement analyze a person's relations to work more or less independently of other life activities. However, people do have other life roles: they study and educate themselves, they have home and family obligations, they perform various duties as members of the local community or they participate actively in politics, and they spend a certain amount of time in leisure activities. The existence of different life roles raises the questions of how the roles interact and what their relative importance is. Recently, in the context of meaning-of-work studies, much attention has been paid to the relative importance of work in relation to other life roles. A new concept has evolved within this line of research—the concept of *work salience*, which can be defined as the relative importance of work in relation to an individual's other important life roles. Super (1976, 1980) introduced this conceptualization of work salience, which is how the WIS project consistently treats it.

In similar vein the Meaning of Work Study (MOW International Research Team, 1987) conceived *work centrality*, defined as a "general belief about the value of working in one's life" (p. 17). The team developed two measures of work centrality: an absolute rating of work importance on a Likert-type scale and a relative rating of the importance of work as compared with the importance of other major life areas (family, community, religion, and leisure). The second measure of work centrality is very close to the WIS conceptualization of work salience.

However, we should note that Dubin (1956) also operationalized his construct of central life interest by relativizing the importance of work in relation to nonwork. He developed a questionnaire that asked subjects to indicate their preferences for several life spheres. Subjects were classified as "job oriented" and as "non–job oriented" according to the relative number of preferences for either sphere (work or nonwork). In 1977 Dubin and Champoux introduced a third neutral classification, which they used to describe people with no clear preference for work or nonwork activities. Dubin and Champoux assumed that such people have a flexible focus of central life interest.

Dubin (1956) administered his questionnaire to a sample of industrial workers. The analysis of their responses revealed that only 24 percent were job oriented, whereas 75 percent found their central life interests in the sphere of non-job activities. Dubin assumed that this was not surprising, given the job content and work organization of the majority of industrial jobs at that time. Although Dubin's instrument seems convenient for wider use, it has some weak points. It does not measure the degree of relative importance of work but offers just a rough (and somewhat arbitrary) classification of subjects in three broad categories. It does not differentiate among various non-job activities: negative definitions such as "nonwork" are nondefinitions. Its metric characteristics are unknown.

The Salience Inventory (SI), which the WIS developed and which is described in Chapter Four, overcomes some weaknesses of Dubin's instrument. Using a number of 4-point Likert-type scales, the SI is intended to assess the degree of importance of five life roles that are manifested in five essential fields of human activity: work, study, homemaking, community activities, and leisure. In accordance with the attitudinal approach to work importance, the WIS evaluates each life role according to three scales: one measures the behavioral aspect of a role (role participation), the second measures the affective aspect (role commitment), and the third taps a mixed affective-cognitive aspect (perception of the possibilities of value realization in a role). An overview of the results obtained by the SI, discussed in detail in several later chapters, delineates the advantages of such an approach.

Work Alienation: Attempts to Use a Philosophical Concept

The meaning of work has been studied from another point of view, its negative aspect—when work becomes meaningless or alienating. As Wilensky (1981) pointed out, the theme of alienation is closely connected with the notion of the quality of life. People living in modern societies, if not strongly dissatisfied with their jobs or occupations, feel at least estranged from workplaces that are embedded within the centralized, technocratic, and bureaucratic structure of modern organizations. Research concerning work alienation dominated the 1960s and the 1970s, although the concept has a much longer tradition in philosophy and social theory. One of the most significant elaborations and conceptualizations of the phenomenon can be found in the analyses of Karl Marx, especially in his early writings.

Marx considered work an important characteristic of human existence, a lifelong creative activity that should provide opportunity for self-fulfillment, the realization of human "generic essence." However, Marx assumed that the conditions of capitalistic production—private ownership, hired work force, and technical division of labor—do not allow the realization of the essence of being human but lead to alienation from work and consequently from life itself. In such work, a worker

> does not confirm himself but denies himself, does not feel
> content but unhappy, does not develop freely his physical and

mental energy but mortifies his body and ruins his mind. The worker therefore only feels himself outside his work, and his work feels outside himself. He is at home when he is not working, and when he is working he is not at home [Marx, 1844/1969, p. 110].

Because many empirical studies on work alienation are based on Marx's concept of alienation, it is useful to recall that he discerned four basic aspects of the concept:

1. Alienation of labor from the act of production, implying that work has lost its intrinsic value and holds only its instrumental function, acquiring a character of forced activity
2. Alienation of labor from its product—the product does not belong to the worker, who feels estranged from it, because it does not appear as an expression of the worker's intrinsic efforts and creative potential
3. Alienation of the individual from other people—representative of a social estrangement that is a consequence of the first two forms of alienation
4. Self-alienation—alienation from nature and hence from the human generic essence

The first three forms of alienation can be considered empirical manifestations of exploitation, owner-employee relations, and division of labor, but self-alienation is a dubious concept because it assumes the possibility of a defining generic essence, a concept of a highly abstract and normative nature.

Empirical attempts to study alienation use the subjective or phenomenological approach: they are mostly oriented toward the examination of feelings, beliefs, and attitudes. However, many Marxist theorists criticize the approach, claiming that alienation possesses an objective reality and cannot be reduced to the phenomenological level of analysis. They recall the notion of false consciousness, which refers to people who are not aware of their alienation. Without entering the deeper epistemological issues implied in discussions of this kind, we would like to point out that every objective state also has its subjective repercussions, which can and should be examined. As we have shown, Marx himself mentioned personal feelings as indicators of alienation.

One of the first and most influential approaches to the empirical investigation of alienation was formulated by Seeman (1959). Using an eclectic approach in unifying the notions of different authors (Marx, Weber, Durkheim, Mannheim, Fromm, and others), Seeman operationalized alienation as a multidimensional variable, consisting of five basic components:

1. *Powerlessness:* lack of conviction (expectation) about being in full control of the powers necessary for people to realize their values and satisfy their needs

2. *Meaninglessness:* people's inability to understand what is going on in their world and lack of conviction (expectation) about the predictability of the results of their actions
3. *Anomie:* belief (expectation) that personal goals can be realized only by forbidden, socially unacceptable activities
4. *Isolation:* feeling of loneliness and low expectation of social acceptance
5. *Self-estrangement:* the degree to which behavior is extrinsically motivated

In 1968 Faunce proposed that powerlessness, meaninglessness, and normlessness (anomie) are predisposing conditions to alienation, whereas only social isolation and self-estrangement are modes of alienation.

Although most researchers have adopted these dimensions, or at least some of them, they have operationalized them in significantly different ways. Because the WIS project found self-estrangement (also called work alienation [Seeman, 1972]) to be the most interesting mode of alienation, we detail how different authors have operationalized the concept.

Wilensky (1981) defined work alienation as the feeling that the routine enactment of the obligations and rights of a person's work role is incongruent with the person's prized self-image. Thus, in order to measure work alienation, it is necessary to measure the central attributes of the self-concept to which the individual attaches strong positive affects. Then the data obtained on the prized self-image must be related to the attributes of the specific work role. Wilensky assumed that people whose work role fits poorly with their prized self-image are work-alienated. Evidently, his concept of work alienation originated from role theory and, more specifically, from the part of it that concerns the person-role conflict.

Wilensky tested this hypothesis in research conducted in the Detroit area of the United States during the 1960s on a sample of 1,156 employed men. The research included measurement of five attributes of the self-image that the work role could most clearly endanger: sociability, intelligence, competence, autonomy, and ambition. He derived the measures from extensive interviews, together with five attributes of the work role that correspond to the attributes of the self-image: opportunity for people to relate socially, use their abilities, perform efficiently, exercise independence in work, and compete for promotion.

Wilensky measured the degree of fit between the two classes of attributes by constructing an index of alienation. If, for example, sociability is a salient part of a person's self-image and the job blocks it, and furthermore if this situation is frustrating for the worker, the person receives a point for "alienated." If, on the other hand, the person has a good chance to mix socially at work and enjoys the social aspect, the fit is good and the person receives a point for being "attached"; if the opportunity to mix socially suits but does not provoke strong affects, the person gets a point for being "indifferent." The multiple classification analysis showed that the best independent predictors of work alienation are

1. A work situation and organizational setting that provide little discretion in pace and schedule, combined with a tall hierarchy above
2. A career that has been blocked and chaotic
3. The stage in the life cycle that exerts strong pressure (children at school and low income)

It is interesting to note that only 15.3 percent of the subjects were alienated in at least one category of attributes. The principal finding was that the majority of middle-class subjects were generally indifferent to work: their jobs neither confirmed their self-image nor denied it for most of the attributes analyzed. Wilensky concluded that the majority of "middle mass" employees in America (the research did not include marginal groups—youth, older workers, women) play it cool, neither strongly attached to their jobs nor feeling them as a serious threat to self-esteem.

Gardell's research (1971) in pulp and paper mills defined alienation at work as the impossibility of satisfying three basic categories of needs, which, when satisfied, make an individual feel involved and highly motivated intrinsically by the work: people's need for influence and control over their own work situation, meaningful work, and interaction and camaraderie with other people. Within the process model Gardell proposed, alienation from work is regarded as a mediating variable, preceded by objective work conditions and affecting workers' mental health. Gardell described the content of work as two main variables that strongly affect the feeling of alienation: first the degree of independence enjoyed by the individual in decision making and the person's control over work pace, work methods, developing aptitudes, and initiating contacts; and second the level of qualification required of a worker for tasks that could be performed efficiently. Mental health was operationalized, not in terms of the mental illness concept used by medical science but in terms of positive emotional states underlying the prized self-image and related to the norms and values of the larger society. In order to measure the degree of mental health, Gardell constructed five attitude scales, which he labeled General Life Satisfaction, Self-Esteem (Feeling of Competence), Self-Esteem (Feeling of Prestige), Contact-Avoiding Feeling, and Feeling of Self-Realization. The results clearly showed that restrictions in the two aspects of work structure (worker freedom and control), and the qualification level required, are related to higher levels of alienation in work and to poor mental health. Also, with respect to the mechanization level (craft work, machine-paced work, and process control), a U-shaped relationship is demonstrated between both control and qualification aspects of the job content, on the one hand, and work alienation and mental health, on the other.

In sixty firms in Croatia, Bahtijarević-Šiber (1980) studied a sample of 847 industrial workers. The aim of the project was to identify psychological indicators of work alienation, their factor structure, and their relationship with the individual's position in the work process. Using Marxist theory as a starting point, she operationalized three modes of alienation:

1. *Alienation of labor from products:* the degree to which workers feel in control of the means and results of production, including their perception
   of their influence on important organizational decisions
2. *Alienation of labor from the act of production:* the subject's relationship with
   the work content, perception of possibilities for self-fulfillment in work,
   and general job satisfaction
3. *Social alienation:* the workers' perception of their social position and satisfaction with the social interaction in the organization

The data, comprising the subjects' answers to forty-three questionnaire
items, were factor analyzed. Five factors were obtained that only partly corresponded to the hypothetical set of alienation components. Because the
intercorrelations of factors were fairly high, a second-order factor analysis
was performed, obtaining one second-order factor that was identified as the
"general factor of work alienation." Scores on this factor were related to
demographic variables as well as to sociopolitical activity and position in the
work process. The two variables showed a significant correlation with the
degree of alienation: low degree of political involvement and low position
within the organizational hierarchy were positively associated with the higher
levels of alienation.

Our review of empirical studies of alienation reveals that the conceptualization of alienation varies across studies. The analyses of the measures used reveal that alienation is operationalized in different ways: sometimes as extrinsic motivation or the instrumental meaning of work,
sometimes as perception of inadequate opportunities for self-fulfillment,
and sometimes, again, as negative affect toward work, such as a feeling of
detachment from work, work dissatisfaction, a feeling of isolation, and helplessness. The term appears to have different meanings for different authors.
In addition, Rus and Arzenšek (1984) claimed that the concept of alienation
not only means different things to different authors but also is used to
explain different concepts, that is, different social problems and their con-
troversies, such as conformity and deviation, political passivity and social dis-
turbance, status aspirations and marginalization, heteronomous life-style
and asocial tendencies (hippies). They concluded that a construct with
pretensions to explain all diverse attitudes and behaviors cannot explain
anything. Therefore, it is proper to ask whether there is indeed a need for
such a concept.

The concept of alienation was important in nineteenth-century
sociopolitical theory: it played a prominent role in the critical reexamination
of the contemporary social reality. But for the purpose of modern empirical
research, the concept is ill defined and incorporates excess meaning. The
ambiguity of its conceptualization in different studies has reached such a level
that the reason for its existence as a unique concept is lost. We accept the
view that in empirical studies it is better to name the variables by their real
names, or by the names of empirically verified constructs that are being

examined, and perhaps to refer to the concept of alienation only as an interpretative frame of reference.

Origin of Individual Differences in the Meaning of Work: A Model of Work Importance in the Life of an Individual

The results of the studies we reviewed indicated the existence of notable individual differences in work involvement, as well as in its opposite: work alienation. Questions have been raised about the origin of these differences. We should note that we are interested in the meaning of work as a general category and not in attitudes toward specific jobs. This difference has already been pointed out, particularly by Kanungo (1981, 1982), who differentiated between work involvement and job involvement and assumed that different antecedent factors underlie the concepts. Kanungo claimed that job involvement is mainly a function of the concrete job situation. On the other hand, work involvement can be conceived as a relatively stable personality characteristic that is determined by the person's previous experiences: it is a "normative belief" formed by "cultural conditioning or socialization" (Kanungo, 1982). Such an attitude fits into the sociological view of the importance of early socialization (for instance, Dubin, 1961), which leads to the internalization of norms and values concerning work. In accordance with this view, work involvement can be defined as "internalization of values about the goodness of work" (Lodahl & Kejner, 1965).

However, such an approach is open to two criticisms. First, it is vague and general, which means it cannot be useful in explaining the cognitive process or the nature of the intervening variables that underlie the formation of individual differences in work involvement. Second, it is one-sided because it describes the person's relationship to work as a mere product of early socialization. Although the value orientations acquired in the period of early socialization are certainly important, it is not correct to assume that the totality of individual differences can be explained solely in terms of early experience, denying the dynamic nature of individual structure as it interacts with its environment throughout the lifetime. The results of a number of studies indicated also that the nonredundant part of total variance of work involvement can be explained not only by individual variables but also by situational characteristics (Rabinowitz & Hall, 1977; Saal, 1981; Sekaran & Mowday, 1981). Therefore, in an attempt to construct a model that describes the relations of work involvement determinants, the researcher should also take into consideration the dynamic influence of situational variables. Figure 1.1 presents a model (Šverko, 1989) that tries to overcome some of the criticisms.

The central concept of the model is work values: these are important and relatively stable goals that people seek to attain in their work—economic security, stimulative social interaction, and use of their abilities. It is generally supposed that the more important such values are to individuals, the more important the work role will be in their lives. However, the model pos-

Figure 1.1. A Model of Work Importance Determinants.

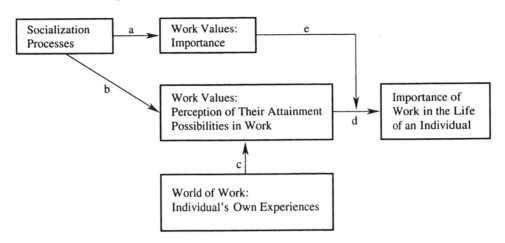

Source: From "Origin of individual differences in importance attached to work: A model and a contribution to its evaluation" by B. Šverko, 1989, *Journal of Vocational Behavior, 34,* p. 30. Copyright 1989 by Academic Press, Inc. Reprinted by permission.

tulates that the work values aspect, which exerts a major influence on the importance attached to work, is not the importance of values but the subject's perceptions or expectations about the possibility of attaining these goals through work, as shown by arrow *d*. The importance of work values has the effect of a moderator variable within the proposed model (shown by the arrow *e* directed toward the arrow *d*).

The model also proposes that work values are primarily determined by the process of socialization, which influences the degree of their importance (arrow *a*) but also has an influence on the perception of value attainment possibilities (arrow *b*). The perceptions are also influenced by experience of the world of work (arrow *c*), that is, by perception of situational factors. The experience is available primarily to people who have been employed, although even those who have not been fully employed, primarily youth or homemakers, can have certain limited insights into the worker role, one that moderates expectations about the realization of work values in some future job.

The model we have described assumes that certain cognitive processes, such as evaluations, expectations, and anticipations, underlie people's attitudes and behavior. Therefore, its origin can be traced to the cognitive approach proposed by Tolman (1932) and Lewin (1938) and further developed in different expectancy theories that attempted to explain the decision-making process (Edwards, 1954), the cognitive structure of attitudes (Rosenberg, 1956, 1960), and work motivation (Vroom, 1964; Porter & Lawler, 1968; Graen, 1969; Lawler, 1973; Campbell & Pritchard, 1976). In terms of cognitive motivation theories, work values correspond to outcomes from work that bear positive valences. Perceptions of their attainment possibilities in work correspond to the perceived instrumentality of work for achieving desired outcomes.

Congruent with this approach was Kanungo's theoretical outlook (1979) stating that work involvement depends on whether the work is perceived to have the potential for satisfying an individual's salient needs. Because it is rather difficult to operationalize the concept of needs, Šverko's WIS model used the concept of work values, which is supposed to reflect the person's needs and is easier to operationalize. Finifter (1972) offered a similar explanation in his analysis of alienation. He assumed that alienation is a consequence of incongruity between a person's aspirations, norms, and values, internalized in the socialization process, on the one hand, and in the person's perception of the socially structured possibilities for their realization, on the other.

The WIS model achieves empirical support by testing four hypotheses derived from the model. The four hypotheses (Šverko, 1989) state that

1. Correlations between the important work values and the importance attached to work should be mainly positive but low.
2. Correlations between value attainment perceptions and work importance should, without exception, be positive and high.
3. The correlation between perceptions of value attainment and work importance should be proportional to the degree of importance of the value in question.
4. A larger part of work importance variance can be explained on the basis of the degree of importance of different work values and the person's perception of possibilities for their realization in work.

The study, carried out on four different Croatian samples, largely confirms the hypotheses (Šverko, 1989). The study has been replicated on six Australian samples with essentially the same results (Lokan, 1989). Thus the correlational analyses strongly support the basic proposition of the model, according to which the importance or salience of work in individuals' lives depends mainly on their perception of the opportunities for the realization of salient values within their work roles.

Conclusion

Because of its manifold functions, work plays an important role in the life of an individual. But the assumption about the central role of work in human life is not universally applicable. Research has shown significant individual differences in various aspects of the meaning of work: work values, work involvement, and alienation from work. Work plays a central role indeed in the lives of some individuals, who recognize it as a source of satisfaction of important personal needs. To others work means toil and drudgery, monotonous and meaningless activity that provides for basic needs. For them work usually represents a discouraging, "alienated," and low-salience activity. Work salience or relative importance depends primarily upon individuals' perceptions of possibilities for the realization of dominant work values through the work role. Therefore, attempts directed toward changing individual orientations to work should be based on a restructuring of the job content and a reorganization of the work context. Only work that is perceived as providing an opportunity for the realization of various needs and values can be the source of real job satisfaction and intrinsic work motivation.

References

Bahtijarević-Šiber, F. (1980). *Socijalno-psihologijski aspekti otuđenja u samoupravnom socijalističkom društvu* (Sociopsychological aspects of alienation in the socialist society). Unpublished doctoral dissertation, University of Zagreb, Zagreb.

Blood, M. R., & Hulin, C. L. (1967). Alienation, environmental characteristics, and worker response. *Journal of Applied Psychology, 51,* 284–290.

Campbell, J. P., & Pritchard, R. D. (1976). Motivation theory in industrial and organizational psychology. In M. D. Dunnette (Ed.), *Handbook of industrial and organizational psychology* (pp. 63–130). Skokie, IL: Rand McNally.

Centers, R. (1948). Motivational aspects of occupational stratification. *Journal of Social Psychology, 28,* 187–217.

Centers, R., & Bugental, D. E. (1966). Intrinsic and extrinsic job motivations among different segments of the working population. *Journal of Applied Psychology, 50,* 193–197.

Dubin, R. (1956). Industrial workers' worlds: A study of the "central life interests" of industrial workers. *Social Problems, 3,* 131–142.

Dubin, R. (1961). *Human relations in administration.* Englewood Cliffs, NJ: Prentice-Hall.

Dubin, R., & Champoux, J. E. (1977). Central life interests and job satisfaction. *Organizational Behavior and Human Performance, 18,* 366–377.

Edwards, W. (1954). The theory of decision-making. *Psychological Bulletin, 51,* 380–418.

Faunce, W. (1968). *Social problems of an industrial civilization.* New York: McGraw-Hill.

Fein, M. (1977). Why job enrichment does not work. In M. G. Miner & J. B. Miner (Eds.), *Policy issues in contemporary personnel and industrial relations.* New York and London: Macmillan.

Finifter, A. (Ed.). (1972). *Alienation and social system.* New York: Wiley.

Fridlander, F. (1965). Comparative work value systems. *Personnel Psychology, 18,* 1–20.

Friedman, E. A., & Havighurst, R. J. (1954). *The meaning of work and retirement.* Chicago: University of Chicago Press.

Gardell, B. (1971). Alienation and mental health in the modern industrial environment. In L. Levi (Ed.), *Society, stress and disease* (Vol. 1, pp. 148–180). Oxford, England: Oxford University Press.

Graen, G. (1969). The instrumentality theory of work motivation: Some experimental results and suggested modifications. *Journal of Applied Psychology Monograph, 53,* 1–25.

Kanungo, R. N. (1979). The concept of alienation and involvement revisited. *Psychological Bulletin, 86,* 119–138.

Kanungo, R. N. (1981). Work alienation and involvement: Problems and prospects. *International Review of Applied Psychology, 30,* 1–15.

Kanungo, R. N. (1982). Measurement of job and work involvement. *Journal of Applied Psychology, 67,* 341–349.

Lawler, E. E. (1973). *Motivation in work organizations.* Pacific Grove, CA: Brooks/Cole.

Lawler, E. E., & Hall, D. T. (1970). Relationship of job characteristics to job involvement, satisfaction, and intrinsic motivation. *Journal of Applied Psychology, 54,* 305–312.

Lewin, K. (1938). *The conceptual representation and the measurement of psychological forces.* Durham, NC: Duke University Press.

Lodahl, T. M., & Kejner, M. (1965). The definition and measurement of job involvement. *Journal of Applied Psychology, 49,* 24–33.

Lokan, J. (1989, November). *Value attainment perceptions in work and leisure.* Paper presented at the Australian Association for Research in Education Annual Conference, Adelaide.

Marx, K. (1969). *The economic and philosophic manuscripts of 1844.* New York: International Publishers. (Original work published 1844)

Morse, N. C., & Weiss, R. S. (1955). The function and meaning of work and the job. *American Sociological Review, 20,* 191–198.

MOW International Research Team. (1987). *The meaning of working.* London: Academic Press.

Porter, L. W., & Lawler, E. E. (1968). *Managerial attitudes and performance.* Belmont, CA: Dorsey Press.

Rabinowitz, S., & Hall, D. T. (1977). Organizational research on job involvement. *Psychological Bulletin, 84,* 265–288.

Rosenberg, M. J. (1956). Cognitive structure and attitudinal affect. *Journal of Abnormal and Social Psychology, 53,* 367–372.

Rosenberg, M. J. (1960). An analysis of affective-cognitive consistency. In C. J. Howland & M. J. Rosenberg (Eds.), *Attitude organization and change* (pp.15–64). New Haven, CT: Yale University Press.

Rus, V. & Arzenšek, V. (1984). *Rad kao sudbina i kao sloboda—podjela i alijenacija rada* (Work as a destiny and liberty: Division and alienation of work). Zagreb: Liber.

Saal, F. E. (1981). Empirical and theoretical implications of a purely cognitive definition of job involvement. *International Review of Applied Psychology, 30,* 103–120.

Saleh, S. D. (1981). A structural view of job involvement and its differentiation from satisfaction and motivation. *International Review of Applied Psychology, 30,* 17–30.

Saleh, S. D., & Hosek, J. (1976). Job involvement: Concepts and measurements. *Academy of Management Journal, 19,* 213–224.

Seeman, M. (1959). On the meaning of alienation. *American Sociological Review, 24,* 783–791.

Seeman, M. (1972). Alienation and engagement. In A. Campbell & P. Converse (Eds.), *The human meaning of social change.* New York: Russell Sage Foundation.

Sekaran, U., & Mowday, R. T. (1981). A cross-cultural analysis of the influence of individual and job characteristics on job involvement. *International Review of Applied Psychology, 30,* 51–64.

Steers, R. M., & Porter, L. (1979). Work and motivation: An evaluative summary. In R. M. Steers & L. Porter (Eds.), *Motivation and work behavior* (pp. 555–564). New York: McGraw-Hill.

Super, D. E. (1976). *Career education and the meanings of work.* Washington, DC: U.S. Government Printing Office.

Super, D. E. (1980). A life-span, life-space, approach to career development. *Journal of Vocational Behavior, 16,* 282–298.

Šverko, B. (1989). Origin of individual differences in importance attached to work: A model and a contribution to its evaluation. *Journal of Vocational Behavior, 34,* 28–39.

Tilgher, A. (1962). Work: What it has meant to men through the ages. In S. Nosov & W. H. Form (Eds.), *Man, work, and society.* New York: Basic Books. (Original work published 1930)

Tolman, E. C. (1932). *Purposive behavior in animals and men.* New York: Century.

Vroom, H. V. (1964). *Work and motivation.* New York: Wiley.

Weber, M. (1922). *Protestantische Ethik und der Geist des Kapitalismus* (Protestant ethics and the spirit of capitalism). Tübingen, Germany: Mohr.

Wilensky, H. L. (1981). Family cycle, work and the quality of life: Reflections on the roots of happiness, despair, and indifference in modern society. In B. Gardell & G. Johansson (Eds.), *Working life.* New York: Wiley.

TWO

The Role Concept in Career Development

David J. Gouws

An actor in a play generally plays a particular part or character in a story, shows a characteristic and more or less coherent pattern of behavior, follows a script, interprets the character and plays it according to a personal style while being faithful to the script, and wins applause or hisses from the audience.

A member of society generally occupies one or more positions in a particular social system, shows a more or less coherent pattern of behavior characteristic of or at least consistent with each position, is implicitly or explicitly aware of social norms and the expectations of others regarding appropriate conduct in each position, has personal ideas or conceptions of what behavior is appropriate for each position and a personal coping and expressive style that affects behavior in each position, and, like the actor, receives feedback (rewards or punishments) from others.

Sociological formulations of role theory in the twentieth century have built on this comparison of social life and the theater, emphasizing some aspects, such as societal norms and expectations, and giving less attention to other aspects, such as the moderating influence of personality and the effect of feedback on actual role performance. Use of the concept of roles grew rapidly after World War II. Psychologists increasingly emphasized the individual as a self-directing actor. Many writers see the concept of roles as a crucial link in the sociological, anthropological, psychological, educational, and management literature. Role theory helps to explain the individual's interaction in the family, neighborhood, school, work, and in the community and society at large.

Summaries of role theory and its constituent concepts are available in dictionaries and encyclopedias (e.g., Mitchell, 1968; Sarbin, 1968; Sills, 1968; Harré & Lamb, 1983; Corsini, 1987). Also available are critical reviews of role theory in its wider social science context (e.g., Biddle, 1986; "Roltheorie," 1979), as are scholarly articles that focus on specific aspects, such as role theory in the organizational setting (Levinson, 1959), role conflict (Van Sell,

Brief, & Schuler, 1981), sex roles (Miller & Garrison, 1982), and the development of role identities (Gordon, 1976).

This chapter considers the usefulness of role theory and some of its many conceptual and practical elaborations in lifelong career development when the latter is seen as many faceted, interdisciplinary, and an exercise in a personal, educational, therapeutic, and organizational life management. It is graphically represented in the Life-Career Rainbow (Super, 1980, 1990) and assessed by the Salience Inventory (Chapter Four).

In somewhat affluent developed countries the traditional stakeholders in this theoretical, research, and practical enterprise—researchers (Super et al., 1957), educators (Herr & Cramer, 1988), and young people entering the adult world—are increasingly being joined by two important new groups. One consists of established adults reassessing their lives and searching for relevant information, helpful conceptual frameworks, and substantive assistance in handling their own career development crises (Howard & Bray, 1988; Lee & Kanungo, 1984). The other is made up of leaders in business, industry, and government who are seeking to facilitate and increase the effectiveness of their employees (Hall, 1986).

A Comprehensive, General Framework for Career Development

The term *career*, originally used to refer to the sequence of work-related positions in a person's working life, from blue-collar workers to professionals and managers (Louis, 1980), has more recently been expanded to cover all major life roles, as well as those that relate to work. Academics now use it to refer to all roles in a person's lifetime (Hall, 1972; Super et al., 1957; Super, 1980; Van Maanen & Schein, 1979) and to the interaction of factors in the domains of work, family, and leisure throughout that life (Rapoport & Rapoport, 1980; Lee & Kanungo, 1984). In defining career as "the combination and sequence of roles played by a person during the course of a life-time" (Super, 1980, p. 282) and as "the constellation of interacting, varying roles" (p. 284), Super favors the more inclusive usage. The Work Importance Study and one of its major instruments, the Salience Inventory (Chapter Four), use this definition.

To conduct meaningful cumulative research on career development, teach it effectively, and be most helpful to clients in analyzing their careers and improving their career-management skills, counselors need a comprehensive conceptual framework for lifelong career development. The function of such a framework should be to order the bewildering array of phenomena and important concepts in a manageable structure or model that makes clear the potentially significant dimensions, aspects, and considerations. Development of such a framework is an imaginative and creative effort; the result will not necessarily be correct in all respects and for all purposes, but it can significantly aid investigation and communication.

A few authors have proposed a general framework that considers life

Figure 2.1. The Life-Career Rainbow: Six Life Roles in Schematic Life Space.

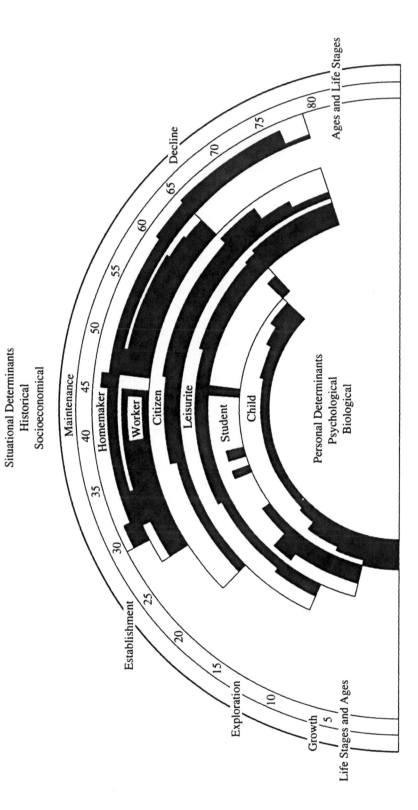

Source: D. E. Super (1990). A life-span, life-space approach to career development. In D. Brown, L. Brooks, & Associates, *Career choice and development: Applying contemporary theories to practice* (2nd ed.). San Francisco: Jossey-Bass, p. 212.

stages and developmental tasks (e.g., Erikson, 1963; Havighurst, 1973; Levinson, 1978; Super et al., 1957), at least for Western industrialized societies. Among the contributions from the career development wing, Super's Life-Career Rainbow (1980, 1990) and the Rapoports' Triple Helix Model (1980) are probably the best-known examples of comprehensive, fairly detailed frameworks.

In fact, Super's Life-Career Rainbow is the only widely used and comprehensive career development framework that explicitly uses "role" as a major classification and explanation. Levinson, coauthor of a book on roles in organizations (Hodgson, Levinson, & Zaleznik, 1965), later chose *not* to use role (or, for that matter, career) as a central organizing concept in studying the developmental stages in the lives of American males (Levinson, 1978). Kotter, Faux, and McArthur's 1978 manual on self-assessment and career development invites the reader to create visual life-style representations without referring to roles explicitly. The examples suggest that the concept of role, although used by many authors in the field, is not indispensable. But it is useful.

Super's Life-Career Rainbow (Super, 1980, 1990) provides a map of career development for an entire life (see Figure 2.1). It presents a manageable number of significant concepts and dimensions, which are arranged around the core concept of role. It indicates the personal and situational determinants of role choice, development, and coping and relinquishment and portrays the pervasive influence of age and life stage. In a sense, it provides a framework into which a client can insert personal particulars to generate an actual and potential life picture that shows the nature and relative temporal and affective importance of each role at each life stage.

The supporting descriptions and subsidiary diagrams in Super's work (1980, 1990) provide an outline for thinking about the dynamic process of career development and emphasize the importance of problem solving and decision making as a frequent subroutine. They introduce such higher-order concepts as life-style and career pattern and illustrate some probable or observed interactions of such factors as cross-role effects of success and failure in an important role and the connections of performances in preoccupational, occupational, and postoccupational roles. In constructing a comprehensive conceptual framework, the dilemma is how to balance scientific comprehensiveness with the parsimony of concepts so that the result is easy to understand. At an early stage of organizing concepts and data, comprehensiveness appears to be the more weighty criterion because it is impossible to be certain which items are more and less important. Super's Life-Career Rainbow is one of the most comprehensive frameworks available. It should stimulate researchers and practitioners to investigate more intensively and develop its various elements and their relationships and to help students and clients to attain a balanced overview of what constitutes and determines a career.

In the Life-Career Rainbow roles are the components of careers and of life-styles (see also Havighurst, 1973). The model defines roles in terms of expectations and performance. But it does not clearly define the concepts that constitute role, although they may be viewed as tasks that produce desired results (products, services, esprit de corps, a managerial team, etc.). The literature on management by objectives, a framework within which management positions are analyzed and sometimes designed or redesigned in terms of types of key result areas (McConkey, 1983), suggests that a role could be described as consisting of a coherent cluster of key areas in each of which effective performance is expected. Achieving such results requires playing a role, performing its tasks.

A related question concerns the level of generality or inclusiveness of the concept of role in Super's rainbow. Because the expectations and performances relating to a given role—for example, the role of child—can vary dramatically with the child's and the parent's ages, the role of child is really a class or category of perhaps quite different and successive roles that have as their major common feature a biological and social connection between specific role partners. Of course, this would also be valid for other roles. Because Super chose the roles in the rainbow so that any one person could be involved in all of them during the course of a lifetime, regarding them as generic roles may be useful. This implies that the specific form and content of such a generic role may vary from person to person, as well as over time. Such generality and oversimplification is the essence of models. Although "the individual pursuing the career . . . may be viewed as at the center of the scene" (Super, 1980, p. 296), the rainbow has no explicit representation for the self apart from "personal determinants." Activities concerned with maintenance of the self (and not directly relatable to any one of the generic role activities), such as sleeping, eating, and grooming, take up a significant proportion of an individual's life. Thus practical application of the rainbow may be difficult because clients trying to precisely determine their relative investments of time find that they cannot allocate certain time-consuming activities to specific roles. Furthermore, explicit inclusion of the self in the model (see, e.g., Holahan & Gilbert, 1979) would be a reminder of the importance of the self-concept in career development (Super, Starishevsky, Matlin, & Jordaan, 1963; Super, 1990).

The selection and naming of roles will probably never prove completely satisfactory. For example, the role of economic provider may be subsumed under that of worker or, in some cases, that of homemaker, or it may be important enough to warrant specific mention, especially in work with less affluent clients or in a culture of poverty, in which it may be of overriding importance.

At the risk of making the rainbow an unwieldy instrument, it might also be desirable to make the important distinction between internal (as construed by the individual) and external (as seen by the organization) careers (Van Maanen & Schein, 1979). Relationships could then, for example, be the internal career counterpart of reciprocal roles in the external career.

Complementary and supplementary roles of role players and their role sets, and the reciprocal and interdependent nature of relationships, need more emphasis in the "dynamic process" aspects of the schema. Although the notion of complementarity was prominent in earlier formulations of role theory (see, e.g., Spiegel, 1957; Turner, 1968), later work has tended to concentrate on the individual role player and to neglect the interdependencies among members of the role set. In complementary roles the emphasis is on matching the interactive behaviors of people playing interdependent roles. For example, the mentor gives advice in a friendly, supportive manner, and the protégé may accept the advice. In supplementary roles the strengths of one member in a particular area make up for the weaknesses of another member in that area. For example, as a homemaker, one spouse may be a good planner but an indifferent executor of plans, whereas the other may be an active, competent executor with little aptitude for systematic planning. In this respect, "dual careers" studies have generally been narrow in their conceptualization.

A related notion about interdependent roles, whether dyadic or involving a larger group, is the importance of rewards, or rights or privileges, that are earned when role expectations are adequately met (Turner, 1968; Sieber, 1974).

Finally, the importance of perceptions, assumptions, and construing or inference processes (systematic, or triggered by the immediate situation) in the development of role conceptions and expectations needs comment because different people can perceive the same objective reality quite differently.

Role Choice

Choice and decision-making processes come into play whenever a person assumes a new role or undergoes or anticipates a role transition. Much work regarding these processes has been done in the areas of vocational guidance and personnel selection and placement, but relatively little has been done for the other generic roles (Biddle, 1986).

The objective and the perceived opportunity structure regarding career choices varies with the person, the role, and the context. Astin (1984) used perceived "structure of opportunity" as an important concept in her model of women's career choice and work behavior. The concept gains force when it is applied to the contextual and situational role and career barriers faced by less privileged individuals and groups (Belbin, 1990; Roberts, 1977). Endemic poverty, poor educational facilities, lack of employment opportunities, and, often, disregard of personal potential seem to be the common fate of people in underdeveloped countries. These problems are often exacerbated by racial and minority group discrimination and oppression and by restrictive cultures that offer little opportunity or tolerance for alternative life-styles. All these factors contribute to a serious diminution of the objective opportunity structure.

Learned helplessness, externality of locus of control, lowered achievement motivation, and a lower level of career maturity all seem to be consequences of growing up and living in underdeveloped countries (Kohn, 1969, 1976; Phares & Lamiell, 1977; Krumboltz, Becker-Haven, & Burnett, 1979). Yet some individuals do not succumb to these hardships and develop instead a sense of autonomy and self-efficacy in the face of adversity. Their apparent immunity to and resilience in deprivation and their "deviant" (in this case, more positive) perceptions, as compared to the modal view of their circumstances, pose a challenge to our understanding and deserve special attention in cross-cultural investigations (Caplan, Whitmore, & Choy, 1989; Sowell, 1981).

Several types or levels of role choice are distinguishable. At a basic level people can, in the case of at least some of the generic roles (e.g., spouse or parent), decide whether and how to become involved. They may fashion a generic role, such as student, worker, or leisurite, to suit their preferences. (*Leisurite* is the term coined by the WIS project to meet the need for a noun denoting the pursuer of leisure.) Most of the voluminous work on career counseling has focused on the choice that involves such generic roles.

A second type of choice occurs when a person already in a role, by choice or otherwise, evaluates the importance of that role in terms of the amount of time and self actually or to be invested in that role. Super (1982) proposes the notions of absolute and relative role salience for such a choice. The adult life course sees repeated reassessments and shifts in the pattern of investments in generic roles (Levinson, 1978), often called *recycling;* so do the child and adolescent stages.

A third type of choice revolves around the degree of adjustment, or shaping (Super, 1980), of role demands that a person should attempt in order to bring the role more into line with the role player's preferences, capabilities, and conception of the role. Some roles in some situations evidently leave less room for this than others, but the literature (and people's perceptions generally) probably is on the side of underestimating the latitude or degree of flexibility of role demands. The work of Harrison (1972) on role negotiation and of Graen (1976) on role making showed that organizational roles, at least, often exhibit a considerable degree of latitude that individuals may use to better shape the roles to suit their preferences and capabilities. Normative role expectations may be more difficult to shape than the expectations for many organizational roles, which supposedly reflect rational patterns of expected behavior rather than ideals.

A fourth type of choice is more stylistic. Having assumed a role, made a certain personal investment in it, and adjusted to the role demands, a person can—at least theoretically—still choose *how* to play that role. Having decided to remain single and unencumbered by family obligations, a young professional may choose to make a significant investment in the role of leisurite. The person may then play the role in such a way as to promote a network of influence in a profession, visibility in a yuppie subculture, prowess in sports, or knowledge and enjoyment of art or some other field.

The choice and decision-making processes we have described are often not very explicit, rational, or systematic (Osipow, 1986). People may be analytic and deliberate about some decisions, whereas they seem to drift into other, equally important, decisions. A general rule could be that the more a particular decision reduces the degree of freedom, the more attention and deliberation that decision should receive.

Clients with favorable opportunity structures may have little need for decision assistance with regard to discrete roles but may well need help in attaining a balanced, effective, and satisfying constellation of roles, with related priorities and commitments for the life stage in question. This is help in career development.

This appears to be a recurring need. Levinson (1978, p. 54) stated,

> No matter how satisfactory a structure is, in time its utility declines and its flaws generate conflict that leads to modification or transformation of the structure. It is as Marx said: every system contains within itself the seeds of its own destruction [but, we might add, also the seeds of its own reconstruction]. The once-stable structure passes into a new transitional period. The seasons change. Developmental tasks are undertaken anew, and the lessons of growth are gathered and stockpiled against the new period coming. The pattern of adult development continues.

The once dormant seeds now bear fruit.

In helping people through these transitions, counselors need measures of individual differences in *patterns* of motivational, stylistic, attitudinal, and other characteristics. Among these are learning style (Kolb & Fry, 1975), locus of control (Rotter, 1954; Lefcourt, 1976; Spector, 1988), career anchors (Schein, 1978; Derr, 1980), psychological hardiness (Kobasa, 1979), and self-efficacy (Bandura, 1977, 1986; Taylor & Betz, 1983). These may be more useful than measures of single traits. Self-explanatory experiential learning approaches (Kotter, Faux, & McArthur, 1978) may be superior to didactic expert-focused interventions, at least with self-efficacious clients. Of major concern in industrialized societies is the need to work out acceptable variants of a life-style in which the central role of worker, although not neglected, is brought into a more positive—and, if possible, synergistic—relationship with the other roles, especially the family and leisure roles (Derr, 1980; Lee & Kanungo, 1984).

Effective choosing presupposes self-knowledge and knowledge of the critical characteristics of the role being contemplated. Neither is easily attained. Most professional work has been done in the educational, vocational, and employment areas, where feedback, achievement or performance appraisal, and educational goals or job analysis and specifications may be standard fare. However, as Schein stated, "One of the major causes of career dissatisfaction is a lack of realism in the internal career and the absence of any corrective mechanisms or feedback from the employer" (1980, p. 359). We might add, "or from earlier teachers or counselors." Career centers in universities (Tyler, 1969), assessment centers (Thornton & Byham, 1982), and the technique of accomplishment analysis (Mahler & Drotter, 1986) in industry represent serious attempts to instill greater realism in the self-assessment of students and managers and in assessments by their institutions or organizations.

However, this lack of realism is probably even greater when it comes to choosing with regard to the family, civic, and leisure roles, within which such feedback and supporting procedures and actions are less available and less often used by potential clients.

Role Changes, Role Transitions, and Role Development

Major social roles, such as those of mother or cleric, evolve within a cultural and historical context. When contextual circumstances change, the concomitant change in roles often starts only after a considerable time lag. This means that, in a rapidly changing society, some aspects of traditionally defined roles may be obsolete. A case in point is gender-role typing and casting in cultures and in organizations (Frieze, Parsons, Johnson, Ruble, & Zellman, 1978; Miller & Garrison, 1982). In many dual-career families the woman, although employed full time, still shoulders the major part of homemaking and often also of parenthood (Crosby, 1984; Lewis & Cooper, 1987). Many husbands, even those who are well disposed toward their wives' occupational aspirations, apparently find it hard to change to a true sharing of work in the home.

Astin (1984) listed major trends in American society likely to lead to continuing changes in women's roles. Among these were increased longevity, declining birth rate, increasing divorce rate, proliferation of nontraditional life-styles, advancements in reproductive technology, and, of course, equal opportunity legislation and practices.

The home, and later the school and workplace, are the major theaters in which people develop conceptions about their role behaviors and their expectations concerning other players' behaviors. The socialization process, probably best described in terms of social learning theory (Bandura, 1977; Mitchell & Krumboltz, 1990), takes place at both conscious and subconscious levels. The presence of suitable role models can significantly promote the development of appropriate role behaviors (Kram, 1985; Mitchell & Krumboltz, 1990).

A central feature of this early learning concerns the aforementioned complementarity and supplementarity of roles. Role conceptions and expectations do not develop for single players in isolation but for pairs or groups of players, whose preconceptions and mutual expectations are expected to converge to some degree in a reciprocity of relationships. Spiegel (1957) commented on the economy of the complementary role system in the traditional family, ideally operating in a mutually supportive and largely automatic fashion. In military aviation this has been called "cooperative" as opposed to "standing" (formal) operational procedure.

Comparing changes in the generic role of worker or leisurite with those of child, parent, or spouse suggests that some roles can change more rapidly and with less disruption than others. Furthermore, although many institutions and organizations have established procedures for handling their role transitions, few formal procedures are available to ease transitions in some other roles, especially those relating to the home and family. The gradual, almost imperceptible, role changes in continuously evolving cultures generally occur far too slowly for comfort during periods of rapid and pervasive social change such as society is now experiencing.

Role changes, whether the result of changes in the environment or self-initiated, imply active role transition and development work for the person concerned. Several authors, (e.g., Havighurst, 1973; Erikson, 1963; Levinson, 1978) have considered developmental tasks in a general way. Systematic and explicit approaches, such as Havighurst's life-span tasks and Campbell, Cellini, Shaltry, Long, and Pinkos's taxonomy of adult career tasks (1979), can be of great help in gaining a clearer understanding of a client's needs (Osipow, 1986). But working out new constellations of modified roles and attaining a relatively consistent, enduring, and satisfying personal life-style are seldom if ever easily done alone. Transition phases in complementary and supplementary roles are particularly demanding because they require simultaneous or synchronized anticipation, revision, planning, adaptation, and development efforts and action by the members of the interdependent role set. Although supplementarity and complementarity of roles evolve almost automatically in the stable family in a culturally homogeneous society, they now more often have to be effected by deliberate cooperative analysis, adjustment, and accommodation. The people involved in interdependent roles, often in close and intense personal relationships, therefore need to become involved in role negotiation and joint problem solving. These require skills different from those used in personal problem solving; in any case, they represent significant social innovation and modification of traditional role stereotypes and the division of labor, with the attendant resistance to change.

Probably because the price of institutional or organizational neglect of role transitions can be determined and demonstrated fairly objectively (e.g., Mahler & Drotter, 1986), many organizations have worked out ways to help newcomers adapt to new roles (London & Stumpf, 1982; Schein, 1971; Walker, 1980).

Organizations usually expect that people occupying new positions will require some time, even with the guidance and support of a supervisor, to adapt to the new role. Using a path-analytic technique, Toffler (1981) studied the role development of a group of physicians' assistants from one month before graduation through the assistants' first five months in their first jobs and found several distinct stages. Nicholson (1984) proposed a theory of work-role transitions in which he distinguished two dimensions—personal development and role development—and proposed four modes of adjustment to transitions that depend on the degree of development in the two dimensions. Using Nicholson's theory, West, Nicholson, and Rees (1987) studied the transitions of a large group of British managers to new and, for a significant subgroup, newly created jobs. They reported that proactive growth models of anticipatory adjustment are more generally applicable to job change than reactive stress-coping models.

Another important development in the workplace is that employers are gradually beginning to recognize the importance of their employees' involvement in other theaters of life, in other roles (London & Stumpf, 1982).

Unfortunately, institutions, organizations, and individuals qualified to facilitate the transition process in roles other than work are not so visible, and those that are available often devote their attention to only a single generic role or life theater, such as child guidance, family counseling, or individual psychotherapy.

Criteria of Role Performance

Because the concept of role links individuals and the social matrix in which they function, criteria of role performance generally contain individual and collective, internal and external, aspects.

From the vantage point of the role set or social unit, the key evaluation criterion is the effectiveness or satisfactoriness of role performance. Because the different parties in the role set do not necessarily have congruent expectations, judgments of effectiveness may become complicated, with one participant proclaiming effective performance and the other seeing only ineffective performance.

Although judgments of effectiveness focus on the actual content and style of the role player's behavior, role theory suggests that several antecedent variables could affect the degree of effectiveness. The variables include the validity of the role players' perceptions of the expectations of their role sets and their own general and specific skills (Sarbin, 1968). On the basis of their study of embarrassment, Gross and Stone (1964) suggested three categories of antecedent conditions for effective role performance: appropriate identity, personal poise, and the maintenance of confidence. The Work Importance Study (Super, 1982) proposes a model of work importance that suggests that degree of affective commitment, active participation, and possession of relevant knowledge are the antecedents of effective role performance. Some of the antecedents may prove useful as intermediate criteria of effectiveness.

An important question about the validity of the effectiveness criteria is whether role *senders'* expectations (that is, expectations of other people who define a player's role) really reflect what is best for *them*. In discussing organizational effectiveness, Schneider (1983) referred to the usefulness of the type of organization member who creates suspicion, conflict, and strain by asking uncomfortable but pertinent questions—behavior that may run counter to the expectations of his or her role set. Similarly, Janis's work (1972) on groupthink provides dramatic illustrations of just how dysfunctional compliance with the cohesive work group's expectations regarding concurrence can be.

When there is marked complementarity or supplementarity of roles, the judgment of effectiveness should also take into account the degree of support and coordination of effort received from complementary and supplementary role partners. Judgments of effectiveness should therefore often reflect the articulation of the interdependent roles as much as individual role performance. This seldom seems to happen. However, one field in which role effectiveness assessments are commonly made, performance appraisal of staff, lends itself to this approach.

From the vantage point of the role player, the key criterion is the satisfaction gained from performing the role. Role theory suggests that an important aspect of satisfaction is self-perceived efficacy in performing the role (as defined by the role player), thus providing a link with the role set's effectiveness criterion. For a largely college- and university-educated group of women, Hall (1972) found that simply coping (as opposed to not coping) with role demands may be more strongly related to satisfaction than is the type of coping strategy a person uses.

As in the case of the role set, the adequacy of the satisfaction criterion in specific cases may be questioned. How realistic, for example, is satisfaction gained from "working harder" (IIIc coping type, [Hall, 1972]) in terms of the longer-term survival and health of the role player?

Whether judgments of effectiveness by members of the role set and assessments of satisfaction by the role player should both be supplemented by contributions from competent third parties is frequently answered by the use of outside consultants.

Other important aspects of the internal criterion for role performance may be satisfaction with the choice of role, when choice is possible; the actual personal expenditure on it, as compared to what the person would have preferred to invest; the degree of control over the investment in the role, as perceived by the role player; the support, comradeship, and recognition received from interdependent role partners; the nature and meaningfulness of the role action; the degree of self-actualization experienced; the external rewards received; and the congruence of the person, the role, and the setting (Schneider, 1985; Seybolt, 1980). Numerous organizational studies have confirmed the importance of these and related factors in job satisfaction. They have also revealed the often complex relationships between effectiveness and satisfaction.

To the extent that performance in separate roles is judged by different role senders, more or less independent judgments of effectiveness are possible. Because it is the role player who assesses the satisfaction gained from performing different roles, the role player has to recognize that satisfaction in one role may affect satisfaction in other roles. This means that the role player must make a conscious effort to assess satisfaction from or in one specific role. Practitioners are well acquainted with the phenomenon of displacement, wherein discontent attributed to one role sometimes represents spillover of dissatisfaction with another role.

For clients, a more important and meaningful criterion than satisfaction with a single role may be satisfaction with the current role constellation, or life structure (Lee, 1984). Quality-of-life studies have shown that satisfaction with work and leisure generally correlates significantly with overall life satisfaction over different demographic groups (Super, 1940; Crandall, 1984). For people in developed countries work, family, and leisure seem to form the triad within which they must attain satisfaction with the life structure (Derr, 1980; Lee & Kanungo, 1984).

Few researchers have attempted to develop comprehensive criteria for role performance that incorporate both the internal and external perspectives. Holland's Person-Environment Fit approach (1976, 1985), although developed for a different purpose, could provide useful leads. Caplan's notion (1987) of assessing both individual abilities against organizational "supplies" and individual abilities against organizational demands, and Muchinsky and Monahan's notions (1987) of supplementary and complementary congruence, are cases in point.

Researchers, such as Heron (1954), and formal organizations with sophisticated views on human resource management have been aware of the dual criteria of role effectiveness and satisfaction for a long time. In other roles, notably such gender-typed roles as homemaker, concern among the role set for effective performance seems to be much greater than concern for the satisfaction the role player gets from the role: spouses want results.

Role Disengagement and Relinquishment

Role disengagement refers to the process of diminishing investment in a role that leads to eventual relinquishment. For upwardly mobile executives, job changes (relinquishing one position to enter a new one) are a recurring experience, but the change is seldom dramatic in the sense of involving radically new role sets and role demands (Kotter, 1982; Mahler & Drotter, 1986). When the prospect of the new role is attractive and those in transit are well prepared, the transition can be and often is a positive experience. However, if the new role requires skills and resources that individuals sense they lack, the transition may be more difficult, with resulting reluctance to move. The baggage syndrome (carrying into a new position satisfying but unnecessary and even dysfunctional tasks and activities that were appropriate to a previous role) is a common occurrence in organizations and probably equally prevalent, even if less studied, in the process of disengagement from and relinquishment of other generic roles, such as that of parent.

But people also experience role disenchantment, or burnout. Here a dwindling subjective investment in the role, for whatever reasons, is coupled with progressively more perfunctory role performance. The issue may be faced and resolved, as by role relinquishment, job redesign, rotation, or, where this is not possible, apathetic resignation.

Role relinquishment can be voluntary, as in choosing early retirement, or involuntary, as in losing an executive position in a hostile takeover. A person can anticipate and prepare for graduation or retirement or may face a sudden and unexpected change, such as losing a spouse in a fatal accident. Specific types of role relinquishment have received some attention—for example, those associated with widowhood (Lopata, 1975), aging and retirement (Lozier, 1975; Ferrini & Parker, 1978; Havighurst, 1973), and loss of position because of redundancy, job abolishment, ineffective performance, or takeovers (Abdelnour & Hall, 1980; Manuso, 1977). Many role relinquishments, in contrast with role acquisitions, are associated with personal pain, sadness, and despair because they are sudden and because the individuals involved have no meaningful new roles that could replace those which were relinquished (Gordon, 1976).

The gradual aging of the population in industrialized countries indicates that role disengagement and relinquishment should become, and indeed are becoming, more significant issues in career development, human resource management, and the helping professions.

Problematic Aspects of Role Demands

Judging from their prominence in the research literature and professional vocabulary, problematic role demands and how to deal with them are among the most important and useful aspects of role theory. Role conflict is the modal concept and may refer to person-role conflict (a person's aspirations lead to a role conception and behaviors unacceptable to members of the role set), intrasender conflict (a role sender makes mutually contradictory demands with respect to the same role, such as in the double-bind type of relationship), intersender conflict (different senders have contradictory expectations with respect to the same role), and interrole conflict (the demands of one role, such as high school teacher, are incompatible with the demands of another role played by the same person, for example, being a part-time bartender in a strip joint).

Other types of role demands that may be problematic are role overload and underload, role ambiguity, and lack of articulation of complementary or supplementary roles. The problematic aspect can be quantitative (e.g., the role demands excessive amounts of time) or qualitative (e.g., different roles have contradictory value orientations).

Such problematic role situations are generally assumed to occur quite commonly and with increasing frequency, and some evidence supports this. Pleck, Staines, and Lang (1980) showed that more than a third of a representative sample of American workers experienced either moderate or severe work-family conflicts. Hall (1972) reported that 65 percent of a sample of mainly college-educated women ($N = 261$) experienced role conflicts. Havighurst (1973) commented on the growing salience of flexible life-styles, implying more role choices and transitions. Astin (1984) referred to dramatic changes in young women's occupational expectations. Lee and Kanungo (1984) mentioned pervasive social changes, such as the increasingly common single-person, single-parent, and dual-career households in the United States, which signify basic changes in life-style, and Rapoport and Rapoport (1980) referred to the changing character of American education, with its critical stance toward socially sanctioned roles and values. All spell additional and potentially problematic new role demands.

A further assumption is that problematic role demands are often dysfunctional, leading to undesirable outcomes. The view is that role conflict and ambiguity tend to hinder performance and that, to the extent that the individual's need to achieve and be productive is frustrated, they may also be unpleasant and stressful (Schuler, 1984; Van Sell et al., 1981; Biddle, 1986).

The research on role conflict and related conditions often suffers from such methodological defects as insufficient differentiation between the different types or facets of role conflict (Rabinowitz & Stumpf, 1987); over-reliance on verbal descriptions of anticipated role behaviors in certain situations, rather than observation of actual behavior (Van De Vliert, 1979); using inadequate criterion measures of role performance, as in measuring achievement without measuring satisfaction or dissatisfaction (Crosby, 1984); and measuring only one role player's performance or satisfaction in a highly interdependent role set, as in some dual-career studies.

Reviewers caution against uncritical acceptance of broad generalizations about the negative effects of problematic role demands (Biddle, 1986; Rabinowitz & Stumpf, 1987). Tension stemming from the demands of different roles, some ambiguity in role demands, and some lack of articulation between supplementary and complementary role players is not only a fact of life but may on occasion provide the stimulus for growth and development.

Counselors and researchers need to become more knowledgeable about the necessary and sufficient conditions for dysfunctional performance and experience of stress; the specific type or facet of role conflict involved; the personalities of the role players and their commitment to the roles in question; immediate situational variables, such as the availability of a support system and perceived control over situational factors; and the broader context of cultural norms regarding the primacy of the several roles and occupational statuses.

Many examples of interrole conflict and role overload—such as the woman in a dual-earner situation, or ambitious young executives actively extending their domain of influence and visibility—have to do with attempts to handle the demands of multiple roles successfully.

Addressing the issue of multiple roles and role strain, Sieber (1974) argued that the benefits of role accumulation tend to outweigh any accompanying stress, whereas Marks (1977) critically examined the underlying ideology of the scarcity approach to human energy and proposed "energy expansion" as an alternative explanation for the *abundance* of energy people often have for things to which they are highly committed, even if they seemingly are already fully occupied.

In this connection Havighurst (1973) reported a preponderance of positive correlations between performance in the various life roles for Kansas City men and women aged 40 to 70 and, to a lesser extent, for some cross-national samples of men aged 70 to 75. The data support the hypothesis that each individual has a certain quantum of time and energy, that this varies from person to person, and that the amount depends upon the person's health, vigor, and motivation.

Significant *positive* relationships exist between amount of role conflict (measured in terms of overall role conflict, intersender conflict, and role overload experienced) and the rated administrative performance of full-time faculty members (Rabinowitz & Stumpf, 1987). Fisher and Gitelson (1983) showed that role conflict and role ambiguity, in an assortment of studies, consistently correlated 0.20 to 0.35 with variables such as organizational commitment and job involvement. Such a result contradicts the general contention that problematic role demands have dysfunctional results.

Women in dual-career marriages, especially if they also are mothers, expand their constellation of roles. Unless some accommodation takes place, as in the husband's supplementing her efforts or in the use of such external support systems as part time child care, role overload and conflict in the roles of worker, spouse, homemaker, and parent would seem inevitable. Crosby (1984) provided a useful summary of typical studies that showed, among other things, that working wives generally do much more of the household labor than their husbands. A second set of studies presented an equivocal picture with regard to the spouses' marital satisfaction as a function of the wife's employment status. Crosby's own investigation of job satisfaction and domestic life in a relatively affluent Boston suburb (1984) led to the unexpected finding that the best single predictor of satisfaction among the employed women and men in her sample was family status, with single people expressing most dissatisfaction with their jobs and parents the least. Citing supporting findings by other researchers, she saw multiple roles as providing a fuller life, better health, and generally greater psychological protection and security.

Holahan and Gilbert (1979) investigated conflict in four major life roles. They related it to a number of personal and situational variables in a small sample of dual-career couples, some with children and some with no children, at a large university in the American Southwest. The correlates of role conflict differed markedly from the parent to the nonparent couples. The addition of the parent role evidently complicates the life of the dual-career couple, yet the parent couples reported equal or greater satisfaction with the relevant other roles than the nonparent group. The high levels of career commitment and aspiration, of feminist attitudes, and of the spouse's emotional support for career pursuit, all of which characterized the men and women in this sample, may account for their successful coping with the demands and challenges of a dual-career marriage.

Investigating stress in two-earner couples in England, Lewis and Cooper (1987) reported some significant relationships among measures of parental role pressure, gender, quantitative overload (much to do and little time in which to do it), Type A behavior, and work commitments and aspirations, on the one hand, and measures of dependent variables, such as anxiety and depression, somatic symptoms, job dissatisfaction, life dissatisfaction, and alcohol consumption, on the other. The sequence of best predictors in the multiple regression equations was quite different for couples with and without children, suggesting that work-family interference is largely work-parenting interference and that the traditional gender-role attitudes of individuals and of organizations continue to underlie much of this work-parenting conflict. Although role pressures were high for their entire sample, in general "the level of symptoms of stress . . . was low, confirming considerable evidence that multiple roles can be well managed" (1987, p. 300).

From a career development point of view it may be useful to consider in which roles, and at what stage of the life cycle, particular facets of role conflict most commonly occur. It would appear that potential or actual person-role conflicts will be much in evidence when role choices are made or reconsidered, whereas the concept of intrasender conflicts may be most applicable to close and intense interpersonal relationships, such as those between spouses or between parent and child. Intersender conflicts are likely when the role set contains more than one significant member, as in the work situation. Interrole conflicts may be especially relevant in considering and developing a satisfactory life-style. Role overload could often become an issue for dual-career couples or for successful professionals who become progressively more involved in ancillary or subroles, such as administration.

Coping with Role Demands

Compliance with role demands need not always be onerous. Indeed, efficacy in role performance is a basic source of satisfaction and joy in life (Andrews and Withey, 1976). As we have discussed, many people succeed in managing their lives well, at least in the short-term perspective used in most research studies, despite problematic and taxing role demands. Understanding how people cope with such situations is clearly of central importance in the field of career development.

In common parlance, coping generally means to deal or contend successfully with tasks, challenges, and the like. The opposite of coping is failing or not coping. In the professional literature the concept of coping has been used most frequently within the context of stress theory. It has been defined in several different ways (Kessler et al., 1985; Haan, 1982). For our purposes we can define coping as the degree of success of the cognitive, behavioral, and emotional efforts made to master, change, tolerate, or otherwise manage role demands that tax or exceed a person's resources (Pearlin & Schooler, 1978; Cohen & Lazarus, 1979). Any one problematic role situation, such as role overload, role conflict, or the lack of articulation of complementary or supplementary roles in the role set, may singly or in combination tax the role player's resources. Also, role demands that usually are not difficult to meet may become problematic when the person's resources are diminished because of illness or a loss in the support system.

A significant early attempt at theorizing about coping arose from Gross, Mason, and McEachern's 1958 study of school superintendents, in which they focused on the behavior of the role player who faces conflicting demands from two role senders (an intersender conflict situation). They used as independent variables the legitimacy of the role senders (as judged by the role player) and the expected negative sanctions from role senders should the role players fail to comply with the role senders' demands. The role player could have one of three orientations. First was the "moralist," who, when faced with conflicting demands, is concerned primarily with the respective legitimacies of the two senders—that is, is more concerned with whether a role sender has the right to make certain demands than with the sanctions that might result from noncompliance. Second was the "expedient," who is more concerned with sanctions than legitimacy and will do anything to avert the worse sanctions. Last was the "moral expedient," who takes into account both legitimacy and sanctions and tries to find an acceptable compromise.

Extensive application of this theory, and its derivations to more than six thousand cases of intersender conflict, resulted in a median proportion of correct predictions of 0.69 (Van De Vliert, 1979). Note that stakeholder theory, an important contribution to organization theory, reemphasizes the importance of effective management of intersender conflicts by the organization rather than by a single role player (Pearce, 1982; Mason & Mitroff, 1981; Gouws, 1988).

Unfortunately, the theory of conflict resolution advanced by Gross et al. (1958) addressed only one facet of the spectrum and did not take into account more proactive ways to cope with role conflict, such as directly influencing and changing role senders' expectations.

Coping behavior can take many forms, depending on the person, the situation, and the context. Dubin (1973) suggested segregation of roles as a form of coping—to not let experiences and feelings in one role affect behavior and experiences in other roles. Wilensky (1960) proposed an alternative view, namely, that positive or negative feelings and experiences in one role will spill over positively or negatively into other roles. A third possibility is compensation, wherein the individual tries to make up for the discontent experienced in one role by gaining satisfaction from one or more other roles. Empirical research in the United States and Europe has shown that all three processes occur, with spillover between work and nonwork apparently the most frequent and segregation the least frequent (Near, 1984).

Lee (1984) proposed three other broad strategies for coping with stress: reducing the uncertainty in a situation, reducing the importance of a situation, and diminishing the negative effects of stress.

In contrast are more specific forms of coping behavior. Folkman and Lazarus (1980) compiled a checklist of sixty-eight specific coping strategies. The meager evidence available suggests that people may show consistent coping responses to the same type of stressor over time but little consistency across different life situations, such as work and family (Kessler et al., 1985).

Starting from a stress and health orientation, Moos and Billings (1982) provided an overview of attempts at classifying coping strategies in meaningful clusters or categories. They also proposed their own classification of coping responses in nine types, grouped in three clusters, according to whether the coping effort focuses mainly on the appraisal aspect, on the problem itself, or on handling the emotions aroused by the situation.

Working with samples of largely college-educated women, Hall (1972) identified sixteen coping strategies they used in handling role conflict situations. Hall grouped the strategies into three main categories: structural role redefinition, personal role redefinition, and reactive role behavior. Amatea and Fong-Beyette (quoted by Phillips et al., 1988) added two dimensions to Hall's classification: active-passive, and emotion focused/problem focused.

In studying coping techniques in marriage, Ilfeld (1982) identified four factors that correlated significantly with marital stress—optimistic-action (negative correlation), and withdrawal-conflict, rationalization-resignation, and seeking outside help (the latter three all positively correlated).

Focusing on coping and the treatment of stress-related problems, Cameron and Meichenbaum (1982) stated four fundamental prerequisites for effective coping with stress: accurate (or at least adaptive) appraisal of the world, the self, and the transactions between the two; having available an adequate response repertoire, especially such universally important social skills as communication and assertive behavior, and palliative skills (e.g., self-relaxation); appropriate deployment of available skills; and efficient recovery from a stress-coping episode (quick return to normal levels of psychological and physiological functioning).

Missing from the list is the availability and use of external resources in the form of a support system that consists of people in or outside the role set, or of facilities that may promote coping. Other classifications of coping behavior could involve reactive-proactive behavior and changing the situation (Nicholson, 1984).

The different approaches suggest the following as minimum perspectives or categories for considering the different ways to cope with role demands:

1. Identification of role demands of role senders and of own conception
2. Available resources: internal (e.g., personal values, attitudes, and interests, repertoire of pertinent knowledge and skills, energy, discretionary time) and external (potential support system within or outside the role set)

3. Actual role behavior: balance of role sender's demands and own conception of role; handling unavoidable intersender role conflicts (i.e., those that are not resolved by identifying role demands); separation, combination, addition, or integration of roles; control of time characteristics (e.g., sequential versus simultaneous role performance)
4. Resistance to stress: mastery of stress-inoculation skills and state of health and fitness

Space does not permit full explication of the classifications, but a few examples may illustrate their potential usefulness in focusing attention on relevant issues and identifying meaningful patterns.

Role demands of role senders often allow some latitude or leeway. Proactively supplying relevant information and explanations to role senders may result in modified demands that are closer to the role player's conception and capabilities. Graen's role-making processes (1976) and Harrison's role negotiation technique (1972) are examples of this approach in work organizations, and a similar approach may resolve problems of work division, such as between dual-career spouses. Biddle (1986) drew attention to three different meanings of *role expectations,* which may refer to normative prescriptions, subjective beliefs, or personal preferences about how a role player should behave. The distinction may be important in assessing the available latitude for adapting or shaping a role.

Practitioners are familiar with situations in which the limiting factor in modifying role perceptions resides not so much in the role sender(s) as in the role player and her or his role conception. For example, some women who work and are spouses, mothers, and homemakers continue to set the same high standards for their homemaker role as they did before the change, despite reassurances from concerned family members that some relaxation of standards is acceptable and desirable. Such people need help in restructuring their role conceptions and explicitly renegotiating their role contracts with their role senders.

The available personal resources, such as values, knowledge, attitudes, and skills, have been the subject of intensive and extensive study, especially in the counseling profession. (We mentioned some examples of inclusive measures of relevant individual differences in the section on role choice.) On the other hand, the contributions of available external resources to improve coping have not been so numerous. Notable are the numerous studies of social support in community mental health (Kessler et al., 1985; Gesten & Jason, 1987), the dramatic influence that systems theory has had on the field of family counseling (Bednar, Burlingame, & Masters, 1988), and management, which highlighted the importance of implementing networks (Kotter, 1982, 1985) and supporting relationships (Clawson, 1980; Kram, 1985).

The control and affection dimensions in social interaction (Leary, 1957; Lorr & McNair, 1963; Benjamin, 1974; Gouws, 1982) suggest a fruitful approach to classifying coping behaviors in terms of the balance in role behavior between role senders' demands and the role player's conception of the role. A situation of high perceived control by the role senders, coupled with positive affect between role senders and role player (as might be expected in a complementary teacher-pupil-parent relationship), will probably result in the following kind of role behavior description: "complies and tries to please members of role set; readily accepts their guidance and help."

On the other hand, a situation in which the role player recognizes that some minimum compliance with the demands of the role set is necessary, experiences a fair amount of personal autonomy, and has a detached affective relationship with the role senders, may lead to role behavior described as performing the role in a perfunctory manner (going through the motions) while signaling distance from the role. Goffman (1961) and Mayntz (1970) discussed other circumstances in which role detachment or distancing might occur.

The work of Gross et al. (1958) and Mason and Mitroff (1981) suggested ways in which to further subdivide behaviors in order to resolve intersender conflicts.

Mintzberg (1980) gave interesting examples of how the shrewd manager uses a role obligation (e.g., officiating at a ceremonial occasion) as an opportunity to initiate role performance (e.g., lobby for a cause). The synergistic integration of roles, when simultaneous or near-simultaneous performance of two roles leads to better results than the performance of either by itself, has not been further explored in the literature and could well be an important explanatory mechanism in beneficial role accumulation (Sieber, 1974; Marks, 1977).

One way to promote coping with multiple roles is to separate their geographical and time domains as clearly as possible and to handle them consecutively. Hall (1972) pointed out that the husband's roles generally allow for more of this approach than the working homemaker's and mother's; she almost inescapably tends to face simultaneous demands from competing role senders.

Increased resistance to stress can be vital when lack of control over the situation or some other circumstance rules out proactive coping strategies and indicates that the role player will have to make the major adaptation without much recourse to external resources. The relevant stress-inoculation skills (Meichenbaum, 1977) include relaxation as a generalized coping strategy (i.e., applicable whenever stress is experienced), cognitive restructuring of stressful events, anxiety-management training, and anger control.

It is interesting that the effects of stressful experiences on health receive much attention, but the generally positive effect on coping ability of being healthy and fit is a relatively neglected topic (see, e.g., Holroyd & Lazarus, 1982; Schuler, 1984).

Finally, variety and flexibility of coping behavior are clearly beneficial. Pearlin and Schooler (1978) found that the more varied an individual's coping repertoire, the better protected that person is from distress. They also concluded that the most effective coping strategies tend to be exhibited by men, by the educated, and by the more affluent members of society. It follows that those people who may be most exposed to hardship are generally least equipped to handle it.

Personal, Contextual, and Situational Factors in Role Behavior

It would be unrealistic to try to summarize here the voluminous research on individual differences (many of which represent interactions with the environment) that could be relevant to role behavior. Useful reviews and contributions include Osipow (1987) on career counseling, Guion and Gibson (1988) on personnel selection, and Gilbert (1978), Schroder (1989), and Sundberg, Snowden, and Reynolds (1978) on assessment of competence. Unfortunately, similarly focused, convenient references are not available except in Gilbert and in Sundberg et al.

One nonspecific personal variable that looms large in all comprehensive accounts of career development is age, most often represented in the more functional form of life stages (Erikson, 1963; Super et al., 1957; Super, 1980, 1990), eras and developmental periods (Levinson, 1978), or similar concepts. An important practical question is how career development as a function of age is seen: many writers, including Super (1980), have used a terminology and the rainbow figure that suggest a curve that rises to a plateau and gradually goes downhill. This view correctly represents the course of certain abilities such as psychomotor skills. Super (1980, 1990) also recognizes "minicycles" (similar to Levinson's 1978 terminology of seasons and eras) as repeated cycles of transitional uncertainty, perhaps even confusion, emerging clarity, growth, and then establishment and consolidation, which eventually give way to the next transitional period. In working with mature clients, I have found strong empathy with and appreciation for the Levinson symbolism of seasons, which may more correctly represent such cognitive, affective, and conative aspects of adult living as growth in wisdom, perspective, and balanced judgment.

An important question in career development is whether individuals should focus on their strengths or aim for all-around effectiveness, giving as much or more attention to the elimination of weaknesses (most typical of clinicians) as to the development and use of strengths (most typical of counselors). Beneath much of the current popular and even more serious literature on management development, for example, lurks the implicit assumption that individual superiority, self-sufficiency, and all-around capability are attainable. Two interesting contrary views have been expressed.

In his style-expression theory, Crandall (1984) proposed that individuals should understand themselves, clearly project their strengths, and look for other people or situations that will reinforce and supplement those strengths. In a research program of more than nine years and the study of about 120 management teams, Belbin (1981) identified nine team roles, each distinctive in terms of psychometric profile and typical behavior in team situations. He also found that teams composed of people who played different but mutually complementary and supplementary roles outperformed more homogeneous teams composed of mentally highly superior members. The Belbin study suggested that in management and team development, at least, aiming for development of superteams may be more realistic, effective, and satisfying than trying to develop superindividuals. This again underscores the importance of looking at role-set performance whenever interdependence between the members is appreciable, and not concentrating too exclusively on solo role performance.

There is no hard-and-fast distinction between longer-term contextual and shorter-term situational determinants. Generally, the individual is relatively powerless with regard to the more enduring and pervasive contextual factors, such as national and organizational culture, the level of wealth or poverty in the country, the quality of the educational system, and the nature of the ruling ideology. When one or more is adverse, the result will almost certainly be some curtailment of the objective opportunity structure.

Situational factors refer to the more transient influences flowing from the characteristics of the settings in which events and time-limited sequences of events take place, such as the kind of boss or colleagues the person has, the availability of particular types of community leisure activities, illness in the family, access to facilities for continued education, number and variety of people in the individual's age group, circumstances and interests in the neighborhood, number and importance of recent changes in the person's life theaters, and the design and content of the person's job. Attempts at developing a general taxonomy of situations have so far not been very successful (Sundberg et al., 1978), presumably because an important consideration is how the person perceives the situation, and that depends significantly on such personal variables as values, interests, and attitudes.

A weak distinction between contextual and situational factors may be the greater degree of influence and control the individual generally has, or may attain, over the situation. Because the arena is smaller, the variables fewer, and the coplayers more tangible and visible, situations generally leave more scope for constructive proactive approaches than is the case with most contextual factors.

Perhaps the most important complex of personal variables in role behavior is that which determines whether a person can perceive positive aspects in even seriously discouraging circumstances. For most of the world's population, the circumstances of poverty, malnutrition, poor education, overcrowding, lack of opportunity, and oppression are objectively present. Presumably, an internal locus of control (Rotter, 1954)—that is, some belief in a person's ability to influence outcomes—and the judgment that achieving something worthwhile is possible, with whatever skills a person has, are both necessary ingredients for beginning to cope constructively with adverse circumstances (Bandura, 1986; Caplan et al., 1989).

Conclusion

This discussion demonstrates the utility of the role construct and of role self-concepts in career development. They can appropriately be used for describing and discussing some of the most important aspects of careers and career development—for example, roles as core components of careers; role choice and development as including some of the most weighty decisions and actions in a person's life; coping with role demands as representing a significant part of how life's problems and difficulties are managed; and role transition, with its phases of reassessment, disengagement and new investment or reinvestment, as central to recurrent personal renewal processes.

This is an impressive and wide-ranging list.

On the negative side, role theory development has so far been restricted to such specific segments of the field as conflict handling (Gross et al., 1958), role making (Graen, 1976), and personal versus role development (Nicholson, 1984). Perhaps the very versatility of the role construct makes it difficult to manipulate in a conventional hypotheticodeductive mode of theory building.

In addition to its advantages for descriptive purposes, the role construct is a valuable heuristic device. Adult clients often need assistance in making sense of the raw data of their career experiences and their feelings about them. Encountering reality does not automatically lead to new insights. A systematic approach to assisting clients in the process of interpreting, understanding, and enriching their experience is necessary. Kolb and Fry's 1975 model of the experiential learning cycle has been quite useful, especially if relevant additional concepts are introduced to the sequence at the abstract conceptualization stage of the cycle.

The various aspects of the role concept lend themselves very well to simple verbal and pictorial presentations (Hall, 1972; Schein, 1978; Super, 1980), which appeal to clients because they are helpful in ordering their experiences, in self-analysis, and in considering future courses of conduct.

When the experiential learning activities are supplemented by more sophisticated measures of role salience, values, interests, self-concepts, and stylistic variables, the task of joint exploration by client and counselor becomes an exciting and worthwhile venture. Different clients appear to profit from different perspectives, and some prefer multiple perspectives, even if this results in what the practitioner may feel is a logically inconsistent array of data and insights (Kolb & Fry, 1975; Linstone, 1984; Lee & Kanungo, 1984).

Three promising directions for further exploration and development emerge from this overview. The first, which is not new but needs a fresh look, concerns the importance of the interdependence of roles and today's one-sided emphasis on the tasks, actions, and effectiveness of the individual role player, with concurrent neglect of the contributions from the other members of the role set. In this chapter we have tried to demonstrate that a more balanced, multiple-actor approach is essential, especially in determining role demands and in assessing the effectiveness of role performance within highly interdependent role sets.

The second area of promise is that of multiple roles and the notion of energy creation (Marks, 1977). More intensive study of how happy and productive people integrate multiple role demands into their daily living, along the lines of the Kotter (1982), Mintzberg (1980), and Super (1940) studies but covering the total spectrum of roles, would be highly instructive.

The third area of promise concerns the relevance of role and career development theory for the disadvantaged multitudes of underdeveloped countries. In the relatively affluent developed countries, a great deal of experimenting with new role conceptions and life-styles is under way among adolescents and adults of all ages. Role and career development theory has much to offer to this type of person and client. Do counselors and clinicians have anything worthwhile to offer to people in severely curtailed opportunity structures, or is career counseling an enterprise with relevance mainly for the privileged? The research of Cherry (1981) and Kidd (1984) in England suggested that these theories do have something to offer. The problems may lie in how they are delivered—that is, the problems may be in the intervention systems.

References

Abdelnour, B. T., & Hall, D. T. (1980). Career development of established employees. *Career Development Bulletin, 2,* 5–8.

Andrews, F. A., & Withey, S. B. (1976). *Social indicators of well-being in America: The development and measurement of perceptual indicators.* New York: Plenum.

Astin, H. S. (1984). The meaning of work in women's lives: A socio-psychological model of career choice and work behavior. *Counseling Psychologist, 12,* 117–126.

Bandura, A. (1977). *Social learning theory.* Englewood Cliffs, NJ: Prentice-Hall.

Bandura, A. (1986). *Social foundations of thought and action.* Englewood Cliffs, NJ: Prentice-Hall.

Bednar, R. L., Burlingame, G. M., & Masters, K. S. (1988). Systems of family treatment: Substance or semantics? *Annual Review of Psychology, 39,* 401–434.

Belbin, R. M. (1981). *Management teams: Why they succeed or fail.* Portsmouth, NH: Heinemann Educational Books.

Belbin, R. M. (1990). *The job promotion: A journey to a new profession.* Portsmouth, NH: Heinemann Educational Books.

Benjamin, L. S. (1974). Structural analysis of social behavior. *Psychological Review, 81,* 392–425.

Biddle, B. J. (1986). Recent developments in role theory. *Annual Review of Sociology, 12,* 67–92.

Cameron, R., & Meichenbaum, D. (1982). The nature of effective coping and the treatment of stress-related problems: A cognitive-behavioral perspective. In L. Goldberger & S. Breznitz (Eds.), *Handbook of stress*. New York: Free Press.

Campbell, R. E., Cellini, J. V., Shaltry, P. E., Long, A. E., & Pinkos, D. (1979). *A diagnostic taxonomy of adult career problems* (NIE Project NO. G-78-0211). Columbus, OH: National Center for Research in Vocational Education.

Caplan, N., Whitmore, J. K., & Choy, M. H. (1989). *The boat people and achievement in America*. Ann Arbor: University of Michigan.

Caplan, R. D. (1987). Person-environment fit theory and organizations: Commensurate dimensions, time perspectives, and mechanisms, *Journal of Vocational Behavior, 31*, 248–267.

Cherry, N. (1981). Ability, education and occupational functioning. In A. G. Watts, D. E. Super, & J. M. Kidd (Eds.) *Career development in Britain* (pp. 193–212). Cambridge, England: Hobson's.

Clawson, J. G. (1980). Mentoring in managerial careers. In C. B. Derr (Ed.), *Work, family, and the career*. New York: Praeger.

Cohen, F., & Lazarus, R. S. (1979). Coping with the stresses of illness. In G. C. Stone, F. Cohen, & N. E. Adler (Eds.), *Health psychology*. San Francisco: Jossey-Bass.

Corsini, R. J. (Ed.). (1987). *Concise encyclopedia of psychology*. New York: Wiley.

Crandall, R. (1984). Work and leisure in the life space. In M. D. Lee & R. N. Kanungo (Eds.), *Management of work and personal life*. New York: Praeger.

Crosby, F. (1984). Job satisfaction and domestic life. In M. D. Lee & R. N. Kanungo (Eds.), *Management of work and personal life*. New York: Praeger.

Derr, C. B. (1980). More about career anchors. In C. B. Derr (Ed.), *Work, family, and the career*. New York: Praeger.

Dubin, R. (1973). Work and nonwork: Institutional perspectives. In M. D. Dunnette (Ed.), *Work and nonwork in the year 2001*. Pacific Grove, CA: Brooks/Cole.

Erikson, E. H. (1963). *Childhood and society* (rev. ed.). New York: W. W. Norton.

Ferrini, P., & Parker, L. A. (1978). *Career change*. Cambridge, MA: Technical Education Research Centers.

Fisher, C. D., & Gitelson, R. (1983). A meta-analysis of the correlates of role conflict and ambiguity. *Journal of Applied Psychology, 68*, 320–333.

Folkman, S., & Lazarus, R. S. (1980). An analysis of coping in a middle-aged community sample. *Journal of Health and Social Behavior, 21*, 219–239.

Frieze, I. H., Parsons, J. E., Johnson, P. B., Ruble, D. N., & Zellman, G. L. (1978). *Women and sex roles: A social psychological perspective*. New York: W. W. Norton.

Gesten, E. L., & Jason, L. A. (1987). Social and community interventions. *Annual Review of Psychology, 38*, 427–460.

Gilbert, T. F. (1978). *Human competence*. New York: McGraw-Hill.

Goffman, E. (1961). *Encounters*. New York: Bobbs-Merrill.

Gordon, C. (1976). Development of evaluated role identities. *Annual Review of Sociology, 2*, 405–433.

Gouws, D. J. (1982). *Die interpersoonlike diagram (intergram) as 'n opleiding-*

shulpmiddel [The interpersonal diagram as a counseling tool]. Paper presented at the Convention of the Psychological Association of South Africa.

Gouws, D. J. (1988). Stakeholders in innovation. *RSA 2000, 10,* 25–30.

Graen, G. (1976). Role-making processes within complex organizations. In M. D. Dunnette (Ed.), *Handbook of industrial and organizational psychology.* Skokie, IL: Rand McNally.

Gross, E., & Stone, G. P. (1964). Embarrassment and the analysis of role requirements. *American Journal of Sociology, 70,* 1–15.

Gross, N., Mason, W. S., & McEachern, A. W. (1958). *Explorations in role analysis: Studies of the school superintendency role.* New York: Wiley.

Guion, R. M., & Gibson, W. M. (1988). Personnel selection and placement. *Annual Review of Psychology, 39,* 349–374.

Haan, N. (1982). The assessment of coping, defense, and stress. In L. Goldberger & S. Breznitz (Eds.), *Handbook of stress.* New York: Free Press.

Hall, D. T. (1972). A model of coping with role-conflict: The role behavior of college educated women. *Administrative Science Quarterly, 17,* 471–486.

Hall, D. T. et al. (1986). *Career development in organizations.* San Francisco: Jossey-Bass.

Harré, R., & Lamb, R. (Eds.). (1983). *The encyclopedic dictionary of psychology.* Cambridge, MA: MIT Press.

Harrison, R. (1972). Role negotiation: A tough-minded approach to team development. In W. W. Burke & H. A. Hornstein (Eds.), *The social technology of organization development.* Fairfax, VA: NTL Learning Resources.

Havighurst, R. J. (1973). Social roles, work, leisure, and education. In C. Eisdorfer & M. P. Lawton (Eds.), *The psychology of adult development and aging.* Washington, DC: American Psychological Association.

Heron, A. (1954). Satisfaction and satisfactoriness: Complementary aspects of occupational adjustment. *Occupational Psychology, 28,* 140–153.

Herr, E., & Cramer, S. H. (1988). *Career guidance and counseling through the life span.* Glenview, IL: Scott, Foresman.

Hodgson, R. C., Levinson, D. J., & Zaleznik, A. (1965). *The executive role constellations: An analysis of personality and role relations in management.* Boston: Harvard Business School.

Holahan, C. K., & Gilbert, L. A. (1979). Conflict between major life roles: Women and men in dual career couples. *Human Relations, 32*(6), 451–467.

Holland, J. L. (1976). Vocational preferences. In M. D. Dunnette (Ed.), *Handbook of industrial and organizational psychology.* Skokie, IL: Rand McNally.

Holland, J. L. (1985). *Making vocational choices: A theory of vocational personalities and work environments* (2nd. ed.). Englewood Cliffs, NJ: Prentice-Hall.

Holroyd, K. A., & Lazarus, R. S. (1982). Stress, coping, and somatic adaptation. In L. Goldberger & S. Breznitz (Eds.), *Handbook of stress.* New York: Free Press.

Howard, A., & Bray, D. W. (1988). *Managerial lives of transition.* New York: Guilford Press.

Ilfeld, F. W., Jr. (1982). Marital stressors, coping styles, and symptoms of depression. In L. Goldberger & S. Breznitz (Eds.), *Handbook of stress*. New York: Free Press.

Janis, I. L. (1972). *Victims of groupthink: A psychological study of foreign policy decisions and fiascoes*. Boston: Houghton Mifflin.

Kessler, R. C., Price, R. H., & Wortman, C. B. (1985). Social factors in psychopathology: Stress, social support, and coping processes. *Annual Review of Psychology, 36,* 531–572.

Kidd, J. M. (1984). The relationship of self and occupational concepts to the occupational preferences of adolescents. *Journal of Vocational Behavior, 24,* 48–65.

Kobasa, S. C. (1979). Stressful life events, personality, and health: An inquiry into hardiness. *Journal of Personality and Social Psychology, 37,* 1–11.

Kohn, M. L. (1969). *Class and conformity*. Belmont, CA: Dorsey Press.

Kohn, M. L. (1976). Social class and parental values: Another confirmation of the relationship. *American Sociological Review, 41,* 538–548.

Kolb, D. A., & Fry, R. (1975). Toward an applied theory of experiential learning. In C. L. Cooper (Ed.), *Theories of group processes*. New York: Wiley.

Kotter, J. P. (1982). *The general managers*. New York: Free Press.

Kotter, J. P. (1985). *Power and influence: Beyond final authority*. New York: Free Press.

Kotter, J. P., Faux, V. A., & McArthur, C. C. (1978). *Self-assessment and career development*. Englewood Cliffs, NJ: Prentice-Hall.

Kram, K. E. (1985). *Mentoring at work: Developmental relationships in organizational life*. Glenview, IL: Scott, Foresman.

Krumboltz, J. D., Becker-Haven, J. F., & Burnett, K. F. (1979). Counseling psychology. *Annual Review of Psychology, 30,* 555–602.

Leary, T. (1957). *Interpersonal diagnosis of personality*. New York: Ronald Press.

Lee, M. D. (1984). Life space design. In M. D. Lee & R. N. Kanungo (Eds.), *Management of work and personal life*. New York: Praeger.

Lee, M. D., & Kanungo, R. N. (Eds.). (1984). *Management of work and personal life*. New York: Praeger.

Lefcourt, H. M. (1976). *Locus of control: Current trends in theory and research*. New York: Wiley.

Levinson, D. J. (1959). Role, personality, and social structure in the organizational setting. *Journal of Abnormal and Social Psychology, 58,* 170–180.

Levinson, D. J. (1978). *The seasons of a man's life*. New York: Knopf.

Lewis, S.N.C., & Cooper, C. L. (1987). Stress in two-earner couples and stage in the life-cycle. *Journal of Occupational Psychology, 60,* 289–303.

Linstone, H. A. (1984). *Multiple perspectives for decision making: Bridging the gap between analysis and action*. New York: North-Holland.

London, M., & Stumpf, S. A. (1982). *Managing careers*. Reading, MA: Addison-Wesley.

Lopata, H. Z. (1975). Widowhood: Societal factors in life-span disruptions and alternatives. In C. Datan & L. H. Ginsberg (Eds.), *Life-span developmental psychology*. San Diego, CA: Academic Press.

Lorr, M., & McNair, D. M. (1963). An interpersonal behavior circle. *Journal of Abnormal and Social Psychology, 67,* 68–75.

Louis, M. R. (1980). Toward an understanding of career transitions. In C. R. Derr (Ed.), *Work, family, and the career.* New York: Praeger.

Lozier, J. (1975). Accommodating old people in society: Examples from Appalachia and New Orleans. In C. Datan & L. H. Ginsberg (Eds.), *Life-span developmental psychology.* San Diego, CA: Academic Press.

McConkey, D. D. (1983). *How to manage by results* (4th ed.). New York: AMACOM.

Mahler, W. R., & Drotter, S. J. (1986). *The succession planning handbook for the chief executive.* Midland Park, NJ: Mahler.

Manuso, J.S.J. (1977). Coping with job abolishment. *Journal of Occupational Medicine, 19,* 598–602.

Marks, S. R. (1977). Multiple roles and role strain: Some notes on human energy, time, and commitment. *American Sociological Review, 42,* 921–936.

Mason, R. O., & Mitroff, I. I. (1981). *Challenging strategic assumptions.* New York: Wiley.

Mayntz, R. (1970). Role distance, role identification, and amoral role behavior. *European Journal of Sociology, 2,* 368–378.

Meichenbaum, D. (1977). *Cognitive-behavior modification: An integrative approach.* New York: Plenum.

Miller, J., & Garrison, H. H. (1982). Sex roles: The division of labor at home and in the work place. *Annual Review of Sociology, 8,* 237–262.

Mintzberg, H. (1980). *The nature of managerial work.* Englewood Cliffs, NJ: Prentice-Hall.

Mitchell, G. D. (Ed.). (1968). *A dictionary of sociology.* New York: Routledge & Kegan Paul.

Mitchell, L. K., & Krumboltz, J. D. (1990). Social learning approach to career decision making. In D. Brown, L. Brooks, and Associates, *Career choice and development* (2nd ed.). San Francisco: Jossey-Bass.

Moos, R. H., & Billings, A. G. (1982). Conceptualizing and measuring coping resources and processes. In L. Goldberg & S. Breznitz (Eds.), *Handbook of stress.* New York: Free Press.

Muchinsky, P. M., & Monahan, C. J. (1987). What is person-environment congruence? Supplementary versus complementary models of fit. *Journal of Vocational Behavior, 31,* 268–277.

Near, J. P. (1984). Predictive and explanatory models of work and nonwork. In M. D. Lee & R. N. Kanungo (Eds.), *Management of work and personal life.* New York: Praeger.

Nicholson, N. (1984). A theory of work role transitions. *Administrative Science Quarterly, 29,* 172–191.

Osipow, S. H. (1986). Career issues through the life span. In M. S. Pallak & R. O. Perloff (Eds.), *Psychology and work: Productivity, change, and employment.* Washington, DC: American Psychological Association.

Osipow, S. H. (1987). Counseling psychology: Theory, research, and practice in career counseling. *Annual Review of Psychology, 38,* 257–278.

Pearce, J. A. (1982). The company mission as a strategic tool. *Sloan Management Review, 23,* 15–24.

Pearlin, L. I., & Schooler, C. (1978). The structure of coping. *Journal of Health and Social Behavior, 19,* 2–21.

Phares, E. J., & Lamiell, J. T. (1977). Personality. *Annual Review of Psychology, 28,* 113–140.

Phillips, S. D., Cairo, P. C., & Blustein, R. A. (1988). Career development and vocational behavior, 1987: A review. *Journal of Vocational Behavior, 33,* 119–184.

Pleck, J. H., Staines, G. L., & Lang, L. (1980). Conflicts between work and family life. *Monthly Labor Review, 103,* 29–32.

Rabinowitz, S., & Stumpf, S. A. (1987). Facets of role conflict, role-specific performance, and organizational level within the academic career. *Journal of Vocational Behavior, 30,* 72–83.

Rapoport, R., & Rapoport, R. N. (1980). Balancing work, family, and leisure: A triple helix model. In C. B. Derr (Ed.), *Work, family, and the career.* New York: Praeger.

Roberts, K. (1977). The social conditions, consequences, and limitations of career guidance. *British Journal of Guidance and Counseling, 5,* 1–9.

Roltheorie [Role theory]. (1979). [Special issue]. *Nederlandse Tijdscrift Voor De Psychologie, 34,* 87–152.

Rotter, J. B. (1954). *Social learning and clinical psychology.* Englewood Cliffs, NJ: Prentice-Hall.

Sarbin, T. R. (1968). Role: Psychological aspects. In D. L. Sills (Ed.), *International encyclopedia of the social sciences.* New York: Free Press.

Schein, E. H. (1971). The individual, the organization, and the career: A conceptual scheme. *Journal of Applied Behavioral Science, 7,* 401–426.

Schein, E. H. (1978). *Career dynamics: Matching individual and organizational needs.* Reading, MA: Addison-Wesley.

Schein, E. H. (1980). Career theory and research: Some issues for the future. In C. B. Derr (Ed.), *Work, family, and the career.* New York: Praeger.

Schneider, B. (1983). An interactionist perspective on organizational effectiveness. In K. S. Cameron & D. A. Whetten (Eds.), *Organizational effectiveness: A comparison of multiple models.* San Diego, CA: Academic Press.

Schneider, B. (1985). Organizational behavior. *Annual Review of Psychology, 36,* 573–611.

Schroder, H. M. (1989). *Managerial competence: The key to excellence.* Dubuque, IA: Kendall/Hunt.

Schuler, R. S. (1984). Organizational and occupational stress and coping: A model and overview. In M. D. Lee & R. N. Kanungo (Eds.), *Management of work and personal life.* New York: Praeger.

Seybolt, J. W. (1980). The impact of work role design on career satisfaction. In C. B. Derr (Ed.), *Work, family, and the career.* New York: Praeger.

Sieber, S. D. (1974). Toward a theory of role accumulation. *American Sociological Review, 39,* 567–578.

Sills, D. L. (Ed.). 1968. International encyclopedia of the social sciences. New York: Free Press.

Sowell, T., (1981). *Ethnic America.* New York: Basic Books.

Spector, P. E. (1988). Development of the work locus-of-control scale. *Journal of Occupational Psychology, 61,* 335–340.

Spiegel, J. P. (1957). The resolution of role conflict within the family. *Psychiatry, 20,* 1–16.

Sundberg, N. D., Snowden, L. R., & Reynolds, W. M. (1978). Toward assessment of personal competence and incompetence in life situations. *Annual Review of Psychology, 29,* 179–221.

Super, D. E. (1940). *Avocational interest patterns: A study of the psychology of occupations.* Stanford, CA: Stanford University Press.

Super, D. E. (1980). A life-span, life-space approach to career development. *Journal of Vocational Behavior, 16,* 282–298.

Super, D. E. (1982). The relative importance of work: Models and measures for meaningful data. *Counseling Psychologist, 10,* 95–103.

Super, D. E. (1990). A life-span, life-space, approach to career development. In D. L. Brown, L. Brooks, and Associates (Eds.), *Career choice and development* (2nd ed.). San Francisco: Jossey-Bass.

Super, D. E., Crites, J. O., Hummel, R. C., Moser, H. P., Overstreet, P. L., & Warnath, C. F. (1957). *Vocational development: A framework for research.* New York: Teachers College Press.

Super, D. E., Starishevsky, R., Matlin, R., & Jordaan, J. P. (1963). *Career development: Self-concept theory.* Princeton, NJ: College Entrance Examination Board.

Taylor, K. M., and Betz, N. E. (1983). Application of self-efficacy theory to the understanding and treatment of career indecision. *Journal of Vocational Behavior, 22,* 63–81.

Thornton, G. C., & Byham, W. C. (1982). *Assessment centers and managerial performance,* San Diego, CA: Academic Press.

Toffler, B. L. (1981). Occupational role development: The changing determinants of outcomes for the individual. *Administrative Science Quarterly, 26,* 396–418.

Turner, R. H. (1968). Role: Sociological aspects. In D. L. Sills (Ed.), *International encyclopedia of the social sciences.* New York: Free Press.

Tyler, L. E. (1969). *The work of the counselor.* East Norwalk, CT: Appleton & Lange.

Van De Vliert, E. (1979). Gedrag in rolconflictsituaties: 20 jaar onderzoek rond een theorie [Behavior in role conflict situations: 20 years of research on a theory]. *Nederlands Tijdschrift voor de Psychologie, 34,* 125–146.

Van Maanen, J., & Schein, E. H. (1979). Toward a theory of organizational socialization. In B. M. Staw (Ed.), *Research in organizational behavior* (Vol. 1). Greenwich, CT: JAI Press.

Van Sell, M., Brief, A. P., & Schuler, R. S. (1981). Role conflict and role ambiguity: Integration of the literature and directions for future research. *Human Relations, 34,* 43–71.

Walker, J. W. (1980). *Human resource planning.* New York: McGraw-Hill.

West, M. A., Nicholson, N., & Rees, A. (1987). Transitions into newly created jobs. *Journal of Occupational Psychology, 60,* 97–113.

Wilensky, H. L. (1960). Work, careers, and social integration. *International Social Science Journal, 12,* 543–560.

THREE

Values: Their Nature, Assessment, and Practical Use

Donald E. Super

The concept of values is an ancient one that also is of great concern to contemporary behavioral scientists. Originally matters for philosophers, values have become the concern of social scientists, social service workers, politicians, and journalists, which compounds confusion in the use of the word. This is no place in which to trace the history of the use and misuse of terms, but in a project such as this, concerning the importance of work in everyday life and how to improve treatment, intervention, and facilitation methods, it is important to define terms and to select objective methods for assessing the constructs thus denoted.

Three terms are of special relevance to this task: *needs, values,* and *interests.* While the Work Importance Study was under way several psychologists in Australia, Belgium, Canada, Portugal, and the United States conducted parallel preliminary studies that built upon earlier formulations (Super, 1949, 1973; Super & Bohn, 1970) and reported their work in symposia at international congresses of psychology (Sydney in 1988, Kyoto in 1990). The definitions used in this work are as follows:

- *Needs* are wants, manifestations of physiological conditions such as hunger, and they are related to survival. They are the result of interaction between the person and the environment, and some thus manifest in the seeking of help from others and, in more refined form, in the need to help others.
- *Values* are the result of further refinement through interaction with the environment, both natural and human. The result of socialization (see Chapter One) is the establishment of the types of objectives that people seek in order to satisfy their needs. The need *for* help thus becomes love, and the need *to* help becomes altruism.
- *Interests* are the activities within which people expect to attain their values and thus satisfy their needs. Valuing the well-being of others (altruism) leads a person to choose a social service occupation such as social work,

54

teaching, some aspects of personnel work, or even a business or industrial enterprise. Thus Robert Owen, an early nineteenth-century manufacturer, founded "ideal" factories and communities in Scotland and the United States. Similarly, Eleanor Roosevelt, homemaker in the sense that she was a wife, mother, and manager of a household, devoted much of her time, energy, and affect to voluntary public and social service.

According to this theoretical formulation, interests are closer to actual behavior than are needs and values. Needing (lacking, wanting) something leads to valuing something that seems likely to meet that need. The something is at this point rather abstract, as are the labels attached to values, for instance, "material," "altruistic," "power," and "beauty." Valuing material things may lead to seeking wealth; power, to seeking positions of authority; beauty, to painting, gardening, collecting art, or just having an attractive home or workplace. People generally seek wealth through managerial, investment, and other presumably remunerative occupations, or perhaps in marriage; they may hope to achieve power in the ownership or management of an enterprise or in politics. The people who seek beauty may be interior decorators, clothing designers, or sculptors. All are examples of value attainment through choice of occupation, but some are notable in other behavioral terms, such as leisure or voluntary community activities. Valuing may lead to action, and action involves occupation with an activity, which may be paid employment or voluntary participation.

One practical implication of this theory of the structure of personality is that those who seek to understand motivation (why people do things) must study needs. On the other hand, those who want to understand what people's needs will lead them to seek should study values. But most important in practice is that if researchers seek to know how people are likely to try to achieve a goal or goals, they should know in which activities people are likely to seek them—that is, researchers must know their subjects' interests.

Although they had no clear theoretical formulation of this type, applied psychologists in the 1920s used it implicitly and developed interest inventories, which Fryer (1931) described in a landmark book and which Strong (1943) reported in definitive detail. In the United States, Strong's work, and that of others using his instrument, has been second in importance and volume only to the use of aptitude tests in vocational or career counseling, personnel selection, and career development. In this case, theory has followed application—if indeed there can be said to be a body of interest theory rather than just a body of interest knowledge.

Research on needs and values, as contrasted with speculation by observers of society and with philosophizing by more systematic and logical thinkers, such as Spranger (1928), did not appear until well after the work on interests: Allport and Vernon pioneered values in 1931 and Murray pioneered needs in 1938. And these were only the beginnings: empirical validation against behavioral criteria (other than reports on individual cases) has even now hardly begun, because personality theorists have shown little interest in the observable behavior of careers or work, and most vocational and organizational psychologists have despaired—perhaps too easily—of finding promising measures of needs or values. Using projective measures of needs, such as Murray's Thematic Apperception Test, is too demanding of skill and time to have been well validated against occupational criteria; the Edwards Personal Preference Schedule has not proved promising. The Minnesota Importance Questionnaire, a measure of values when judged by its content and construct validation studies (although called a needs measure by its authors), does show promise, which supports the idea that traits closer to the environment are more predictive than those nearer to the psychological core of personality. It is worth noting that traits, assessed by such instruments as the California Psychological Inventory (Gough, 1987), measure modes of behavior, not needs, values, or interests as defined here.

Research on the Construct of Values

The theoretical model of personality outlined here is hypothetical and requires empirical testing. Such is the nature of models. Furthermore, because models are hypothetical, they are simplistic. They must be, in order to convey a complex message briefly and clearly. Projects now testing this model are not part of the WIS, but they are relevant to the development and use of the values measure devised and used by that study, and we therefore draw on them here.

Do Values Differ from Needs and Interests?

In a study that used the Canadian version of the WIS Values Scale, Macnab and Fitzsimmons (1987) essayed a multitrait multifactor test of the construct validity of the WIS project's measure of values. Their work, and an earlier study of another instrument by the authors of the Minnesota Importance Questionnaire, may help provide a logical and empirical basis for a definition of values.

Macnab and Fitzsimmons (1987) used data from the WIS Values Scale of the Canadian Life Roles Inventory, the Work Aspect Preference Scale (WAPS; Pryor, 1982), the Minnesota Importance Questionnaire (MIQ; Rounds, Henley, Dawis, Lofquist, & Weiss, 1981), and the Work Values Inventory (WVI; Super, 1970) for their statistical analysis of the similarity of measures of needs, values, and interests. Macnab and Fitzsimmons chose the MIQ as a measure of needs, but its items, when scanned, are like items used in values measures. They chose the WVI (Super, 1970) and the Canadian Values Scale (Fitzsimmons, Macnab, & Casserly, 1986) as values instruments; their content resembles that of other values measures. Macnab & Fitzsimmons chose the WAPS as a measure of *preferences*, a word rarely used in measurement: in the literature it is generally used to denote expressed as opposed to measured interests. The items, when examined by a number of informed psychologists, were deemed to resemble values more than interests. Indeed, Pryor (1982) was in search of "a conceptual and comprised integration" in his work, whereas earlier he had stated that he was "in search of a concept: Work Values" (Pryor, 1979). He seems thus to have muddied his own thinking, and also that of Macnab and Fitzsimmons, by introducing disused and ill-defined terms and to have in fact produced one more measure of values. Despite the confusion of labels and constructs, we may accept as valid the statistical results of this study. Macnab and Fitzsimmons therefore helped to establish, in our judgment, that even when values are assessed with measures devised from somewhat different perspectives but with similar item content, it is possible to measure them objectively. One set of authors may call them needs, another values, and another interests, but the items maintain their integrity and group according to the logic of needs-values-interests (NVI) theory. Chapter Four describes the WIS Values Scale; Chapters Five to Fifteen, the national versions and their respective manuals (e.g., the American manual in Nevill & Super, 1989).

In the work presented at the international symposia to which we referred earlier, the other constructs, those of needs and interests, also appear to maintain their theoretical identities, although more work must be done on needs before this can be stated with any certainty. But the validity of the construct of interests, as related to but differing from values, does appear to have been supported in the preliminary work of several projects in Australia (Lokan, 1990), Canada, and the United States (Dagley, Super, & Lautenschlager, 1990). Dagley et al. show that the WIS Values Scale (Super & Nevill, 1986)—seen in its virtually identical Canadian version (Macnab & Fitzsimmons, 1987) to be a good representative of existing measures that have value content—has significantly lower intercorrelations with the Vocational Preference Inventory (Holland, 1985), the Strong Interest Inventory (Hansen, 1985), the Kuder Occupational Interest Schedule (1979), and the Tetreau-Trahan Visual Test of Interests (Tetreau & Trahan, 1986) than these four instruments do among themselves. Thus several instruments clearly establish interests as a valid psychological construct, whereas it is equally clear that values, as we have seen, are another related but clearly identifiable construct.

Do Values Differ from One Country to Another?

Popular stereotypes suggest that values do differ from one country to another. The results of prior cross-national studies, such as that by Ronen (1977), discussed by Šverko in Chapter Sixteen, and a later study by Hofstede (1980), are perhaps flawed for our purposes because they dealt with employees in single international corporations, who may therefore be deemed to have been both selected and molded by common corporate subcultures. But the studies do agree in finding the dominant values of Japanese employees to be somewhat different from those of, for example, American employees in ways suggestive of differences observed by anthropologists, sociologists, and journalists. But it is the hierarchy that differs, not the actual values that constitute the hierarchies. People seem to want the same good things from life, but in different countries and in different subcultures they attach differing emphases to them.

In Chapters Sixteen and Seventeen, Šverko, and Trentini and Muzio, respectively, address the cross-national question, using the same data from the same countries, with samples that are not truly identical but are not limited to any one subculture of any given country (except Poland, where only university students were studied). The data were objectively obtained with internationally developed measures and scored by internationally agreed-upon objective methods. The answers to the question of national differences are essentially in agreement, despite some variations in statistical methods, but they are not simple answers. In Chapter Fourteen, Langley reports intercultural differences in one country.

Do Values Differ with Age, Gender, and Other Demographic Variables?

The answers proposed by earlier studies with such instruments as the Allport-Vernon Study of Values (a 1931 American-British measure based on German philosophical speculation and designed for university students), and on less refined methods in studies by Rokeach (1973) and others, suggested that they do thus differ, at least on some variables. Values do change somewhat with age and experience, as during the years of university study or of work experience after leaving school (Bloom, 1964); girls and women, for example, have tended to value human relations more and authority less than have boys and men (Nevill & Super, 1989). Other demographic variables, generally in studies with samples that are more limited than are most of the WIS samples, have also shown value differences.

The national teams in the Work Importance Study have studied some of the differences that may be attributable to demographics; these are examined briefly in the chapters dealing with their work. Thus Chapter Fourteen, on the South African WIS, reports comparisons between language groups that are essentially ethnic groups (e.g., Afrikaans, English, Xhosa, and Zulu speakers) and gives due regard to the fact that all subjects were being educated in either Afrikaans (generally South Africans of Dutch descent) or in English (descendants of British settlers, Indian immigrants, and of native tribes). Chapter Seven compares Anglophones and Francophones in Canada, and other chapters look at students at different year levels in most countries and examine occupational samples in the countries that studied adults (e.g., Belgium, Canada, and Croatia in Chapters Six, Seven, and Eight). The national chapters in this volume do not report all analyses of national data, because they attempt to provide no more than a sample of what is becoming available in national reports published in the twelve member countries.

Of special interest, because they break new ground, are the analyses of the values of individuals who attach differing degrees of importance to the major life roles of student, worker, homemaker, citizen, and pursuer of leisure. Such analyses, where available, should prove valuable in career guidance and counseling; Lokan reports some here in Chapter Nineteen.

In addition, several countries have measures of vocational or career maturity, as do Australia, Canada, Japan, Portugal, South Africa, and the United States. Not all report such research in this volume, but Nevill and Super (1988) and Super and Nevill (1986) have reported elsewhere on studies of career maturity, work salience, and demographic data, pointing the way to studies of the values of students who have vocationally mature attitudes and who are informed about the opportunity structures, educational requirements, life-styles, and career patterns of occupations and who know the principles and determinants of occupational choice.

Are Values Related to Occupational Choice, Stability, and Satisfaction?

The most thorough earlier studies on these questions were part of the Minnesota Work Adjustment Study (Weiss, Dawis, & Lofquist, 1981), with two instruments, the Minnesota Importance Questionnaire (MIQ) and the Minnesota Satisfaction Questionnaire (MSQ). The work adjustment study measured values (called *needs* by the authors), and the latter two measured satisfaction, with comparable items and scales. Both the MIQ and the MSQ were developed for use with blue-collar workers and have proved usable and useful. Generally they find that values are related to occupational choice, stability, and satisfaction. But the same questions need to be addressed with items perhaps more appropriate for white-collar workers, managers, and professionals.

The WIS Values Scale has proved applicable to and appropriate for the full range of occupational levels, given (as is true of all such measures) the ability to read at the secondary school level. Whether work and other major lifelong career roles, such as those of homemaker and leisurite, satisfy a person's specific values has not yet been studied with the Values Scale, which might well be adapted (like the MIQ and MSQ) to yield comparable satisfaction scores.

It is in the nature of books such as this that topics in various chapters overlap a bit—although *interlock* might be a better term, not only because each national project has procedures and data to report but because a chapter on the meaning of work, such as that prepared by our Croatian colleagues (Chapter One), inevitably deals with values, as must also a chapter on roles, such as that by our South African writer (Chapter Two). Furthermore, in Chapter Nineteen, the leader of the Australian project reports an analysis of the relationships of values to commitment to the five major life roles studied by the WIS, using data from four participating countries in Australasia, North America, and Europe; unlike this and the preceding chapters, which are reviews of literature and theory, it reports data. Readers interested in the content of Chapter Nineteen should also read Chapters One and Two, as well as

Chapter Four, which describes the development of the cross-national Values Scale; Chapters Eighteen, Twenty-three, and Twenty-four; and, of course, the chapters on individual countries that are of special interest to them.

Conclusion

Clearly, values can be measured, and they are related to a number of important psychological and sociological variables. On the other hand, evidence about their relation to such behaviors as occupational choice and entry, satisfaction, and success is limited. The University of Minnesota studies in work adjustment have, as we have seen, pursued some questions intensively and with some success, but such studies are still exceptional: employers are not keen to let outsiders study their workers, and studies of satisfaction by employers tend to be available to a limited audience. Furthermore, longitudinal studies of what people seek and what they find are needed more than are cross-sectional surveys. Thus there is much room for further work on the predictive validity of values for occupational choice, stability, and satisfaction. That a well-researched instrument such as the WIS Values Scale is now available, in a number of major and some less widely known languages, should make such studies easier to conduct and their findings easier to compare from one study to another.

References

Allport, G. W., & Vernon, P. E. (1931). *A study of values.* Boston: Houghton Mifflin.

Bloom, B. S. (1964). *Stability and change in human characteristics.* New York: Wiley.

Dagley, J. C., Super, D. E., & Lautenschlager, G. J. (1990, June). *Needs, values, and interests: Empirical relationships.* Paper presented at the International Congress of Applied Psychology, Kyoto, Japan.

Fitzsimmons, G. W., Macnab, D., & Casserly, C. (1986). *Technical manual for the Life Roles Inventory: Values and salience.* Edmonton, Alberta, Canada: Psican Consulting.

Fryer, D. H. (1931). *The measurement of interests in relation to human adjustment.* Troy, MO: Holt, Rinehart & Winston.

Gough, H. M. (1987). *The California Psychological Inventory.* Palo Alto, CA: Consulting Psychologists Press.

Hansen, J.-I.C. (1985). *Strong-Campbell Interest Inventory.* Stanford, CA: Stanford University Press.

Hofstede, G. H. (1980). *Culture's consequences: International differences in work-related values.* Newbury Park, CA: Sage.

Holland, J. L. (1985). *The Kuder Occupational Interest Survey.* Chicago: Science Research Associates.

Kuder, G. F. (1979). *Occupational Interest Survey: General manual* (2nd ed.). Chicago: Science Research Associates.

Lokan, J. J. (1990). The Work Importance Study: Australian young people's values in international perspective. In M. E. Poole, (Ed.), *Education, work, and society.* Hawthorn: Australian Council for Educational Research.

Macnab, D., & Fitzsimmons, G. (1987). A multitrait, multimethod study of work-related needs, values, and preferences. *Journal of Vocational Behavior, 30,* 1–15.

Murray, H. A. (1938). *Explorations in personality.* New York: Oxford University Press.

Nevill, D. D., & Super, D. E. (1988). Career maturity and commitment to work in university students. *Journal of Vocational Behavior, 32,* 139–152.

Nevill, D. D., & Super, D. E. (1989). *Manual to the Values Scale* (rev. ed.). Palo Alto, CA: Consulting Psychologists Press.

Pryor, R.G.L. (1979). In search of a concept: Work values. *Vocational Guidance Quarterly 27,* 250–258.

Pryor, R.G.L. (1982). Values, preferences, needs, work ethics, and orientations to work: Toward a conceptual and comprised integration. *Journal of Vocational Behavior, 20,* 40–52.

Rokeach, M. (1973). *The nature of human values.* New York: Free Press.

Ronen, S. (1977). Personal values: A basis for motivational set and work attitude. *Organizational Behavior and Human Performance, 21,* 80–107.

Rounds, J. B., Henley, G. A., Dawis, R. V., Lofquist, L. H., & Weiss, D. J. (1981). *Manual for the Minnesota Importance Questionnaire.* Minneapolis: University of Minnesota.

Spranger, E. (1928). *Types of men* (P.J.W. Pigors, Trans.). New York: Hafncr Publishing.

Strong, E. K., Jr. (1943). *The vocational interests of men and women.* Stanford, CA: Stanford University Press.

Super, D. E. (1949). *Appraising vocational fitness by means of psychological tests.* New York: HarperCollins.

Super, D. E. (1970). *The Work Values Inventory.* Boston: Houghton Mifflin.

Super, D. E. (1973). The Work Values Inventory. In D. G. Zytowski (Ed.). *New approaches to interest measurement.* Minneapolis: University of Minnesota Press.

Super, D. E., & Bohn, M. J., Jr. (1970). *Occupational psychology.* Pacific Grove, CA: Brooks/Cole.

Super, D. E., & Nevill, D. D. (1986). *The Values Scale.* Palo Alto, CA: Consulting Psychologists Press.

Tetreau, B., & Trahan, M. (1986). *Test visuel d'intérêts: Manuel.* (Manual for the Pictorial Interest Inventory). Montreal, Canada: SECPREP.

Weiss, J. J., Dawis, R. V., & Lofquist, L. H. (1981). *The Minnesota Work Adjustment Study.* Minneapolis: University of Minnesota Press.

FOUR

Developing the Work Importance Study

J. Ferreira-Marques
M. J. Miranda

The origins of the Work Importance Study (WIS) lie in the International Congresses of Applied Psychology: the idea germinated after a symposium at the Munich congress of 1978; four years later, the Edinburgh congress of 1982 first devoted a symposium to WIS progress reports. The European Research Office of the U.S. Army Research Institute and the International Association for Educational and Vocational Guidance gave it impetus.

Under the international coordination of Donald Super, the project started in March 1979 with its inaugural conference in Cambridge, England. Psychologists from eight countries attended.

The project's aim is to investigate the relative importance of work in comparison with other activities and the rewards that youth and adults seek in their major life roles, especially the role of worker. From the beginning, WIS teams paid particular attention to theoretical models and empirical methods pertaining to the assessment of values and work salience. As Super described it early on, a major goal was, "through a network of coordinated national projects, to clarify the constructs of work salience (job involvement, career commitment, etc.), to make them operational by developing assessment methods, and to relate them to work values and work motivation" (Super, 1979, p. 1).

International and National Organization

The WIS was developed as a network of national projects. Each team had a national project director, with international coordination assured by Super, first in Cambridge, England; next at Columbia University, in New York; and finally in Savannah.

By late 1979 delegates from the following countries were actively involved in the project: Australia, Canada, Croatia, the Federal Republic of Germany, France, Greece, Italy, the Netherlands, Poland, Portugal, Spain,

Switzerland, the United Kingdom, the United States, and Zimbabwe. Joining later were participants from Belgium, Czechoslovakia, India, Israel, Japan, and South Africa. Some later withdrew because of lack of financial support. Eleven national teams completed their projects. See Table 4.1 for a list of the participating teams and their directors.

Planning the WIS

At the first conference of the Work Importance Study, in March 1979, participants identified and agreed upon four stages:

> Stage I—literature reviews (national and international) and pilot study planning
> Stage II—pilot studies and instrument development
> Stage III—the definitive or main study
> Stage IV—follow-up

From 1979 to 1989 participants held twelve international working conferences to discuss and analyze project developments and current issues.

Literature Reviews and Refinement of Models

To take into account the increasingly changing structure of work in contemporary societies and the contributions of psychologists, educators, and sociologists to the meanings of work in general and for the individual, the WIS gave special attention to a review of the literature.

The network of national projects adopted its "Guide to Searching the National Literature for the Work Importance Study," including some key words and the initial model of role salience and values. The guide includes sociological, philosophical, and psychological works; literature reviews from Australia and New Zealand, Canada, Croatia, Greece, the Netherlands, Poland, Spain, and Switzerland and from France, England, the United States, and Zimbabwe were presented to the second WIS planning conference in England in December 1979. On the basis of the reviews, Donald Super, Jennifer Kidd, and Edward Knasel (1980) and Jean-Pierre Descombes (1980) prepared international literature reviews. Descombes's paper was in French and covered only the literature on work values.

Discussing the national reviews and identifying the main issues were particularly useful in refining theoretical concepts and models during the WIS planning conferences held in 1980—in March in Lisbon, and in mid-October in Dubrovnik. Participants made progress on a general taxonomy and a taxonomy of work values and refined constructs related to work salience.

They agreed to conceptualize *value* as "an objective, either a psychological state, a relationship, or a material condition, that one seeks to attain

Table 4.1. WIS National Teams and Their Directors.

Country	Director	Affiliation
Australia	Jan J. Lokan	Australian Council for Educational Research
Belgium	Pol Coetsier	University of Ghent, Laboratory of Sociopsychology of Work and Organization
Canada	Catherine Casserly	Canada Employment and Immigration Commission
Croatia	Branimir Šverko	University of Zagreb, Department of Psychology
Israel	Edgar Krau	University of Tel-Aviv, Department of Psychology
Italy	Giancarlo Trentini	University of Venice
Japan	N. Nakanishi	University of Osaka, Faculty of Human Sciences
Poland	B. Hornowski, succeeded by Elzbieta Hornowska	University of Poznań, Institute of Psychology
Portugal	J. Ferreira-Marques	University of Lisbon, Faculty of Psychology and Education
South Africa	Ronelle Langley	Human Sciences Research Council. After 1989: Rand Africans University, Student Counseling Service
United States	Donald E. Super and from 1981, Dorothy D. Nevill	Wolfson College and the National Institute for Careers Education and Counselling, Cambridge, England
		University of Florida, Department of Psychology

or achieve" (Super, 1980, p. 82). At the Dubrovnik conference they adapted a set of twenty-three values applicable to any role:

    Ability Utilization
    Achievement
    Advancement
    Aesthetics
    Altruism
    Associates
    Authority
    Autonomy

Creativity
Economic Rewards
Economic Security
Environment
Intellectual Stimulation
Life-style
Participation in Organizational Decisions
Prestige
Responsibility
Risk
Spirituality
Supervisory Relations
Variety
Cultural Identity
Physical Activity

They made Cultural Identity and Physical Activity optional for the national projects, because some teams considered the Cultural Identity scale irrelevant in their culture, and some countries do not make a distinction between Physical Activity and Physical Prowess.

Using a glossary of terms relevant to work importance (see Super, 1980) and the review of British and American literature, Kidd and Knasel (1979) developed and submitted a hierarchical model of role salience that consists of the important behavioral, cognitive, and affective components.

A working conference of national directors refined the initial model to clarify and standardize terminology in a domain in which terms have been variously and confusingly used. They defined *Salience* as importance or prominence as shown by behavior, attitudes, and knowledge. The directors construed the fundamental elements of salience as combining *Involvement* (affective attachment with use of time and effort) and *Engagement* (use of time and effort with knowledge and understanding). The model also views *Commitment* (affective attachment), *Participation* (use of time and effort), and *Orientation* (knowledge and understanding) as fundamental components.

Figure 4.1 shows the revised model of role importance for the Work Importance Study (Knasel, Super, & Kidd, 1981). Commitment, participation, and knowledge are considered fundamental and logically discrete features of the importance of any role and as such empirically distinguishable. They and their combinations are applicable to all major life and career roles, not to only the work role from which literature the model of importance was derived. Emotional attachment (commitment) to a role can exist without participation in and with little knowledge of the role. The behavioral component, participation, is the use of time and energy in an activity and can occur with or without affective attachment and significant knowledge. Knowledge, being cognitive, means information and understanding of at least some requirements and expectations of a role: it can exist without significant affect

Figure 4.1. The Work Importance Study Model of Role Importance.

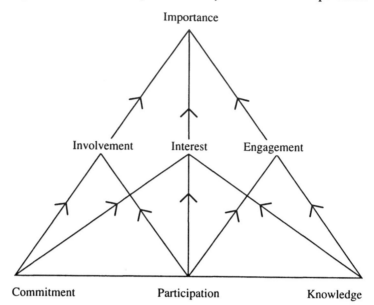

Source: Adapted from Knasel, Super, & Kidd, 1981.

or behavior. The combination of two of the three basic components of Importance produces the intermediate level: Involvement is Commitment with Participation, Interest is Commitment and Knowledge, and Engagement is Participation with Knowledge. Importance can be viewed as a combination of Involvement, Interest, and Engagement and thus of Commitment, Participation, and Knowledge. The arrows in Figure 4.1 show the hierarchy for all combinations possible.

Development of the Field Trial Forms
of the Values Scale and of the Salience Inventory

At least two national teams prepared draft specifications and sample items for each of the values in the Values Scale (VS) and each component of the Salience Inventory (SI). The two international working conferences held in 1980 discussed and revised them, and they led to the Values Scale and the Salience Inventory. Thus the final products are not those of any one country but are instead truly international instruments with versions in each country's language prepared by its national team (Ferreira-Marques, 1982).

Participants agreed at the Dubrovnik conference of 1980 that the field trial forms of the Values Scale should have 210 items (twenty-one scales, ten items per scale) or 230 items if the two optional scales were included. The directions ask subjects to assess, on a 5-point scale, how important to them are various values or satisfactions that most people seek in life. Among the ten items for each value (Creativity, for example), the first five are general and applicable to any role (the "general" subscale) and the last five items are clearly related to work and a job (the "work" subscale). The score for each scale and for each subscale is the sum of the weights given by the subject to the respective items.

The SI asks what people do or might do during, and how they feel about, five types of activities: Study, Work, Community Service, Homemaking, and Leisure. At this point the SI had three sections: the Involvement grid, the Role Values grid, and the Time scale.

The Involvement grid—a "ratings" type of instrument—asked respondents to tell about the things they *do* in each of five kinds of activities or roles (the Participation measure) and how they *feel* about doing them (Commitment). The answers to each question were ranked on a 5-point scale. The score for Participation in and Commitment to each role was the sum of the weights (1 to 5) given to each item.

The teams planned to approach the relationship of role values and role salience through a values realization, or expectation, measure. The Role Values grid consisted of one item for each value in the VS. Subjects were asked what values they find or hope to find in each of the five types of activities, using a scale of 1 to 5. The final method of scoring was the same as for Participation and Commitment, decided upon after trying other methods.

The approach to Participation and to Commitment represented by the Time scale was rather different from that of the Involvement grid. The Time scale asked subjects to use linear graphics to show the time they actually devoted to the five types of activities during a typical working day, then during an "ideal" working day, and finally during a typical nonworking day. The hypothesis was that the actual time scale would relate to Participation and the ideal time scale to Commitment.

The Field Trials and Revision of the Instruments

The national project directors planned to try out all WIS instruments in each country with a few subjects and the VS with large samples. The age groups to be sampled were to include secondary school pupils from eighth grade to the last grade of secondary education and, whenever possible, prefinal or final year of higher education, and adults after six months in the labor force, both employed and unemployed.

Reports on the field trials from Australia, Canada, Portugal, Spain, the United States, and Croatia were presented at the fifth WIS planning conference in Lisbon in October 1981 (Ferreira-Marques, 1982).

The Australian team reported the results obtained with two versions of the VS, the first administered to students in year 11 (two separate groups of about 350 pupils) and the second one to approximately 1,400 pupils in year 10. In Canada the English and French forms of the VS were used with a total of about 3,000 subjects, including secondary students and adults. In

Portugal the VS was administered to 953 ninth-year students, 322 twelfth-year students, and 156 adults in the labor force; the SI was administered to 187 year-9 and 71 year-12 students, and 46 adults. In Spain both instruments were used with secondary school students ($n = 252$ for the VS; $n = 135$ for the SI) and with adults in the labor market ($n = 183$ for the VS; $n = 58$ for the SI). Data from the United States were based on large samples of secondary and higher education students: VS, $n = 686$ eleventh-year (secondary) and 1,042 higher education students; the SI was given to 511 secondary and higher education students, and to two groups of about 20 adults. The Croatian team reported VS results obtained with a group of 930 high school and university students ($n = 726$, years 10 and 12; $n = 204$ for higher education students).

The statistical analysis of the VS includes means and standard deviations of the a priori scales and subscales and of each item, gender differences between scale means, alpha coefficients for every scale and subscale, correlations between the general subscale and the work subscale of each value, scale intercorrelations and factor analysis, item-scale correlations, scale intercorrelations, and factor analysis of the items.

The large amount of empirical evidence was the basis for agreement during the Lisbon conference (October 1981) on the revision of the VS. The participants selected the scales the WIS would retain after they saw the comparison of factor loadings by each national team. Four of the original twenty-one scales were either absorbed by other scales or dropped for lack of retainable items. These were Intellectual Stimulation, Participation in Organizational Decisions, Responsibility, and Spirituality—each much favored a priori by more than one project director. Two scales, Economic Rewards and Economic Security, were combined in a single scale on the basis of cross-national and most national data but retained as separate scales in national projects when data warranted doing so (for example, the United States). The Associates scale split into two new scales: Social Interaction and Social Relations, the latter also incorporating some Supervisory Relations items. The directors agreed to focus the Environment scale on Working Conditions and to rename it accordingly; they found that other aspects of the Environment scale would fit into the Life-Style scale. Another decision was to accept Physical Activity for cross-national comparisons and to retain Physical Prowess and Cultural Identity as optional. So, by including a new scale named Personal Development, the twenty-one a priori values (plus two optional values) became eighteen (plus two optional) in the final revised form of the VS. Table 4.2 presents a synthesis of the major changes.

High internal consistencies of the scales (alpha coefficients of generally 0.80 and above) made it possible to reduce to five the number of items in each scale of the revised VS, which resulted in fewer criticisms of item repetition by respondents. The first three of the five items are common to all countries and used for international comparisons; each national project selected two other items in each scale from the remaining items that had the highest

Table 4.2. WIS Values Scales.

Field Trial Form	Revised Form
1. Ability Utilization	1. Ability Utilization
2. Achievement	2. Achievement
3. Advancement	3. Advancement
4. Aesthetics	4. Aesthetics
5. Altruism	5. Altruism
6. Associates	6. Social Interaction
	7. Social Relations
7. Authority	8. Authority
8. Autonomy	9. Autonomy
9. Creativity	10. Creativity
10. Economic Rewards	11. Economics
11. Economic Security	
12. Environment	12. Working Conditions
13. Intellectual Stimulation	
14. Life-style	13. Life-style
15. Participation in Organizational Decisions	
	14. Personal Development
16. Prestige	15. Prestige
17. Responsibility	
18. Risk	16. Risk
19. Spiritu,aliy	
20. Supervisory Relations	
21. Variety	17. Variety
22. Cultural Identity (optional)	18. Cultural Identity (optional nationally)
23. Physical Activity (optional)	19. Physical Activity
	20. Physical Prowess (optional nationally)

internal consistency nationally and conceptual adequacy. The directors also decided to keep the instrument as a general values inventory and to include one or two work-related items among the three cross-national items in each scale (except, of course, in the Working Conditions scale). The merger of work and nonwork items in the statistical analysis of the two types of subscales resulted in the final revised form. As in the field trial form, items occur in the same order as the scales in Table 4.2, making it easy for scorers to place items in their scales. In the revised form, answers are on a 4-point scale.

The statistical analysis of the data of the field trial form of the SI provided the usual psychometric data on the Participation, Commitment, and Role Values measures for the five roles or types of activities. Directors decided during the Lisbon conference of October 1981 to keep Participation, Commitment, and the Role Values grid (renamed Value Expectations) as parts of the SI (revised form), with a 4-point response scale in terms of time and degree. The Time scale became optional, retained by only a few countries. The directors reduced the Participation and Commitment scales to the ten best items in each, on the basis of empirical evidence. The results made possible the selection of the one item for each value to be included in the renamed Value Expectations scale.

International Edition of the Values Scale—
Description of the Instrument

The WIS Values Scale includes eighteen values plus two optional values, which are listed in Table 4.2, column 2. The international VS contains fifty-four items (eighteen values); three of the five items of each scale are cross-national.

The items are sentence completions introduced by the incomplete sentence, or stem, "It is now or will be important for me to _____." Responses are on a 4-point scale of

1.   Of little or no importance
2.   Of some importance
3.   Important
4.   Very important

Table 4.3 lists the Values scales and gives sample items.

The VS can be administered to people of secondary school age; the reading level is about the eighth year. Administration time is from thirty to forty-five minutes. More information about this instrument can be found in the American manual (Nevill & Super, 1986a) and in other national manuals. (People interested in making national versions for countries without one should contact one of the national directors.)

International Edition of the Salience Inventory—
Description of the Instrument

The five kinds of activities pertaining to the five roles assessed by the Salience Inventory are defined as follows:

Studying: taking courses, going to day or night school classes, lectures or laboratory work; preparing for class, studying in a library or at home; independent formal or informal study

Working: activities that produce pay or profit, on a job or for self

Community Service: activities with community organizations such as recreational groups, Scouts, Red Cross, social service agencies, neighborhood associations, political parties, and trade unions

Home and Family: taking care of bedroom, apartment, or house; fixing or cleaning up after meals; shopping and caring for dependents, such as children and aging parents

Leisure: taking part in sports, watching television, pursuing hobbies, going to movies, theater, or concerts, reading, relaxing or loafing, being with family and friends

The Participation measure consists of ten items (eight cross-national plus two selected from a list of six optional ones). The Commitment measure

Table 4.3. Values Scales and Sample Items.

Values Scales	Sample Items
1. Ability Utilization	Use all my skill and knowledge
2. Achievement	Have results which show that I have done well
3. Advancement	Get ahead
4. Aesthetics	Make life more beautiful
5. Altruism	Help people with problems
6. Authority	Tell others what to do
7. Autonomy	Act on my own
8. Creativity	Discover, develop, or design new things
9. Economics	Have a high standard of living
10. Life-Style	Living according to my ideas
11. Personal Development	Develop as a person
12. Physical Activity	Get a lot of exercise
13. Prestige	Be admired for my knowledge and skills
14. Risk	Do risky things
15. Social Interaction	Do things with other people
16. Social Relations	Be with friends
17. Variety	Have every day different in some way from the one before it
18. Working Conditions	Have good space and light in which to work

has ten cross-national items. The Role Values measure has fourteen items (the one best item from fourteen of the cross-national Value scales).

Standard phrases introduce the items: "What do you actually do or have you done recently?" (Participation); "How do you feel about it?" (Commitment); and "What opportunities do you see now or in the future to _____?" (Value Expectations). The items pertain to each of the five activities or roles—Studying, Working, Community Service, Home, and Leisure. The same stem is used for each activity. The Value Expectations scale includes the following fourteen VS values:

Ability Utilization
Achievement
Aesthetics
Altruism
Autonomy
Creativity
Economics
Life-style
Physical Activity
Prestige
Risk
Social Interaction
Variety
Working Conditions

Responses to each item of the SI are rated in a 4-point scale meaning of

1. Never or rarely/little or none
2. Sometimes/some

3. Often/quite a lot
4. Almost always or always/a great deal

The raw scores are computed for each activity in each scale by totaling the weights for each item of the scale for that activity.

The SI can be administered to populations from secondary school level and up. Administration time runs thirty to forty-five minutes. This instrument is presented in more detail in the national manuals, for example, the American (Nevill & Super, 1986b).

Throughout the chapters of this book, references to scales from the Salience Inventory often use the activity domains listed above, such as Studying and Home and Family. The English-language inventory, however, provides scores (such as Participation) for each of the corresponding *roles* (Student and Homemaker). These role terms are used in such tables as Appendix B.2. The two forms should be considered equivalent in their reference to scales from the Salience Inventory.

Development of the Main Study

The directors decided at the Lisbon conference of October 1981 to carry out a preliminary study with the revised forms of the VS and SI, using a small sample in each country before starting the main study. With satisfactory results from the preliminary studies in mind, all the research teams attending the Edinburgh conference in 1982 agreed not to make further changes in the international instruments. During the conferences and other meetings of the Work Importance Study up to 1984, participants examined the plan of the main study in detail, including the specifics of sampling at the secondary school, higher education, and adult levels.

As we mentioned earlier, difficulties in pursuing the main study in some countries arose from funding problems, which led some national groups to withdraw. Others that later were able to join or rejoin the original group followed the procedures of the international network. Jai B. P. Sinha of Patna, India, although not participating fully in the WIS, took part in the symposium of the Work Importance Study held during the Jerusalem Congress of Applied Psychology in 1986. As described in his paper, a study of managers, he adapted the VS to India, adding a new scale for Peace of Mind. He thus reconfirmed two important WIS hypotheses: so-called Western values can be meaningfully assessed elsewhere, and in some countries additional values can be identified, with resulting enrichment.

Progress reports from the national teams were presented and discussed at WIS conferences. Cross-national comparisons and the analysis of related issues paved the way for this book, which has been the main concern of the network since the Venice conference in 1987.

Contributions (by participants) have dealt with empirical tests of the WIS models, validation of the instruments, studies of group differences according to gender, education, occupation, employment status, life stage, and cultural differences. Some cross-national comparisons have attracted a good deal of interest. Psychologists not involved in the WIS have often been active in discussion of the papers and have occasionally been invited to participate. Among them were Lenore W. Harmon of the University of Illinois, who joined the Edinburgh congress, and Rabindra N. Kanungo of McGill University, who participated in Montreal. A good example of spin-off studies and symposia was the symposium "Needs, Values, and Interests: Theoretical and Psychometric Contributions to the Clarification and Conceptual and Practical Confusion," which was held during the International Congress of Psychology in Sydney in 1988 and involved some members of the Work Importance Study.

This book presents the activities of the national projects, major cross-national studies, and research on special topics and issues. Journal articles and other publications by members of the network in our twelve countries have reported other studies.

Finally, we should emphasize that one objective of the Work Importance Study, as originally proposed and as described in some national chapters, was to "yield instruments useful in psychological assessment for career or vocational counseling, for personnel selection, and for programme evaluation" (Super, 1979, p. 1). The value of this idea has already been demonstrated by the increasing interest of other countries in adapting and using the WIS instruments in guidance, counseling, and personnel selection, as described in the national chapters, such as those pertaining to Belgium and the United States.

References

Descombes, J. P. (1980). Cinquante ans d'études et d'évaluation des valeurs professionnelles (1925–1975) (Fifty years of studies and assessment of work values, 1925–1975). *Révue de Psychologie Appliquée, 30,* 1–101.

Ferreira-Marques, J. (1982, July). The planning and instrument development of the Work Importance Study. Paper presented at the symposium The Relative Importance of Work, Reports from Eight Countries, 20th International Congress of Applied Psychology, Edinburgh (Mimeo).

Kidd, J. M., & Knasel, E. G. (1979, December). *Work values and work salience: A review of research.* Paper presented at the second WIS conference, Cambridge, England (Mimeo).

Knasel, E. G., Super, D. E., & Kidd, J. M. (1981). *Work salience and work values: Their dimensions, assessment, and significance.* Cambridge, England: National Institute for Careers Education and Counselling (Mimeo).

Nevill, D. D., & Super, D. E. (1986a). *The Values Scale: Theory, application, and research* (Manual). (Research ed.) Palo Alto, CA: Consulting Psychologists Press.

Nevill, D. D., & Super, D. E. (1986b). *The Salience Inventory: Theory, applica-*

tion, and research (Manual). (Research ed.) Palo Alto, CA: Consulting Psychologists Press.

Super, D. E. (1979). *Work salience and work values: Their dimensions, assessment, and significance.* Cambridge, England: National Institute for Careers Education and Counselling (mimeo).

Super, D. E. (1980). Perspectives on the motivation to work: Some recent research on work values and work salience. In *Actes du IXe Congrès mondial de l'AIOSP,* Königstein/Taunus 1979 (pp. 70–87). Nürnberg, Germany: Bundesanstalt für Arbeit.

Super, D. E., Kidd, J. M., & Knasel, E. G. (1980). *Work values and work salience: A survey of literature in fourteen countries.* Cambridge, England: National Institute for Careers Education and Counseling (Mimeo).

PART TWO

The National Projects

In Part One we sought to develop a background for the main body of work reported in this book. The four chapters summarize our state of knowledge concerning roles, values, personality, the human aspects of work, and the history and objectives of the Work Importance Study.

In Part Two we take up the national projects and describe the beginnings, methods, and findings of each. Of the eleven projects, seven were among the original starters, although the course of events interrupted the participation of teams from two countries. Three teams joined the project soon after it started and, like the starters, played major roles in the development of the international—and therefore the national—studies. One other joined the WIS late but had a running start, thanks to another, comparable project, and quickly caught up with the original teams.

The differences in institutional bases, support, and particular histories are notable, as seen in Chapter Four, the historical chapter, and in the national chapters that follow, Five to Fifteen. Government agencies, universities both public and private in U.S. terminology (the latter are *libres* or autonomous in some countries), consulting firms, and independent researchers played major roles. Readers who are oriented to industrial/organizational psychology or organizational sociology may be interested in reading Chapters Five to Fifteen to see whether type of sponsorship made any systematic difference in the projects' methods, samples, foci, or outcomes; compare, for example, Canada, South Africa, and the United States. Financing also differed, and the same questions may be relevant.

The variety of successful project strategies is also notable. The best-supported project, one that also may be considered to have done the best sampling, was a public agency that involved representatives of major public and private organizations in its planning and execution. Two projects that started with public funding lost their government support as a result of policy changes; only one died as a result. The other managed to operate by piecing together funding from miscellaneous sources (including some money from a commercial publisher) and getting access to subjects with the help of many friends and even strangers, not through official, power-wielding channels. Chapter Twelve recounts the results, but not the details, of the work of a psychologist's daughter who, joined by her husband, picked up a project shattered by the death of the principal investigator and carried it through with a small sample of one kind of student—their effort kept the flag flying and provided the instruments for further and more substantial work. As researchers occasionally note in lectures but rarely in print, the path from idea to product is often not a smooth one, and the rarely heralded lessons of doing research are often as important as the findings. Research can be successfully supported and managed in many ways.

Some countries—actually research teams *in* countries but not the governments *of* countries—studied only high school students, others only university students, others all categories, although the general WIS plan was to study at least secondary (tenth- or eleventh-year) students. The national samples were drawn in a variety of ways, making the cross-national comparisons sometimes questionable, which is duly noted in appropriate places. That the instruments, as described in Chapter Four, were truly international and cross-national, not merely translated or adapted imports, and that they were used in eleven countries on five continents and thus are now globally available, makes the projects unique, especially interesting, and worthwhile. The reader interested in cross-national comparisons will therefore need to keep in mind the descriptions of instrument development in Chapter Four and the accounts of developmental work and sampling in the national chapters that follow.

Because of the commonly developed instruments, this multifaceted multinational book is more cohesive and more cumulative as it proceeds than the seemingly repetitious series of reports of national projects might suggest. As a Victorian author might have written, "Bear with us, gentle reader, there *is* a beginning, a plot, and an end to this tale," and what lies between offers ample variety.

FIVE

Studies of Work Importance in Australia

Janice J. Lokan
Meredith Shears

According to Maas (1979, p. 2), "Work, and its rewards, is of singular, central importance within our culture. It influences our pattern and level of living, our leisure, our relationships, our psychological and mental health, and our view of the world." This statement reflects the attitude that work is central for Australians, but that attitude has rarely been seriously questioned. The work role has been prominent in Australian life from the country's earliest days of convict labor. For the early convicts, most of whom had been transported for only petty crimes, the passport to freedom was granted in return for hard work. The pioneers had to toil long and hard, often in difficult conditions of terrain and climate, merely to survive. From these early days of adversity Australians developed a strong belief in the right to work for all. Unionism has traditionally been strong in Australia, with the result that many reforms in working conditions have been pioneered here. As early as 1910, workers in Australia had better conditions than their American or European counterparts (Conway, 1976).

Even with the changes in the distribution of the work force that have occurred during the twentieth century, and the disappearance since the mid-1970s of the opportunity for full employment, Australians still believe that everyone has a basic right to a job. The belief in the right to work is not necessarily associated with the practice of working hard, however, if we accept the views frequently expressed in the popular media. "The stereotype is that Australian workers treat their jobs as an annoying interlude between weekends" (Best, 1985, cited in Murdoch & Starford, 1989, p. 135). Or, as Conway insisted, there exists in Australia "a reflexive hatred of work itself and any doctrine which preaches that work is a worthy and necessary function. The old puritan work-ethic still persists among the executive classes. Elsewhere the shirk-ethic . . . marks the climate of the day" (1976, p. 24). However, the data do not support this view of the Australian worker.

Australia has had a tradition of thorough large-scale surveys of populations and of randomly selected samples of young people, sometimes undertaken by an official committee of inquiry. Available is a wealth of descriptive information, going back at least to the early 1960s, of the nature, destinations, and often aspirations of the school-leaver (dropout or recent graduate) population for the country as a whole (Radford, 1962; Radford & Wilkes, 1975; Rosier, 1978; Williams, Clancy, Batten, & Girling-Butcher, 1980) and for more localized regions (Connell, Stroobant, Sinclair, Connell, & Rogers, 1975; Poole, 1983). In contrast to the view put forth in the popular press, the results of these and other studies have revealed the importance that Australians assign to working. In interviews of a nationally representative sample of one thousand young people (Hansen–Rubinsohn–McCann-Erickson, 1978), only 6 percent of those aged 20 to 25 preferred to be unemployed rather than working or studying, whereas two-thirds of those still at school said they would prefer to be in the work force. A poll of two thousand adults aged 18 or older conducted in 1986 by one of Australia's leading newspapers found that the group overall perceived unemployment to be the biggest problem facing young people; the younger the age group, the more concerned respondents were with unemployment as a key problem (*Age,* 1986, cited in Murdoch & Starford, 1989).

Studies that focus on reasons for working rather than the importance of work in a global way also have suggested that the popular media's view of Australia as the land of the shirk ethic is not substantiated, at least as far as self-report data are concerned. Few respondents to the McCann-Erickson survey (Hansen-Rubinsohn, 1978) said they were looking for a quiet life or not having to work too hard. Even most respondents in low-skilled jobs who were interviewed as part of the federal government's Commission of Enquiry into Poverty were seen to "cling tenaciously to work as something meaningful and worthwhile" (p. 17) and to find enjoyment in learning on the job despite adverse circumstances in their work histories (Wright, Headlam, Ozolins, & Fitzgerald, 1978). A survey carried out in 1985 by the Roy Morgan Research Centre, in which the attitudes of Australian workers were compared with those of workers in the United States, Europe, and Japan, reported that "Australia has a relatively conscientious, job-oriented workforce" (p. 135) and that Australian workers gave a higher priority than workers of other nationalities to having interesting jobs that allow for achievement and initiative. The researchers said they could find little evidence of decline in the work ethic (Murdoch & Starford, 1989, pp. 135–136).

The studies cited thus far have been carried out mostly by sociologists or labor market economists, and they tend to lack any emphasis on psychological constructs relating to aspirations, choice, or the meaning of work to individuals. But research on values and attitudes as psychological constructs has grown considerably in Australia since the early 1970s. This is particularly true of studies concerned with the psychological effects of unemployment (e.g., O'Brien & Kabanoff, 1979; Tiggemann & Winefield, 1984; Winefield & Tiggemann, 1985; Feather, 1985; Feather & O'Brien, 1986). Feather (1972,

1975), Poole (1983), and Musgrave (1984) have published significant research on general life values held by large samples of Australians. Also, a strand of research has looked into the social environment of the workplace and its relation to the community in general. For example, Emery and Phillips (1976) carried out in Australia a replication of the O'Toole (1974) study on work in America.

In the domain of work-related values, Feather (1979) carried his interest in societal values to viewing school as a workplace and demonstrated the importance of the opportunity for exercising skills as a "determinant of increasing happiness" for students (p. 135). An early study of work-related values for Australia was done by Underwood (1966), who studied the patterns of values of beginning university students in different courses. Underwood's work led Sweet (1975) to use thirteen statements representing values in Super's Work Values Inventory (1970) in a study of more than fourteen hundred year-12 students in twenty-two occupational choice groups. Sweet found in discriminant analyses that the simple values statements accounted for almost twice as much of the between-group variance as did a set of abilities measures. Recognizing the potential of such values for vocational counseling, Sweet's colleague, Pryor, set to developing an Australian measure of what he has opted to call "work aspect preferences." Starting with nineteen dimensions deduced from the literature, a 5-point scale, and 38 items, Pryor's instrument went through several revisions and much scrutiny before he published the thirteen-scale, 52-item Work Aspect Preference Scale (WAPS) in 1983.

The scales in the WAPS are factor based, and its manual contains considerable evidence of construct-, concurrent-, and criterion-related validity. The latter evidence, in terms of the scales' ability to differentiate occupational choice and actual occupational groups, is particularly impressive. In a subsequent paper, Pryor (1985) reported second-order factor analyses of the thirteen scales in several samples. In all samples, he extracted three factors that he showed, through their coefficients of congruence, to correspond closely to each other. Pryor named the factors Human/Personal Concern, Nonwork Orientation, and Freedom and was able, in comparisons of these factors among occupational choice and occupational groups, "to confirm the expected outcomes, given the characterizations of the preference dimensions." (1985, p. 3).

Some significant studies of work orientation and career salience—more than were identified in any of the other Work Importance Study countries—have also been done in Australia since the early 1970s. For example, Parsler (1971) studied the relative importance of work, family, community activities, and leisure for almost six hundred blue-collar, clerical, and middle-class workers in Melbourne. For the sample as a whole, family relationships were considered the major source of life satisfaction, career was second, and leisure activities third. However, the middle-class respondents ranked career more firmly in second place than the other two groups of respondents, many of whom judged that they gained more satisfaction from leisure activities than from work.

Taylor (1975) classified existing occupational choice theories in three categories: Self-Actualization, Calculation, and Destiny. He then constructed a thirty-three-item questionnaire designed to assess attitudes toward careers and the work role along the three dimensions. After doing factor analysis of responses from a group of young adult males, he decided that the instrument better reflected dimensions that he named Responsibly Committed, Traditionally Comfortable, and Passively Unconcerned. We used Taylor's instrument, which he called the Work Quiz, in one stage of the Australian WIS, and we discuss it further later in this chapter.

In 1981 Sheridan constructed the unidimensional Orientation-to-Work Scale, based partly on Greenhaus's Career Salience Inventory (1973). In a study involving a large sample of secondary school students in years 8 to 12 in western Australia, Sheridan found positive associations between his orientation-to-work dimension and all scales of a prepublication edition of the Australian version of the Career Development Inventory (CDI) (Lokan, 1983). For the Career Planning scale of the CDI, the average correlation with orientation to work for several groups was about 0.4, for career exploration it was about 0.3, and for the career development knowledge scale it was about 0.2.

WIS in Australia

Through the Australian Council for Educational Research (ACER), Australia has participated in all but the earliest planning stages of the WIS. Our team developed draft items for two of the originally specified values (Creativity and Intellectual Stimulation) and the Physical Activity value, which was included later because Pryor's research had indicated it to be an important value for Australians, at least in the adolescent stage of development. Altogether, the Australian Values Scale (VS) went through three revisions, and our Salience Inventory (SI) had two. The instruments were used in five different data-collection exercises as part of the WIS. We regard the fourth, which involved random sampling on a national basis, as our main study. However, because of some departures from the cross-national content in the versions of the VS and SI that we used in our fourth stage, the results we report here are mostly from the third and fifth stages.

Stage I

The main purpose of our first stage was the preliminary assessment of the VS in terms of the suitability of its vocabulary and the coherence of its hypothesized scales. We omitted the Cultural Identity scale, which we thought Australian secondary school students might have difficulty interpreting, leaving us with twenty-two values to test with ten items (five general and five work-related) for each. This made for a long questionnaire, so we split the items across two forms. One contained mostly the internally oriented values, and the other contained mostly the externally oriented. We administered each form to about 350 year-11 (secondary school) students from several large government schools in metropolitan Melbourne.

Stage II

We used results from stage I, particularly the item-scale correlation indexes, to select the best three work-related and the best three general items for each value, to achieve a single instrument of more acceptable length that covers all values. In our revised VS we arranged the values randomly rather than alphabetically, because the alphabetical listing sometimes resulted in highly similar questions in succession. We gave our first version of the SI, which contained fourteen each of Commitment and Participation items and twenty Value Expectations items per role, and the revised VS to about fourteen hundred year-10 students from a variety of secondary schools (independent, religious, state technical, and state high schools) in and around Melbourne. The authors administered all the questionnaires. This allowed us to obtain comments on the general nature of the instruments from the students, who almost universally said they found it tedious to respond to so many similar questions in a session. To obtain some information on the criterion-related validity of the WIS instruments, we made a second trip to several schools and asked students to complete Taylor's Work Quiz and an adaptation of the occupational scales from Holland's Vocational Preference Inventory that had been prepared under Taylor's auspices for research purposes at Melbourne University. On a second visit to other schools, we had students complete either Pryor's WAPS or the Australian CDI. We made the second visits approximately six weeks after the first.

Stage III

Along with several other countries, we presented the results from our second stage at a meeting of the international WIS group. It was during this meeting that the team directors chose the three best-functioning items for each value for all countries for the cross-national version of the Values Scale. Each country agreed to use the items and the next two best-functioning items for each national scale. They specified a basic list of eighteen values for cross-national use, with Cultural Identity and Physical Prowess as optional additions. Thus for our third stage we prepared a one-hundred-item version of the VS according to the cross-national plan and included both the Physical Prowess and Cultural Identity dimensions—the first time that Cultural Identity was scrutinized in our country. Of the 100 items, 47 were worded in terms of life in general and 53 were work related. We reverted to alphabetical ordering of the values, because no other country had tried a random order and the results we had obtained with our stage II VS were similar to those the other countries obtained. Agreement was also reached at the international meeting about retaining only ten of the fourteen items in each of the Participation and Commitment sections of the SI. The directors also specified a preferred list of fourteen of the twenty values from the Value Expectations part. The version of the SI used in the Australian stage III conforms to this plan.

Our main purposes in stage III were to assess the properties of the revised instruments and to examine score differences in different groups of respondents. For the first time, we administered the questionnaires to respondents beyond year 11. Unless a researcher obtains access to schools early in the school year, it is difficult to include year-12 students in research studies: it is a year of high-pressure preparation for university entrance examinations, and both teachers and students resent extraneous activities. However, in our third stage we managed to obtain responses from about 160 year-12 students from four Melbourne schools. We also tested about 260 year-10 students from the same schools; about 190 higher education students from two universities, an advanced education college, and a technology institute; and about 100 adult workers. Table 5.1 describes the groups in terms of some key characteristics. The groups provided the basis for some intergroup and intragroup comparisons and yielded data on the versions of the VS and SI that turned out to be the cross-national versions.

Stage IV

We collected the Australian main study data in mid-1983. The sample included secondary students in years 9, 10, and 11 (in most states, year 9 is the third year of secondary school, although in some it is the second). We used two-stage cluster sampling—first selecting schools with a probability proportional to their enrollment size from the sampling frame for the entire country that is maintained by the ACER. Altogether, we selected seventy-two schools. Then we acquired class lists from schools and drew random samples of ten students, on the basis of date of birth, from each of the target-year levels. We specified lists of replacement students for any students absent on the day of testing.

When we undertook our stage III data collection early in 1982, we thought that there would be a further round of instrument revision cross-nationally before the main studies took place. (In many ways, it is a disadvantage to be half a year out of synchronization with most of the world's population.) Our stage III experience indicated strongly that respondents still found the SI tedious to do and that the Personal Development items introduced to the VS for that stage had not worked as a factor. Nor had the Cultural Identity items functioned well, despite our targeting of schools with high immigrant enrollments. In preparing for our main study, then, we made further modifications to the instruments, which were communicated to other countries early in 1983 but not acted on by them. We shortened the SI by

Table 5.1. WIS Main Stages and Samples in Australia.

	Sample Level					
	Secondary				Higher Education	Worker
Stage	Yr 9	Yr 10	Yr 11	Yr 12		
III N	—	272	—	162	192	97
Percentage male	—	48	—	50	48	59
Modal age	—	15	—	17	19	30–39
IV N	630	630	616	—	—	—
Percentage male	53	51	51	—	—	—
Modal age	14	15	16	—	—	—
V N	—	837	—	—	—	—
Percentage male	—	41	—	—	—	—
Modal age	—	15	—	—	—	—

Occupational Status of Head of Household (percentage)

	Professional	Semiprofessional	Clerical	Skilled Trade	Semiskilled	Unskilled	Unemployed/ Unknown
III Secondary	30	17	8	18	8	12	7
Higher education	23	12	4	18	5	3	35
Worker	63	3	11	5	6	4	5
IV Secondary	15	26	10	16	10	13	10
V Secondary	na	na	na	na	na	na	na

Course type (percentage)

	Arts/Law/Education	Psychology	Business/Commerce	Science/Engineering/ Medicine	Other
III Higher education	34	23	12	29	2

retaining the best six items for each role in the Participation and Commitment sections, with negligible loss of reliability (as established by reanalysis of the stage III data). We reached this decision reluctantly, because of the possibility that it would affect cross-national comparability. But for the instrument to be of most use in our country, it had to be in a format that teachers and counselors would accept. On the basis of our stage III results, we prepared a 90-item version of the VS that contains 5 items in each of 18 scales, only 17 of which are common to the cross-national version because of our omission of the Personal Development items.

Completed WIS questionnaires were returned by 1,876 of the intended 2,160 students, who came from sixty-nine of the seventy-two schools that agreed to participate in the research. The students also took a general scholastic aptitude test, and about two-thirds completed a prepublication version of the Australian edition of *The Self-Directed Search* (Lokan, Shears, & Taylor, 1988). We collected a variety of other background and achievement data by means of two brief questionnaires. One, which sought information on family ethnicity and parental occupations, was completed by the students. The other was completed by teachers; it asked for ratings of the students' achievement on a 5-point scale in a wide range of their school subjects. Thus a wealth of data exists from our stage IV against which we could assess the properties of the WIS instruments.

Of the total sample, 48.3 percent were female; 33 percent were in year 9, 33 percent in year 10, and 34 percent in year 11; 7 percent were younger than 14, 24 percent were aged 14, 36 percent were 15, 26 percent were 16, and the remainder were 17 or older. Seventy-nine percent were in government schools, 12 percent were in schools run by the Roman Catholic church, and 9 percent were in schools run by other churches or by other independent bodies. As Table 5.1 shows, 15 percent of the students had household heads with professional or paraprofessional jobs, 26 percent with managerial jobs, 10 percent with other clerical or office jobs, 16 percent with skilled trade jobs, and 10 percent with semiskilled jobs. Thirteen percent of the household heads had unskilled jobs, and the remainder were either unemployed (7 percent) or the information was not provided (4 percent). Of the students, 88 percent were born in Australia, 7 percent in another English-speaking country, and 5 percent in a non-English-speaking country. Of their fathers, 70 percent were born in Australia, 13 percent in another English-speaking country, 6 percent in a northern or eastern European country, 6 percent in a southern European country, and 4 percent in another non-English-speaking country. On each of the characteristics measured, the distribution of the sample was close to the national distribution at the time.

Stage V

We went to yet another stage of data collection, this time with the version of the VS as used in stage III because of its correspondence with the cross-national version. We did this in 1988, when we collected data from 840 year-10 students from six schools in the Melbourne area for a study of needs, values, and interests. In addition to the VS, the students completed the Australian Self-Directed Search and the Adjective Check List (Gough, 1984).

The remainder of this chapter reports basic results mostly from the third and fifth stages to correspond with the international WIS work, describing the results for the three-item Values scales. Detailed results from the Australian main study are reported elsewhere (Lokan, 1992; in press). The chapter also contains a number of findings from additional analyses, including validity evidence from the main study.

Basic Results: Values Scale

Reliability

As an indication of internal consistency, we computed Cronbach's alpha coefficient for each three-item scale of the VS in each main sample group from stages III, IV, and V. More than 70 percent of the resulting 118 coefficients reach 0.6 or better, with about 40 percent reaching 0.7 or better. The lowest reliability value, 0.32, is obtained for the Personal Development scale in the adult worker group, but after this the next lowest is 0.44 for the Economics scale in the year-10 group of the main study. For three-item scales, which in any case are being used only for cross-national research, the results overall seem quite acceptable.

Item and Scale Intercorrelations and Factor Structure

For each group in the third, fourth, and fifth stages, we computed intercorrelations between the five-item a priori VS scores and between the three-item a priori VS scores. When the number of respondents was large enough to justify item-level factor analysis (that is, in all but the higher education and worker groups in stage III), we also computed intercorrelations at the item level. We discuss here only results of factor analyses from the largest sample for which Australian data on the cross-national items are available (stage V). We used the principal components followed by Varimax rotation method for all factor analyses.

For the sample concerned, all members of which were students in their last year of compulsory schooling (year 10), the item-level analysis of the cross-national part of the instrument indicates that the items are best allocated to twelve factors. Fourteen eigenvalues are greater than unity, but the last two factors have only single items with loadings worth considering. Of the twenty a priori dimensions, only the Physical Activity and Variety scales, closely followed by the Creativity scale, are the same in the factor analysis solution. Items on the two Social scales group together, as do the Risk and Physical Prowess items and the Cultural Identity and Working Conditions items. The Aesthetics items (work context) group with the Achievement and Prestige items in one factor, whereas the general context Aesthetics items align with the Altruism items in another factor. The Advancement, Economics, and Work Conditions (one item only) items group together, as do the Personal Development items with some of the Ability Utilization and Achievement items. Finally, the Autonomy items load about equally with the Authority items on one factor, as they do with the Life-style items on another. Taken together, the results show that, at least for respondents in midadolescence, the a priori dimensions are only partially factor based.

When we force a five-factor solution, corresponding to the number of eigenvalues greater than two, from the item-level data, the items group together in quite meaningful ways. Considering only factor loadings at or above 0.35, we could not assign four items to any factor (one each from the Authority, Creativity, Personal Development, and Cultural Identity values), and only two items (both intended as measures of Authority) appear in two factors. The Economics, Advancement, Prestige, Working Conditions, and Cultural Identity items group together in a Material Conditions dimension; the Autonomy, Life-style, and Creativity items form a Freedom (or perhaps Independence) dimension; the Physical Prowess, Physical Activity, and Risk items come together in a dimension reflecting Adventure; the Altruism, Personal Development, Aesthetics, and Ability Utilization items form a Human/Personal Concern dimension; and the Social and Variety items cluster as a Social dimension.

A factor analysis of the matrix of a priori scale intercorrelations for the stage V sample yields five eigenvalues greater than unity, accounting for about 60 percent of the variance. The Varimax-rotated factor loadings from this analysis reveal structure similar to that suggested by the item-level analysis just discussed. It is also similar to the factor structure we find in most other countries or in the global, transnational pooled sample shown in Appendix A.2.

Relative Importance of Values

Appendix A.4 shows the values ranked most important and least important by the third-stage Australian samples. Although the values are listed in rank-order of the mean scores obtained within a group and shown in Appendix A.4, it is usually not the case in the top groups that adjacent, or even adjacent-but-one, pairs of values are significantly different. In the bottom groups are more instances, but not the majority, of pairs that are significantly different.

The appendix reveals similar value priorities across the Australian sample groups, with self-improvement, social, and economic values usually the most important. Older respondents also rank an independent life-style as among the most important, displacing Economics from the top five. The least important values across the groups are also quite similar. Risk and heavy work (Physical Prowess, one of the optional values, occupies a bottom place in all samples) do not appeal, and, at least at the level of self-reporting, opportunities for using authority or gaining prestige are less important than most other sources of work and life satisfaction. For Australian respondents, Cultural Identity (another optional scale, not shown in Appendix A.2) issues rank among the least important, although Variety displaces this value from the bottom five for the sample with the greatest overrepresentation of immigrant respondents (year 10, stage III).

Values Differences Among Subgroups

Again, for reasons of space, we are not including here full results of analyses by subgroups such as gender, socioeconomic status, ethnic background, and so on. In the ensuing discussion, because of the usually large sample sizes that can result in disproportionately significant mean scores from very small actual differences, we consider only subgroup differences significant at the 0.01 level or better. In most samples, differences by gender run according to stereotype. Males are higher on such values as Authority, Economics, Physical Activity, Physical Prowess, Prestige, and Risk; females are higher on Altruism, Personal Development, and Social Interaction. The younger the group, the more stereotypic the pattern. The latter finding probably reflects the more representative nature of the year-10 groups rather than a trend to narrower views among younger respondents. About half of a cohort in Australia has already left school before year 12, and a further fifth does not undertake any kind of higher education. Hence a year-12 group is more select than a year-10 group, and a higher education group is still more select. It is interesting to note that in the higher education sample (stage III), women value opportunities to use their abilities and to achieve more than do the men, and there is no difference in Physical Activity or Social Interaction. In the worker sample, dominated by incumbents of professional and semiprofessional jobs, significant gender differences occur only on the two Physical scales.

Appendix A.1 presents the means on all of the three-item Values scales for the four stage III sample groups. The results of one-way analyses of variance (ANOVAs) followed by Scheffé tests show a number of significant differences among the Australian samples. In all but one case, the scores of the year-10 group are higher than in the other groups. The exception is Lifestyle, which is rated as more important by the higher education group. The results probably reflect a combination of the more representative nature of the year-10 group and the greater maturity and more realistic view of life possibilities expected in older groups.

We find few value differences at stage III among groups of different socioeconomic status (SES), judged by whether the household head held a professional/semiprofessional or nonprofessional job. In the school group, with years 10 and 12 combined, the professional group scores significantly higher on Autonomy, and the nonprofessional group scores significantly higher on Social Interaction. The higher education group shows no difference on any of the Values scales when the respondents are categorized according to type of occupation held by the household head. Among the workers, the professionals value Ability Utilization, Autonomy, and Life-style more highly, whereas the non-professionals value Advancement, Physical Prowess, and Risk more highly. In stage IV the professional/semiprofessional group again scores significantly higher on Autonomy and scores higher on Ability Utilization. The lower-SES groups are significantly higher on Physical Prowess. We find interesting results by type of school attended, which also has a socioeconomic component, because nongovernment schools charge fees. The students in government schools score lower than students in nongovernment schools on the academic motivation scales (Ability Utilization and Achievement) and higher on the less academic scales (Economics, Physical Prowess, and Risk), as would be expected in the Australian context.

Comparisons were also made in stages III and IV for secondary students of differing ethnic backgrounds. For about half the values assessed we find in stage III significant differences between three groups classified according to whether fathers were born in Australia, in another English-speaking country, or in a non-English-speaking country. The only value endorsed more highly by the Australian group is Life-style, which involves a desire to live life as a person wishes—the "independent-minded Aussie" stereotype. All other differences are in favor of the non-English-speaking origin group compared with one or both other groups and include such aspects as Ability Utilization, Advancement, Aesthetics, Authority, Physical Prowess, Prestige, Social Interaction, and Working Conditions. The non-English-speaking origin group also scores significantly higher on Cultural Identity than the English-speaking origin groups when we combine these two groups, but not when we consider the three groups separately. To some extent, the results by ethnic background may be bound up with socioeconomic status (the non-English-speaking group on the whole would be overrepresented in the nonprofessional group), but it is a well-established finding that immigrant parents have high aspirations for their children's futures in their new country—as do the children for themselves.

In the stage IV sample, which is accurately representative of Australia as a whole, the ANOVAs by ethnic background yield significant differences on a smaller number of the values dimensions, but in a direction consistent with the differences we find in the stage III sample. The non-English-speaking origin group scores higher than the Australian origin or than both the English-speaking origin groups on Aesthetics, Authority, Creativity, Prestige, Risk, and Physical Prowess. This seems to reflect a greater desire for status and adventure, coupled with more appreciation of opportunities for individual expression. A lack of appreciation of the "finer things of life" has also been traditionally a part of the stereotyped Aussie image (Horne, 1971); the results here concerning Aesthetics, in both the secondary student samples and Creativity in the stage IV sample, offer some support for that image.

We analyzed the data from the stage III higher education sample for the students grouped into four main categories according to the type of course they were studying. The four areas, as shown in Table 5.1, are arts, law, and education; psychology; business and commerce; and science, engineering, and medicine. Analyses of variance and Scheffé tests were then carried out to locate differences in importance of values among the four groups. Among the significant findings are that the arts/law/education and psychology students score higher than the other groups on Ability Utilization; the arts/law/education and business/commerce groups each score higher than the science/engineering/medicine group on Achievement; the psychology and arts/law/education groups each score higher than the science/engineering/medicine group on Altruism; the business/commerce and science/engineering/medicine students score higher than the arts/law/education students on Risk and lower on Aesthetics; and the business/commerce students score higher than the science/engineering/medicine group on Social Interaction. (In retrospect, we should have omitted the small number of medicine students from these analyses because earlier research [Feather, 1982] showed that medicine students as a group are characteristically different in their values—for example, in Altruism—from other kinds of students.) We did two-way ANOVAs with both gender and course type as factors, to gauge the importance of the gender composition of the course groups in the results. The supplementary analyses show that the main effect of gender is significant only for Ability Utilization and Altruism, but the main effect of course type also remains significant for these values. Taken together, the results by course type provide considerable evidence for the criterion-related validity of the Values scales.

Correlations with Other Variables

We computed correlations between the six-item Australian VS scales from stage II with factor-based scale scores from Taylor's Work Quiz and with Pryor's Work Aspect Preference Scale (WAPS). Table 5.2 shows all correlation coefficients with the Work Quiz scales. For reasons of space, we show only the highest two correlations between each scale from the VS and the scales from the WAPS. To obtain the Work Quiz scales, we factor analyzed the data from the stage II respondents in an attempt to replicate the results Taylor had obtained in an all-male, older sample. The analysis for the year-10 students yields a better solution than Taylor found, with factors showing orientations toward work that are self-actualizing and instrumental and that view work as a necessity.

If the WAPS and WIS items can justifiably be considered substantively different methodologically, the results in Table 5.2 demonstrate quite strong support for the validity of the VS dimensions. The WAPS scales are usually most highly correlated with the WIS scales to which they would be expected to correspond. The Work Quiz Self-Actualizing scale, typefied by a person seeking competent performance for both personal and altruistic reasons, positively correlates with values such as Altruism, Aesthetics, Creativity, Achievement, and Ability Utilization and does not correlate with less abstract

Table 5.2. Correlations of the VS with the WAPS and Work Quiz Scales, Stage II.

Values Scale	Self-Actualizing	Work Quiz Scale Instrumental	Necessity	Work Aspect Preference Scale[a] Highest	2nd highest
Ability Utilization	25**	23**	–04	31** (SDe)	24** (Cre)
Achievement	30**	23**	–13*	37** (Pre)	33** (SDe)
Advancement	23**	35**	00	42** (Pre)	36** (Man)
Aesthetics	20**	18**	10	36** (Cre)	35** (Pre)
Altruism	30**	–10	04	55** (Alt)	26** (CoW)
Associates	06	13*	09	50** (CoW)	30** (Sur)
Authority	20**	31**	–04	51** (Man)	44** (Pre)
Autonomy	17**	23**	–01	42** (Ind)	30** (Mon)
Creativity	26**	24**	02	57** (Cre)	38** (SDe)
Economic Rewards	–03	52**	11	62** (Mon)	38** (Pre)
Economic Security	11	27**	06	40** (Sec)	31** (Sur)
Environment	10	29**	10	48** (Sur)	32** (LSt)
Intellectual Stimulation	35**	12	–09	39** (SDe)	38** (Cre)
Life-style	03	24**	14*	43** (Ind)	35** (LSt)
Participation in Decision Making	19**	12	–07	28** (SDe)	26** (Sec)
Physical Activity	13**	26**	10	40** (PAc)	29** (Pre)
Prestige	11	34**	11	48** (Pre)	37** (Mon)
Responsibility	33**	07	–02	27** (SDe)	22** (Cre)
Risk Taking	07	15*	07	29** (Ind)	25** (PAc)
Spiritual Values	28**	09	11	45** (Alt)	36** (Pre)
Supervisory Relations	10	17**	03	40** (CoW)	40** (Sur)
Variety	09	22**	01	33** (Ind)	31** (SDe)

Note: Decimal points omitted.
* Significantly different from zero at $p < 0.01$ level.
** Significantly different from zero at $p < 0.001$ level.

[a] Key to Work Aspect Preference Scale:

Alt	Altruism	LSt	Life-style	Pre	Prestige
CoW	Co-workers	Man	Management	Sec	Security
Cre	Creativity	Mon	Money	SDe	Self-Development
Det	Detachment	PAc	Physical activity	Sur	Surroundings
Ind	Independence				

values, such as Working Conditions, Life-style, Economics, and the Work Associates and Supervisory Relations values that we included in stage II. The Instrumental scale of the Work Quiz correlates with almost all less abstract values. Those values that do not correlate significantly with the Self-Actualizing orientation do, together with others, do so with the Instrumental orientation. We expected a relationship with Achievement for the Instrumental scale, but we also found other relationships that we had not expected—for example, Aesthetics, Creativity, Autonomy, and Ability Utilization. Perhaps this occurs because students with this orientation desire a high standard of living, although they may not expect a high level of personal satisfaction from their work. Finally, we found only two significant correlations for the Work Quiz "Necessity" scale—an expected negative relationship with Achievement and a positive relationship with Life-style, which can perhaps be attributed to a desire to spend time in other activities.

We also obtained correlations of the VS scores with the general scholastic aptitude measures and teacher ratings of school achievement from stage IV. In brief, these are mostly small (0.2 or lower), although often statistically different from zero. Notable is the Physical Prowess scale, which has several correlations of about 0.3 to 0.4 with scholastic aptitude or with achievement in academic subjects, always in the negative direction. The overall pattern of correlations between the VS and achievement ratings support the validity of the VS.

Basic Results: Salience Inventory

Reliability

As with the VS, we computed Cronbach's alpha coefficient for each SI scale in each sample group. The results, especially in the early stages of the project, are extremely high, usually exceeding 0.9. Such high coefficients in a measure of attitudes suggest either that the questions within the scales are overly similar or that the respondents so perceive them (Kline, 1979). With the Participation and Commitment sections reduced from ten questions per role to six, the reliability indexes remain high enough to justify use of the scales in individual counseling. The lowest is 0.82, the highest 0.93.

Item and Scale Intercorrelations and Factor Structure

For the third and fourth stages, we computed sample intercorrelations by group for the SI scales, but only the stage IV total group was large enough to use item-level intercorrelations. We carried out factor analyses of each scale-level correlation matrix and for three subsets, corresponding to the three main sections of Participation, Commitment, and Value Expectations, of the stage IV item-level matrix. We used the principal components plus Varimax rotation method throughout. The factor matrixes we obtained are similar to that presented in Chapter Nineteen. In all cases, clear five-factor solutions corresponding to the five roles emerge. At the scale level, this supports the intended role structure of the instrument. However, at the item level it shows that the hoped-for by-product of some differentiation of potential sources of satisfaction within roles (from the Value Expectations scales) was not achieved.

Role Salience Differences Among Subgroups

The stage III means by sample group, which appear in Appendix B.1, reveal differences in SI scale scores according to age and status. The workers are less committed to and participate less in the Study role, with the reverse for the higher education student group. The secondary students rate themselves as neither particularly committed to nor participating much in the Study role, no doubt revealing a general attitude of disaffection with school. No group feels committed to or is doing much about assisting its Community. The level of commitment to the Home role is relatively high in all groups but significantly higher for the workers, as is participation in Home activities for this group. Ratings of the Leisure role are highest for the secondary student group, lowest for the worker group.

Analyses of the SI scales by gender within the various sample groups from stages III and IV reveal somewhat common patterns throughout. The younger the student sample, the fewer the significant differences by gender. In almost all instances in which differences are significant, the women score higher than the men. In the student samples, the only exceptions to this pattern are for Participation in Work at stage IV and for Value Expectations from Leisure at stage III for the higher education students. The latter result also emerges from the stage III worker sample. In the higher education student sample we find significant differences on ten of the fifteen SI scales, whereas in the worker sample there is only one other difference apart from the Value Expectations from Leisure difference already cited. This is in Commitment to Study, on which the women score higher. Overall, more of each of the Commitment and Value Expectations scales yield significant differences by gender than the Participation scales. That women may more readily give higher ratings than men to attitudinal statements could be a confounding variable in the results, but one that the present data are unfortunately not adequate to monitor.

Analyses by socioeconomic status (the worker or household head holding a professional/semiprofessional or nonprofessional job) reveal few significant differences. In the stage III year-10 group the children of professionals are more committed to Study, in the stage III year-12 group the children of nonprofessionals expect more satisfaction from Home activities, and in the worker group the professionals are participating more in Study. In the stage IV sample the children of professionals score higher on all the SI Study scales than do the children of nonprofessionals.

Differences by degree of family ethnicity, on the 3-point scale of whether the father's birthplace was in Australia, another English-speaking country, or a non-English-speaking country, were assessed for the stage III student sample and for the more representative stage IV sample. Those stage III students whose fathers were born in a non-English-speaking country score higher than the Australian origin group on commitment to and valuing Study and higher than both of the other groups on their self-rated participation in Study. They also report significantly more participation in Home activities than the other two groups. All the findings concerning the Study role are replicated in the stage IV sample. In addition, in the stage IV sample, members of the Australian-origin group said they are more committed to and expecting more satisfaction from Community activities than did the other groups, and both the Australian-origin and other English-speaking origin groups score significantly higher on all the Leisure scales than the non-English-speaking, origin group. On the whole, the results further reinforce the stereotype of the leisure-loving Australian, with recent immigrant groups striving more for education, which they see as a pathway to success in their new country.

Correlations with Other Variables

We also analyzed results of the SI from stage II with respect to the factor-based scales of Taylor's Work Quiz; Table 5.3 shows the correlations we find. The Work Quiz Self-Actualizing scale relates positively to four of the five role activities—all but Leisure. Students with self-actualizing orientation to the Worker role thus seem to see themselves as committed to a wide spectrum of roles but are either too busy or perhaps not interested enough to take part in many Leisure activities. On the other hand, those with an Instrumental view of the Worker role tend to participate in and value Leisure rather than other life-role activities. We find no relationship between participating in or being committed to any of the five life roles for the Work Quiz Work as Necessity scale. In addition to not showing any positive affect for Work, individuals with this orientation appear not to care about other kinds of activities, although our data do no more than suggest this as a possibility.

We computed correlations between the SI scales and measures of scholastic aptitude and school achievement for the stage IV group, and many are significantly different from zero. Lokan (1985) reports detailed results. The correlations significant at the 0.01 level or better are mostly quite low, in the range 0.15 to 0.25, but present a picture consistent with what would be expected. All the aptitude and achievement variables correlate positively with Participation in Study, and most correlate similarly with Commitment to and Valuing Study. By contrast, relationships with Participation in Work are significant but negative, as are the scholastic aptitude correlations with Participation in Home and Valuing Home activities.

We analyzed the relationships of SI scales with the scales of the Australian version of the Career Development Inventory (CDI) (Lokan, 1983) in a small study with a subgroup of the stage III secondary sample. Levy (1987), who undertook a study of career maturity and related variables in a group of students followed from year 9 through to year 12, also analyzed them in doctoral research. In both studies the correlation values are not high, but they are consistent in supporting expectations. The cognitive scales of the CDI correlate significantly only with the SI Study or Work scales, apart from the Commitment to Community scale. Because the CDI attitudinal scales assess orientation to the need for career planning and exploration as well as self-rated amount of exploration the subject has undertaken, we would expect students with more involvement in and commitment to their present

Table 5.3. Correlations of the SI with the Australian Career Development Inventory Scales from Two Separate Studies.

	Career Development Inventory Scale					
SI Scale	Career Planning	Career Exploration	Career Attitude Total	World of Work Information	Career Decision Making	Career Knowledge Total
(A) Participation						
Study	25*	39**	36**	25*	19*	26**
Work	29**	14	28**	08	06	09
Community	23*	15	24*	02	08	06
Home	04	24*	13	-11	-12	-13
Leisure	-09	-02	-08	03	05	04
Commitment						
Study	15	39**	28**	26**	20*	27**
Work	32**	19*	32**	31**	26**	32**
Community	20*	20*	24*	17	18	20*
Home	11	28**	21*	07	03	06
Leisure	-07	-02	-07	04	08	06
Value Expectations						
Study	17	28**	25*	18	15	19*
Work	25*	22*	28**	30**	21*	29**
Community	10	22*	17	15	17	16
Home	05	20*	12	-05	-07	-05
Leisure	-16	06	-09	-06	-04	-06
(B) Participation						
Study	29**	31**	35**	09	02	07
Work	33**	19**	30**	-02	-02	-02
Community	11	19**	17*	03	01	03
Home	13*	30**	24**	-04	-05	-05
Leisure	19**	14*	19**	05	06	06
Commitment						
Study	26**	28**	31**	13	06	11
Work	24**	16*	23**	08	06	07
Community	16*	24*	23**	18**	15*	18**
Home	10	23**	18**	02	03	03
Leisure	12	07	11	10	12	12
Value Expectation						
Study	24**	27**	29**	09	04	07
Work	25**	18**	26**	09	09	10
Community	07	22**	16*	10	11	12
Home	16*	25**	23**	-02	02	00
Leisure	13*	09	13*	04	07	06

Note: Decimal points omitted. Section A is from stage III of the Australian Career Development Inventory Scales. Section B is from Levy (1987).
* Significantly different from zero at *p* < 0.01 level.
** Significantly different from zero at *p* < 0.001 level.

and future vocational (rather than avocational) roles to score higher on these dimensions. On the whole, the results show just that—the CDI attitudinal scales relate significantly to most SI scales, except those for the Leisure role. The exception here was that Participation in Leisure correlates positively with both the CDI attitude subscales (and, of course, with the total CDI attitude scores) in Levy's study.

Salience Inventory and Values Scale Relationships

We initially assessed the relationships between scores on the VS and SI through correlation coefficients. To obtain a better picture of the functioning of the dimensions of the instruments, we performed multivariate (discriminant function) analyses on the stage IV (main study) data, using the three-item Values scales only. We made similar analyses of the data sets from three other countries; the results are presented in Chapter Nineteen. Overall, the patterns of relationships again support expectations, for example, with the Leisure scales relating to the Life-style, Physical Activity, and Social Values scales, the Study scales relating to the Ability Utilization scale, and the Community scales relating to the Altruism scale.

Uses of WIS Instruments in Australia

To date, the WIS instruments have been used in Australia only in research. In addition to the work of Lokan and Shears, the Salience Inventory has been used in one doctoral and two master's dissertations, and the VS is likely to be used in one soon. The instruments' value for research has been recognized. Manuals to accompany published versions of the instruments are in preparation to facilitate their use in actual counseling situations.

Pryor's Work Aspect Preference Scale is quite widely recognized as a tool useful in working with students as they begin their career exploration in earnest—in Australia this is encouraged, particularly in the middle secondary years. The advent of the WIS VS, which also is backed up with extensive Australian data, will give users the opportunity to choose an alternative that has a broad base. A further benefit of the VS is that it has been studied extensively in relation to the SI, for which there is no existing alternative in Australia.

With regard to the SI, we expect practicing counselors and researchers to welcome the opportunity it provides to help people examine their life-role priorities. This, together with consideration of value priorities from the VS, should provide the basis for life-span counseling, not just in the years leading up to choice of educational program or occupational field but also in the mid-career and later years. Midlife counseling that arises from redeployment needs is becoming increasingly necessary in Australia, as in other industrialized countries. Relatively few instruments suitable for this purpose are available, and we hope that the WIS instruments will prove a useful addition for psychologists, other counselors, and clients.

Conclusion

The Australian literature on work is rich, and it shows work in a light different from that reflected in popular opinion. Aussies work: they value jobs and the right to work. Descriptive writings to this effect abound; hard data support them. The large amount of research on values—objective psychometric research—is not as well known outside Australia as it should be.

So what has the Work Importance Study added to the picture, other than perhaps to help Australia stand front and center on the world stage?

Two new world-class instruments, the Values Scale and the Salience Inventory, are now available for use in Australia. The VS agrees moderately with the Australian WAPS and somewhat less well with the Australian Work Quiz. This appears to be a multimethod multitrait validation. Which instrument is best? We need external criteria in order to make that judgment.

The VS is about as reliable in Australia as most such scales: alphas of 0.60 and above are useful for research, which is the purpose of the cross-national three-item scales, but not for individual assessment (which is of course done only with the longer national versions). Fourteen factors appear to underlie the twenty-two scales: the a priori scales do overlap in adolescence, but the factors group items in ways that are, post hoc, logical and that agree with data from other countries. The a priori scales were not meant to be pure—they were meant to be *meaningful*, to be criteria-related. Were they?

The answer is yes. We found the differences we expected in gender, educational (age and SES) level, parental occupational level (in secondary but not in university students), occupational level in employed adults, and ethnicity. Immigrants from more recently industrialized societies tend to be more oriented to achievement or personal development and their own culture. The study bears out the curricular differences we expected: arts, law, education, and psychology students value Ability Utilization more than do others, and business, commerce, science, engineering, and medicine students score higher on Risk and lower on Aesthetics than do arts, law, and education students.

Values tend to show small but significant relationships with scholastic aptitudes and achievement, as we expected. The SI, WIS's innovative measure of the relative importance of five major life roles (Student, Worker, Homemaker, Community Service, and Leisurite), is a reliable measure of both behavioral participation and affective commitment. The scales are factorially pure in Australia as elsewhere.

Group differences are as expected: workers consider Study less important than do students in higher education, but secondary school students, a larger part of the general population, tend to value some roles as the workers do: homemaking is valued, community service is not. Is volunteerism dead in Australia? Is it alive and well even in Canada or the United States? And what of Portugal, Poland, or Japan?

Gender differences in role importance tend not to be great in secondary school, but where we do note a difference is that women tend to value a role more than men do except in the case of Work Participation. Commitment showed more differences than did Participation. Children of professionals value Study more than do other children, and those of nonprofessionals tend to expect more of Home and Family. Among ethnic groups, the Australian-origin group appears more leisure-oriented than are other groups: because they are established, they can perhaps enjoy life more.

Correlations with Taylor's Work Quiz suggest this type of construct is valid. Aptitude and achievement data tend to correlate as expected—positively but only slightly—with considering Study important.

We examined career development (CDI) scores in relation to role salience. Those with higher Career Attitude scores tend to value Study, Work, and Home more highly than do those with lower scores on Career Planning and Exploration, whereas those with higher scores on Decision Making and World of Work Information tend to value the Study and Work scales more than do low scorers.

In Chapter Nineteen the relationships between roles and values are reported to be as expected in Australia and three other countries.

Finally, although only researchers have used the SI and VS in Australia to date (a period of about five years), we expect both scales will soon find their way into practice. The experiences reported in some other countries—for example, Belgium, Canada, South Africa, and the United States—already show how they can be used in counseling. What their effect will be is a matter for time and further research to show.

References

Age. (1986, May 10). Problems facing the young (p. 5). Cited in L. H. Murdoch & P. Starford (1989). *Work in perspective* (p. 5). New York: Macmillan.

Best, B. (1989). Survey rejects work shy image. Cited in L. H. Murdoch & P. Starford (1989). *Work in perspective* (pp. 135–136). New York: Macmillan.

Connell, W. F., Stroobant, R. E., Sinclair, K. E., Connell, R.W.F., & Rogers, K. W. (1975). *Twelve to 20: Studies of city youth.* Sydney: Hicks Smith.

Conway, R. (1976, July 31). Is work a four-letter word? *Bulletin,* pp. 24–27.

Emery, F. E., & Phillips, C. (1976). *Living at work.* Canberra: Australian Government Publishing Service.

Feather, N. T. (1972). Value similarity and school adjustment. *Australian Journal of Psychology, 24,* 193–208.

Feather, N. T. (1975). *Values in education and society.* New York: Free Press.

Feather, N. T. (1979). Human values and the work situation: Two studies. *Australian Psychologist, 14,* 131–141.

Feather, N. T. (1982). Reasons for entering medical school in relation to value priorities and sex of student. *Journal of Occupational Psychology, 55,* 119–128.

Feather, N. T. (1985). Attitudes, values, and attributions: Explanations of unemployment. *Journal of Personality and Social Psychology, 48,* 876–889.

Feather, N. T., & O'Brien, G. E. (1986). A longitudinal study of the effects of employment and unemployment on school-leavers. *Journal of Occupational Psychology, 59,* 121–144.

Gough, H. (1984). *Adjective Check List.* Palo Alto, CA: Consulting Psychologists Press.

Greenhaus, J. H. (1973). A factorial investigation of career salience. *Journal of Vocational Behavior, 3,* 95–98.

Hansen–Rubinsohn–McCann-Erickson Pty. Ltd. (1978). *Youth in Australia: The McCann report.* Sydney: McCann-Erickson.

Horne, D. (1971). *The lucky country.* Ringwood, Australia: Penguin.

Kline, P. (1979). *Psychometrics and psychology.* San Diego, CA: Academic Press.

Levy, B. (1987). *A longitudinal study of vocational maturity.* Unpublished doctoral dissertation, Monash University, Melbourne.

Lokan, J. J. (1983). *Career Development Inventory, Australia.* Hawthorn: Australian Council for Educational Research.

Lokan, J. J. (1985, September). *Some correlates of commitments and life satisfactions for secondary students in Australia.* Paper presented at International Association of Educational and Vocational Guidance Conference, Dubrovnik.

Lokan, J. J. (1992). The Work Importance Study: Australian young people's work values in international perspective. In M. E. Poole (Ed.), *Education and work.* Hawthorn: Australian Council for Educational Research.

Lokan, J. J. (in press). *Life Roles Inventory, Parts I and II* (Manual).

Lokan, J. J., Shears, M. J., & Taylor, K. F. (1988). *The self-directed search* (Australian ed.). Hawthorn: Australian Council for Educational Research.

Maas, F. (1979, May). *Unemployment is not working: The importance and meaning of work.* Paper presented at the Annual Conference of the Australian College of Education, Perth.

Murdoch, L. H., & Starford, P. (1989). *Work in perspective.* New York: Macmillan.

Musgrave, P. (1984). The moral values of some Australian adolescents: A report and discussion. *Australian and New Zealand Journal of Sociology, 20,* 197–217.

O'Brien, G. E., & Kabanoff, B. (1979). Comparison of unemployed and employed workers on work values, locus of control, and health variables. *Australian Psychologist, 14,* 143–154.

O'Toole, J. (Ed.). (1974). *Work and the quality of life.* Cambridge, MA: MIT Press.

Parsler, R. (1971). Some social aspects of embourgoisement in Australia. *Sociology, 5,* 95–112.

Poole, M. E. (1983). *Youth: Expectations and transitions.* New York: Routledge & Kegan Paul.

Pryor, R. G. L. (1983). *Work Aspect Preference Scale.* Hawthorn: Australian Council for Educational Research.

Pryor, R. G. L. (1985). The measurement of second-order factors in Work Aspect Preference Scale. *Bulletin for Psychologists, 38,* 2–11.

Radford, W. C. (1962). *School leavers in Australia 1959–60.* Hawthorn: Australian Council for Educational Research.

Radford, W. C., & Wilkes, R. E. (1975). *School leavers in Australia 1971–72.* Hawthorn: Australian Council for Educational Research.

Rosier, M. J. (1978). *Early school leavers in Australia.* Stockholm: Almqvist and Wiksell, and Hawthorn: Australian Council for Educational Research.

Sheridan, B. (1981). *Career development in Adolescents: Its relationship to orientation to work and locus of control.* Unpublished doctoral dissertation. University of Western Australia, Perth.

Super, D. E. (1970). *The Work Values Inventory.* Boston: Houghton Mifflin.

Sweet, R. (1975). *The occupational choices of sixth form students in relation to aptitudes, vocational interests, and work values* (Research report). Sydney: New South Wales Department of Labour and Industry, Division of Vocational Guidance Services.

Taylor, K. F. (1975). *Orientations to work.* Unpublished doctoral dissertation. University of Melbourne, Melbourne.

Tiggemann, M., & Winefield, A. H. (1984). The effects of unemployment on the mood, self-esteem, locus of control, and depressive affect of school-leavers. *Journal of Occupational Psychology, 57,* 33–42.

Underwood, K. (1966). *Work values of university entrants.* Unpublished manuscript. University of New South Wales, Student Counselling and Research Unit, Sydney.

Williams, T., Clancy, J., Batten, M., & Girling-Butcher, S. (1980). *School, work, and career: Seventeen-year-olds in Australia.* (Research monograph No. 6.) Hawthorn: Australian Council for Educational Research.

Winefield, A. H., & Tiggemann, M. (1985). Psychological correlates of employment and unemployment: Effects, predisposing factors, and sex differences. *Journal of Occupational Psychology, 58,* 229–242.

Wright, A., Headlam, F., Ozolins, U., & Fitzgerald, R. T. (1978). Poverty, education, and adolescents. In Report of the Commission of Enquiry into Poverty, *Outcomes of schooling: Aspects of success and failure.* Canberra: Australian Government Publishing Service.

SIX

The Flemish Work Importance Study

Pol Coetsier
Rita Claes

Belgium consists of two independent states (Flanders and Wallonia) with two different cultures and two different languages (Dutch and French). The assessment of the importance of life roles and life values, somehow embedded in a community's culture, should be through instruments adapted for that community. The Flemish WIS instruments (for the Dutch-speaking part of Belgium) have been developed by the Laboratory of Sociopsychology of Work and of Test Construction of the State University Ghent. The Research Council of the State University Ghent partially funds the project. The adaptation of the WIS instruments for the French-speaking part of Belgium has not started yet.

The Flemish WIS started with the translation to Dutch and back to English of the U.S. version of the international WIS instruments (Super & Nevill, 1986a, 1986b). In line with the WIS procedure we developed new items for each of the VS and SI scales that accounted for about one-third of all items. This led to the Flemish pilot versions—127 VS items and 225 SI items. The pilot study of July 1987 ($N = 80$) checked the translation of the items and the answer sheets for clarity and verified their acceptability to respondents. Interviewers instructed to observe the respondents' reactions and comments administered the instruments individually. Their observations and the results of simple statistical analyses (means, standard deviations, internal consistency, intercorrelations) led to the conclusion that the pilot versions were acceptable.

In the instrument development phase (October 1987 to May 1988) we administered the extended versions of the instruments to about fourteen hundred respondents. The instrument development sample consisted of male and female respondents of varying ages, life stages, and labor market situations. This sample of convenience covered the main future user groups of the WIS instrument in Flanders. Seven interviewers gathered the data. Item analyses and factor analyses led to modifications of the instrument development versions and resulted in the final Flemish VS and SI.

The Flemish VS is called *Belang van Waarden* and contains twenty-one scales with five items each, three cross-national and two specifically Flemish, in keeping with WIS policy. The Flemish SI is called *Belang van Levensrollen* with scales *Deelname* (Participation), *Inzet* (Commitment), and *Verwachtingen* (Value Expectations). Thus the Flemish SI is like the cross-national SI. The manual of the Flemish VS and SI (Coetsier & Claes, 1990) contains a complete report of instrument development, reliability, and validity and includes norms for various samples.

This chapter presents Flemish data on the cross-national version of the VS (eighteen scales of three items) and the SI for three groups of subjects: secondary school students, higher education students, and adults. Table 6.1 reports the characteristics of the three samples. Two test administrators gathered the data for the secondary and higher education groups in group settings. For adults we preferred to conduct individual interviews at the home of the respondent.

The Flemish Research on Life Values and Roles

The Flemish WIS results should be seen in light of the main findings of recent Flemish research on life values and roles. The European Value Systems Study Group studied, in some thirty countries, the values attached to work and leisure, family and sexuality, religion, politics, and social ethics (for Belgium, see Delooz, 1984; Kerkhofs, 1984a, 1984b; Kerkhofs & Rezsohazy, 1984). The studies showed continuity but also intergenerational differences in such areas as motivations at work, the life-style sought, and the importance attached to having children. Using repeated-inquiries data, De Coster and colleagues (1987, 1988) showed that adolescents' and parents' value hierarchies are quite similar. They valued most the human and social values, insofar as their place in society was secure. The basic concerns of the adolescents as well as their parents were harmonious relations within the family and the prospects of success in study and meaningful work.

The main focus of the Flemish research is work values and the importance of the role of worker, sometimes compared to other life values and life roles. Flemish working-class people work for a good life away from the job, and at work they simply want to get on with their jobs, have good company, and a little advancement (Rosseel, 1979). One international study, *The Meaning of Working* (Meaning of Work [MOW], 1987; Coetsier & Spoelders-Claes, 1984), showed that in Flanders family was a more important life area than work and leisure, and social service and religion were far less important than family. The main values sought in working were an interesting job, good pay, job security, and good interpersonal relations. According to Degroote and Cossey (1988), students had a traditional image of work: working was a central facet of life, and they considered not wanting to work unethical. Since the late 1980s work has become a more central life interest, and the values associated with work have become increasingly instrumental for youths entering the labor market (Claes, 1990).

Table 6.1. Characteristics of the Three Flemish Samples.

	Secondary Education	Higher Education	Adults
Number of subjects	442	172	770
Age (median)	17	22	33
Gender (percentage of males)	39%	36%	49%
Education Level Attained (by percentage)			
Primary school	—	—	13%
Lower secondary school	100%	—	16%
Higher secondary school	—	88%	27%
Higher nonuniversity	—	7%	15%
University	—	5%	20%
No certificate at all	—	—	9%
Marital Status (by percentage)			
Single	100%	93%	21%
Married/living together	—	7%	73%
Widowed/separated	—	—	6%
Occupational Level (by percentage)			
Professional and managerial	Not applicable		19%
Clerical and sales			20%
Skilled			31%
Semiskilled or unskilled			30%
Kind of Work (by percentage)			
Science, research	Not applicable		9%
Teaching, social services			9%
Business			37%
Technical work			25%
Manual, physical work			20%

One way to examine the meaning and the value of working is by looking at the effects of unemployment. The main finding of Van Loon and colleagues (1982) was that female unemployment had an inhibiting effect on family creation. De Witte (1986, 1988) pointed to one consequence of youth unemployment: the inhibition of personality development and of integration in society by, for example, undertaking family responsibilities. However, it is also true that young unemployed women withdraw from the labor market and take up the traditional roles of housekeeper and mother to escape unemployment. Analysis of the time budget of the unemployed (Elchardus et al., 1984; Enhus et al., 1986) pointed to the importance of work as a source of social contact. The unemployed compensate for not working by undertaking activities with social meaning and even seeking to increase the social significance of those activities (Elchardus & Glorieux, 1988; Glorieux, 1988).

But De Witte (1988) reported that the majority of unemployed youth became indifferent to politics.

Studies on multiple life roles have dealt mostly with women. Degroote and Cossey (1988) found that, when confronted with the duality of worker and homemaker roles, young women were inclined to drop the occupational role in favor of the family responsibilities.

Research on women's daily activities has revealed the values of major life roles for contemporary Flemish women. Pauwels and colleagues (1988) concluded that homemakers have become a minority struggling to have their activities valued, both morally and economically. Homemakers can be differentiated by educational level and by their motivation to raise children, respect their husbands' wishes, and achieve self-realization, and by their feeling the impossibility of combining employment and homemaking. Research has shown that the number of homemakers wanting to enter or reenter the labor market is increasing. Paid occupational activity is increasingly becoming the societal norm for women. The major influences on the participation of married women in work are educational level, number of children, and husband's income. Their reasons for entering the labor market are the intrinsic nature of the job, social contact, and income. Although husbands of employed women are taking on more homemaking tasks, there has been no real role redefinition as yet (Van Dongen et al., 1988).

Flemish research has revealed a sharp focus on values considered attainable in two roles: Family and Work. Making available Flemish instruments that measure the salience of life roles and values throughout the life span will no doubt stimulate further research and strengthen the theoretical underpinnings as well as the tools of life-career counseling.

Values: Their Structure, Hierarchy, and Correlates

We must briefly discuss the reliability of the Values Scale. We computed two measures of reliability for each scale: internal consistency (alpha coefficients) for the three samples, and stability (test-retest) for the higher education sample. The alphas of seven scales lie above 0.70 in every sample. The following scales reach an alpha of at least 0.60 in every group: Ability Utilization, Autonomy, Economics, Life-style, and Physical Activity. The scales for Social Relations and Variety have the lowest internal consistency in the Flemish VS, 0.50 and 0.46, respectively; both occur in the secondary education sample. The stability for eleven VS scales reaches the 0.60 level. The Aesthetics scale shows the weakest stability (0.47).

Factor Structure of the VS

The interscale correlations and the factors derived from them reflect the structure of the VS. An analysis of the interscale correlations (not shown here for reasons of space) reveals that the number of significant and sizable *r*'s is related to age and educational level. For the adults, 95 percent of the r's reach the 0.01 significance level; for the youngest group, the secondary school sample, this is the case for 69 percent of the r's. In the higher education sample, which falls between the high school students and the adults by age, only 42 percent of the interscale r's reach the 0.01 significance level. It may be that younger people distinguish values better than older people and that more highly educated people differentiate values better than the less educated. We examine these questions later, in connection with the hierarchy and correlates of values.

To get at the underlying dimensions of the eighteen values, we factor analyzed their interscale correlations. We used principal factoring, with R^2 as the initial estimate of communality and Varimax rotation for factors with eigenvalue of 1.0. We performed the factor analysis for each of the three samples. The three factor analyses yield congruent structures that reveal a quite high degree of factorial similarity of VS in the three samples. We found five factors and identified them as follows:

1. *Self-Realization,* defined by Ability Utilization, Personal Development, and to some extent Achievement, Creativity, and Aesthetics
2. *Material Career Progress,* consisting of Economics, Advancement, Achievement, and to some extent Prestige and Authority
3. *Group Orientation,* defined by Social Interaction, Social Relations, Altruism, Aesthetics, and to some extent Variety
4. *Challenge,* comprising Risk and Authority
5. *Autonomy,* defined by Autonomy and Life-Style.

Hierarchy of Values

Appendix A.4 provides the hierarchy of the eighteen values in the three samples. The hierarchies are based on sample means, shown in Appendix A.1. An analysis of within-sample differences for the means of different values (paired t tests) reveals that the secondary school sample does not differentiate as much as the two older samples in the importance of the values, although the hierarchies of values in the three samples are similar. The four most important values in the three samples are Personal Development, Ability Utilization, Social Relations, and Aesthetics. This finding points to the high salience of the Self-Realization and Group Orientation values. The low end of the hierarchy of values for the three samples in Flanders includes Risk and Authority, or the dimension of Challenge.

Correlates of Values

A number of personal and situational variables presumably correlate with the importance of any given value at one stage in life. The personal correlates of values with which the Flemish WIS project dealt are age, gender, and occupational level. We studied employment status to determine whether it is a situational correlate. We used a series of covariance analyses that take a hierarchical approach, combined with a series of multiple classification analyses on the aggregate of the three samples, to assess the relationship of age to values as a covariate, and of gender, employment status, and occupation level as main effects. Table 6.2 summarizes the analyses and includes the Pearson correlation coefficients (significant beyond the 0.05 level) of age with the eighteen scales.

The relationships of values and age point to the important role of this personal correlate. The older the person, the less important are the values of Self-Realization and Material Career Progress as well as the specific values of Physical Activity and Variety. The effect of gender on values is classically gender stereotypical: men attach more importance to Self-Realization and Challenge, whereas women attach more importance to Group Orientation values.

A strong correlate of values is actual employment status. Respondents concerned with work (employed or unemployed) value Self-Realization and Material Career Progress more than do students, homemakers, and retired people. Employed respondents attach more importance to Authority than do all other categories of respondents. Unemployed subjects not looking for work and students value Autonomy more than do all other respondents. Quite strongly related to the importance people attach to their life values is occupational level; the higher the occupational level, the greater the importance of Self-Realization and Challenge. The higher the occupational level, the lower the importance of Material Career Progress, perhaps because these people feel that they have reached the peak of their career.

Roles: Their Structure, Hierarchy, and Correlates

We computed two measures of reliability for the SI: internal consistency (alpha coefficients) for the three groups and stability (test-retest) for the higher education sample. The alphas are high for all groups: in the three samples no alphas are lower than 0.80. The stability coefficients after an interval of two months, for eight of the fifteen scales, lie above 0.70; the lowest test-retest reliability is 0.52, for the Participation scale of the Leisurite role.

Factor Structure of SI

An analysis of intercorrelations of the fifteen SI scales for each sample shows a strong positive relationship for the three aspects of life-role salience (i.e., Participation, Commitment, and Value Expectations). Furthermore, the relationship between Commitment and Value Expectations seems stronger (in the sense of positive relations for all roles) than between Participation and either Commitment or Value Expectations. The two affective scales clearly cluster together more, whereas the behavioral scale tends to assess another, more independent dimension of role salience. Finally, the Participation scale

Table 6.2. Correlates of the Importance of Values: Summary of Series of Covariance Analyses and Multiple Classification Analyses.

	Age	Gender	Employment	Occupational Level
	r	Highest Score	High to Low	High to Low
Self-Realization				
Ability Utilization	-21	Men	1/6/3/2/7/4/5*	A/C/B/D**
Personal Development	-18		7/1/3/6/2/4/5	A/C/B/D
Creativity	-06	Men	1/7/6/3/2/4/5	A/C/B/D
Material Career Progress				
Economics	-06		6/1/7/3/2/4/5	D/C/B/A
Advancement	-22	Men	1/2/7/6/4/3/5	A/D/C/B
Achievement	-10		1/7/2/6/4/3/5	A/D/B = C
Prestige	-06		7/1/4/6/2/3/5	
Group Orientation				
Aesthetics	12	Women		
Altruism	-12	Women	7/3/5/1/4/6/2	C/D/B/A
Social Interaction	-12	Women		
Social Relations	-14	Women		C/B/A/D
Challenge				
Authority	08	Men	1/2/7/4/3/6/5	A/B/D/C
Risk	-13	Men		A/D/C/B
Autonomy				
Autonomy	-10		3/7/1/6/2/4/5	A/C/B/D
Life-Style			7/3/6/1/4/5/2	
Physical Activity				
Variety	-08	Men	5/7/4/2/6/1 = 3	B/A/C/D
Working Conditions	-17	Women	7/2/6/1/3/5/4	D/C/B/A

Notes: *1 = Full-time employed; 2 = part-time employed; 3 = full-time student; 4 = homemaker; 5 = retired; 6 = unemployed, looking for job; 7 = unemployed, not looking for job.

**A = Specialist/management; B = administration/sales; C = skilled; D = semiskilled to unskilled.

shows more relationship with the Commitment scale (for more roles) than with the Value Expectations scale. As Super and Nevill (1986b) stated, this could have to do with format similarity.

Role Importance

We computed means, standard deviations (given in Appendix B.1), and the corresponding paired t tests between means of the fifteen salience scales and used them to infer the hierarchy of the five life roles for each sample. The two younger samples attach the greatest importance, expressed by the time and the energy expended, to the roles of Leisurite and Student; this finding was to be expected. Although the SI covers vicarious and symbolic participation, having no real working experience could affect the answers of the respondents: work is rather remote. The same reasoning could explain their low Participation in Community Service: only Flemish citizens aged 18 and older have rights and duties in society (voting duty, driver's license right, and so on). Home and Family holds for these respondents a moderate position as far as Participation is concerned; peer relationships have often been found more important at this stage in life. The secondary school sample differentiates more than does the higher education sample in Commitment to life roles. The former have a clear-cut hierarchy of Leisure, Home, Work, Study, and Community Service; the latter rank Study first, then equally Home, Work, and Leisure, and at the bottom of the hierarchy is Community Service.

While a person is still in school, Work looms as the primary way to realize life values, at the cost of Leisure. The two younger samples are still studying or have just finished training; they are mentally preparing for work, and they are educated to attain their values as workers. They are affectively concerned with the problems of the labor market. The young people do not feel involved in the community, and they do not expect much involvement in it in the future. The analysis of the relative importance of the five roles in adulthood shows that the overall salience of the Homemaker role is the greatest, followed by Worker and then by Leisurite. This finding seems a contradiction, given the time that people spend in working and at home. Yet respondents report greater Participation in the Homemaker role, feel more emotionally tied to it, and expect to realize more of their values in it. The Citizen role is the lowest-ranked role in the adult sample too.

Correlates of Roles

A number of personal and situational variables may be expected to correlate with the importance of a certain role at a certain stage in life. This study looked at age, gender, and occupational level as potential personal correlates of role salience and at employment status as a potential situational correlate. Through a series of covariance analyses that used a hierarchical approach, combined with a series of multiple classification analyses on the aggregate of the three samples, we assessed the effect on role salience of age as a covariate and of gender, employment status, occupational level, and kind of work as main effects. Table 6.3 reports these analyses and includes the correlation coefficients (significant beyond the 0.05 level) of age with the fifteen scales of the SI.

The relationships of role salience and age show clearly the evolution of life roles during various life stages, if we may infer longitudinality from cross-sectional samples. The oldest people in our samples were about 54 years old, usually full members of the labor force (only about fifteen subjects were actually semiretired or retired). The relationship of age and the roles of Student and Leisurite is negative both for the affective and the behavioral component of role salience; the relationship between age and the salience of the Homemaker role is positive for the affective and behavioral component. The relationship of age and the Worker role is positive for the time and the energy expended but negative for the emotional tie and the values expected to be realized in it.

Gender shows a consistent relationship with role salience for the three importance aspects of Work and Home. The findings confirm the classical stereotypes of males' attaching more importance to Work and females' attaching more importance to Home and Family. Furthermore, male respondents report higher Participation in Leisure than female respondents. Women report higher Commitment to Study than do men.

A strong correlate of role salience seems to be the employment status of the respondents. This characteristic has significant relations with all fifteen SI scales, consistent over the three aspects of role salience. Students attach the most importance to Study. The greater the actual participation in employment, the higher the salience of the Worker role is. Little or no participation in employment goes with high salience of Community Service. Homemakers show consistently high scores on the importance of Home and Family. Respondents who have the most free time value the role of Leisurite more than other respondents do.

The relationship between the salience of life roles and occupational level is ambiguous and inconsistent. For the Study role we find some clarity in the relationship of occupational level and salience: the higher the occupational level, the higher the Participation in, Commitment to, and the Value Expectations of Study. For the Worker role, people at the highest occupational levels score highest on Work salience; for the Citizen role, the lowest occupational level scores the lowest on Community Service.

Values and Roles in Relation to Other Variables

We used multiple discriminant analyses to examine the power of the VS and the SI to discriminate among eight groups of potential future users of the WIS instruments. We analyzed the data for 16-year-old secondary students (n = 165), school leavers (dropouts and recent graduates) (n = 300), university

Table 6.3. Correlates of Role Salience: Summary of Series of Covariance Analyses and Multiple Classification Analyses.

	Age	Gender	Employment	Occupational Level
	r	Highest Score	High to Low	High to Low
Participation				
1. Study	−49		6/3/1/7/2/5/4*	A/B/C/D**
2. Work	36	Male	1/2/6/7/3/5/4	A/D/B/C
3. Community			5/7/4/3/6/2/1	A/B/C/D
4. Home	37	Female	4/1/2/6/5/7/3	D/B/C/A
5. Leisure	−34	Male	5/4/3/7/6/2/1	
Commitment				
1. Study	−45	Female	3/7/6/1/2/4/5	A/B/C/D
2. Work	−07	Male	1/6/2/7/3/5/4	A/D/C/B
3. Community			7/3/5/4/1/6/2	A/C/B/D
4. Home	21	Female	4/1/6/2/5/3/7	
5. Leisure	−28		4/5/7/6/3/2/1	B/D/C/A
Value Expectations				
1. Study	−51		3/7/6/1/2/5/4	A/B/C/D
2. Work	−32	Male	1/2/6/7/3/5/4	A/C/D/B
3. Community			7/3/5/4/1/2/6	B/C/A/D
4. Home	07	Female	4/7/5/2/1/6/3	C/D/B/A
5. Leisure	−29		4/3/5/7/6/2/1	

Notes: *1 = Full-time employed; 2 = part-time employed; 3 = full-time student; 4 = homemaker; 5 = retired; 6 = unemployed, looking for job; 7 = unemployed, not looking for job.

**A = Specialist/management; B = administration/sales; C = skilled; D = semiskilled to unskilled.

students ($n = 161$), young adults aged 30 to 45 ($n = 150$), 40-year-old employed women at mid-career ($n = 120$), older adults aged 50 to 54 ($n = 150$), the unemployed ($n = 208$), and job applicants. Figures 6.1 and 6.2 illustrate the location of the eight subsamples on the discriminant functions of the VS and the SI.

For the VS (Figure 6.1) it seems of primary relevance to look at scores on the scales for Advancement, Personal Development, and Working Conditions. Indeed, the three younger samples and especially the job applicants—all by definition preoccupied with career development—score high on Advancement and Personal Development and low on Working Conditions. This can be explained by their lack of experience with Working Conditions, whereas the job applicants do not stress this aspect of work as they look for work. The contrary is true of adults who have a position to defend in the labor market. All three adult samples, and especially the 50-year-olds, attach great importance to good Working Conditions and little importance to Advancement and Personal Development. The VS scales for Advancement, Social Relations, and Authority also differentiate. School leavers score high on Advancement and Social Relations and low on Authority. The job applicants and the 50-year-olds, on the other hand, appear to be rather ambitious and striving for power.

As Figure 6.2 indicates, a first way to classify people on role salience is to look at sequential participation in two roles, those of Student and Worker. Older employed groups (employed women, 50-year-olds, and 30-year-olds) are spending time and energy largely in Work, whereas younger groups (16-year-olds, school leavers, and university students) are mainly participating in Study. A second way to differentiate people on the SI is to consider simultaneous participation in the roles of student and worker. Not engaged in these roles at the same time in life are 50-year-olds, whereas job applicants are spending time and energy on two roles simultaneously.

Uses of WIS Data and WIS Instruments in Flanders

As we pointed out earlier, no scientifically developed psychodiagnostic instruments are available for assessing the importance of life roles and values in the Dutch-speaking area of Belgium. The Salience Inventory and the Values Scale are the first instruments to fill the void. Thus we anticipate the use of the Flemish WIS instruments in ongoing and future research and applications, especially in industrial/organizational psychology and vocational guidance. Their use in research should be helpful for assessing changes in the salience of life roles and values over time and in analyzing intra- and inter-role conflicts in individuals and dual career couples. We anticipate using the WIS instruments in a longitudinal study of the early working careers of youth in the ongoing study "Work Socialization of Youth". We can further envisage the relevance of the instruments in analyzing changing patterns of the meaning of working when following up specific target groups, such as the unem-

Figure 6.1. Discriminant Analysis of Eight Flemish Groups:
The Location of Group Centroids in the Space Defined
by Two Discriminant Functions of the Values Scale Scores.

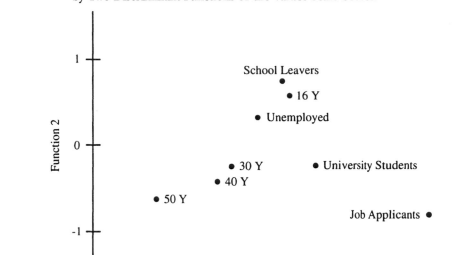

ployed, preretirement and temporary workers, and the self-employed. In the context of problems studied in Flanders nowadays, such as the division of available labor, alternative work schedules, and the increase of leisure time, researchers will certainly welcome the WIS instruments.

The Flemish WIS data gathered thus far can be used to illuminate other research findings. The Flemish SI and VS manuals make available to interested researchers cross-sectional data of the salient life roles and values for nine specific samples in Flanders: 16-year-olds, school leavers (aged 17 to 19), university students (20 to 22), 30- to 34-year-olds, 50- to 54-year-olds, 40-year-old homemakers, 40-year-old employed women, the unemployed, and employment applicants.

We consider the WIS instruments highly relevant for psychologists working as consultants in vocational guidance in Flanders. In this context the application of the SI and the VS lies mainly in three domains: in orientation and counseling of school leavers in educational and vocational choices, in vocational reorientation and guidance of the unemployed, and in personnel selection. We have developed an approach for the use of the WIS instruments

Figure 6.2. Discriminant Analysis of Eight Flemish Groups:
The Location of Group Centroids in the Space Defined
by Two Discriminant Functions of the Salience Inventory Scores.

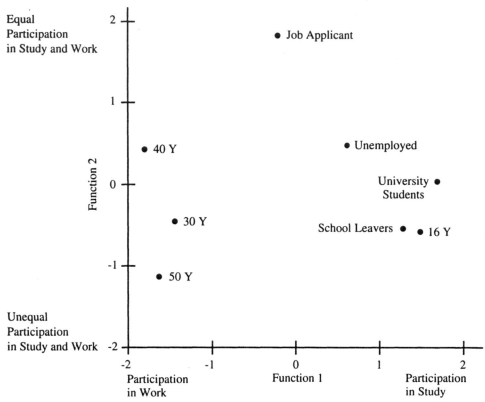

in the three fields. The psychologist's approach with the Flemish WIS splits into three phases:

1. After a short introductory discussion of life careers, respondents fill out a self-report on the importance of life roles and values. This is done in a rather direct and explicit way by rank-order and forced-choice techniques.
2. The WIS instruments are administered on paper or interactively with a computer.
3. After approximately one week (after scoring, comparison with norms, printing, and plotting for feedback), or interactively when computer equipment is available, the three-step feedback process starts: (a) respondents study their WIS results in pie charts for the SI and in bar charts for the VS, compare them with their self-reports, and draw tentative conclusions; (b) respondents compare their results with the results of a relevant norm group and make notes; (c) respondents discuss the WIS results during an in-depth interview with the psychologist.

Psychologists working in Flemish centers for the educational and vocational guidance of pupils through the age of 18 often express the need for instruments like those of the WIS. Vocational guidance psychologists consider it desirable for pupils to be actively involved in the career-choice process. The WIS instruments allow pupils to learn what their central life roles and values are and how these develop in the course of about three years. The SI and VS scores offer an objective starting point for discussions between the psychologist and the counselee, which should lead to better decision making.

As an experiment, one center for educational and vocational guidance is trying the WIS instruments out in two classes of about twenty pupils in the fifth year of secondary school. The objective is to gain better insight into the self-concept of the youth and to have the pupils more personally involved in the decision process. Evaluation of the use of the WIS instrument to stimulate involvement of the pupils in the counseling process is favorable. The pupils are attracted by the real interaction with the psychologist on the basis of their WIS results. They try to look deeper inside themselves when contradictions between their self-reports and WIS results appear. They search for concrete examples to justify themselves when striking deviations from their classmates' results or norms occur. The psychologist is no longer "just an answering machine to questions you have to phrase yourself" but a valued partner in guidance discussions.

All Flemish unemployed are enrolled in the State Employment Service, which has established "job clubs" all over the country to help them find jobs, sometimes after retraining or reorientation. In this context the WIS instruments can be a tool to help the unemployed clarify their important life roles and values. Because most centers for the unemployed are equipped with optical scanners and PCs plus printers and/or plotters, it will be possible to administer the instruments, score them, and give people the results in a truly interactive way. We anticipate both individual and small group approaches (in the sense of self-help groups) with the guidance of psychologists.

In selection situations in which psychologists try to guide work-career decisions, it is useful to know about the applicant's important life roles and values. For instance, is Work the dominant role or are other roles, such as Home and Family or Leisure, also important? If so, could part-time employment be a suitable solution? Is the candidate still keen on studying? Which values does the candidate expect to realize in which life roles? Our evaluation of these uses of the WIS instruments is positive. Clients, especially those at higher occupational levels, welcome an approach that is different from classical paper-and-pencil tests. The confrontation between self-report and WIS instrument results increases the clients' interest and in general increases their engagement in the whole selection procedure. The self-confrontation eventually restricts faking socially desirable behavior: the client feels invited to talk more openly about plans for a work career. The individual comparison with a group of peers aids in self-discovery. The client gladly experiences this consciousness raising, although it sometimes stirs up feelings of doubt and uneasiness. The WIS instrument results are a rewarding starting point for the in-depth selection interview. Combined with other data gathered in the selection procedure, they allow the consultant to guide the candidate toward suitable planning for a balanced work and life career.

Conclusion

On the whole, Flemish men and women attach the greatest importance to self-realization and social life values. Values in Flanders are affected both by personal qualities of gender, age, occupational level, and a major situational factor, the labor market.

In Flanders, three life roles appear to be quite important: Homemaker, Worker, and Leisurite. The extremely low salience of the Citizen role is striking. The importance of the various life roles seems to be determined by gender, age, and employment status.

The effect of age on the salience of life roles and values in Flanders follows a trend generally expected in life-span theories. The effect of occupational level on the WIS variables is also more or less in the direction seen in other studies. The effect of gender reflects rather traditional Flemish male-female stereotypes of men as breadwinners (Workers) and women as Homemakers. We wonder whether this is also the case in other countries. Belgian Flanders may have some special determinants of employment status, such as Flemish laws and Flemish experiments in work-study training programs for youngsters.

In summary, from the researcher's and from the practitioner's point of view, the Flemish Salience Inventory and Values Scale are important additions to psychodiagnostics. They are reliable and valid instruments that have various potential uses in Flanders. The information provided by WIS scores can be a rewarding starting point for a counseling session, an in-depth interview, or a small group discussion. More generally, the WIS instruments could lead the way in Flanders to a more interactive approach to individual life-career counseling.

References

Claes, R. (1990). Work motivation of youngsters entering the labor market. In U. Kleinbeck et al. (Eds.), *Work motivation.* Hillsdale, NJ: Erlbaum.

Coetsier, P., & Claes, R. (1990). *Belang van levensvollen en waarden* [Salience of life roles and values]. Ostende, Belgium: Infoservice. (Dutch.)

Coetsier, P., & Spoelders-Claes, R. (1984). *Waarde en betekenis van werken in Vlaanderen* [Meaning of working in Flanders]. Ghent: Laboratorium en Seminarie voor Toegepaste Psychologie. (Dutch.)

De Coster, W., et al. (1987). Value hierarchies in Flemish adolescents and parents. *Psychologica Belgica, XXVII-2,* 99–111.

De Coster, W., et al. (1988). L'échelle des valeurs des adolescents Flamands [Value hierarchies in Flemish adolescents]. *Scientia Paedagogica Experimentalis, XXV-2,* 267–288. (French.)

Degroote, A., & Cossey, H. (1988). *De beeldvorming van jongeren over beroepen in handenarbeid* [Youngsters' image of technical-manual occupations]. Louvain, Belgium: HIVA. (Dutch.)

Delooz, P. (1984, January). Une enquête européenne sur les valeurs [European value survey]. *Revue Nouvelle* (French.)

De Witte, H. (1986). Psycho-sociale gevolgen van werkloosheid bij jongeren [Psychosocial consequences of youth unemployment]. In Hoger Institut voor de Arbeid–Stuurgroep (Eds.), *Met een stempel door het leven?* [Lifelong unemployment?] (pp. 111–170). Louvain, Belgium: HIVA.

De Witte, H. (1988). Individuele en maatdschappelijke gevolgen van jeugworkloosheid [Individual and societal consequences of youth unemployment]. In Hoger Institunt voor de Arbeid–Werkgroep Jeugdwerkloosheid (Eds.), *En de jongeren, zij stempelden voort?* [And youth continue to be unemployed?] (pp. 33–49). Louvain, Belgium: HIVA.

Elchardus, M., & Glorieux, I. (1988). Signification du temps et temps de la signification [Significance of time and time of significance]. In D. Mercure & A. Wallemacq (Eds.), *Les temps sociaux* [The social times] (pp. 97–119). Brussels: De Boeck Universite. (French.)

Elchardus, M., et al. (1984). *Tijdsbesteding en maatschappelijke integratie van werklozen* [Time budget and societal integration of unemployed]. Brussels: Vrije Universiteit, Centrum voor Sociologie. (Dutch.)

Enhus, E., et al. (1986). Werkloosheid en sociale isolatie: Een herorintatie [Unemployment and social isolation: Reorientation]. *Mens en maatschappij, 2,* 116–146. (Dutch.)

Glorieux, I. (1988). Werkloosheid en sociale zingeving: Resultaten van een tijdsbudget-onderzock [Unemployment and social significance: Results of a time-budget study]. In *Sociologisch en Antropologisch Jaarboek 1988–1989* [Sociological and anthropological yearbook, 1988–1989], Tijdschrift voor Sociologie. (Dutch.)

Kerkhofs, J. (1984a). Les valuers du temps présent: Une enquête européenne [Present day values: A European survey]. *Choisir, 289,* 13–18. (French.)

Kerkhofs, J. (1984b). Young people and values in Western Europe. *Pro Mundi Vita Dossiers Europe–North America, 27.*

Kerkhofs, J., & Rezsohazy, R. (1984). *De stille ommekeer: Oude en nieuwe waardenin het Belgie van de jaren tachtig* [Silent changes: Old and new values in Belgium in the eighties]. Thielt, Belgium: Lannoo. (Dutch.)

Meaning of Work International Research Team (1987). *The meaning of working.* San Diego, CA: Academic Press.

Pauwels, K., et al. (1988). *De thuiswerkende, de buitenshuis werkende en de werkzoekende vrouwen in Vlaanderen. Samenvattend rapport.* [Women of Flanders: Homemakers, employees, unemployed: Summary report]. Brussels: Centrum voor Bevolkings en Gezinsstudien. (Dutch.)

Rosseel, E. (1979). Work orientations of the Flemish working people: Methodology and preliminary results. *British Journal of Sociology, 30-1,* 362–372.

Super, D., & Nevill, D. (1986a). *The Values Scale.* Palo Alto, CA: Consulting Psychologists Press.

Super, D., & Nevill, D. (1986b). *The Salience Inventory.* Palo Alto, CA: Consulting Psychologists Press.

Van Dongen, W., et al.(1988). *Een studie van de tijdsbesteding inzake betaalde beroepsarbeid en onbetaalde gezinsarbeid van de thuiswerkende, de buitenshuis werkende en werkzoekende vrouwen in Vlaanderen* [Time-budget study for paid employment and unpaid homemaker's work of Flemish women]. Brussels: CBGS-Werkdocument, 55.(Dutch.)

Van Loon, F., et al. (1982). Werkloosheid en de verwachte en gewenste herintreding in hetarbeids proces [Unemployment and expected and desired reintegration in the labor market]. *Tijdschrift voor Sociale Wetenschappen, 2,* 153–158. (Dutch.)

SEVEN

The Canadian Study of
Life Roles and Values

Catherine Casserly
George Fitzsimmons
Donald Macnab

The Canadian Work Importance Study (WIS) was carried out as a national project under the sponsorship of the Canada Employment and Immigration Commission. The twenty-four members of the Canadian WIS team, formed immediately after the first planning meeting of the international group, represented public (federal and provincial), private, nonprofit, and educational sectors across the country. The team membership also balanced the two national languages. The project brought together counselors, researchers, employers, and program developers interested in the psychological importance of work and of other life roles. They sought to identify the values and objectives Canadians seek in these roles, as well as the importance of work relative to other roles. A senior project officer with the Canada Employment and Immigration Commission served as staff for the team, and two consultants were contracted to carry out all psychometric work. These three people are the authors of this chapter.

Because of the mandate of the primary sponsor, the major focus of the research team was to identify how the importance placed on work and other life roles by Canadians affects the functioning of the Canadian labor market. In the early 1980s Canada was experiencing unusually high levels of unemployment, record numbers of youth looking for first-time jobs, and record numbers of reentrants to the labor market, in particular women with young children. The labor market needed to integrate large numbers of immigrants who often had no knowledge of either English or French.

As an initial step, the Canadian team carried out two separate literature reviews. The first, *The Work Importance Study in the Canadian Context,* by Casserly and Cote (1980), was a review of literature published in English-language Canadian sources. The second, *Work Importance and Work Values: A Review of the French-Canadian Literature,* by Bujold (1980), focused on the work done in the province of Quebec, Canada's major French-speaking province. The research team perceived a need for two distinct reviews because

117

research in one language is often not available in the other language. Further, in Canada the best sources of ideas are not necessarily professional journals but rather government publications, theses, and texts developed for specific counselor education courses. The two reviews provided a thorough examination of what was known to date about Canadians' work-related values. Their conclusions confirmed the importance of the main values subsequently selected at the international level and also identified the value of cultural identity as one of some importance to many Canadians, in particular to French speakers living outside the province of Quebec and to recent immigrants.

The classic study *Canadian Work Values* (Burstein, Tienhaara, Hewson, & Warrander, 1975) asked Canadians to describe ideal jobs. The most important characteristics stressed in the early 1970s were that the work be interesting, that people have enough information and authority to do the job, and that they be given the opportunity to develop special abilities. Of lesser importance were job security, promotional considerations, pay, hours of work, and fringe benefits. Not surprising, professional and managerial workers expressed greater satisfaction at being able to achieve the goals. But even here, the results were confounded by such other variables as age, gender, and education.

One primary finding of the research was that no single criterion characterized members of the Canadian labor force. A distinctive feature of Canada is that it is essentially a nation of immigrants with two dominant but not exclusive cultures. Forcese (1980) summarized the socioeconomic situation in Canada by saying that it is a country of extremes. The pattern of relative advantage points clearly to regional, rural-urban, and ethnic disparities.

In Canada the two primary cultural groups are labeled by language of communication. Francophones are the French-speaking Canadians, most of whom live in the province of Quebec but with substantial communities in the bordering provinces of New Brunswick and Ontario. Within this cultural group exists a subgroup of Acadians in the Atlantic provinces who speak a different dialect. Since the late 1960s the groups have fought hard and successfully for educational and employment opportunities and the provision of social and medical services in their language. Their political influence far outweighs their actual numbers. Hence cultural identity is in the daily consciousness.

Non-Francophones are referred to as *Anglophones* and include the rest of the population. In fact, many Canadians labeled as Anglophones speak other native tongues, such as Italian, Ukrainian, German, and Chinese, and the children in these groups often do not speak English before beginning school, although they may be second- and third-generation Canadians. The designation of language, then, is really an oversimplification for purposes of research and politics.

In 1975 Nightingale explored in a controlled and systematic fashion a broad range of attitudes and reactions of French- and English-Canadians in their work organization. He found no discernible differences in management philosophy in the two cultures. Top managers in both cultures were oriented more to theory Y than theory X (i.e., their assumptions about human nature were optimistic) and, interestingly, were generally more theory Y than their middle managers. On virtually all dimensions of work-related opinion and attitude, when differences existed, French-Canadian employees at all levels (from top management to rank-and-file workers but especially at the rank-and-file level) felt more positive than their English-Canadian counterparts. French-Canadians at all levels had more direct and open relationships with their superiors, higher trust and confidence in their superiors, and a good deal more perceived freedom to approach their superiors with personal problems than did their English-Canadian counterparts. Among French-Canadian workers Nightingale found a corresponding feeling of confidence and trust in other workers and an encouragement of hard work, which was not as evident among English-Canadian workers. French-Canadian workers also reported more positive attitudes toward management and were more satisfied with their salaries than were English-Canadian workers. Interestingly, there were no differences in job satisfaction. From a variety of measures Nightingale determined that although the English-Canadian rank and file had much more say in the affairs of the company than their French-Canadian counterparts, they also expected far more and therefore ended up much less satisfied with their role in decision making in the company.

Nightingale also found that English-Canadian employees at all levels valued freedom more highly than French-Canadian employees and that English-Canadian top managers desired advancement opportunities and time for their families more than did French-Canadian top managers. Nightingale had not anticipated the importance of time for family for English-Canadian top managers.

Kanungo and Dauderis (1974) and Jain, Normand, and Kanungo (1979) studied groups of Anglophone and Francophone managers. Both studies revealed that "interesting nature of work" is the most important job outcome for both groups of employees. Second, in both studies Anglophones showed greater concern for autonomy and achievement than Francophone employees. On the other hand, Francophone employees in both studies showed greater concern for security and fringe benefits. Finally, in both studies Francophones exhibited more job satisfaction than Anglophones.

Another major dimension of cultural differences in Canada is that between the native and white population. Primarily, the natives are Amerindians who live below the tree line, Metís who are of mixed white and Amerindian backgrounds, and the Inuit of the far north. There are about eight hundred thousand recognized Native Canadians. Native Canadians have many barriers to employment, and the salience of jobs in their lives has evolved with dimensions different from those of non-native Canadians. The largest majority are of working age and unemployed. The average unemployment rate on reserves is 48 percent. The majority live in rural environments, often hundreds of miles from cities where unskilled jobs are available. They perceive relocation as a frightening experience. The level of education tends to be much below the national average. Further, many natives are not fluent in either English or French. The cultural orientation of natives is also different. In isolated regions a person does not work on fixed shifts but when necessity or opportunity arises, and the seasons of the year control many opportunities. Hence the concept of time in these regions is different from that in industrial centers. The time factor and others, such as the impersonality of urban life, usually result in cultural shock for the native who relocates to the city. However, urban locations are still the choice of work for most younger natives.

Another factor is the involvement of women in the labor force and the rapid and dramatic changing of their involvement. Today's pattern is that most women of employment age are working, including the majority of mothers with preschool-age and school-age children. Total predicted working life for women is now thirty years, compared to thirty-five years for men. The time away from the labor force has dropped dramatically in one generation, from an average of fifteen years to an average of five years, and is continuing to decrease. Further, the level of education and training for women is increasing, which contributes to the probability of long-term attachment to the labor force. We expect the differences in how men and women view work will diminish.

Age groups are also likely to show differences in values. The Canadian work values study (Burstein et al., 1975) showed that both younger and older Canadians viewed work as the primary means of attaining success. The differences between age groups lay not in the importance they placed on work but on the relative emphasis they placed on friends and family; younger people more often considered friends the key to self-fulfillment and a means of attaining personal goals, whereas older people more frequently felt that family provided such rewards. Commitment to the family was of primary importance to all age groups, but for those younger than 25 commitment to friends was secondary, whereas for those older than 25 commitment to work was secondary.

Data Collection

We developed the Values Scale in English and French. We developed items in English, translated them into French, and retranslated them into English as a check on comparability across languages. After preliminary trials with 2,886 subjects that used both language versions, we decided that the Canadian inventory would include all twenty values, including Physical Prowess and Cultural Identity. All aspects of development, other than that of language, conform to the international specifications for the project.

We administered the Values Scale and the Salience Inventory simultaneously in the summer and fall of 1984. To obtain background information for use in evaluation and presentation of the research, each participant also received a personal information sheet to fill out.

The total Canadian sample is 10,120 and represents most regions, major demographic variables, major occupational categories, and age groupings for members of the labor force (ages 14 to 65). It consists of three subsamples: adults, postsecondary students, and secondary students in grades 10 and 12.

The Canadian Classification and Dictionary of Occupations (CCDO) classifies all occupations according to twenty-three categories. Because of its comprehensiveness, the CCDO system is used for census, research, and counseling purposes. It was our intention to capture adult subjects from as many groups as possible in order to ensure our sample was representative of the Canadian labor force. Occupations in the major group of managerial, administrative, and related occupations are included in samples drawn from a national department store chain, federal government departments, and a national transportation company. People working in the natural sciences, engineering, and mathematics group came from the National Research Council of Canada and from Novacor, an oil exploration company, as well as from a national computer software developer. Those in the social sciences were represented by employees who were counselors in school systems and of a national nongovernment voluntary organization, the United Way of Canada. People who teach and were in related occupations came from secondary schools and postsecondary institutions (colleges that offer diplomas, professional registration and certification, and universities that offer degree programs) in several parts of the country. The Canadian Broadcasting Corporation provided staff in the area of the artistic and performing arts. Clerical and related occupations were represented by all employers involved. Sales occupations came from the Bay, a national department store that operates in every part of the country, including remote areas; Bay employees were both minimum-wage and highly paid commission sales staff. Occupations in medicine and health were represented by the staff of a large general hospital and by almost 80 percent of the members of the Canadian Association of Occupational Therapists who completed the inventories. The category of mining and quarrying, including oil and gas field occupations, was represented by the field staff of the oil exploration company. Trade groups were represented by the staff and students of two technical institutes and by trades staff within the federal government. In all cases we obtained both management and union support before requesting the voluntary cooperation of staff. Of the twenty-three major occupational groups, approximately fifteen are part of the study, but they constitute more than 80 percent of occupations in Canada. In general, only primary resource occupations, such as fishing, hunting, and trapping, were not included.

Unemployed people across the country and in all occupational categories were asked to complete the inventories as part of their registration process for assistance in the job search process and to obtain unemployment insurance. They represent a variety of backgrounds but with an emphasis in the semiskilled and skilled occupations.

Finally, to ensure that native groups would be sufficiently represented, the National Indigenous Peoples Program cooperated by having its members complete the inventories.

Of the total adult sample ($n = 6,382$) the largest group was employed (79 percent), whereas 8 percent were unemployed, 8 percent were homemakers, and the rest fell into special categories. More than half (57 percent) were professionals, whereas the rest were clerical (17 percent), skilled (15 percent), semiskilled (8 percent), or unknown (3 percent). The median family income for both the English and French sample was in the $30,000–$39,999 (Canadian) range, which put it in the average family income range. Both linguistic groups had a median of fourteen to sixteen years of education. Approximately 20 percent were immigrants and 10 percent Amerindian and Inuit.

We gathered the higher education or postsecondary student sample ($n = 623$) from a number of institutions across Canada. They were in arts, sciences, engineering, nursing, education, and commerce programs. Most were single and came from a professional, managerial, or skilled family background. They came from the first and final years of their programs. Because only forty-four Francophone postsecondary students completed the forms, we do not include their results in this report.

The secondary school students also came from across Canada and equally represented genders and programs of studies. The year-10 (grade 10) sample is 1,481, and the year-12 (grade 12) sample is 1,634. In Canada each province and territory establishes its own final year of secondary education, which varies from grade 11 to grade 13 but most typically is grade 12. The students represent the three main streams of programs: academic (university entrance), general (postsecondary institute entrance or work force entry), and technical-vocational (usually immediate entrants to the work force). Both language groups are represented. In some schools students were fluently bilingual and were involved in the two-language test-retest group.

Although the sample is not scientifically statistically selected, it is a logical approximation of representativeness. Only minor groups and categories were excluded because of lack of availability or access. This is particularly true of those in remote areas. Further, Canadians who do not use either English or French were also excluded.

The final instruments produced by the project constitute a single booklet called *The Life Roles Inventory* (LRI), which measures career values and role salience and is designed to be used in vocational and general counseling, career guidance, and job placement. It consists of two parts: the LRI Values Scale (LRI VS) and the LRI Salience Inventory (LRI SI). The VS is a 100-item inventory that is scored for twenty values, some of which are somewhat interrelated and some of which are independent. The SI is a 170-item inventory that measures Participation, Commitment, and Value Expectations for five major life roles: Study, Work, Community Service, Home and Family, and Leisure.

Major Results on the Values Scale

Reliability and Validity of the Values Scales

We carried out several studies to investigate the reliability of the LRI Values Scale (Macnab, 1985; Fitzsimmons, Macnab, & Casserly, 1986). They provide strong support that the instrument is quite reliable. The alpha coefficient (Cronbach, 1951) indicates good internal consistency for both language versions and across age groups. In repeated administrations we found that short interval test-retest correlations done after four to six weeks range from 0.53 (for the French version of Cultural Identity) to a high of 0.82 (for Physical Prowess and Physical Activity on the English version). In repeated administrations we had secondary school students first complete one version in one language and a second in the other language. The alternate form reliabilities range from 0.62 (Achievement) to 0.88 (Physical Prowess), with a median coefficient of 0.74.

Similarly, studies of convergent and discriminant validity support the construct validity of the instrument (Fitzsimmons et al., 1986).

In order to explore the factor structure of the Values Scales, we carried out a series of principal components analyses with Varimax rotation on the data obtained on adult, postsecondary, and secondary school samples. An inspection of the results (included in Fitzsimmons et al., 1986) indicates a consensus on the factor structure of all groups, except French grade-10 students. In general, we found five factors:

- Personal Achievement and Development, with highest loadings on Ability Utilization, Achievement, Advancement, Prestige, and Personal Development
- Social Orientation, with highest loadings on Altruism, Social Interaction, and Social Relations
- Independence, with highest loadings on Autonomy, Creativity, Life-style, and Variety
- Economic Conditions, with highest loadings on Economics, Working Conditions, and Cultural Identity
- Physical Activity and Risk, with highest loadings on Physical Activity, Physical Prowess, and Risk

Tables containing information on the correlation matrixes and rotated factor matrixes are available from the senior author.

Appendix A.1 presents means and standard deviations for all sample groups on the Values Scale (i.e., English and French) based on the three international items. The values that have the highest ratings for adults in Canada are Personal Development, Ability Utilization, Achievement, Social Relations, and Economics. The values that have the lowest ratings are Physical Prowess and Risk. This is true for the respondents to both the English and French forms.

An analysis of the gender differences reveals that male and female samples are similar to the total sample. However, they reveal certain traditional differences: women rate Social Relations and Working Conditions as more important than men do. Within categories of occupations the primary difference across groups is that the professional subsample rates Autonomy as very important, whereas the other three groups (clerical, skilled, and unskilled) rate Economics higher. This is not surprising, given that professionals tend to have professional security and to be among the best-paid workers.

Higher education students in all programs have the same ranking of values as do adults for the first four values. But women in particular give much greater importance to Altruism and Autonomy than do all older adults.

Secondary students in both languages show several differences that appear to reflect an interaction of age, gender, and cultural background. English-speaking female students have the same top six values in grade 10 and in grade 12 (Social Relations, Personal Development, Ability Utilization, Economics, Achievement, and Altruism). English-speaking male students in the two groups have a somewhat different ranking. The same six values remain highest but their ranking changes slightly (Economics, Ability Utilization, Social Relations, Achievement, Personal Development, and Advancement). The samples confirm cultural stereotypes that women are more people-oriented. French-speaking female students show a similar picture. In both grades 10 and 12 the five highest-ranked values are Social Relations, Personal Development, Advancement, Achievement, and Ability Utilization. However, what is noteworthy is that female students also rate Aesthetics as a major value and rate Economics as of moderate importance. Similarly, the French-speaking male students show differences from the adults and other students. Although they rate Social Relations and Personal Development as the two most important values in both grades 10 and 12, in grade 10 they rate Physical Activity third and in grade 12 they put it sixth. In neither grade does Economics appear in the top five values.

What is consistent across all groups and ages is the emphasis on Personal Development, Social Relations, Ability Utilization, and Achievement. And what is consistently not important across all categories are Physical Prowess and Risk. The value profile of Canadians is generally consistent across age, education, gender, linguistic group, and geographical region.

Major Results of the Salience Inventory

We administered the revised version of the Salience Inventory at the same time to the same sample as the revised Values Scale. Statistical analysis of the Salience Inventory included item-scale intercorrelations, reliability analysis, and a validity study. A description of the procedures for standardization and for norming appears in the national team's technical report (Fitzsimmons et al., 1986).

Reliability and Validity of the Salience Inventory

The national technical manual presents the reliability of the Salience Inventory scales by describing internal consistency coefficients, test-retest coefficients, and alternate form correlations. Alpha coefficients range from 0.84 to 0.95; retests at intervals of four to six weeks range from 0.68 to 0.81 for secondary school students.

We assured the content validity of the Salience Inventory by using the literature on life stages and career development to select the major life roles of adolescents and adults. The intercorrelation matrixes provide evidence of construct validity—correlations between the different measures of the same role are higher than the correlations between the same measures of different roles. Furthermore, Madill (1985) finds few significant relationships between the scales of Holland's Vocational Preference Inventory and the Salience Inventory, providing evidence of discriminant validity of the Salience Inventory. Macnab (1985) finds that the correlations between the activity ratings of students and the Salience Inventory roles are significant and highest for corresponding roles and activities. Thus ratings of academic activities have the highest correlations with Participation, Commitment, and Role Values for Work. In general, the highest correlations are between the Commitment measures and their corresponding activity ratings.

Other studies conducted in Canada and referred to in the national technical manual provide additional evidence of the validity of the Canadian versions of the Salience Inventory.

The influence of life-span developmental psychology and its advocates in vocational psychology has led to fundamental changes in the way careers are examined. Such theorizing and research are exemplified by the work of Super (1980, 1981), who advocates the view of a career as a multifaceted multirole developmental concept. The model used in WIS is an attempt to provide a more precise definition of the concepts of importance (salience). The Canadian Salience Inventory and its components were based on the International WIS version and developed and refined similarly to the Values Scale, including parallel development in two languages and in cooperation with the national and international teams.

The overall results, as presented in Appendix B.1, again indicate a relatively consistent national pattern. In the adult sample the role rated as highest for participation by both English and French respondents is Work. The lowest-ranked role in all cases is Community Service. This also holds true for levels of occupational groups. Although there are no differences between genders in the French sample, women in the English sample rate their Participation in the Home and Family role higher than does the male sample.

The ratings of postsecondary students show similar characteristics to the adult sample for Commitment and Role Values. They rate Study as the major role in which they participate. Again, female students are more likely to rate Commitment to and Role Values for Home and Family higher than the male student sample.

All secondary school samples rate Participation in Leisure Activities as highest and Community Service lowest. All female secondary school samples rate Participation, Commitment, and Role Values of Home and Family and of Community Service higher than the corresponding male samples.

Conclusion

The Values Scale and Salience Inventory of the Canadian Life Roles Inventory are designed for use in English or French with secondary school students, postsecondary students, and adults. The psychometric properties of the LRI Values Scale and the LRI Salience Inventory indicate that the instrument has good structural reliability and validity characteristics for these populations. It is now being used in secondary schools and universities across Canada and in many career counseling offices. It has been put to particular use in rehabilitation centers where adults are forced to make major decisions about new directions in their lives. The LRI measures have already proved useful not only with junior secondary school students and secondary school students but also in counseling adults about midcareer change, midcareer evaluation, labor force or employment entry, education reentry, and retirement and preretirement.

In guidance counseling the Life Roles Inventory is now a valuable introduction to the vocabulary of values and career roles with junior secondary school and secondary school students. Completing the LRI is an educational experience for them as they learn more about themselves and are offered a linguistic framework with which to express what they are learning. Employment counselors find the LRI helpful in providing a standardized description of clients' values and of the importance clients attach to different life roles. The instrument has also proved practical in research because a wealth of technical information pertains to the psychometric characteristics of the scale, the scale is available in both French and English, norms are available for a number of groups for a Canadian sample, and the scales are truly cross-national in character, allowing their valid use in cross-cultural research in a multicultural society.

References

Bujold, C. (1980). Signification du travail et valeurs de travail: Revue de la littérature canadienne de langue française [Work importance and work values: Review of the Canadian French-language literature]. *L'Orientation Professionnelle, 16*(1), 5–47.

Burstein M., Tienhaara, N., Hewson, P., & Warrander, B. (1975). *Canadian work values: Findings of a work ethic survey and a job satisfaction survey*. Ottawa: Department of Manpower and Immigration.

Casserly, M. C., & Cote, L. (1980). *The Work Importance Study in the Canadian context.* Ottawa: Canada Employment and Immigration Commission.

Cronbach, L. J. (1951). Coefficient alpha and the internal structure of tests. *Psychometrika, 16,* 297–334.

Fitzsimmons, G. W., Macnab, D., & Casserly, C. (1986). *Technical manual for the Life Roles Inventory: Values and salience.* Edmonton: PsiCan Consulting.

Forcese, D. (1980). *The Canadian class structure.* Toronto: McGraw Ryerson.

Jain, H. C., Normand, J., & Kanungo, R. N. (1979). Job motivation of Canadian Anglophone and Francophone hospital employees. *Canadian Journal of Behavioural Science, 11,* 160–163.

Kanungo, R. N., & Dauderis, H. J. (1974). *Motivational orientation of Canadian Anglophone and Francophone managers.* Montreal: Faculty of Management, McGill University.

Macnab, D. (1985). *Work related needs, preferences, and values: An empirical integration.* Unpublished doctoral dissertation, University of Alberta, Edmonton, Alberta, Canada.

Madill, H. M. (1985). *A cross-sectional analysis of work-related issues in occupational therapy.* Unpublished doctoral dissertation, University of Alberta, Edmonton, Alberta, Canada.

Nightingale, D. V. (1975). The French-Canadian work shows up well in study. *Canadian Personnel and Industrial Relations Journal, 22*(5), 28–30.

Super, D. E. (1980). A life-span, life-space approach to career development. *Journal of Vocational Behavior, 16,* 282–298.

Super, D. E. (1981). The relative importance of work. *Bulletin of the International Association of Educational and Vocational Guidance, 37,* 26–36.

EIGHT

Life Roles and Values in Croatia: Some Results of the Work Importance Study

Branimir Šverko
Željko Jerneić
Alija Kulenović
Vlasta Vizek-Vidović

The Croatian research team has been involved in the Work Importance Study from the beginning, since the first planning conference in Cambridge in 1979. The team contributed to all stages of the study, from reviewing literature and refining theoretical models through pilot work on instrument development and preliminary testing to planning and carrying out the main study and final cross-national analyses.

The purpose of the study in Croatia was twofold: to obtain two psychometrically sound inventories to use in assessing values and life roles in both research and counseling, and to contribute data for the cross-national study of values and roles in a number of countries participating in the Work Importance Study.

The WIS research undertaken in Croatia was supported by grants from *Samoupravna zajednica za znanstveni rad SR Hrvatske* (Association of Research Councils of Croatia) and by *Savez samoupravnih zajednica za zapošljavanje SR Hrvatske* (Employment Bureau Association of Croatia).

Previous Research on Values and Roles: A Short Review

Most of the Croatian value studies are from the 1970s and 1980s, when Croatia was a part of former socialist Yugoslavia. The studies can be divided into three broad groups. The first includes sociological studies of value systems, stressing the conflict between the values of traditional preindustrial culture and a new value system reflecting the introduction of modern industrial technology and socialist ideology. The work has been mostly speculative or has

An earlier version of this and other reports in this project referred to *Yugoslavia*. The label *Croatia* in the final version takes into account the changed circumstances, as well as the fact that all subjects and researchers were from Croatia.

relied on anthropological research into traditional cultures. Various values have been proposed as characteristic of the southern Slavic people: the value of combativeness, or a "heroic code" at the national level (Erlich, 1965), a group of values that includes friendship, solidarity, and equality at the societal level, and improvement of living standards at the individual level (Rihtman-Augustin, 1967). Županov (1978) argued that egalitarianism was the dominant value in former Yugoslavia and speculated about its role in economic development; he suggested that it had a positive effect during the early phases of industrialization, but that by 1978, "when the economic system require[d] reorientation toward the most productive resources, egalitarianism ha[d] an inhibiting effect" (p. 93).

The second group of studies consists of empirical studies of value systems in industry. A review of the studies (Šverko, 1982a) gave particular attention to the position of pay in workers' value hierarchies. The hierarchies underwent considerable change during the three phases studied. During the first phase (1960–1962) people placed the most value on such factors as opportunities for advancement, interesting work, and social relations. They attached less value to pay. During the second phase (1962–1965) pay rose in the hierarchy, and in the third phase (1965 and later) studies consistently revealed pay to be the highest-ranked value. The progression may have been the result of a rapid rise in the actual and desired standard of living and of the economic reform of 1965, which laid greater emphasis on the material rewards for job performance.

A third group of studies was concerned with the values of young people. In her longitudinal study of occupational choices of two thousand secondary school students, Čudina-Obradović (1974) analyzed the values that the students expected to fulfill in their jobs. Students who later did not achieve their educational plans and were dissatisfied with their choice of study exhibited a tendency to increase the importance attached to extrinsic values, such as status and material reward. Šverko et al. (1980) examined the work values of secondary school students and their perceptions of value-attainment possibilities in different occupations in an attempt to understand why the majority of young people avoided vocational schools that offered preparation for "productive," mainly blue-collar, occupations. The results clearly revealed that students perceived that they could attain most of their values more easily in nonproducing white-collar occupations. But in general the studies revealed the prevalence of intrinsic values; it seems that youth put less emphasis on extrinsic values than did adult workers.

The few studies on the life roles that had been done in Croatia focused mainly on the role of worker, dealing mostly with such constructs as job satisfaction, work orientation, and work alienation (e.g., Bjelajac, 1971; Obradović, 1978). No one had attempted a large-scale study using well-studied instruments and seeking to compare different roles. The Work Importance Study, with its constructs and instruments, has therefore been welcomed in Croatia.

Croatian WIS Instruments: Development and Description

The two WIS instruments are available in Croatian and are known as *V-upitnik* (Values Scale) and *S-upitnik* (Salience Inventory). We developed and standardized both instruments by using the elaborate procedure followed by all original WIS teams during the years 1980 to 1983. The procedure comprised the several stages described in Chapter Four:

1. Devising initial versions of the WIS instruments. The first stage included literature searches and reviews, defining initial value taxonomy and role salience dimensions, and writing and refining questionnaire items for the initial versions of the Values Scale and Salience Inventory. The Croatian team, which actively contributed to devising both initial international instruments, immediately used WIS materials and procedures to prepare the Croatian versions.
2. Field trials. The trials collected data for the psychometric evaluation and refinement of the instruments. We used only the Values Scale in the Croatian field trial. In 1981 we administered its initial version, comprising 230 items, to 930 secondary school and university students. We performed conventional item analysis and a complete factor analysis of items, the latter to assess whether the a priori value taxonomy corresponded to the empirical grouping of items.
3. Revising the instruments. We used the field trial data (internal consistency coefficients, item-scale correlations, factor loadings of items, etc.) to revise the Values Scale: we reduced it to twenty five-item scales, each represented by three cross-national items agreed upon at the Lisbon conference in 1981 and two other items chosen by the Croatian team on empirical and logical grounds. We followed a similar procedure (based mostly on Portuguese, Spanish, and U.S. data) in revising the Salience Inventory.
4. Preliminary study with the revised instruments. To check for the psychometric properties of the revised scales, in 1982 we administered the instruments to a sample of 915 subjects (622 secondary school students, 247 university students, and 46 workers). All the analyses performed (factor analyses of both scales and items, reliability estimates, etc.) revealed acceptable properties of both instruments; we deemed no further revisions necessary.

Description of the Final Instruments. The Croatian version of the Values Scale (VS) is a one-hundred-item inventory comprising the following twenty five-item scales:

Ability Utilization
Achievement
Advancement

Aesthetics
Altruism
Authority
Autonomy
Creativity
Economics
Life-style
Personal Development
Physical Activity
Prestige
Risk
Social Interaction
Social Relations
Variety
Working Conditions
Cultural Identity
Participation in Decision Making

The last two are optional scales adopted by interested national projects. Each scale is composed of three cross-national items and two items chosen, according to the WIS plan, by the Croatian team. A detailed description is given in the Values Scale manual (Šverko, 1987a) and in Chapter Four.

The Croatian version of the Salience Inventory (SI) consists of the ten-item Participation scale, ten-item Commitment scale, and twenty-item Value Expectations scale (to allow for cross-national comparability, this last scale is scored as a fourteen-item scale in this report). We used each of the three scales to assess the importance of each of the five life-role activities (Study, Work, Community Service, Home and Family, and Leisure Activities), giving a total of fifteen salience measures.

In addition to the standard salience scales, the Croatian SI contains two simple time scales that required subjects to estimate the daily number of hours they typically devoted and would have liked to devote to each of the five roles.

Main Study: Samples and Procedure

A total of 4,314 subjects from Croatia were questioned in the main study. The subjects belong to the following samples: eighth-year (elementary school) pupils ($n = 1,750$), tenth-year (secondary school) students ($n = 923$), twelfth-year (secondary school) students ($n = 949$), university students ($n = 348$), and adult workers ($n = 344$).

The eighth-year sample and both secondary school samples were planned as representative samples of the populations of all eighth, tenth, and twelfth graders in Croatia. The samples were stratified by districts (associations of communes) of Croatia. Subjects from all districts (Zagreb, Varaždin,

Bjelovar, Osijek, Karlovac, Sisak, Gospić, Rijeka, and Split) were included in the samples in proportion to the total number of pupils or students in each district. However, to cut down on the cost of data gathering, we did not sample individual subjects in each stratum or district directly. Instead, we sampled school classes and took as subjects all individuals within selected classes. Thus, the sampling procedure used a kind of single-stage cluster design.

We collected the university student sample from all universities in Croatia (Zagreb, Osijek, Rijeka, and Split). We selected students from different faculties or departments (mechanical, electrical, and civil engineering; business and commerce; architecture; medicine; social work; education; and psychology).

The adult sample was one of convenience, interviewed and tested by a group of psychology students. Each student was instructed to find and question about six adult workers, who had to be of both genders, different ages, and different educational levels.

Table 8.1 shows the average age, gender composition, and socioeconomic level of the subjects of the five samples.

The secondary school, university student, and adult samples were questioned in the spring of 1983, using both the Values Scale and the Salience Inventory. Trained psychologists collected all data for the student samples in classroom settings. The procedure consisted of a general introduction and information about the purpose of the study, followed by a partly guided administration of both inventories, the VS first. For adults, the administration of inventories was individual.

The elementary school subjects (eighth graders) were questioned in spring of 1986, using only the Values Scale. We used a nineteen-scale version (omitting the Cultural Identity scale). This study was organized by the Employment Bureau Association of Croatia in order to examine the possibility of using the Values Scale in the vocational guidance of youngsters before they enter different types of secondary schools. The VS was administered along with other tests and inventories. It was administered in classroom settings under the direction of trained psychologists.

Participation was not anonymous. It was voluntary, and the subjects were assured that their scores would be used for scientific purposes only.

Basic Results: Values

Here we present the data concerning the average importance of the values and the values hierarchies obtained in the main study. But we first must analyze the reliability and validity of the Values Scale.

Several analyses have demonstrated the validity of the Values Scale, including two types of construct-related evidence: internal construct validity, focusing on the interrelation of the inventory items and scales, and external construct validity, dealing with their relationship to other observable behaviors.

Table 8.1. Description of the Croatian Samples.

| | Age | | Sex | Socioeconomic Level (Percentage) | | | | |
Samples	Mean	Standard Deviation	(Percentage of Men)	1	2	3	4	5
Year-8 students	14.3		50	22.2	34.3	23.1	13.5	8.9
Year-10 students	16.4	0.71	42	23.0	38.6	14.1	19.4	4.9
Year-12 students	18.2	0.86	48	21.8	39.9	14.9	17.6	5.7
University students	22.1	1.71	34	4.4	29.4	22.8	37.0	6.5
Adult workers	33.4	10.75	56	15.8	25.2	24.0	35.1	—

Note: SES codes: 1 = unskilled and semiskilled; 2 = skilled; 3 = clerical; 4 = professional; 5 = unknown. Parental SES is used for students. Year-8 students' ages were not collected; given mean is an appraisal.

Reliability. We computed two measures of reliability of the VS for each sample: internal consistency (Cronbach's alpha) and stability (test-retest) coefficients. The statistical values we obtained are presented elsewhere (Šverko, 1987a). The means and the ranges (across the scales) of the internal consistency coefficients of the three-item scales are as follows: year-8 pupils, 0.53 (0.42 to 0.65); year-10 students, 0.57 (0.38 to 0.73); year-12 students, 0.60 (0.45 to 0.74); university students, 0.66 (0.54 to 0.82); adults, 0.62 (0.46 to 0.76). As expected, the lowest mean coefficient is obtained for the eighth graders and the highest for the university students. We obtained comparable values for the stability coefficients.

The reliability coefficients we obtained are relatively low. They are proportionate to the length of the scales; higher values can hardly be expected for three-item scales. However, the scales are intended for group comparisons in the cross-national and other analyses, not for individual assessment purposes. For research purposes their reliability is satisfactory.

Factor Structure: Internal Construct Validity. We analyzed the factor structure of the VS on both item and scale levels. Both analyses reveal meaningful results that support the internal construct validity of the VS. We performed the item-factor analysis of the one hundred VS items on pooled data from the four older samples ($n = 2,564$). This analysis yields fifteen interpretable factors, logically defined by the homogeneous groups of items belonging to only one or two scales.

On the scale level, analysis of the initial VS data shows that Croatian students have a factor structure similar to the factor structures of students in three other countries (Šverko, 1987b). For the main study data, we explored the factor structure for each Croatian sample separately. In the analysis of the factor structure of secondary school students, university students, and adults, Kulenović, Jerneić, Šverko, and Vizek-Vidović (1984) carried out a number of analyses in which they varied the input matrixes, method of extraction, and methods of rotation (both orthogonal and oblique). The different methods of analysis reveal similar results, and the factor structure of the scales is similar across samples. We find five identical factors, accounting for approximately 63 percent of variance, in each sample and a high degree of congruence among them (all of Tucker's between-samples congruence coefficients were above 0.90). We also submitted the scores of the eighth graders ($n = 1,750$) to factor analysis, with similar results (Šverko, 1987a). The five analogous factors that appear in the analyses of separate samples also appear in the pooled data analysis ($n = 2,564$). We interpreted them as value orientations and labeled them as follows:

1.   Orientation Toward Self-Actualization (sA). This factor is defined primarily by Ability Utilization, Achievement, Personal Development, and Aesthetics—typical intrinsic values that are important in the satisfaction of higher-order needs. Creativity, Participation in Decision Making, and Altruism are also appropriately saturated with this factor.
2.   Individualistic Orientation (In). This factor stresses the importance of independence and an autonomous life-style. It is defined primarily by Life-style and Autonomy. Variety and Creativity are also saturated with this factor but to a lesser degree.
3.   Social Orientation (So). In both analyses this factor is defined primarily by Social Interaction and Social Relations. Some loadings on this factor include Variety, Working Conditions, Participation in Decision Making, and Altruism.
4.   Utilitarian Orientation (Ut). Five typical extrinsic values define this factor: Economics, Advancement, Authority, Prestige, and Working Conditions. It is interesting to note that Cultural Identity also has a projection on this factor, perhaps suggesting that the need for ethnic identification may have a utilitarian meaning.
5.   Adventurous Orientation (Av). This is a tentative label for the fifth factor. It has the highest loadings on Risk and Physical Activity.

Five scales are factorially complex: Altruism (which has projections on sA, So, and Av), Creativity (sA, In), Variety (In, So, Av), Working Conditions (So, Ut), and Participation in Decision Making (sA, So). All fifteen scales remaining have their salient projections on only one logically corresponding factor. The results seem to support the internal construct validity of the Values Scale.

External Construct Validity. Generally speaking, an instrument is valid if it can be shown to be related to other independent manifestations of the measured characteristics. One indication of the validity of an instrument is its ability to differentiate between groups of subjects in a way that can be postulated logically. There are several such contributions to the validation of the VS.

One concerns the differences in the results obtained on certain scales by men and women. On the basis of the gender roles traditionally established in the southern Slavic culture, the expectation might be that women would value more highly such qualities as Altruism, Social Interaction, Personal Development, and Aesthetics, whereas men would give greater weight to Physical Activity, Authority, and Autonomy. Furthermore, as the influence of cultural stereotypes decreases with education, we can predict that the observed gender differences will be least prominent in the student sample. The observed differences between the male and female subjects, reviewed later, largely confirm the predictions.

The next contribution to the validation of the Values Scale are the differences in the scores of people training for different occupations. In theory, people choose their future occupations partly in accordance with their values; in addition, in the process of anticipatory socialization, individuals in training are believed to adopt values like those of their future peer group. We therefore can expect that people preparing for different occupations will score differently on certain scales. Three analyses show that the Values Scale reproduces expected differences, significantly supporting its validity.

We did the first analysis (Šverko, 1982b) with the initial version of the Values Scale, comparing the value profiles (expressed in z scores) of students in three types of secondary schools—technical, humanistic, and medical. We find striking differences (higher than one standard deviation for some values) for the three value profiles, and their direction was in keeping with our expectations. Thus those attending secondary technical schools attach somewhat more importance to more Utilitarian values but do not significantly depart from the general average on any scale. Those attending the secondary schools specializing in the humanities and arts demonstrate a powerful Individualistic and Self-Actualizing orientation, with emphasis on Creativity and Aesthetics. In contrast, those attending secondary medically oriented schools attach little value to Life-style, Autonomy, Variety, and Aesthetics, but, in keeping with an idealized view of their future profession, see great value in Altruism.

Our second analysis (Jerneić et al., 1985) compares the scores on the final version of the VS of secondary school students training for productive (mainly blue-collar) and distributive nonproducing (mainly white-collar) occupations. The first group attaches greater importance to Utilitarian values and the second to Self-Actualizing values.

Our third analysis (Šverko et al., 1987) compares the value profiles of university students pursuing curricula for different occupations. We find significant differences in the value profiles for the six groups we compared. In comparison with others, engineering students tend to be slightly lower on Self-Actualization and Social values and slightly higher on the Utilitarian ones. Business and commerce students have high orientation to Utilitarian values and Achievement but one low on Altruism. Students of architecture tend to be high on Self-Actualization values, with Aesthetics salient. Psychology students score high on Life-style and Autonomy values, low on Utilitarian ones. Medical students tend to be high on Social Orientation and Utilitarian values, low on Creativity. Social work students appear to be high on Social orientation, with Altruism salient. Because we had predicted most of these features, we accepted them as important evidence of the validity of the VS.

Interesting data were obtained by Knezović, Kulenović, Sakić, Zarevski, and Žužul (1989), who used a shortened version of the VS to examine the psychological profiles of prison inmates in Croatia. In one analysis they divided the subjects ($n = 986$), on the basis of the assessment of prison counselors, into those willing to work and those inclined to idleness and then compared their values profiles. Those rated as willing to work were higher on Self-Actualization and Utilitarian values, whereas those rated as inclined to idleness preferred Individualistic and Adventurous orientation values (Autonomy, Life-style, and Risk).

Lihter (1986) compared the Values Scale scores with interview assessments of a small sample of eighth-grade elementary school pupils ($n = 84$). On the basis of the interview, she determined the dominant value orientation of each subject as Self-Actualizing, Utilitarian, Social, or Individualistic. She then compared the VS profiles of the four groups. As expected, the profiles of the groups were congruent with the value orientations established during the interview.

Finally, let us mention one more and very significant contribution to the global validation of group value hierarchies. Jusupović (1984) applied the VS to a group of students ($N = 373$) and asked them at the same time to assess the prospects of attaining each of the twenty values in their future work. He then correlated such estimates of attainment with the degree of satisfaction with the chosen profession. As expected, the correlations were significant but uneven: the highest were those for Personal Development (0.64) and Achievement (0.63) and the lowest for Authority (0.19) and Risk (0.24). The first two refer to values that top the list and the last two to those that stand at the bottom of all the value hierarchies obtained in this country. This is in full agreement with theory: the more important a value, the more pronounced should be the influence on satisfaction of its perceived attainment possibilities. The correlation between the directly determined group hierarchy of values held by his subjects and their indirectly determined hierarchy (based on the correlations mentioned) was high ($rho = 0.80$, $p < 0.01$). Here again is important evidence for the validity of the Values Scale.

The Problem of Faking. Questions about the validity of values inventories arise in view of the subjects' potential to give socially acceptable answers. If present, such a tendency would produce a systematic bias that would directly affect the validity of the measurement. Jusupović's data (1984) suggest that such a bias is not critical, because the indirectly obtained hierarchy of values (over which the subject has no control) shows agreement on the group level with the direct hierarchy. However, we should note that these data were not obtained in a distinctly competitive situation, in which the probability of bias is greater. Therefore, we checked the Values Scale in a competitive situation, with applicants taking the admissions test for the study of psychology. The VS was not used as the selection instrument, but the subjects did not know this. We then tested the accepted students ($n = 52$) again four months later, but this time in a noncompetitive situation and with instructions that encouraged them to be sincere. Šuran (1983) analyzed the results obtained on the two occasions. As we had predicted, Šuran found certain statistically significant differences. Some values of the Self-Actualization and Social orientations (Personal Development, Ability Utilization, Participation in Decision Making, Social Interaction, and Altruism) are more important in the competitive than in the noncompetitive situation, whereas the reverse is true for some Utilitarian and Individualistic values (Prestige, Economics, and Life-style). Such differences seem to reveal the tendency of people to present themselves as suitable candidates for the study of psychology. The differences are, however, small, and the hierarchy of values remains identical in both situations.

Mean Scores and Hierarchy of Values. Appendix A.1 presents mean scores and standard deviations for each of the values scales and for each sample. The obtained means range from 5.51 for Authority to 10.84 for Personal Development (both values obtained for university students), with the majority of the means above 7. Because the theoretical range is from 3 to 12, the means tend to be distributed in the higher part of the theoretical range. Consequently, the score distributions of the scales tend to be negatively skewed.

We used the samples' means to constitute the values hierarchies. The hierarchies of eighteen values for the combined secondary school, university student, and adult samples appear in Appendix A.4. Also similar is the hierarchy for the year-8 sample, which is not shown. The rankings of different sample groups reflect a high degree of agreement, confirmed by computing the rank-order correlations among the value hierarchies of the five samples. All of the *rho* coefficients are high (0.92 on the average), supporting the view of the early internalization of the value system (Vizek-Vidović et al., 1984).

The four most important values in each Croatian sample are the same: Personal Development, Ability Utilization, Achievement, and Social Relations. The four least important values in almost all samples are, from bottom up, Authority, Risk, Prestige, and Cultural Identity (the last was an optional value not shown in the eighteen values hierarchies). Three of the most important values are typical intrinsic values with high projections on the factor identified as orientation toward Self-Actualization. On the other hand, three of the least important values have high projections on the factor identified as Utilitarian orientation. It seems that our subjects from all generations place a strong emphasis on the importance of the higher-order needs of Self-Actualization. At the same time, they attach less importance to Utilitarian values.

Gender Differences. We examined all the values scales for differences between men and women, looking at each sample separately. We find a number of statistically significant gender differences. They are generally consistent with existing gender stereotypes revealed by other studies. In most of the samples women score higher than men on Aesthetics, Altruism, Personal Development, Social Interaction, Social Relations, Variety, and Working Conditions, whereas men score higher than women on Authority, Physical Activity, and Autonomy. Although statistically significant, most differences are not very big. As a consequence, the male and female value hierarchies seem to be quite similar: across-the-scales correlations between male and female means for the five samples (from eighth graders to adults) are 0.96, 0.96, 0.94, 0.96, and 0.92, respectively.

The Influence of Socioeconomic Status. The data presented here show that the prevalence of the orientation toward Self-Actualization and the low placement of Utilitarian values disagree with a number of studies of value hierarchies in Croatian industry (reviewed by Šverko, 1982a), which pointed to the dominance of the Utilitarian orientation. The reasons for the disagreement can be found in the composition of the samples: our samples are general samples, consisting of subjects from all socioeconomic levels, whereas the earlier research in Croatian industrial organizations covered only production workers, mostly unskilled and semiskilled. In order to check this explanation, we divided the WIS sample of employed adults into the following four categories: unskilled and semiskilled, skilled, clerical, and professional and managerial. The analysis of the means of their values scales reveals that socioeconomic status is indeed an influential variable: the four groups of subjects differ significantly on almost all values, and the differences in their means are so great that their hierarchies also differ. The differences are greatest between the two extreme groups: whereas the professional and managerial subjects place the greatest emphasis on values of the orientation toward Self-Actualization, unskilled and semiskilled workers give priority to Utilitarian and Social values. Economics and Social Relations rank first, with practically identical means in the hierarchy of the latter group, which is in full agreement with the results of the earlier studies of adults in Croatian industry.

Basic Results: The Salience of Major Life Roles

Before we present the Salience Inventory (SI) data concerning the relative importance of five major life roles to Croatian secondary school students, university students, and adults, we must analyze the psychometric properties of the SI. In addition to reliability indexes, we analyzed three sources of construct-related validity evidence: internal evidence focusing in the interrelations and factor structure of the salience measures, evidence based on their relationships with time scale measurements, and other evidence.

Reliability of the Salience Measures. We computed two reliability indexes of the fifteen SI measures: internal consistency (Cronbach's alpha), and stability (test-retest). We calculated internal consistency coefficients for each of the four main study samples. To calculate stability coefficients we used data of two additional university student samples that were tested twice, with periods of one month ($n = 78$) and one year ($n = 217$) between the two trials. Let us summarize all the values we obtained.

The internal consistency coefficients indicate the high reliability of all fifteen SI measures. The obtained values vary from 0.80 (Value Expectations scores for the Student role in the university student sample) to 0.95 (Commitment scores for Community Activities in the adult sample), with a mean of 0.90. Because the SI scales are relatively short (ten items for Participation and Commitment; fourteen items for Value Expectations), the obtained values are indeed high.

There may be a question as to whether the internal consistency coefficients are artificially inflated. We cannot completely rule out this possibility because of the specific response format of the SI questionnaire, which enables subjects to see their responses to earlier items. This opens the door to a certain amount of "method variance," the consequence of which can be an unrealistic augmentation of the internal consistency coefficients. The stability coefficients seem to point to such a possibility: they are appreciably lower and amount on average to 0.70 for the interval of one month and 0.55 for the interval of one year. The latter coefficient has a lower value, probably because real and theoretically explainable changes take place in the importance of roles over time. Because the same assumption cannot be made for the stability coefficients obtained after a one-month interval, their average value of "only" 0.70 indicates that the value of the internal consistency coefficient of 0.90 on the average is probably inflated. The real reliability of the salience measures could lie somewhere between the values of 0.70 and 0.90, which are still notably high for an attitude scale.

Factor Structure: Internal Construct Validity. Using the WIS model of role salience based on Super's earlier work, it is possible to state definite hypotheses about the interrelations of the SI measures. Although the model allows for a divergence of salience indexes, it is fair to assume that under normal circumstances there will be significant positive correlations among the different indexes (i.e., Participation, Commitment, and Value Expectations) of the same role. This assumption permits the formulation of a hypothetical factor matrix for the set of fifteen SI measures; it consists of five factors that correspond to the salience of five different roles. It can be expected that the three different measures of the salience of each particular role will correlate highly with a corresponding factor, whereas the loadings of all other variables will be much lower.

To check this hypothetical structure, we performed a separate factor analysis of the fifteen salience measures on data for each of the four samples and on the aggregate data for all four samples. We used the principal components analysis method, with "ones" in the principal diagonal. Five PCs with eigenvalues in excess of 1.00 (explaining 77.5 percent of total variance) were orthogonally rotated in accordance with the Varimax criterion. The factor matrixes of all samples are mutually congruent (cf. Šverko et al., 1984) and similar to the findings from other countries discussed in Chapter Nineteen.

The factor structure we obtained represents a model example of a "simple structure" and is fully in agreement with the hypothesized structure. We obtained five hypothesized factors that explain more than two-thirds of the total variance. Each factor corresponds to one role and is equally defined by high correlations (over 0.70) with each of the three indexes of salience of the corresponding role. The loadings of the other variables are negligible (as a rule, under 0.20). Formally, the data represent maximum support for the validity of the SI. But do not forget that they could be partly an expression of the method variance we have mentioned.

Relations to Time Scale Scores. In addition to Participation, Commitment, and Value Expectations items, the Salience Inventory includes a part that consists of two simple time-allocation scales. One requires subjects to estimate the number of hours devoted on a typical day to each of the five roles (Actual Time scale). The second time scale requires subjects to give the time structure of an ideal day, that is, to estimate the number of hours that they would like to devote to each of the five roles (Ideal Time scale). However, because the administration of the whole inventory was considered to take too long, we collected the time scale ratings for only a part of our sample (467 subjects, comprising 245 secondary school students, 102 university students, and 120 adults). We used their time scale ratings to validate the Salience Inventory scales.

It is fair to assume that the subjects' estimates of the time they devote (or would like to devote) to a particular role at least partly reflect the importance of that role. If so, time scale scores may be used as a criterion for the validation of standard SI scales. The obtained correlations of each of the three basic SI scales with actual and ideal time scale scores for each role (these are in fact coefficients of convergent validity) are all positive and statistically significant, and many are quite high (above 0.50). Therefore, we can conclude that the data support evidence for the validity of the SI.

We sought another contribution to the construct validity in the pattern of the obtained correlations. In this connection, two assumptions appear theoretically justified. We assumed that the behavioral measure of salience (Participation) should correlate better with actual than with ideal time, and that the two affective measures of salience (Commitment and Value Expectations) should show the opposite trend and correlate more highly with the ideal than with the actual time scores. We found that the average correlation values show precisely this trend, although the magnitude of differences among the coefficients is not particularly impressive.

Other Evidence of Validity. An important validity indicator of a given instrument is its ability to differentiate between groups of subjects in a way that is logical and theoretically explainable. Several such analyses exist for the Salience Inventory; distinct and logically explainable differences have been found between men and women, students and working adults, and among working adults of different socioeconomic status. All the differences support the validity of the SI.

Finally, the empirical evaluation of some theoretical models involving salience measures may also be quoted as validity evidence for the SI. Šverko (1989) proposed and evaluated a cognitive model of work salience, which states that the importance of work for an individual depends on an individual's perception of the possibilities for attaining her or his salient work values through working. Working within the framework of expectancy theory, Kulenović (1987) generalized this view to encompass all the roles. Both Šverko and Kulenović used Values Scale and Salience Inventory measures to operationalize the variables in the empirical evaluations of their theoretical assertions. Their analyses, which supported the assertions, at the same time thus indirectly contributed evidence for the validity of Salience Inventory.

Role Salience in Croatian Samples. Appendix B.1 shows the average importance that four groups of subjects attach to each of the five roles on the basic Participation, Commitment, and Value Expectations scales. The data provide answers to two questions: What is the relative importance of the roles within each sample? What are cross-sample differences in role salience?

Both groups of secondary school students have identical role hierarchies. For Participation, the highest-rated activities are Leisure and Study, whereas Community Activities and Work run lowest. The rankings for Commitment and Value Expectations are somewhat different, although in these scales too Leisure ranks first and Community Activities last. The university students have similar hierarchies: they too participate most in Study and Leisure, and these are the activities to which they are most committed.

Adults gave quite different assessments. For them, Work is most important on all three scales: they participate most in Work, they are most committed to it, and they find their best opportunities for value realization in Work. The activities next in importance are those of Home and Family; Community Activities again rank last.

We can observe certain regularities in the data, regardless of the nature of the sample. For instance, the means for all roles are, as a rule, higher for Commitment than for Participation. The differences are greatest (about one standard deviation) for Work in the student samples and for Home in the adult group. In accordance with this, Commitment and Value Expectations hierarchies (both affective) resemble each other more than they do Participation (which is behavioral). This is probably because Work is not yet a real activity for most students.

We used a simple analysis of variance to test the significance of the differences. The F ratios we obtained showed that all the differences are statistically significant. For the most part this is because of the differences between all students on one side and working adults on the other: the students understandably attach much greater importance to Leisure and Study and the adults to Work and Home. However, some differences also exist between secondary school and university students: the latter are more committed to Study, and they consistently rank Community Activities lower. Figure 8.1 illustrates all the differences discussed thus far.

The existence of age differences in role salience is confirmed also by the results of an additional analysis of the adult data. In this analysis we compared three age groups (28 and younger, 29 to 40, and 41 and older). The results reveal several significant differences. Younger subjects attach relatively greater importance to Leisure (on all three scales) and Study (on the Value Expectations scale), and less importance to Work and Home (on the Commitment and Value Expectations scales). The differences between the youngest and oldest subjects in the adult sample are compatible with already discussed differences between the student and adult samples.

Sex and SES Differences. We examined all the salience measures for differences between men and women, for each sample separately. We find significant differences in all samples, although the hierarchies of roles do not essentially differ for men and women. We find the smallest number of statistically significant differences in the university student sample; this is not surprising, because differences between the genders have generally been found to diminish with education.

Among the gender differences we found, the most consistent are those that refer to Home and Family: in all the samples women show greater participation and commitment to the role of Homemaker. Also, with the notable exception of the university student sample, women see in the familial role greater opportunities than do men for the realization of values. We also find differences in the importance subjects attach to Study, but these are not consistent: among secondary school students, females attach greater importance than males to Study on all three scales; among adults, however, the opposite is true, and men attach greater importance to Study on the Participation and Value Expectations scales.

We examined the adult sample data for differences in socioeconomic status. We compared four groups of adult subjects: unskilled and semiskilled, skilled, clerical, and professional and managerial. An analysis of variance of their role salience scores reveals significant SES differences for Study, Home, and Community Activities. The professional and managerial group rates Study higher, and Home and Family Activities lower, than all the other groups. The clerical group shows lower Commitment to Community Activities than the other groups. We noticed no statistically significant SES differences in the importance of Work and Leisure.

Figure 8.1. Life-Role Salience in Croatian Samples.

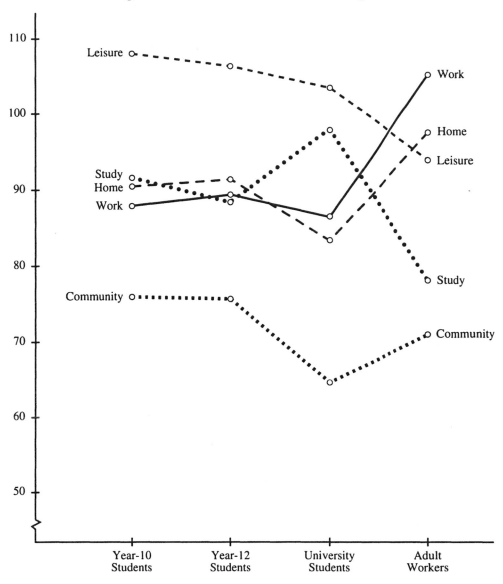

Conclusion

The Croatian work with secondary school students, university students, and adults reveals that both the Values Scale and the Salience Inventory have good psychometric properties for these populations. They have minimally acceptable (VS) or quite respectable (SI) levels of reliability, and their meaningful factor structures and ability to discriminate among different groups of individuals rather strongly indicate their construct validity. Although the instruments have been designed for secondary school students and older subjects, the tryout of the Values Scale with the year-8 pupils reveals that meaningful results may be obtained even with such young subjects.

The factor structure of both values and salience measures appears to be the same across all samples. We identified five factors in the analysis of values and labeled them orientation toward Self-Actualization (sA), Individualistic orientation (In), Social orientation (So), Utilitarian orientation (Ut), and Adventurous orientation (Av). We also found five factors in the analysis of role importance measures; they correspond to each of the five life roles. Because the basic structure of the values and salience measures is the same across the samples, the comparison of their means and hierarchies seems justified.

Hierarchies of values obtained by ranking the arithmetic means of twenty values appear to be very similar across the samples. Although the samples differ with respect to the mean importance they assign to any particular value, their value hierarchies show a high degree of mutual agreement. Top positions on all hierarchies are held by intrinsic values associated with opportunity for self-actualization. However, this general finding, based on the analysis of the total sample means, does not apply equally to all subgroups of our subjects. A breakdown of the adult sample by socioeconomic status uncovers marked differences among socioeconomic groups. Whereas professional and managerial subjects give priority to values associated with Self-Actualization, blue-collar workers place greater emphasis on Utilitarian and Social values.

The analysis of the importance of different life-role activities across the samples reveals noticeable logical differences. For secondary school students, the most important are Leisure Activities; these are followed by Study, Home and Family Activities, and Work. A similar pattern is obtained with university students, although they place a stronger emphasis on the importance of Study. The adults, however, exhibit a quite different but also anticipated picture. The most salient activity for adults is Work, followed in importance by Home and Family Activities, Leisure, and Study. Community Activities consistently obtain the lowest ratings of importance, indicating the relatively peripheral place of the Citizen role in all the samples.

References

Bjelajac, S. (1971). Životno opredjeljenje omladine i njen stav prema radu [Life orientation of youth and their attitude toward work]. *Sociologija, 13*(2), 189–208.

Čudina-Obradović, M. (1974). *Professionalni planovi: Realizacija, frustracija i promjena motivacije* [Occupational plans: Realizations, frustration, and changes in motivations]. Zagreb: Institut za društvena istraživanja.

Erlich, V. (1965). Ljudske vrednote i kontakti kultura [Human values and culture contacts]. *Sociologija, 7*(3), 27–42.

Jerneić, Z., Kulenović, A., Šverko, B., & Vizek-Vidović, V. (1985). Radne vrijednosti i profesionalno-obrazovna orijentacija mladih [Work values and vocational orientation of youth]. *Psihologija, 18*, 174–183.

Jusupović, D. (1984). *Teorija očekivanja i zadovoljstvo izabranom profesijom* [Expectancy theory and satisfaction with chosen occupation]. Unpublished master's thesis, University of Zagreb.

Knezović, Z., Kulenović, A., Šakić, V., Zarevski, P., & Žužul, M. (1989). *Psihološke karakteristike osuđenih osoba* [Psychological characteristics of prison inmates]. Zagreb: Penološko društvo Hrvatske.

Kulenović, A. (1987). *Salijentnost uloga u kontekstu teorije očekivanja* [Role salience in the context of expectancy theory]. Unpublished doctoral dissertation, University of Zagreb.

Kulenović, A., Jerneić, Ž. Šverko, B., & Vizek-Vidović, V. (1984). Faktorska struktura radnih vrijednosti učenika, studenata i zaposlenih [Factor structure of values among pupils, students, and employees]. *Primijenjena psihologija, 5,* 158–165.

Lihter, L. (1986). *Prilog istraživanjima radnih vrijednosti V-upitnikom* [A contribution to assessment of values with Values Scale]. Unpublished diploma thesis, Department of Psychology, University of Zagreb.

Obradović, J. (1978). Effects of technology and participation on attitudes toward work. In J. Obradović & W. N. Dunn (Eds.), *Workers' self-management and organizational power in Yugoslavia* (pp. 296–310). Pittsburgh: University of Pittsburgh.

Rihtman-Auguštin, D. (1967). *Kulturna tradicija i vrednote: Neke pretpostavke i jedno pilot-istraživanje* [Cultural traditions and values: Some assumptions and a pilot study]. Zagreb: Institut za društvena istraživanja.

Šuran, I.(1983). *Primjena V-upitnika u kompetivnoj i nekompeti tivnoj situaciji* [Administration of the Values Scale in competitive and noncompetitive situations]. Unpublished diploma thesis, Department of Psychology, University of Zagreb.

Šverko, B. (1982a). Istraživanja hijerarhije motivacijskih faktora u našoj industriji i mjesto osobnog dohotka u toj hijerarhiji [Investigations of hierarchy of motivational factors in our industry and the position of pay]. In J. Obradović (Ed.), *Psihologija i sociologija organizacije* [Psychology and sociology of organizations] (pp. 281–288). Zagreb: Školska knjiga.

Šverko, B. (1982b). Radne vrijednosti i njihov značaj za izbor zanimanja [Work values and their role in vocational choice]. *Čovek i zanimanje,* No. 6-7-8, 11–15.

Šverko, B. (1987a). *Priručnik za upitnik vrijednosti (V-upitnik)* [Manual for the Values Scale]. Zagreb: Savez samoupravnih zajednica za zapošljavanje Hrvatske.

Šverko, B. (1987b). The structure of work values: A cross-national comparison. *Acta Instituti Psychologici Universitatis Zagrabiensis, 17,* 23–29.

Šverko, B. (1989). Origin of individual differences in importance attached to work: A model and a contribution to its evaluation. *Journal of Vocational Behavior, 34,* 28–39.

Šverko, B., Ajduković, D., Hajnc, L., Kulenović, A., Prišlin, R., & Vizek-Vidović, V. (1980). *Psihosocijalni aspekti izbora obrazovanja i zanimanja* [Psychosocial aspects of vocational choice]. Zagreb: Centar druš tvenih djelatnosti SSO.

Šverko, B., Jerneić, Z., Kulenović, A., & Vizek-Vidović, V. (1984, October). *Work Importance Study: Tables of data for Yugoslavia.* 32 pp. (Mimeo).

Šverko, B., Jerneić, Ž., Kulenović, A., & Vizek-Vidović, V. (1987). Work values of students preparing for different occupations: A contribution to validation of the WIS Values Scale. *Revija za psihologiju, 17,* 59–66.

Vizek-Vidović, V., Kulenović, A., Jerneić, Ž., & Šverko, B. (1984). Hijerarhije radnih vrijednosti, ućenika, studenata i zaposlenih [Hierarchies of values among pupils, students, and employees]. *Primijenjena psihologija, 5,* 166–173.

Županov, J. (1978). Egalitarianism and industrialism. In J. Obradović & W. N. Dunn (Eds.). *Workers' self-management and organizational power in Yugoslavia* (pp. 60–96). Pittsburgh: University of Pittsburgh.

NINE

The Israeli Work Importance Study

Edgar Krau

Since the mid-1980s the problem of values in general and of work values in particular has been an important subject for research in Israel. The reasons for this are social, political, and economic. Israel is a relatively young independent state; it has a heterogeneous ethnic and social base that relies on immigration from various countries and on political forces with various ideologies. The system is reflected in the economy, which is divided into three powerful sectors: the labor-owned enterprises, government-owned enterprises, and the private sector. This heterogeneous base poses a problem not only for the economist but also for the social scientist faced with the question of whether it is possible to identify values that characterize the whole of Israeli society. The problem is being approached from several directions.

Mannheim (1984) compared managerial and worker attitudes in labor-owned enterprises to those in privately owned enterprises; he expected that work centrality and identification with the organization would be higher in labor-owned organizations than in others. He collected data from production managers and production workers in a representative sample of fifty-seven industrial plants stratified by size and sector of ownership. Contrary to expectations, the study found no differences in work centrality, or in workers' identification with their enterprise.

In a different approach Krau (1987) compared the values of secondary school students belonging to high and low socioeconomic levels, to urban and rural environments, and in Jewish, Catholic, Monastic, and Arab schools. He concluded that these groups had a general agreement in regard to the least preferred values and that positive values are strongly influenced by socioeconomic and age factors. Yarr (1984) also found common attitudes in the value of technological innovation. He concluded that in Israel the value differences between blue- and white-collar, and between genders, were small.

Nevertheless, Jacobson and Eran (1980) and Mannheim and Jacobson (1972) found important gender- and age-related differences in work values, especially in adults in their attitudes toward the continuation of work versus their desire for retirement. In general, people who wanted to continue to work emphasized its time-filling function and its function of ensuring belongingness, escape, and health benefits. In particular, men tended to view work more as a structuring element in their lives, conducive to preservation of their health. In other research Mannheim and Schiffrin (1984) found that professional women continued to perform traditionally female tasks in their families, even when their husbands were supportive. Professional women who perceived their jobs as interfering with their family roles exhibited lower work-role centrality.

The studies suggest that despite differences within Israeli society, it has a common value basis. Remaining is the problem of determining the specific factors of value crystallization and value change in Israel. Researchers have approached the question in two ways: by stressing the general factors of value crystallization and modification (Elizur, 1984; Krau, 1987) and by examining the specific factors at work in particular economic situations or organizations (Shapira, 1948; Erez & Tzezana, 1984; Jacobson, 1985; Shamir, 1986).

Elizur (1984) suggested that two facets of the structure of values are the modality of outcome (material, social, psychological) and the type of outcome (reward, resource). Shapira (1984) contended that in examining employees' work values, researchers must make a distinction between the influence of general cultural and socioeconomic factors and the subculture factors specific to the workplace. However, Erez and Tzezana (1984) drew attention to the fact that the organizational culture depends upon the values and the ideology of the owner (labor, government, private).

Studies have found that a strong commitment to values, as it appears in the Protestant work ethic, has a beneficial influence in alleviating the distress of unemployment but that a far stronger influence is commitment to work based on meaning of work to the individual and on the potential satisfactions related to it (Shamir, 1986). Similarly, Jacobson (1985), who studied job-at-risk behavior, stated that the effect of organizational instability varies by subgroup. Depending upon values and beliefs, there is a differential vulnerability in coping patterns. Krau (1987, 1989) postulated that theoretical understanding of the values must rest on analysis of general factors influencing their crystallization and change. Therefore, the appropriate research should be an investigation of values in social groups, with controls for the various potential determinants.

According to Krau's general hypothesis (1987, 1989), the roles people perform during their life cycles are social roles that develop under the guidance of socialization agents. Each life stage has a salient role that confronts the individual with certain developmental tasks (Havighurst, 1964). The assumption is that the socialization agent that introduces the person to a developmental task will be dominant for that period and its dominance should be expressed in the value system of the age cohort. As the cohort moves to another life stage characterized by different developmental tasks, another socialization agent will become dominant, and this change in dominance will produce modifications in the person's value system. In other words, the common and dominant influences of school should determine a certain commonality in the value profiles of secondary school students, regardless of differences in age and socioeconomic level. Similarly, the dominance of the world of work as a socialization agent should produce certain similarities in the salience of life activities and in the value profiles of adults, regardless of occupation.

Socioeconomic level is a comprehensive influence that also represents the culture (Krau, 1987). It ensures the longitudinal preservation (over time) of mores and sociocultural identity while horizontally (at any one time) differentiating between the values of groups within the population. A second factor of age-conditioned experience plays the opposite role, horizontally merging the value profiles of age cohorts while acting as a longitudinal differentiator. Thus the actual value profile of a social group appears as a combination of two identities: the longitudinal identity of social belongingness and the horizontal identity of the various age groups within the general population. Modification in age-related experience may be expected to affect all members of the population, whereas changes in social identity produced by social mobility should occur only in some segments.

The developmental pattern of value formation and of transition in values also holds true for the salience of life domains. This means that the degree of change in life-domain centralities should depend upon the transitions in dominant socialization agencies, whereas age-related experience and socioeconomic status again should appear as factors that mediate and shape the process.

In accordance with the dominant role of school as a socialization agent in early to middle adolescence, the role of Israeli student should constitute the main domain of salience at that stage. School influences fade in late adolescence, but for the offspring of the low and middle socioeconomic levels, school is recognized as the main instrument for achieving a better position. Therefore, paradoxically in Israel at least, school maintains a high centrality for adolescents of low socioeconomic level who continue their studies in secondary school.

Work constitutes an important focus of interest in adult workers, because at this stage it is the dominant socializing agent. However, because a meaningful job is not a part of workers' expectations today (Yankelovich, 1974; Krau, 1983), and because of the realities of family-oriented life in Israel, home is likely to be the salient role, with work occupying second place but still one of substantial importance. For professionals work should occupy the central place. These have long been, and with changing conditions still are, researchable questions.

The Israeli Work Importance Study

We draw the samples on which the Israeli research was based ($N = 930$) from groups of high and low socioeconomic status at the main stages of development in the roles of student and of adult worker:

1. Ninth-year (secondary school) students from high socioeconomic levels, $n = 130$
2. Ninth-year (secondary school) students from low socioeconomic levels, $n = 124$
3. Twelfth-year (secondary school) students from high socioeconomic levels, $n = 123$
4. Twelfth-year (secondary school) students from low socioeconomic levels, $n = 125$
5. Higher education students from various fields, $n = 114$
6. Youth looking for jobs at private employment offices, $n = 85$
7. White-collar employees in semiskilled jobs, $n = 104$
8. Blue-collar workers in semiskilled to skilled jobs, $n = 80$
9. People in professional or semiprofessional jobs who once majored in the specialties that match the majors of students in the higher education sample (e.g., psychologists, teachers), $n = 45$

We used the school neighborhood to establish socioeconomic level. Such a division is typical for Israeli schools, and the samples are therefore representative of the main strata of Israeli society. The sample of higher education students is proportionate to the frequency of their first choices of departments: psychology, education, law, and economics. The private employment offices are very much a part of the economic life of the country. The offices mediate jobs for a fee; as in other countries they therefore are unlikely to be used by individuals who belong to low socioeconomic levels, because they tend to prefer state employment offices, which offer free services.

We used the Israeli version of the Salience Inventory and the Values Scale of the Work Importance Study (WIS) to investigate the salience of life domains and value profiles. The Israeli instruments followed the WIS model of twenty-two values with five items for each value. Of the five, two are general values, two specifically work values, and the last could be either. In order to elaborate the Hebrew version of the instruments, we had the items translated to Hebrew and then retranslated to English for translation control.

To measure life-role saliences, we administered the Participation and the Value Expectations scales of the Salience Inventory. The inventory refers to the domains of Study, Work, Home and Family, Community, and Leisure. The Commitment scale is unreliable in Israel, with an alpha coefficient of 0.48, and had to be omitted. The internal consistency (Cronbach alpha) for the Israeli five-item Values scale is (averaged across values) 0.78 for secondary school students, 0.74 for higher education students, 0.84 for blue- and white-collar employees, and 0.79 for the holders of professional and semiprofessional jobs. The test-retest reliability with higher education students, four months after the first testing, as in the United States, averaged across values, is 0.69. For the Salience Inventory the internal consistency averaged across roles is 0.83 in secondary school, 0.86 in higher education, and 0.88 in the adult samples. The test-retest score is 0.65 (higher education students).

Results

Tables 9.1 and 9.2 present the means (m) and standard deviations (sd) of values in all sample groups.

To provide evidence of the clustering in value profiles that results from the presumed influence of socialization agencies, we computed Spearman's rank-order correlation for the mean hierarchies of value preferences. We submitted the results to Guttman and Lingoe's Smallest Space Analysis (SSA), a general nonmetric method designed to find the minimal number of Euclidean dimensions for the description of a collection of variables (Guttman, 1968). The results yield a space defined by three dimensions with a low coefficient of alienation (0.11), which attests to the significance of the results. The developmental path of value preferences reflects the influence of school and the world of work at different ages.

The cluster comprising the secondary school samples is distinct from the cluster of working adults. Students and youth in search of employment appear as a transitional cluster between the two. The cluster of the secondary school students shows a clear differentiation between the values of the high socioeconomic level and those of the low socioeconomic level. It is possible to use value preferences to trace the developmental paths for the two social strata—one leads through university to professional jobs and the other to clerical or blue-collar jobs.

Table 9.3 reports the qualitative analysis of values in the different socioeconomic strata at different ages. Confirming previous research, the fourth quartile of value preferences shows a greater uniformity than the values appearing in the first quartile. Except for the ninth-grade secondary school students of low socioeconomic status, all the differences between the first and fourth lower quartiles of the value preferences are significant.

The combined influence of age and socioeconomic level appears in the first quartile of value preferences, which produces the differentiation. The fourth quartile shows little differentiation. The average Israeli

Table 9.1. Values in Secondary School.

	Ninth-Year High SES		Ninth-Year Low SES		Twelfth-Year High SES		Twelfth-Year Low SES	
	M	*SD*	*M*	*SD*	*M*	*SD*	*M*	*SD*
1. Ability Utilization	20.77	3.29	20.25	4.10	22.24	2.20	21.48	3.28
2. Achievement	21.53	2.80	20.00	4.46	22.09	3.17	21.44	3.31
3. Advancement	20.17	2.73	20.00	3.82	18.74	4.64	19.52	3.99
4. Aesthetics	17.77	3.82	18.38	3.99	17.00	3.55	18.00	4.57
5. Altruism	17.30	4.41	18.50	4.26	18.65	4.34	20.16	3.26
6. Social Interaction	19.40	3.76	18.96	4.35	19.39	2.67	20.08	3.52
7. Authority	15.70	4.33	16.37	4.28	15.17	3.21	15.28	4.16
8. Autonomy	19.47	3.23	19.38	4.34	20.39	3.66	19.56	4.18
9. Creativity	19.73	3.36	19.42	4.07	18.87	4.87	19.64	4.53
10. Economic Rewards	18.90	3.69	18.96	4.36	18.73	4.48	18.28	4.44
11. Economic Security	22.40	3.14	20.54	4.36	20.74	3.94	22.08	3.02
12. Working Environment	17.71	3.96	17.93	3.62	18.26	4.32	18.40	4.33
13. Intellectual Stimulation	19.20	3.57	19.17	3.88	19.74	3.60	20.76	3.11
14. Life-style	19.23	3.20	19.72	3.95	20.09	3.64	19.00	3.47
15. Participation in Decision Making	19.50	3.55	18.38	4.10	20.30	4.43	20.80	3.95
16. Prestige	18.60	3.49	18.50	3.53	17.17	4.87	15.84	4.27
17. Responsibility	20.07	2.66	20.00	3.82	19.87	2.52	19.08	2.95
18. Risk Taking	16.40	4.38	17.83	3.79	17.13	3.37	14.92	4.49
19. Spiritual Values	20.73	2.72	19.58	4.55	20.26	3.51	21.48	3.56
20. Supervisory Relations	21.47	3.33	19.67	4.31	21.20	3.76	20.43	3.21
21. Variety	18.63	3.12	18.54	3.59	19.09	3.18	18.80	3.41
22. Physical Activity	17.17	4.54	18.29	3.60	14.35	3.60	15.36	4.51

adolescent values Economic Security, Ability Utilization, (good) Supervisory Relations, and Achievement. Least valued are Authority, Physical Activity, and Risk Taking.

Tables 9.4 and 9.5 present the role salience data (Participation and Value Expectations) in secondary school, Tables 9.6 and 9.7 present the role salience data from the samples of students and of adults.

As the tables show, the Student role occupies first place in the ninth year for high socioeconomic status students, in the twelfth year for low socioeconomic status, and in higher education students. Work occupies the first place for professionals and for white-collar workers (also in students as far as value expectations are concerned). Home and Family is the most important life area for ninth-year students of low socioeconomic status, for youth searching for work in employment offices, and for blue-collar workers. In Israel, Leisure seems to be the salient area only for the twelfth-year

Table 9.2. Values in Higher Education Students, Labor Force Youth, and Adults.

	Students		Youth at Employment Offices		White Collar		Blue Collar		Professional Adults	
	M	SD	M	SD	M	SD	M	SD	M	SD
1. Ability Utilization	23.05	1.43	24.30	0.98	20.53	4.96	24.00	0.90	12.11	4.3
2. Achievement	21.86	2.89	23.88	1.99	20.69	5.26	23.60	0.86	23.12	2.4
3. Advancement	19.04	3.41	23.35	2.26	18.84	5.47	23.20	1.23	18.53	4.8
4. Aesthetics	17.62	3.10	22.23	2.70	17.69	6.54	22.70	2.24	18.41	5.0
5. Altruism	17.46	2.27	20.64	2.49	17.61	4.21	20.30	4.30	19.41	4.2
6. Social Interaction	19.84	2.00	20.11	2.49	18.23	5.03	19.50	3.25	19.18	4.1
7. Authority	18.04	4.20	21.11	3.23	19.23	3.78	20.20	3.80	16.60	5.2
8. Autonomy	19.65	3.65	22.05	3.54	21.15	3.43	24.30	1.16	20.18	4.1
9. Creativity	18.66	3.31	24.11	1.79	19.53	6.76	23.80	2.60	21.88	4.1
10. Economic Rewards	18.23	3.64	21.70	4.39	20.92	4.00	23.80	1.06	20.48	3.8
11. Economic Security	19.86	3.60	23.70	2.25	22.69	3.59	24.60	0.80	20.88	4.1
12. Working Environment	17.64	3.46	21.82	3.60	20.07	3.79	23.00	3.60	17.88	5.5
13. Intellectual Stimulation	19.02	3.34	23.17	2.53	10.97	4.38	22.10	2.46	22.53	2.7
14. Life-style	19.59	3.14	22.29	3.42	10.61	4.48	22.20	2.15	21.18	3.4
15. Participation in Decision Making	20.50	4.07	22.11	3.33	19.30	3.81	22.30	3.16	21.82	3.1
16. Prestige	17.47	2.98	22.52	3.87	20.84	3.43	24.20	3.30	19.82	4.1
17. Responsibility	20.12	3.28	22.94	1.91	20.46	3.35	21.90	2.80	21.88	2.5
18. Risk Taking	16.42	3.46	16.47	3.65	13.23	6.00	15.00	4.35	14.06	4.9
19. Spiritual Values	19.23	3.42	23.23	2.58	20.53	2.72	21.60	0.90	20.76	3.2
20. Supervisory Relations	20.78	3.12	23.76	2.04	22.38	3.06	24.40	1.10	22.70	2.9
21. Variety	18.84	3.07	18.05	4.35	17.76	5.15	16.60	3.85	19.76	4.5
22. Physical Activity	12.18	3.88	20.76	2.94	15.97	4.36	21.10	1.45	12.11	4.3

(secondary school) students of high socioeconomic status. Except for students in the twelfth-year of secondary school, Israelis seem to attach little importance to Community. This may be because Israeli schools require participation in community work in the tenth and eleventh years of (secondary) school.

How values relate to role salience is interesting. Table 9.8 presents the correlations.

Ability Utilization has significant links to Study, Work, and Leisure, as do Achievement and Advancement. Altruism is related to Community, Home, and Study (many of the students and professional subjects had studied psychology, education, or economics). It is logical that Intellectual Stimulation and Spiritual Values appear to be linked to Study, that Responsibility is a value expectation of Work, and that Variety is a value expectation of Leisure. It is also logical that Aesthetics is a value expectation of Leisure. However, the relationship of Leisure, Economic Rewards, and Autonomy is interesting—it

Table 9.3. Value Quartiles by Age and Socioeconomic Group.

First Quartile of Values

	Ninth Year High Socioeconomic	Ninth Year Low Socioeconomic	Twelfth Year High Socioeconomic	Twelfth Year Low Socioeconomic	Higher Education Students	Youth at Employment Office	White-Collar Workers	Blue-Collar Workers	Professional Workers
	Economic Security	Economic Security	Ability Utilization	Economic Security	Ability Utilization	Ability Utilization	Economic Security	Economic Security	Ability Utilization
	Achievement	Ability Utilization	Achievement	Achievement	Achievement	Creativity	Supervisory Relations	Supervisory Relations	Achievement
	Supervisory Relations	Responsibility	Spiritual Values	Ability Utilization	Supervisory Relations	Achievement	Autonomy	Prestige	Supervisory Relations
	Ability Utilization	Supervisory Relations	Economic Security	Supervisory Relations	Participation in Decision Making	Economic Security	Economic Rewards	Autonomy	Intellectual Stimulation
	Spiritual Values	Autonomy	Participation in Decision Making	Responsibility	Supervisory Relations	Prestige	Ability Utilization	Creativity	
Averaged Mean*	21.38	20.03	21.47	21.24	21.26	23.95	21.95	24.30	22.77
Mean SD*	3.05	4.10	3.31	3.35	2.95	1.81	3.50	1.45	2.78
T-test with fourth quartile for matched samples	2.65†	1.14	3.21†	2.82†	4.21†	6.20†	2.21†	6.18†	2.26†

Fourth Quartile of Values

Authority	Authority	Physical Activity	Risk Taking	Physical Activity	Risk Taking	Risk Taking	Risk Taking	Physical Activity
Risk Taking	Risk Taking	Authority	Authority	Risk Taking	Variety	Physical Activity	Variety	Risk Taking
Physical Activity	Working Environment	Aesthetics	Physical Activity	Altruism	Social Interaction	Altruism	Authority	Authority
Altruism	Physical Activity	Prestige	Prestige	Prestige	Altruism	Aesthetics	Altruism	Environment
Working Environment	Aesthetics	Risk Taking	Aesthetics	Aesthetics	Physical Activity	Variety	Physical Activity	Aesthetics
Averaged Mean* 16.85	17.76	16.16	15.88	16.23	19.20	16.27	18.64	15.81
Mean SD* 4.32	3.85	3.72	4.40	3.23	3.18	5.25	3.55	4.98

Notes: *Calculations were made on the basis of the data in Tables 9.1 and 9.2.
†Significant at the level of better than 0.05.

Table 9.4. Role Salience (Participation) in Secondary School.

	Ninth-Year High SES		Ninth-Year Low SES		Twelfth-Year High SES		Twelfth-Year Low SES	
	M	SD	M	SD	M	SD	M	SD
Study	17.23	5.14	14.75	3.60	13.86	3.38	17.32	4.26
Work	8.40	1.71	10.12	2.30	9.17	3.21	8.84	3.55
Community	9.83	4.30	10.41	4.30	15.60	5.99	11.16	4.70
Home and Family	14.36	3.62	15.54	3.46	13.17	2.80	13.88	3.73
Leisure	15.56	4.56	14.91	3.70	15.52	4.92	15.20	4.05

Table 9.5. Role (Value) Expectations in Secondary School.

	Ninth-Year High SES		Ninth-Year Low SES		Twelfth-Year High SES		Twelfth-Year Low SES	
	M	SD	M	SD	M	SD	M	SD
Study	37.80	8.58	35.16	8.03	33.21	6.43	40.12	5.99
Work	34.23	9.10	35.66	6.16	35.08	6.24	34.32	8.18
Community	23.76	9.31	26.95	7.43	36.00	7.12	31.04	9.40
Home and Family	35.53	7.66	38.87	5.24	36.86	5.67	36.72	5.48
Leisure	32.60	8.28	32.39	6.79	37.56	5.23	33.36	6.52

Table 9.6. Role Salience (Participation) in Students and Adults.

	Higher Education		Youth at Employment Offices		White-Collar Workers		Blue-Collar Workers		Professional Workers	
	M	SD	M	SD	M	SD	M	SD	M	SD
Study	17.11	2.98	12.94	3.59	11.84	4.54	13.70	3.72	12.95	5.70
Work	11.18	3.29	17.41	4.01	14.84	4.52	18.20	4.67	16.19	4.80
Community	9.66	4.25	9.17	3.71	9.30	3.01	7.30	1.30	8.39	4.21
Home and Family	12.31	3.05	19.05	3.38	14.61	5.20	20.00	6.00	15.46	4.41
Leisure	15.10	3.45	14.58	3.33	13.15	3.31	13.40	5.62	13.00	4.77

Table 9.7. Role (Value) Expectations in Students and Adults.

	Higher Education		Youth at Employment Offices		White-Collar Workers		Blue-Collar Workers		Professional Workers	
	M	SD	M	SD	M	SD	M	SD	M	SD
Study	37.15	5.43	33.23	10.84	28.0	10.05	7.75	0.86	30.40	12.50
Work	37.86	6.45	45.11	2.82	37.69	5.60	38.33	2.49	38.66	6.73
Community	26.60	8.62	28.05	9.54	24.30	9.00	21.58	7.31	17.84	7.31
Home and Family	36.50	5.70	44.94	4.16	36.53	7.07	39.41	0.99	37.98	6.86
Leisure	31.89	4.44	35.52	5.10	33.30	6.07	27.0	6.60	26.44	5.68

Table 9.8. Correlations of Values and Role Expectations.*

Values**	Participation Salience (SI)					Value Expectations (SI)				
	Study	Work	Community	Home	Leisure	Study	Work	Community	Home	Leisure
1. Ability Utilization	.33*	.05	.13	−.06	.25	.39*	.30*	.21	.04	.29
2. Achievement	.27	−.02	.13	.02	.27	.24	.31*	.19	.09	.28
3. Advancement	.31*	.11	.01	.15	.24	.30*	.34*	.10	.08	.25
4. Aesthetics	.19	.06	.00	.03	.25	.27	.22	.16	.04	.29
5. Altruism	.21	−.12	.32*	.19	.01	.32*	.09	.40*	.32*	.18
6. Social Interaction	.06	−.08	.02	−.08	.07	.19	.05	.14	.16	.25
7. Authority	.30*	.21	.10	.03	.34*	.25	.22	.05	−.01	.24
8. Autonomy	.25	−.01	.19	.00	.24	.25	.22	.22	.05	.29
9. Creativity	.28	.10	.20	.12	.21	.20	.16	.24	−.01	.18
10. Economic Rewards	.10	.05	.00	.02	.27	.04	.13	−.02	−.06	.28
11. Economic Security	.30*	−.03	−.07	.25	.38*	.19	.25	.00	.06	.27
12. Working Environment	.07	−.05	.00	−.01	.19	.11	.14	.11	.15	.31*
13. Intellectual Stimulation	.39*	−.04	.18	.12	.23	.46*	.26	.35*	.06	.23
14. Life-style	.11	.02	.01	.00	.23	.12	.16	.05	.05	.21
15. Participation in Decision Making	.31*	−.02	.13	.08	.23	.15	.14	.21	.03	.21
16. Prestige	.23	.03	.05	.03	.19	.12	.12	.01	.02	.18
17. Responsibility	.29	.15	.18	.10	.23	.24	.35*	.22	.06	.25
18. Risk Taking	.05	.19	.28	.18	.09	.06	.21	.28	.10	.15
19. Spiritual Values	.35*	−.03	.22	.18	.20	.29	.24	.27	.14	.23
20. Supervisory Relations	.34*	−.15	.02	.09	.14	.28	.27	.12	.19	.18
21. Variety	.17	.00	.15	.02	.30*	.23	.12	.20	.08	.32*
22. Physical Activity	.01	.06	.00	.16	.09	.04	.08	.14	−.06	.22*

*Correlations above 0.29 are significant at $p < 0.10$.
**Preliminary or developmental form (see Chapter Four).

seems to indicate a certain social realism in Israeli society, in which autonomy is a characteristic of Leisure Activities and not of work.

Conclusion

The WIS project has confirmed the presumed combined influence of age and of socioeconomic status in the value system of the Israeli population. It also confirms the hypothesis concerning the leading role of a dominant socialization agent in value formation at each stage of vocational development, the salience of study for school-leaving youth (dropouts and recent graduates) of low socioeconomic status, and the salience of work for professionals.

Because of the cross-sectional character of the research, we can provide no direct description of the process of value modification. However, because the research samples are cross-sections of the developmental chain of vocational development, and because the research purposely focused on the relationship of age to values, we consider this grounds for believing that the value variance across the developmental line of the samples reflects the modification of values by the socialization agents that become dominant as a person develops.

Thus we see that the process of value modification by exposure to work starts with the groups for which the proximity of work is most real. Such groups are the twelfth-year students of low socioeconomic status and the higher education students (who tend to be of high socioeconomic status). It is noteworthy, however, that our analysis did not isolate low SES higher education students (if such exist). The values emphasized by occupational socialization correspond to career aspirations and expectations. Intellectual Stimulation and Creativity appear in professionals but not in white- or blue-collar workers. The leading motives of the latter, as expressed in their value preferences, are Economic Security and Rewards, good Supervisory Relations, and the wish for Autonomy and Prestige (what used to be called *consideration* in leadership studies).

One of the main findings of the Israeli research is that the first profile to crystallize is that of value rejection. This profile is already formed by the ninth year of schooling in middle adolescence, and it seems to develop no further (see fourth quartile, Table 9.3). Thus the evolution of value profiles between middle and late adolescence appears to be related to the diversification of preferences in accordance with the aspirations characteristic of the subculture to which the subject belongs.

References

Elizur, D. (1984). *Facets of work values: A structural analysis of outcomes.* International Colloquium on Developing Human Resources in a Rapidly Changing Society, Jerusalem.

Erez, M., & Tzezana. (1984). *The congruence between social values and goal-setting strategies and its effect on performance.* International Colloquium on Developing Human Resources in a Rapidly Changing Society, Jerusalem.

Guttman, L. (1968). A general nonmetric technique for finding the smallest coordinate space for a configuration of points. *Psychometrika, 33,* 470–514.

Havighurst, R. J. (1964). Youth in exploration and man emergent. In H. Borow (Ed.), *Man in a world at work.* Boston: Houghton Mifflin.

Jacobson, D. (1985). *Determinants of job at risk behavior.* Tel Aviv: Golda Meir Institute for Social and Labour Research.

Jacobson, D., & Eran, M. (1980). Expectancy theory components and nonexpectancy moderators as predictors of physicians' preference for retirement. *Journal of Occupational Psychology, 53,* 11–26.

Krau, E. (1983). The attitude toward work toward career transitions. *Journal of Vocational Behavior, 23,* 270–285.

Krau, E. (1987). The crystallization of work values in adolescence: A socioculture approach. *Journal of Vocational Behavior, 30,* 103–123.

Krau, E. (1989). The transition in life domain salience and the modification of work values between high school and adult employment. *Journal of Vocational Behavior, 34,* 100–116.

Mannheim, B. (1984). Managerial orientations and workers' job responses in labor-owned and private industrial plants in Israel. *Organization Studies, 5,* 23–42.

Mannheim, B., & Jacobson, D. (1972). Attitudes of older industrial workers toward retirement. In L. Miller (Ed.), *Mental health in a rapidly changing society.* San Diego, CA: Academic Press.

Mannheim, B., & Schiffrin, M. (1984). Family structure, job characteristics, rewards, and strains as related to work-role centrality of employed and self-employed professional women with children. *Journal of Occupational Behavior, 5,* 83–101.

Shamir, B. (1986). Protestant work ethic, work involvement, and the psychological impact of unemployment. *Journal of Occupational Behavior, 7,* 25–38.

Shapira, Z. (1984). *Factors affecting employer work values: Evidence about industrial workers in Israel.* International Colloquium on Developing Human Resources in a Rapidly Changing Society, Jerusalem.

Yankelovich, D. (1974). The meaning of work. In The American Assembly, Columbia University (Ed.), *The worker and the job: Coping with change.* Englewood Cliffs, NJ: Prentice-Hall.

Yarr, E. (1984). *Technological development and the meaning of work: A sociopsychological perspective.* International Colloquium on Developing Human Resources in a Rapidly Changing Society, Jerusalem.

TEN

Life Roles and Values in Italy: Some Results of the Work Importance Study

Giancarlo Trentini

Italy has participated in the WIS project since 1982, with Giancarlo Trentini as national project director. Other members of the group were Massimo Bellotto, Giuseppe Favretto, and Maria Cristina Bolla; Favretto left the group in 1984, and Giovanni Sprini and Antonio Miragliotta joined it. Since 1987 Marisa Sangiorgi and Giovanni Battista Muzio also have collaborated in the project.

The group started its study without formal sponsorship and with no financial support; participants provided their own initial funds. In 1983 SINTAGMA (Communicational and Psycho-Social Problems, Milan) began supporting the research, both by contributing to the expenses and by supporting researchers with its organizational structure and secretarial staff. Some participants were also able to avail themselves of the organizational support of their universities, the Department of Philosophy and Theory of Sciences of the University of Venice, and the Department of Psychology of the University of Palermo.

In Italy studies of values and roles are generally based on interdisciplinary approaches that integrate the approaches of cultural anthropology, psychology, sociology, pedagogics, political science, and organizational science.

In psychology Calegari and Massimini (1976) critically examined the values theory, Calvi (1977) carried out a new psychographic method to measure values and life-styles of Italians, Bosotti Ellenis (1983) studied values and identities in young people, Bellotto and Trentini (1989) created a new model to interpret organizational cultures and values, and Bellotto and Miragliotta (1990) analyzed values trends according to different demographic variables.

In sociology Cavalli, Cesareo, De Lillo, Ricolfi, and Romagnoli (1984) and Cavalli and De Lillo (1988) carried out particularly meaningful research

The chapter author acknowledges the collaboration of Massimo Bellotto, Maria Cristina Bolla, Antonio Miragliotta, Marisa Sangiorgi, and Giovanni Sprini.

on the conditions of young people. Cesareo (1984) and D'Alessandro (1985) studied the meaning of work in the Italian population.

Italian WIS Instruments: Development and Description

In 1982 the Italian WIS team translated the initial versions of the Values Scale (VS) and Salience Inventory (SI) agreed upon at the Dubrovnik conference in 1980. We then administered the translated instruments to a small number of subjects whom we subsequently interviewed for the critical analysis of the inventories. As a result, we made some adjustments and in 1983 administered the improved preliminary versions of the inventories to a convenience sample of 391 students from all regions of Italy. We did a statistical analysis of the data and used the results—together with the results obtained in other countries—to revise the initial 230-item VS. We reduced it to a 105-item inventory consisting of twenty-one scales of five items each. Each scale has three international items, agreed to by the WIS directors, and two additional items chosen by the Italian team. We based our choices of two national items for each scale on the magnitude of their correlations with the three internationally adopted items. At the same time we prepared the final version of the SI in three parts: Participation, 10 items for each role; Commitment, 10 items for each role; and Value Expectations, 14 items for each role.

The final version of the VS (*Questionario Valori* in Italian) contains twenty-one five-item scales. Their international labels are

Ability Utilization
Achievement
Advancement
Aesthetics
Altruism
Authority
Autonomy
Creativity
Economic Rewards
Life-style
Personal Development
Physical Activity
Prestige
Risk
Social Interaction
Social Relations
Variety
Work Conditions
Cultural Identity
Physical Prowess
Economic Security

For national use, the Italian VS contains both the Economic Rewards and Economic Security scales, which in international use are combined as the Economics scale. The Italian team thought it wise to maintain both scales of economic values. Latin cultures seem to show evidence of a conflict between Life-style and weltanschauung, focused on economic security on the one side and economic rewards on the other. We retained the other two optional scales (Cultural Identity and Physical Prowess) because of their potential relevance to the study of sociocultural differences in Italy.

The final version of the Salience Inventory (*Questionario Importanza* in Italian) in all its parts closely resembles the international SI described in Chapter Four.

Main Study: Sample and Procedure

The main Italian study was carried out in1985, during May and June. We administered the WIS instruments, in their final Italian versions, to a total of 3,000 subjects consisting of two subsamples: 2,168 secondary school students (17 to 19 years old), and 832 higher education students (19 to 25 years old). Our work was carried out in two regions (Lombardy and Sicily) that are considered representative of northern and southern Italy, respectively, and therefore of the complex whole of Italian culture.

Both the secondary school and higher education samples are considered representative of the population of Lombardy and Sicily as to gender, urban density, and type of school. The secondary students were drawn from both *licei* (grammar schools) and *istituti* (vocational or technical schools) in proportion to the distribution of students in these types of secondary school. The university students were drawn from both *facoltà umanistiche* and *facoltà scientifiche* in proportion to the distribution of students in these liberal arts and technology and science institutions of higher education. Table 10.1 presents the composition of the sample.

We administered the VS and SI to groups of subjects on university and school premises. Before filling out the questionnaires, we gave the subjects information about the scientific aims of the research project and assured them their participation was voluntary and anonymous. We administered some questionnaires individually.

Values in Italy

We determined the reliability of the VS (eighteen three-item scales) by using internal consistency coefficients (Cronbach's alpha). The alphas we obtained from the three-item scales on the overall sample range from 0.26 (Aesthetics) to 0.65 (Prestige and Risk), with a mean of 0.51. The reliabilities are relatively low, barely acceptable for group comparisons.

We established internal construct validity by analyzing interscale correlations, including factor analysis. The factor analysis reveals a five-dimensional

Table 10.1. Composition of the Italian Sample.

Level of Education	Geocultural Region		Gender		Agglomeration Size		Type of School		Totals
	North	South	Males	Females	Large Agglomeration	Medium/Small Agglomeration	Licei or Facoltà Umanistiche	Istituti or Facoltà Scientifiche	
Secondary school	1,145	1,023	1,158	1,010	1,240	928	689	1,479	2,168
Higher education	554	278	447	385	472	360	336	496	832
Totals	1,699	1,301	1,605	1,395	1,712	1,288	1,025	1,975	3,000

structure of the Italian VS. We interpreted the five Italian value factors as value orientations and named them.

- *Material Orientation,* defined by Advancement, Economics, Prestige, Authority, Achievement, and Working Conditions
- *Self-Orientation,* defined by Ability Utilization, Altruism, Personal Development, Physical Activity, Achievement, and Creativity
- *Social Orientation,* defined primarily by Social Interaction and Social Relations and to a lesser degree by Variety and Working Conditions
- *Independence,* defined by Life-style, Autonomy, Creativity, Personal Development, and Variety
- *Challenge,* defined primarily by Risk and then by Authority, Variety, Creativity, and Physical Activity

The Hierarchy of Values in Italy. The mean scores and standard deviations of the VS scales for the two Italian samples appear in Appendix A.1. The Italian value hierarchies based on these means appear in Appendix A.4. The values in the upper part of the Italian hierarchy (Personal Development, Ability Utilization, and Achievement) reveal the prominence of a non-instrumental meaning of work, which is seen rather as a means for self-actualization and self-achievement. The values in the lower part of the hierarchy in both samples include, from bottom up, Risk, Authority, Prestige, and Advancement.

Although the hierarchies of the secondary and higher education students are quite similar, the analysis of their scores shows some statistically significant differences. The following values are more important to secondary than to university students: Achievement, Advancement, Authority, Economics, Physical Activity, Prestige, Risk, and Working Conditions, whereas only Creativity and Life-style are more important to university than to secondary students. The findings might mean that more advanced education attracts young adults who have greater motivation for a creative and expressive life-style. Another hypothesis is that the maturing process begins to free adolescents from their more youthful conceptions. A third tentative hypothesis is that the differences are generational rather than maturational, but only a longitudinal study could address this question.

Our analysis of gender differences shows that men and women do not differ much in their value hierarchies. The position of top values (Personal Development, Ability Utilization, and Achievement) is the same for both genders, as are the values in the four last places (Prestige, Advancement, Authority, and Risk). However, some statistically significant differences between the genders do appear. In particular, the following scales are more important to men: Advancement, Authority, Economics, and Risk. The following are more important to women: Altruism, Life-style, Personal Development, Social Interaction, Social Relations, and Working Conditions. This seems to fit a cultural stereotype of gender differences.

We also studied regional differences, but the comparison of the hierarchies of the students from northern and southern Italy does not show much difference. Their rankings of values are quite similar. Nevertheless, analysis of the scores shows a number of statistically significant differences. Students from southern Italy attach more importance than northern students to nine of the eighteen values, namely, Ability Utilization, Achievement, Advancement, Altruism, Autonomy, Economics, Prestige, Risk, and Working Conditions.

The Relative Importance of Major Life Roles in Italy

The reliability of the Salience Inventory, assessed by the internal consistency coefficients (Cronbach's alpha), is notably high: all alphas are above 0.80. An analysis of the intercorrelations of the fifteen SI measures supports their internal construct validity.

The mean salience scores and standard deviations for the two Italian samples appear in Appendix B.1. The mean scores for Participation are generally lower than for Commitment and Value Expectations. A hierarchy of life roles may be derived from the mean salience scores. For the overall sample, the hierarchy of the five roles for Participation is Leisure, Study, Home, Work, and Community. For Commitment it is Leisure, Work, Study, Home, and Community. And for Value Expectations the hierarchy is Work, Leisure, Home, Study, and Community.

It seems that, as far as behavior is concerned, the Italian students report spending more time on Leisure and perhaps less on Study (although the mean is very high). The hierarchy is different for psychological involvement (Commitment): in addition to the two areas in which students generally are involved, Leisure and Study, they feel committed to the Work role. Affectively, they give Work as much importance as they do Leisure, but in their actions Work comes after Leisure, Study, and Home. Italian students consider the four roles important, Community Activities less important. Last, the pattern for Value Expectations is clearer: they give the Work role much importance, followed by Leisure, Home, and Study, respectively. Community Service again is valued low. The students believe they can attain the values in various roles and in different degrees, with Work considered the most self-fulfilling.

The comparison of the SI scores of secondary and university students reveals some differences. In Participation, the university students are more engaged in Study, and secondary students give priority to Leisure. The Worker role is valued by higher education students, whereas the Leisurite role is more valued by secondary students. The same trend emerges in affective involvement, although both behavioral patterns consider the Work environment an important area in which to enact a person's role. The data show that university students are more committed to Study and Work than are secondary students. The latter are more involved in Leisure and Home. It is worth noting that secondary students do not report Study as particularly involving. The two groups show fewer differences in the expected value fulfillment of the five roles. Both in fact think that the Work and Leisure roles are the most important roles in which to attain values; the only difference is that higher education students believe that such fulfillment is possible in Study. Secondary students put more emphasis on Leisure.

Our analysis of the gender differences shows that women have higher Participation scores for Study and Home, and men for Work. This seems to support the stereotype. As to Commitment, the women show higher means for all five roles, in particular for the Student and Homemaker roles. A higher female involvement is even more evident in higher Value Expectations scores. Although sharing the importance hierarchy with men (with Work at the top), women seem to hold more strongly to the belief that they can fulfill their values in Study and Home. Whereas we expected the belief in fulfilling values in Home, we did not expect the clear and high female expectations in Work.

The study of the regional differences shows similar results for all three salience measures: students from northern Italy consider Study more important, and they see Work, Home, and Community Service as less important than do southern students. Considering the hierarchies, however, the two groups show significant similarity, especially in Value Expectations. In both regions students give primary importance to Work, which they believe is the prime role for attaining and fulfilling values.

Conclusion

The Meaning of Work

The results presented here thus far suggest that Italian students especially value the Work role. It seems that the popular belief that youth refuse work is no longer valid, if indeed it ever was. On the contrary, it appears that youth see real meaning in work and consider it an area that is important for self-fulfillment. They give Leisure great importance, but that does not mean that they see it is an alternative to Work; instead, they view Work and Leisure as the two most important means for the harmonious achievement of life goals. The family, however, keeps its traditional function, offering opportunities for both men and women to attain a variety of life goals. As for Community, we gather from our data that Italians attach limited importance to formal or informal social service activity. For now, it is difficult to tell whether this reveals a tendency toward a newly revived individualism and repudiation of values related to solidarity or even whether it signals the existence of some other feature that has not yet received "institutional status." The Anglophone tradition of volunteerism appears not to be strong in Italy.

The groups we compared (men and women, secondary and university students, northerners and southerners) have a basic similarity in the values to which they subscribe, as well as in the importance they give to the major life roles in which they seek such values. But some of our findings are difficult to interpret. What should we deduce from the fact that Personal Development, Achievement, and Ability Utilization have the first positions in their hierarchy and that Economics, Advancement, Prestige, Authority, and Risk have the last? The prevalence of intrinsic values and the low valuation of extrinsic values may suggest a society in which material problems are considered largely solved and social conflict absent or unworthy of attention. In such an environment youth can have an optimistic view of their present and a positive outlook on their future, anticipating fulfillment in all areas of life. But another interpretation can also be put forward: our value hierarchy could be an expression of nonfulfillment of the values people feel are important. It could be that because the conditions for their fulfillment are not good, people stress their importance. Values such as Economics and Prestige may be judged easier to attain in Italy. In this case, values could be interpreted not as generally positive objectives that an individual aims to attain but rather as expressions of aims that are not likely to be fulfilled. The answers to the Value Expectations scale of the Salience Inventory shed some light on this issue: in our opinion they support the former scenario more than the latter.

The Epistemology of Values

In our research we do not deal with the ethical aspects of values, which involve the interface between individual and collective rights. The values of this type, such as liberty, justice, and sacredness of the individual, are essential to the concept of an ethical culture. In the WIS research, the concept of value does not directly reflect this important aspect of the European cultural tradition, the political philosophy developed in the eighteenth century. Also, the study does not address the psychology of the unconscious. We hold that values give birth to a motivational system that includes personal, ideal, and emotionally mature motivation in the individual. This happens after and through the process of reality testing; a consistent growth process yields a personal and unique synthesis of primary and secondary needs for the autonomous elaboration of the binomial nature-culture. The WIS research is based on a point of view that is more pragmatic, linked with the particular perspective of psychology. Thus the definition of the term *value* and dimensions that represent it are based on an empirical approach and deal with issues that are intertwined with daily life. Some difficulties and questions may arise from such an approach. For example, how is it possible to translate not only linguistically but semantically a wide range of meanings referring to the human activities our study investigated? Is it possible to compare the value hierarchies of countries that have highly different political and historical points of view? And is it possible to study the value system without referring to values that are expressions of conscious individual motivation?

Interpretation of Affective Codes

It is possible to interpret our data by referring to Fornari's theory of affective codes (1977, 1981, 1985), especially the maternal and paternal. Fornari saw them as two psychodynamic components of individual life, one pertaining to the dynamics of security and the other to the dynamics of growth. As to the maternal code, Trentini (1987) stated that it

> seeks to ensure and reward the group's overall protectiveness in relation to all its members. According to the maternal code, maximum attention is dedicated to the nurturing of an individual with every possible guarantee of support and assistance, defense and backing, safeguarding and preservation, guardianship and help. To each member according to his needs [p. 194].

As to the paternal code, Trentini stated that it

> encourages and rewards initiative and the growth of the individual in relation to the development of the group's culture. It dedicates the maximum attention to the emergence of independent values and norms applicable to each and all, and it strives to provide each individual with every possible guarantee as regards the progress and extension of his own abilities, the recognition of the spirit of enterprise, and the opportunity to cultivate and develop his skills and test his aptitudes, talents and virtues. To each according to his abilities [p. 195].

In Italy the affective codes have been studied in clinical and social-psychological studies, with interesting and fruitful results.

According to this theory, some of the eighteen values scales could, on one hand, match psychodynamic components that are somewhat linked with protection and feeling secure (maternal code). Other values could be better interpreted through a paternal code, in the sense that they are more linked with the acceptance of insecurity, challenge, and change. With such an interpretation, it is possible to put forward a new view of the value hierarchy in which the two codes appear: it seems that values with maternal components prevail in the higher part of the hierarchy, whereas the paternal components prevail in the lower part. This may suggest the idea of a certain "maturity" of the Italian sample.

Uses of WIS Instruments

Until now the Values Scale and Salience Inventory have been used in only research in Italy. We believe that they will be used both in research and application in the future. In research we anticipate (1) further analysis of roles and values in relation to various demographic variables, particularly in reference to specific geographic and cultural identities of Italy today; (2) longitudinal studies to describe and interpret the trend of values and expectations in the world of young people and to foresee life-styles and opinion movements; and (3) correlational studies of values and roles in relation to other aspects that are particularly meaningful, such as birth order, group membership and leadership, anxiety tolerance, and so on. In application, we expect WIS instruments to be used in counseling and assessment, with particular reference to career decision making. They might also be used, together with other instruments, for diagnosis of organizational climates and cultures.

References

Bellotto, M., & Miragliotta, A. (1990). *L'influenza di alcuni fattori sull'intensità degli orientamenti valoriali dei giovani verso il ruolo lavorativo* [The influence of some factors on young people's work role value orientations]. Contributi IV [Contributions]. Palermo: Dipartimento di Psicologia, Università Statale.

Bellotto, M., & Trentini, G. (1989). *Culture organizzative e formazione* [Organizational cultures and formation]. Milan: Franco Angeli.

Bosotti Ellenis, E. (1983). *Valori, identità giovanili e sistema di interazione* [Values, youth identity, and the system of interaction]. Turin: Istituto di Psicologia Sperimentale e Sociale, Università Statale.

Calegari, P., & Massimini, F. (1976). *Introduzione alla teoria dei valori umani* [Introduction to the theory of human values]. Milan: Isedi.

Calvi, G. (1977). *Valori e stili di vita degli italiani: Indagine psicografica nazionale 1976* [Values and life-styles of the Italians: National psychographic study 1976]. Milan: Isedi.

Cavalli, A., Cesareo, V., De Lillo, A., Ricolfi, L., & Romagnoli, G. (1984). *Giovani oggi* [Young people today]. Bologna: Il Mulino.

Cavalli, A., & De Lillo, A. (1988). *Giovani anni 80* [Young people in the eighties]. Bologna: Il Mulino.

Cesareo, V. (1984). *Senso e non senso del lavoro* [Sense and nonsense of work]. Milan: Franco Angeli.

D'Alessandro, V. (1985). *Ethos giovanile e lavoro* [Youth ethos and work]. Milan: Franco Angeli.

Fornari, F. (1977). *Il minotauro* [Minotaur]. Milan: Rizzoli.

Fornari, F. (1981). *Il collettivo e le strutture affettive del* Principe *di Macchiavelli* [The collective and the affective structures of Macchiavelli's *The Prince*]. Milan: Unicopli.

Fornari, F. (1985). *Psicoanalisi in ospedale* [Psychoanalysis in the hospital]. Milan: R. Cortina.

Trentini, G. (1987). *Il cerchio magico* [The magic circle]. Milan: Franco Angeli.

ELEVEN

Work Values and Role Salience in Japanese Culture

Nobuo Nakanishi
Toshiki Mikawa

In the Old Testament (Genesis 3: 17–19) working is considered the punishment for humans' original sin. So in Western tradition Judeo-Christian views regard working as a form of punishment, as a duty or obligation to God. Traditional Japanese culture, however, has no myth of original sin.

In Oriental culture Buddhists especially think that the attainment of nirvana is tantamount to liberation of the self from passions that constrain and impede reaching the peaceful state. In Burma and Thailand nirvana is thought to be attained by meditation. However, a different idea exists in the Buddhist culture of East Asia, especially in Japan. According to Dogen (a Japanese Zen priest of the thirteenth century), the road to nirvana is to execute properly the most simple and basic daily activities. Shosan Suzuki (a Japanese samurai and later a Zen priest of the seventeenth century) extended this notion to the proper conduct of work, which he viewed as a way to minimize the passion-arousing influence of idleness: "When one carries out and suffers from an arduous and difficult task, one is not constrained by passions. One then practices a Buddhist activity." As Suzuki declared, "Farming is a Buddhist activity." Thus nirvana can be reached through hard work. Japanese tradition has regarded work as an activity that harmonizes human beings with nature, an activity that develops the person.

The purpose of this study is to explore the meaning of work in contemporary Japan. Some research on the topic already exists: ten years ago Fujimoto prepared the Japanese edition of Work Values Inventory (Super, 1970), and Fujimoto and Abe (1988) since have completed its standardization. There was no attempt, however, to study life roles. The Japanese WIS project attempted to study both values and life roles in Japanese students and adults, using the methodological approach developed by the Work Importance Study (WIS) consortium (Nakanishi & Mikawa, 1987, 1988).

The Japanese WIS Instruments and Sample

The Japanese WIS adopted the American versions of the WIS inventories (Nevill & Super, 1986a, 1986b). The Japanese edition of the Values Scale (VS) consists of twenty five-item scales that measure the values that most people seek in life:

Ability Utilization
Achievement
Advancement
Aesthetics
Altruism
Authority
Autonomy
Creativity
Economic Rewards
Life-style
Personal Development
Physical Activity
Prestige
Risk
Social Interaction
Social Relations
Variety
Working Conditions
Physical Prowess
Economic Security

The Japanese Salience Inventory (SI) is similar to that adopted in other countries.

We administered both instruments to secondary school students ($n = 502$, 140 men and 362 women) and to higher education students ($n = 371$, 140 men and 231 women). We collected all data in a classroom setting. The samples of secondary and university students are fairly representative of the overall Japanese sociocultural context. In addition, we administered the instruments to adult workers; we used the Values Scale to question 750 workers (648 men and 102 women) and the Salience Inventory to question 883 workers (605 men and 278 women). All responses were collected through voluntary deposit in a box.

Values Scale: Some Results

Reliability of the Japanese edition of the VS proved acceptable. Internal consistency (alpha coefficients) for all samples range from 0.46 to 0.89. We obtained the highest reliabilities in the adult sample and the lowest in the secondary school sample, probably because secondary students are still forming their values. The Advancement and Economic Security scales show the highest alphas in all samples, whereas the Achievement, Autonomy, and Life-style scales show the lowest reliabilities, especially in the female samples.

The means and standard deviations for all scales appear in Appendix A.1, and the hierarchy of the eighteen internationally comparable values appears in Appendix A.4. As the appendixes show, the five most important values in each of the three Japanese samples are Ability Utilization, Personal Development, Aesthetics, Creativity, and Autonomy—the values that indicate strong orientation to self-actualization. On the other hand, the least important values are Risk, Authority, and Advancement, as well as Physical Prowess, which is not shown in the appendix.

Although the global hierarchies of the three samples are quite similar, the three groups also show differences. We studied differences for gender separately. In male samples, higher education students have significantly ($p < 0.01$) higher scores than adult workers in Ability Utilization, Aesthetics, Autonomy, Life-style, Personal Development, Social Relations, and Variety, whereas adult workers have higher scores in Authority and Economic Rewards. Secondary school students have higher scores than higher education students in Advancement, Physical Activity, Social Interaction, Social Relations, Physical Prowess, and Economic Security. Students generally consider the values of Risk, Social Interaction, and Social Relations more important than adult workers do. In female samples, higher education students have higher scores than adult workers in Ability Utilization, Achievement, Aesthetics, Altruism, Personal Development, Physical Activity, Social Interaction, and Social Relations, whereas adult workers have higher scores only in Economic Rewards. Female secondary students have higher scores than female higher education students on Advancement, Altruism, Authority, Physical Activity, Risk, Social Interaction, Variety, Physical Prowess, and Economic Security.

We also analyzed the gender differences in values. We find a number of significant differences at each level, although we find the most differences at the secondary school level. In general, in most samples the men consider Advancement, Authority, Autonomy, Creativity, Economic Rewards, Risk, and Physical Prowess more important than women do, whereas women receive higher scores in Ability Utilization, Personal Development, and Social Interaction.

Salience Inventory: Some Results

Reliability of the Japanese Salience Inventory proved generally high: the internal consistency (alpha) coefficients for all samples range from 0.84 to 0.95. The coefficients are generally higher in the adult samples and lowest in the secondary school samples.

The means and standard deviations of all salience measures appear in Appendix B.1. Although the data are for the pooled samples, we analyzed role importance for each gender separately.

Our analysis of male data reveals that Work is the most important activity for adult men. This finding is indicated congruently by the Participation, Commitment, and Value Expectations scales. For youth in both secondary and higher education, however, the most important activity, as shown by each of the scales, is Leisure. The same is true for female students: they consider Leisure the most important activity, although the female higher education students receive the highest Value Expectations scores for Work. Unlike the adult men, who consider Work the most important activity, the adult women give priority to Home and Family and Leisure activities. The least important activity in all samples is Community Service.

We also studied the differences among the three groups. In both male and female samples the higher education students have higher scores than the secondary students for Study and Work on each of the three salience measures. Adult workers, however, consider Work and Home and Family activities more important than do either of the two student groups, with the exception that the female higher education students receive higher Value Expectations scores for Work than do female adult workers.

The analysis of gender differences reveals a number of significant differences in each of the three groups. In general, men consider Work more important and Home and Family activities less important than women do.

Conclusion

Foreign observers often regard Japanese workers as workaholics. They do have a high achievement need, which has contributed to the economic development of Japan since World War II. They see their work as central to their lives, and their private lives as closely connected with their business. However, as this survey shows, how adult workers and students in Japan view work is now showing some differences. This study reveals that students prefer leisure to other roles; it seems that they are gradually developing work values similar to those in Western countries.

References

Fujimoto, K., & Abe, K. (1988). Standardization of Work Values Inventory. *Career Guidance Study, 9,* 44–49.

Nakanishi, N., & Mikawa, T. (1987). A cross-national study of role salience: The role salience in Japanese adults. *Career Guidance Study, 8,* 17–25.

Nakanishi, N., & Mikawa, T. (1988). A cross-national study of work values: The work values in Japanese adults. *Career Guidance Study, 9,* 10–18.

Nevill, D. D., & Super, D. E. (1986a). *The Salience Inventory: Theory, application and research* (Manual). Palo Alto, CA: Consulting Psychologists Press.

Nevill, D. D., & Super, D. E. (1986b). *The Values Scale: Theory, application, and research* (Manual). Palo Alto, CA: Consulting Psychologists Press.

Super, D. E. (1970). *The Work Values Inventory.* Boston: Houghton Mifflin.

TWELVE

The Work Importance Study in Poland

Elzbieta M. Hornowska
Wladislaw J. Paluchowski

Sociological writings (Nowak, 1979, 1984; Nowakowska-Zakowska, 1980; Sulek, 1984; Swida, 1979) and publications of an ideological character (e.g., Dobrowolska, 1977) have dominated the Polish literature on values, and in particular on values in work. Only a few contributions are more directly related to the psychology of life values (Gliszczynska, 1971; Miluska & Bogacka, 1987).

Life values should be seen in their cultural, economic, and political context. The purpose of the historical outline that follows is to provide such a context for understanding changes in contemporary attitudes, values, and aspirations in Poland. We found two main discrepancies in the literature we reviewed: that between traditional and officially propagated "socialistic" values, and that between the socialistic values people publicly express and those people truly hold.

Medieval Christianity held that work was a necessary evil, intended for lower classes. Later, domination by the nobility reinforced the contempt for manual work. This very ethic contributed to the consolidation of such values as patriotism and dignity after the partition of Poland late in the eighteenth century. The country was treated as a colony and exploited economically, developments that are believed to have considerably delayed the formulation of a contemporary work ethic. When early ideas of capitalism emerged in western Europe, Poles cultivated instead patriotism and self- and family preservation. They associated service to the foreign conquering country with treason. The twenty-two-year period of independence, from 1917 to 1939, and the absence of expansive capitalism in Poland's history slowed the change to a modern industrial economy.

The post–World War II period forced industrialization according to the Stalinist model of martial communism, and the all-pervasive politicization of life was accompanied by the propagation of a new system of values. Work thus became an official value promoted by education. Individual effort, not property as in the old regime, was to determine an individual's position. Work was to become an instrument of planned social change and the basis of planned personal development as a "socialistic personality." Poles associated work discipline with self-awareness and self-control rather than with economic necessity or the risk of being unemployed. Officially proclaimed slogans, such as "Work is your basic good" and "Self-realization through work," found ready acceptance in a country destroyed by war, oppression, and revolution.

In fact the centralized system of planning and administering the economy led to a fatalism that made many people await and accept passively whatever the authorities might decide. The omnipresence of the central administration and institutionalized social life suppressed individual initiative. People felt helpless and lacked a sense of responsibility. Government institutions, propaganda, and the central management of mass culture obstructed initiative and creative activities, fostering passivity and mediocrity. The glorification of unskilled manual work and the depreciation of skill, knowledge, and competence were both the causes and consequences of technological stagnation. All those processes resulted in the devaluing of work: it became an impersonal activity, and Poles considered the workplace either a source of stress or a place to rest before moonlighting.

Paradoxically, the social system that officially has its roots in Marxist philosophy proved the validity of Marxism with regard to at least one aspect: work alienation. According to Marx (see Chapter One), work alienation arises when workers lose direct control of the manufacturing process and work environment, do not understand the links between their work and the general organization of production, and cease or fail to see work as a means of self-expression. The Communist era confronted Polish workers with all those negative aspects of work. The omnipresent, officially declared propaganda success of the system increasingly contradicted the facts of everyday life. The successive socioeconomic crises (1956, 1968, 1970, 1976, 1980), as well as the election of Karol Wojtyla as Pope John Paul II and his two visits to Poland, helped to liberate social thinking from the influence of officially controlled public communication. People found that changes were possible despite the authorities. At the beginning, strikers' dominant goal was to "give everyone his or her due because it has been promised." The rise of the Solidarity movement changed social consciousness, and alternative conceptions of social objectives emerged. The new principal goal was "it is due to us because certain things are owed to everybody, and nobody should live the way we are forced to live." The current expression of this tendency is the "right to a normal (i.e., wholesome) life." It is not an exorbitant aspiration (although perhaps not realizable in the near future) but a worthy one: to "live normally" implies living with dignity and being treated as a human being.

We believe that Polish history is responsible for some distinctive features of current Polish attitudes toward work. We hope the WIS analysis of life values and roles may help to identify the contemporary forms of these features.

Development of the Polish Work Importance Study (WIS)

Poland has participated in the WIS since the first planning conference in England, in 1979. It has been a project of the Institute of Psychology of the University of Poznań. Originally, the research group consisted of Boleslaw Hornowski and his students. Elzbieta M. Hornowska and Wladislaw J. Paluchowski have led the project since 1983. Like those in several other national projects, our group started the study without being funded. For a short period, from 1985 to 1986, our work was supported by the Academy of Physical Education.

We developed the two WIS inventories, known in Poland as *Skala Wartosci* (Values Scale) and *Skala Zaangazowaina w Role* (Salience Inventory), by using the procedure followed by the other WIS teams. After reviewing the Polish literature on values and work importance, we translated to Polish and back to English the 1980 basic version of the Values Scale and Salience Inventory and prepared some additional items for national use. We subsequently tried the initial versions of the instruments out in a pilot study that used individual interviews to check the suitability of the constructs and the vocabulary of the instruments and to estimate the cultural suitability of the items.

Next we undertook the preliminary study. Its purpose was to assess the psychometric properties of the instruments through conventional item analyses. We administered both the VS and the SI to a sample of two hundred students of both genders and diverse ages. Because of their importance to Polish populations, we retained the following VS scales from the 1980 preliminary version: Responsibility, Participation in Organizational Decisions, Intellectual Stimulation, and Supervisory Relations. At this stage we omitted these scales: Personal Development, Social Relations, Cultural Identity, and Physical Prowess. We calculated the descriptive statistics of the scales (means, standard deviations, and intercorrelations) and some psychometric properties (i.e., indexes of discrimination power, alpha coefficients).

We developed the final versions of the VS and SI in 1988. In line with the standard WIS procedure, we chose two national items that had high correlations with the total scale and added them to the three cross-national items for that scale. The final Polish VS consists of twenty-one five-item WIS scales:

Ability Utilization
Achievement
Advancement
Aesthetics
Altruism
Authority
Autonomy

Creativity
Cultural Identity
Economic Rewards
Economic Security
Life-style
Personal Development
Physical Activity
Physical Prowess
Prestige
Risk
Social Interaction
Social Relations
Variety
Working Conditions

The Polish SI consists of three parts (Participation, Commitment, and Value Expectations) and is like the cross-national SI.

We also did the main study in 1988. We administered the questionnaires to 252 students enrolled in various programs at the University of Poznań: 42.8 percent were men, and 57.2 percent were women; 31 percent of the subjects were in their first year at the university, 22 percent in the second, 16 percent in the third, 16 percent in the fourth, and 15 percent in the fifth; 8.7 percent had some job experiences, and 91.3 percent had none. The sample was planned as a quota sample. For each characteristic considered, the distribution of the sample was similar to the distribution of the population of students in Poznań.

The Values Scale: Basic Results

Reliability. We calculated the internal consistencies (alpha coefficients) for the total sample, as well as for males and females separately. For three scales (Prestige, Social Interaction, and Economic Security) the alphas lie above 0.70 for all three groups. For seven scales (Advancement, Aesthetics, Altruism, Creativity, Economic Rewards, Physical Activity, and Risk) the alphas are above 0.60. For Life-style and Physical Prowess, however, the alphas are quite low, especially in the female subgroup: 0.30 and 0.33, respectively.

Factor Structure. We analyzed the factor structure of the Values Scale on the scale level only. The principal components analysis, followed by the Varimax rotation, revealed a six-dimensional structure (eigenvalues greater than one). We labeled the factors as follows:

- Self-Realization, defined by Personal Development, Autonomy, Ability Utilization, Creativity, Aesthetics, and Life-style
- Security and Material Conditions, defined by Economic Security, Working Conditions, Economic Rewards, Cultural Identity, and Achievement

- Career and Status Progress, defined primarily by Advancement, Authority, and Prestige, and with some loadings on Achievement
- Group Orientation, defined by Social Interaction, Altruism, Social Relations, and to a lesser degree by Cultural Identity
- Brute Force (Physical Prowess), defined only by Physical Activity and Physical Prowess
- Hazardous and Exciting Life (Adventure), defined by Variety and Lifestyle and to a lesser degree by Risk

Hierarchy of Values. The Polish sample's means and standard deviations appear in Appendix A.1. Part of the hierarchy of values derived from these means appears in Appendix A.4 (optional values are omitted). The most important values for Polish university students are Personal Development, Life-style, Ability Utilization, Aesthetics, and Autonomy. The least important are Risk, Cultural Identity, Advancement, Authority, and Physical Prowess. All of the more important values might be called personal or individual. Living according to personal ideas and conscience, using personal abilities, self-determination, and beauty seeking are the values that serve an individual more than society. These are values that a person can acquire autonomously, and self-governing becomes a value itself. Comparing the Polish with other national data, the relatively high ranking of Life-style and low ranking of Advancement and Authority are noteworthy. The low standing of Physical Prowess, managing things at work, and promotion in the hierarchy suggest an idealistic rather than realistic attitude toward work. We should bear in mind, however, that the Polish sample consists of university students, which may account for the unwillingness to risk and to face a life of paid work. In Poland, studying represents to many a way to prolong adolescence, and the low ranking of these values indicates a desire for self-development. To students the types of paid work available do not signal progress.

Correlates of Values. We studied gender as a factor in value importance. The analysis revealed noticeable gender differences. Of the twenty-one scales, twelve showed statistically significant differences between men and women. The differences correspond to the traditional stereotypic images of the genders. Men place higher value on Physical Activity, Physical Prowess, Advancement, and Authority, whereas women stress the importance of Altruism and Social Interaction.

The Salience Inventory: Basic Results

Reliability and Factor Structure. We computed alpha coefficients to assess the internal consistency of the Salience Inventory. All the coefficients are quite high; almost all exceed 0.80. The internal reliability coefficients are below 0.80 for only four scales for the women (Participation in Studying, Working, Leisure, and Homemaking) and for two of the scales for the combined samples (Participation in Studying and in Working).

Factor analysis of the fifteen salience measures using the principal components method with Varimax rotation reveals in all instances (overall sample, male and female subgroups) a clear five-factor solution, each factor corresponding to one of the five roles that the SI is designed to measure. The Polish SI thus resembles psychometrically the SI in other countries.

Importance of the Life Roles. The means and standard deviations of the Salience Inventory appear in Appendix B.1. In all three aspects of salience (Participation, Commitment, and Value Expectations) the highest means are obtained for the Homemaker and Leisurite roles and the lowest for the role of Citizen. This holds for both men and women, although there are some gender differences. Women attach more importance than men to Home and Family. Interestingly, women show greater Commitment to Work and to Community Service, as well as higher Value Expectations in Studying and Work, than do men. We find no significant differences in favor of men.

Conclusion

The proposition of a specifically Polish attitude toward work, which we put forward early in the chapter, is only partly confirmed by our data. We find both the hierarchy of values in Polish students and their role salience to be quite similar to the value and role hierarchies reported for other countries. On the other hand, gender differences in Poland are somewhat different in that we find women students to be more committed to work than their male counterparts are.

References

Dobrowolska, D. (1977). Watrosc pracy dla jednostki [Work value for an individual]. In *Przemiany osobowosci w spoleczenstwie socialistycznym* [Changes of personality in the socialistic society]. Warsaw: PWN.

Gliszczynska, X. (1971). *Psychologiczne badania motywacji w srodowisku pracy* [Psychological research on motivation in work environment]. Warsaw: PWN.

Miluska, J., & Bogacka, H. (1987). Wartosci studentow: Preferencje, znaczenie i ich zmiana [Values of students: Preferences, their importance, and change]. *Przeglad Psychologiczny, 2*, 386–429.

Nowak, S. (1979). System wartosci spoliczenstwa polskiego [Value hierarchy of the Polish society]. *Studia Socjologiczne, 4*, 155–173.

Nowak, S. (1984). Postawy, wartocy i aspiracje spoleczenstwa polskiego [Attitudes, values, and aspirations of the Polish society]. In S. Nowak (Ed.), *Spoleczenstwo polskie czasu kryzysu* [Polish society in time of crisis]. Warsaw: Uniwersytet Warszawski.

Nowakowska-Zakowska, E. (1980). *Hierarchiczne wartosci peocownikov a efektynosc pracy* [Hierarchy of values and the effectiveness of work]. Unpublished master's thesis, Instytut Psychologii, Poznań.

Sulek, A. (1984). Przemiany wartosci zyciowich mlodziezy polskiej: Wyniki badan-obserwacje-spekulacje [Changes of life values of Polish youth: Results, observations, speculations]. In S. Nowak (Ed.), *Spoleczenstwo polskie czasu kryzysu* [Polish society in time of crisis]. Warsaw: Uniwersytet Warszawski.

Swida, H. (1979). Wartosci i mlodziez [Values and youth]. Warsaw: PWN.

THIRTEEN

The Portuguese Work Importance Study

J. Ferreira-Marques

The Portuguese project of the Work Importance Study (WIS) is based at the Faculty of Psychology and Education in Lisbon. The National Research Council, through the Psychometrics Center of the University of Lisbon, partially funds the project.

The director of the Portuguese project, Professor José Ferreira-Marques, attended the first two WIS meetings (1979) at Cambridge University (England), organized the third planning conference in Lisbon in 1980, and participated actively in the discussion of the literature reviews and in the refinement of the models at the international level. Given the small extent of previous research on roles and values in Portugal, we did no separate review of the literature.

In 1980 the Portuguese WIS research group was formed at the University of Lisbon. Since then, Maria José Miranda, Jorge H. Alves, Helena R. Pinto, and Eduarda Duarte have worked with Ferreira-Marques on this project. Maria João Afonso, Odília Teixeira and Rosário Lima later became collaborators and members of the research team.

The group was directly involved in the pilot work on the development of the international instruments and in the preparation of the Portuguese versions (Ferreira-Marques, 1982). We administered the Values Scale in Portugal to 953 students in year 9, to 322 students in year 12, and to 156 adults in the labor force. We tried the Salience Inventory out on smaller samples (187 students in year 9, 71 students in year 12, and 46 adults). The data obtained in Portugal and in the five other countries then active in WIS made possible the international revision of both instruments in October 1981. We administered revised forms (1982) to a small sample of Lisbon secondary school students in a preliminary study of the instruments. We subsequently used the forms in further research.

This chapter presents data on research and development work with the Portuguese version of the cross-national Values Scale (eighteen scales of three items each) and of the Salience Inventory from the WIS main study in Portugal.

The Portuguese Samples

Secondary Education Samples

For the WIS main study the Portuguese samples of year-10 ($n = 1,199$) and year-12 ($n = 1,189$) students are national samples collected from high schools in all districts across the country (with the sole exceptions of the autonomous island regions of Madeira and the Azores). The two samples include both genders and were designed to be representative of urban and rural populations in the major regions of Portugal: northwest (districts of Viana do Castelo, Braga, Porto, Aveiro, Viseu, and Coimbra), northeast (districts of Vila Real, Braganca, and Viseu) and south (districts of Leiria, Santarem, Lisboa, Setubal, Castelo Branco, Portalegre, Evora, Beja, and Faro).

Higher Education Sample

About half the Portuguese students in higher education are enrolled in universities and colleges situated in the Lisbon area. We collected these data ($n = 580$) for the main study in this area, including male and female students in veterinary science, fine arts, philosophy, history, management, accounting, and civil engineering (there are only male subjects in this last group). The potential occupations of the students correspond to five of the Holland types: investigative (civil engineering, veterinary science), artistic (fine arts and philosophy), social (history), enterprising (management), and conventional (accounting).

Values: Their Structure and Hierarchy

We calculated internal consistency measures (alpha coefficients) for the three-item and five-item scores for the two national samples of secondary school pupils. In the sample of year-12 students the alpha coefficients for the three-item scales are all above 0.60, most of them reaching 0.70. However, in the sample of year-10 students the internal consistency is lower, especially with the three-item scores.

We intercorrelated the eighteen values scores of the Values Scale at each year level and factor analyzed (principal components analysis) the resulting matrix. We used the eigenvalue of one to determine the number of factors. Four factors emerge in both samples that explain 53 percent of the variance in year-10 and 58 percent in year-12 students. We examined each rotated factor matrix to identify the highest loadings (scales with loading of 0.50 or more) in each factor.

In the national sample of year-10 students the first factor includes the self-oriented values: Ability Utilization, Personal Development, Achievement, and Aesthetics. The second factor concerns the material values: Economics, Authority, Advancement, and Prestige. The third factor concerns Life-style, Autonomy, and Risk; these may be called the self-expression values. The fourth factor includes the socially oriented values—Social Interaction, Altruism, and Social Relations—as well as Physical Activity and Variety. It is interesting to note that the younger group associates Physical Activity with social values.

In the national sample of year-12 students the first factor is both socially oriented (Altruism, Social Interaction, and Social Relations) and self-oriented (Personal Development, Aesthetics, and Ability Utilization). The second and third factors for the year-12 factors II and III students correspond to the second and third factors in year 10. However, the fourth factor is different in year 12; it includes Risk, Physical Activity, and Variety.

We also intercorrelated the eighteen values scores for the students in higher education and factor analyzed the matrix by using principal components analysis. We used the same criterion to determine the number of factors: five factors emerge, accounting for 63.2 percent of the variance. In these data, the first factor corresponds to the values related to the first factor at year 10 but with the addition of Autonomy and Life-style. The second factor includes the material values, as in year 10, and the third factor the social values, not including, however, Physical Activity and Variety. The fourth factor includes Risk and Variety, as in year 12; the fifth factor, Physical Activity and Working Conditions.

Inspection of the means of the Values Scale in Appendix A.1 and the corresponding hierarchy in Appendix A.4 shows Personal Development, Ability Utilization, and Achievement—all of which are self-oriented values—as the highest and Prestige, Authority, and Risk as the lowest in the total sample of year-10 students (true also for each gender group). The results in year 12 are similar. We interpret this hierarchy as showing that the average Portuguese secondary school student in years 10 and 12 has the following main objectives in life: to develop as a person (Personal Development), use skills and knowledge (Ability Utilization), and do things well (Achievement). Valued to a much smaller degree are being admired and recognized (Prestige), telling others what to do (Authority), and being able to take risks (Risk). The Portuguese sample of higher education students scores Ability Utilization, Personal Development, and Life-style as most important and, again, Prestige, Authority, and Risk as the least important values. The ranking of values in this group suggests that Life-style is much more important in higher education than in secondary school.

Values: Relationship with Potential Determinants

We also looked at gender, age, and education as potential determinants of the importance of values.

Gender

The rankings of the means for male and female students are similar in all secondary school samples and in the higher education sample, with one exception: in years 10 and 12 female students attach significantly more importance to Altruism than do males. However, we find expectable differences between means. Female students in year 12 give higher rankings than their male counterparts to Altruism, Personal Development, Social Interaction, Social Relations, and Variety, and female students in years 10 and 12 favor Altruism and Variety more than the male students do. Male students in year 10 give higher priority to Economics than do their female classmates. Among higher education students, women place greater value on Altrium, Autonomy, Social Relations, and Variety, whereas men favor Authority and Economics.

In general we find few differences in value scores by age or education, except that living according to personal ideas (Life-style) is relatively more important to students in higher education than in secondary school.

Roles: Their Structure and Hierarchy

We computed alpha coefficients for the Salience Inventory scores for the national samples of secondary school students. In years 10 and 12 the alphas are high, always above 0.80.

We studied the structure of the Salience Inventory by looking at the intercorrelations of the fifteen scores. For the Portuguese national sample of year-10 students the correlations of the Participation and Commitment sections within the same role are generally quite high, as are the correlations of the commitment and role values scores.

In general, there is within the same type of activity a close relationship between Participation and Commitment and between Commitment and Value Expectations (and, to a lesser degree, between Participation and Value Expectations) for the roles of Student, Community Service volunteer, Homemaker, and Leisurite. It is much lower for the role of Worker among secondary school students. We found the same relationship both within the Portuguese national sample of year-12 students and within the college and university sample.

Inspection of the means of the Participation scores in year 10 (Appendix B.1) shows the following hierarchy: Leisure and Study are the highest, with Home, Work, and Community rather lower. Leisure appears of high average salience in both Participation and Commitment for the tenth-year students, and the mean Commitment score for Work is close behind; Study comes third, and Community and Home have the lowest mean scores. The rank order of Value Expectations and Commitment scores is the same, with one exception: in Value Expectations, Leisure comes second, after Work. Students in year 12 tend to rate Participation in Studying and in Leisure as most important, and Home, Work, and Community Service as least important. Work and Study are the most important activities for Commitment, and Leisure, Community, and Home, respectively, have the lowest mean scores. The ranking of Value Expectations is different: Work, Leisure, and Study are highest, and Home and Community are rather lower.

We administered the Salience Inventory and the Values Scale to a group of 580 higher education students from the Lisbon area. The rank order of the means in each section of the Salience Inventory shows results similar to those obtained from the year-12 students, but higher education students place Study second after Work, and before Leisure in Value Expectations.

Roles: Relationships with Potential Determinants

Gender

We examined all fifteen salience scores for differences between males and females in the national samples of students in years 10 and 12. Tests for the significance of differences between means of the two genders reveal more scales with significant differences (0.05 and 0.01 levels) in year 12 (female students favor Participation-Study, Participation-Home, Commitment-Study, Commitment-Work, Commitment-Community, Commitment-Home, Value Expectations-Study, Value Expectations-Work, Value Expectations-Community, and Value Expectations-Home, and male students favor Participation-Leisure) than in year 10 (similarly, the female students favor Participation-Home, Commitment-Home, Value Expectations-Home, whereas the male students favor Participation-Work). Using the Salience Inventory, we also find differences between means of the genders in the higher education sample in the three SI sections for the roles of Student and Homemaker. These are statistically significant in favor of women, as are Commitment-Community and Value Expectations-Community. We should also note that the ranking of the means for one gender is quite similar to that for the other gender group in the same educational level, especially in grade 10.

Age and Education

Comparisons of the ranks of the means for the total sample at each educational level show important differences. In contrast with the sample of year-10 students, the scores for the two older samples show Study is more important than Leisure in both Participation and Commitment. Another interesting difference is that higher education students have the highest expectations for Work and Study and that in secondary school students have the highest expectations for Work and Leisure.

Values and Roles in Relation to Other Variables

Members of the Portuguese project carried out two different studies. They investigated values and roles in relation to such variables as interests and career maturity. Both studies use the instruments developed by the Work Importance Study.

Teixeira (1988) analyzed the relationships between values and inventories interests. The team administered the Portuguese versions of the WIS Values Scale and of the Kuder General Interest Survey (Form E) in Lisbon to a sample of year-11 students ($n = 366$). A major finding is the low correlation between values scores and interest scores, with only one exception (Altruism correlates substantially with Community Service). This supports the distinction between values and interests and the idea that a given value may be attained through more than one type of preferred activity.

Afonso (1987) studied role salience (the SI) in relation to career maturity. The team used the Portuguese adaptation of Super's Career Development Inventory (high school form) with an eleventh-year group ($n = 151$) in Lisbon.

Uses of the WIS Data and Instruments in Portugal

The Values Scale and the Salience Inventory were the first instruments developed in Portugal for assessing values and role salience, and it is already possible to anticipate their use in research and applications, especially in guidance and counseling.

Within the context of the Work Importance Study, Ferreira-Marques (1983) reports the development of the Values Scale and the results obtained in Portugal during its field trial in years 9 and 12 and with adults. Members of the Portuguese project (Ferreira-Marques et al., 1985) published another paper on the revised form and its use in educational and vocational guidance in secondary schools.

A 1986 study by Ferreira-Marques provides data on values and role salience for higher education students in different fields. The Values Scale has proved useful in identifying the objectives considered especially important by each group of students and by Holland type. However, distinctive role patterns do not emerge in most groups of students taking the Salience Inventory.

Conclusion

Examination of the results of the Values Scale and of the Salience Inventory in years 10 and 12 shows how value scores and role scores are structured. The dimensions of values and of role salience are more or less similar at the two levels we examined. Looking at the mean scores in both secondary school and in higher education, we find the most important values are Personal Development and Ability Utilization, and the roles of Student and Leisurite rank highest in Participation. In contrast, Commitment and Value Expectations as a Worker are of high average salience in comparison with other roles, except for the Commitment scores of the younger group, which place Leisure before Work. We also established differences between men and women, but we should emphasize that extensive overlapping characterizes the distributions of the genders in all values and in all roles.

The conclusions that may be drawn from this study—supported by studies carried out by other colleagues of the WIS group in other countries (for example, Nevill & Super, 1986a, 1986b)— also suggest that both the Values Scale and the Salience Inventory may be useful in psychological assessment in different settings. Now we need to focus on the relative emphasis that an individual places on each value or on each role and the implications of that emphasis for career (educational and occupational) decisions. This is a question of differential validity. The reliability of the scores on the national forms is generally adequate for that purpose. We have seen good evidence of content validity and of construct validity. Studies of predictive validity will complete the picture.

References

Afonso, M. J. (1987). *Estudo da maturidade vocacional e da saliência das actividades em estudantes do ensino secundário* [The study of vocational maturity and role salience in secondary school students]. Lisbon: Faculdade de Psicologia e de Ciências da Educação (Mimeo).

Ferreira-Marques, J. (1982, July). *The planning and instrument development processes of the Work Importance Study.* Paper presented at the 20th International Congress of Applied Psychology, Edinburgh (Mimeo).

Ferreira-Marques, J. (1983). A investigação psicológica sobre os valores: Desenvolvimento de uma nova Escala de Valores [The psychological research on values: Development of a new values scale]. *Revista Portuguesa de Psicologia.* Lisbon: Sociedade Portuguesa de Psicologia.

Ferreira-Marques, J. (1986, July). The relative importance of work in Portuguese students. Paper presented at the 21st International Congress of Applied Psychology, Jerusalem (Mimeo).

Ferreira-Marques, J., Alves, J. H., Duarte, M. E., & Afonso, M. J. (1985). A Escala de Valores WIS e sua utilização em orientação [The WIS Values Scale and its use in guidance]. In J.F.A. Cruz, L. S. Almeida, & O. F. Gonçalves (Eds.), *Intervenção psicológica na educação* [Psychological intervention in education] (pp. 447–455). Oporto, Portugal: Associação Portuguesa de Licenciados em Psicologia.

Nevill, D. D., & Super, D. E. (1986a). *The Values Scale: Theory, application, and research* (Manual). (Research ed.) Palo Alto, CA: Consulting Psychologists Press.

Nevill, D. D., & Super, D. E. (1986b). *The Salience Inventory. Theory, application, and research* (Manual). (Research ed.) Palo Alto, CA: Consulting Psychologists Press.

Teixeira, M. O. (1988). *Estudo dos valores e dos interesses em estudantes do ensino secundário* [The study of values and interests in secondary school students]. Lisbon: Faculdade de Psicologia e de Ciências da Educação (Mimeo).

FOURTEEN

The South African Work Importance Study

Ronelle Langley

The Institute for Psychological and Edumetric Research of the Human Sciences Research Council (HSRC), an autonomous research organization, conducted the South African Work Importance Study (WIS).

Ten staff members of the HSRC, representing the different language groups that participated in this study, assisted with instrument development according to WIS guidelines, the pilot study, and the main study, aided by more than twenty participants from other agencies. This group, from a variety of Western, Asian, and African cultures, was involved in the development of items for the Values Scale (VS) and Salience Inventory (SI) for South African use.

Pilot Phase

We administered an Afrikaans (a language related to Dutch) version of the VS and SI to a sample of 978 secondary school students. The organizers of the African languages groups suggested that the VS and SI should not be adapted for any of the eleven indigenous African languages, such as Zulu, spoken in South Africa. They based their arguments on the fact that English is the medium of instruction for secondary school students who speak an African language at home, and that certain abstract words such as *moral,* used in the VS and SI, do not translate well into the African languages, because the languages tend to be concrete, practical, and colorful. The organizers of the different language groups subsequently assisted in writing the WIS-specified additional items for the VS to ensure that the ten items contained in each subscale would be appropriate for all cultural groups. We arranged a trial run at an African secondary school with a view to identifying words that are difficult to understand in the African culture. Examples are certain words for abstract concepts, such as *abilities, accomplishments,* and *high esteem;* to explain them we used circumlocutions or practical examples in brackets after the problematic terms.

During 1987 we conducted a pilot study involving at least six hundred secondary school students in each of the following groups:

English-speaking in a predominantly Western culture
English-speaking in the Asian culture
English-speaking in the so-called colored culture
Afrikaans-speaking in a predominantly Western culture
Afrikaans-speaking in the so-called colored culture
Zulu-speaking in the African culture
Northern Sotho–speaking in the African culture

The aim of the pilot study was to determine whether the VS and SI had acceptable psychometric properties for use in the African, Asian, and Western cultures of South Africa, and to perform item analyses of the VS and SI with a view to standardizing the instruments for South African use.

The pilot study revealed that the SI and VS indeed had acceptable psychometric properties for all the major language and culture groups in South Africa, and the subjective experience of administration and review confirmed that we could conduct the main study. The statistical analyses included means, standard deviations, internal consistency, intercorrelations, and factor analysis. We used item analyses to reduce the VS to five items per subscale. The three international items, as well as the two items that proved the most appropriate for all test groups involved in the pilot study, constitute the South African VS.

Main Study

We conducted the main study between May and August 1988. We based our investigation on a representative sample of all secondary schools in South Africa, which involved more than five thousand students countrywide. We administered the VS and SI in English to students whose home language was English or an African language and in Afrikaans to Afrikaans-speaking students. The first three test groups in the pilot study (English speakers, English speakers in the Asian culture, and English speakers in the so-called colored culture) together constitute the test group that we refer to as the English-speaking students. The fourth and fifth groups—namely, Afrikaans speakers and Afrikaans speakers in the so-called colored culture—formed the test group of Afrikaans-speaking students. We extended the sixth and seventh groups of the pilot study to include all the African language groups in South Africa, using English versions of the instruments, because English is the medium of instruction in these schools.

South African WIS Instruments

The South African Values Scale (VS) consists of twenty-two subscales of five items each, including the three cross-national items common to all twelve countries. We included the original subscale for Spirituality (WIS Planning Conference, 1979) after the organizers agreed that the value is probably important and measurable for all the major culture groups in South Africa, although it is manifested in different ways (African, Eastern, and Western religions). Statistical analyses show that the Spiritual Values scale is indeed internally consistent and correlates only moderately with the Altruism and Social Relations scales. Other optional subscales included in the South African VS are Cultural Identity, Economic Security, and Physical Prowess.

The South African Salience Inventory (SI) resembles that of the other WIS countries with the examples of each role adapted to the local culture. The manuals of the South African VS and SI include a comprehensive report on the development of the instruments, as well as the reliability and validity of the final questionnaires (Langley, 1989b).

As part of the study, we administered two other instruments, the South African Career Development Questionnaire (a measure of career maturity; Langley, 1989a) and the Self-Directed Search (SDS) (Holland, 1985; Bisschoff, 1987).

Here we report the results of the South African WIS for three major language groups: English, Afrikaans, and African languages.

South African Research on Values and Roles

The few studies on values and roles in South Africa focused mainly on the values of adult male workers in industrial organizations. Most of this research involved African language–speaking respondents or representative samples from all population groups. Little is known about the values and roles of younger people and adult females. The South African WIS is therefore the first national study of the values and roles of secondary school students in South Africa and is particularly valuable in filling the gaps in knowledge of the values and roles of students in all population groups.

Academics in various disciplines emphasize the importance of research on values. In his keynote address at the annual congress of the Psychological Association of South Africa in 1986, Simon Biesheuvel stressed that South African society needed among other things, research into values to help resolve the problems confronting the country (Biesheuvel, 1987). Dian Joubert, a leading sociologist, maintained that if South Africa recognized, investigated, criticized, and changed its values and socioeconomic political realities, it would have an approach to human sciences that is meaningful, liberating, and humanitarian (Joubert, 1986). He stated that it was worthwhile to ask whether South African society was such that value studies and therefore knowledge of values were more urgent than in other societies (Joubert, 1986). Raddall (1984) felt strongly that research on values should be accorded priority. He maintained that South Africa, with its sensitive racial situation, had a greater urgency to evaluate values pertaining to work than other countries did. Bluen and Barling (1983) and Munro (1986) stressed the importance of cross-cultural factors when studying values in Africa. Orpen and Bernath (1979) found that a Westernized group of black supervisors more freely endorsed the values of the Protestant ethic than did a group of traditionally oriented black supervisors. Munro (1985) found that a group of black students at a teacher-training college in Zimbabwe ranked the values "support family," "have cooperation," and "use abilities" as the highest of forty-two values. He also found a difference between the traditional (more group-dependent and conformist) values and the individualistic personal achievement values of modern industrial society. Steenekamp (1983) determined the value orientations of a group of English-speaking and a group of Afrikaans-speaking adults: the value orientations of the Afrikaans-speaking respondents pointed to the role played by religion, obedience to authority, and a desire for freedom and patriotism in the Afrikaner, whereas the value orientation of the English-speaking respondents was characterized by individualism and dialogue.

The results of the South African Value Associations Study, conducted among urban adults from all population groups, revealed similarity within diversity (Burgess, 1988). Although South African consumers from different racial groups exhibited some different values, all the groups shared the same orientations with regard to most of the values (twenty-four of thirty-six). Burgess (1988) suggested that the level of training and socioeconomic status had a greater effect on the values of South Africans than did race.

Research into roles has been limited mainly to black males in their role as workers. Orpen and Bernath (1979) found that an overload on the worker role related negatively to job performance among a group of black supervisors at a gold mine. Coldwell (1979) confirmed that there was a considerable gap between the traditional black social systems and Westernized industrial subsystems that black male workers in industry have had to bridge. Bloom (1984) found in a study of urbanized black male and female workers that individuals who displayed a greater need for achievement, autonomy, and clarity (concern for attention to detail) were generally better able to deal with the stress of their role as worker.

From these studies we can conclude that research into values is accorded high priority in scientific circles in South Africa. Although studies of values and roles have been done within certain organizations, many gaps remain in the different phases of life, socioeconomic status groups, levels of education, cultures, and gender. The availability of the SI and VS for South African use has already started to stimulate research into values and roles for a wider range of subjects.

The South African Sample

We took a random sample of ninety-nine secondary schools drawn from all secondary schools in South Africa. In each secondary school we drew equal numbers of year-10 and -12 students and equal numbers of male and female respondents. Each major language group (English, Afrikaans, African languages) was represented almost equally in the South African sample (Table 14.1). The African languages group consists of more than eleven indigenous South African languages, but only nine language groups had more than fifty respondents who could be used for statistical analysis. For the purpose of this chapter we regard the African-language groups as a single group.

Table 14.1 shows the average age of the South African sample. It varies from 15 years, 4 months, to 22 years, 7 months, because students from the African culture often commence their school careers at a relatively late stage (Munro, 1985). We should note that the sample of English-speaking and Afrikaans-speaking students is more representative than is that for African students, because a lower percentage of the latter cohort attends secondary school. In general, adolescence also occurs later in this culture, so we assumed that almost all respondents in the South African investigation were in the adolescent phase, although some were older chronologically. Genders are generally equally represented in all three South African subsamples.

We indexed the socioeconomic status of subjects by coding the parental occupation to a 5-point scale (1 = professional, 2 = managerial, 3 = clerical and sales, 4 = skilled, 5 = semiskilled and unskilled). The sample is somewhat skewed to the upper levels.

Values: Their Structure, Hierarchy, and Reliability

Structure. Interscale correlations for all three subsamples are positive throughout and indicate the interdependence of the scales. The correlation pattern for the three groups is similar. When we compare data from the South African investigation with data from other WIS countries, the larger number of significant correlations with Economic Security and Advancement is noteworthy (Fitzsimmons, Menab, & Casserly, 1984; Super & Nevill, 1988). Such values may have a greater influence on other values in South Africa.

We performed a factor analysis of the VS items on the pooled data of the three subsamples ($N = 5,350$). To form a better understanding of the constructs underlying the values, we did a principal components analysis. It results in six factors with eigenvalues larger than one. These factors were rotated (Varimax), and they explain 76.3 percent of the total variance.

In South Africa the six factors and the values that define them are as follows:

- Inner Orientation: Ability Utilization, Economic Security, Personal Development, Advancement, Achievement, Life-style, Working Conditions, Cultural Identity, Economic Rewards, and Aesthetics
- Material Orientation: Prestige, Economic Rewards, Authority, Advancement, Achievement, and Working Conditions
- Autonomous Life-style: Autonomy, Life-Style, Variety, Creativity, and Risk
- Humanism and Religion: Altruism, Spirituality, and Aesthetics

Table 14.1. Description of the South African Sample.

Language Group	Number of Subjects			Sex (percentage male)	Mean Age	
	Year 10	Year 12	Total		Year 10	Year 12
English	890	953	1,843	44%	16.3	18.2
Afrikaans	909	803	1,712	50%	16.4	18.3
African language	922	837	1,795	50%	17.6	19.2

- Social Orientation: Social Interaction, Social Relations, Cultural Identity, and Working Conditions
- Physical Orientation: Physical Prowess, Physical Activities, and Risk

The South African factors for the total sample correspond reasonably well with those found in other countries (Nevill & Super, 1986; Macnab, Fitzsimmons, & Casserly, 1987; Šverko, 1987). The four factors—Inner Orientation, Material Orientation, Autonomous Life-style, Physical Orientation—correspond to a great extent with other international findings. A unique factor in South Africa is Humanism and Religion.

Hierarchy. The hierarchy of the twenty-two subscales of the VS for the South African samples appears in the means and standard deviations in Appendix A.1 and the rankings in Appendix A.4.

The five most important values for secondary school students in South Africa are Ability Utilization, Personal Development, Achievement, Economic Security, and Advancement. The five values with the lowest ranking for the South African sample are Social Relations, Variety, Authority, Physical Prowess, and Risk. When we compare the results of the subgroups with one another, Ability Utilization emerges as the most important value for all subgroups. Economic Security and Personal Development share second place for the English-speaking as well as for the Afrikaans-speaking students. The second value for the African language–speaking students is Altruism. Other values falling into the first five rankings are Achievement (all three groups), Advancement (Afrikaans and English), and Spirituality (African languages).

In the total sample we find significant gender differences on a number of scales. The largest differences, with higher values for women, are Altruism, Personal Development, Social Interaction, and Social Relations. Men receive higher scores on Authority, Creativity, both Physical scales, and Risk.

When we compare the South African data with data from other countries, it is clear that the outstanding values for South Africa are Economic Security and Advancement and that the relationship between these and other values in South Africa is stronger than in other countries (Fitzsimmons et al., 1984; Super & Nevill, 1988; Chapter Nineteen). Among the lowest values, Social Relations is the distinctive South African value.

Reliability. The reliability index of the VS for the three subgroups in the South African WIS show a pattern of ethnic differences. For the English-speaking students seven of the values scales obtain alphas higher than 0.70, whereas six of the Afrikaans-speaking students' scales are higher than 0.70. The English-speaking and Afrikaans-speaking students obtain alphas higher than 0.60 on sixteen scales. In the African languages sample, the internal consistency is considerably lower, with only ten subscales with alphas of at least 0.50. The internal consistency of the VS for the English-speaking and for the Afrikaans-speaking students compares favorably with that of other countries, but the internal consistency for secondary school students who speak African languages is lower than that for other countries. It is important to note, however, that the internal consistency is higher for the 5-item VS that contains two additional items particularly applicable to the culture and that it correlates well with the cross-national anchor items (standard WIS practice).

Potential Correlates of Values

Potential correlates of values on which we collected data are gender, educational level, language, and socioeconomic status. We did a regression analysis to determine the relationship of these variables with values. Table 14.2 contains a summary of the results for the twenty-two scales, with $p < 0.05$.

The relation between gender and values is suggestive of gender stereotyping in South Africa. The female respondents attach more importance to Personal Development and Achievement and to humanitarian and religious values. On the other hand, the male respondents are more materialistic and physical in their values, since they regard Risk, Physical Activities, and Physical Prowess as important.

The relationship of socioeconomic status (SES) and values is apparent in the greater importance accorded humanitarian and religious values by respondents from the lower socioeconomic group, whereas inner-oriented and social values and an autonomous life-style constitute higher SES values. All socioeconomic status groups share materialistic values, whereas physical values are more important in the lower- and middle-income groups.

An important correlate of values in the study appears to be language, with the English-speaking and the Afrikaans-speaking respondents more inner oriented, materialistic, and social in their values. They also place greater emphasis on an autonomous life-style than students from the African culture. The African language–speaking students as well as the Afrikaans-speaking students are more humanistic, religious, and physical in their value orientations than English-speaking students.

Another variable that has a relationship with values in the investigation is educational level. The grade-12 students regard inner-oriented materialistic values and an autonomous life-style as important, whereas the grade-10 students deem humanitarian, religious, and physical values more

Table 14.2. Correlates of Values: A Summary Table ($N = 5,350$).

Values Scales	Gender Highest Score	SES High to Low*	Language High to Low**	Educational Level*** Highest Score
Inner Orientation				
Economic Security		H/M/L	B = A/C	12
Ability Utilization		H/M/L	A = B/C	12
Personal Development	Females	H/M/L	B = A/C	12
Achievement	Females	H/M = L	B/A/C	12
Working Conditions	Males	H/M = L	A/B/C	
Cultural Identity		H = M/L	A/B/C	
Material Orientation				
Prestige		L = H = M	B/C = A	
Authority	Males	L = H = M		
Economic Rewards	Males	H = M = L	B = A/C	12
Advancement	Males	H = M/L	A/B/C	12
Autonomous Life-style				
Autonomy		H/M/L	B/A/C	12
Risk	Males	H = M/L	A = B/C	10
Creativity	Males	L = H = M	A/C = B	
Life-style	Males	H/M/L	B/A/C	12
Variety	Females	H/M/L	A/B/C	
Humanism & Religion				
Altruism	Females	L/M/H	C/A/B	10
Spirituality	Females	L = M = H	A/C/B	10
Aesthetics	Females	M = H = L	A/B/C	10
Social Orientation				
Social Interaction	Females	H/M/L	B = A/C	
Social Relations	Females	H = M/L	A = B/C	
Physical Orientation				
Physical Prowess	Males	L = M/H	A = C/B	10
Physical Activities	Males	L = M = H	C = A/B	10

*H = High SES (professional and managerial); M = middle SES (clerical, sales, and skilled); L = low SES (semi- or unskilled)

**A = Afrikaans; B = English; C = African languages

***12 = Grade 12; 10 = grade 10

important than do the grade-12 students. There is no difference between these two groups as far as the social values are concerned.

Roles: Their Structure, Hierarchy, and Reliability

Structure. The structure of the SI was derived from the intercorrelations formed by the fifteen subscales. The structure of the South African SI differs somewhat from that of the other countries participating in the WIS (see Chapter Eighteen). Although the South African sample, like those of the other countries, indicates a strong positive relation between the behavioral and affective aspects of role salience, the roles appear to be more interdependent in South Africans than in subjects in the other countries. The Homemaker role shows a significant correlation with the Student and Worker roles, as can be seen from the Participation, Commitment, and Value Expectations scales of the SI. Can this be taken as showing that Home and Family are more important determinants of the Worker and Student roles than is the case in the other countries?

Hierarchy. We obtained the hierarchy of the five life roles by arranging the means and standard deviations of the SI scales in descending order (see Appendix B.1). We analyzed gender differences and education-level differences in each of the language groups. Female students in the combined secondary school sample ($n = 2,819$) report more Participation in Study, Community Activities, and Home and Family than do male students, with the high confidence level of 0.001. Male students participate in Leisure Activities ($p < 0.001$) and Work ($p < 0.01$) more than do females. The same patterns result from the affective scales of Commitment and Value Expectations, but the levels of confidence for the Work role suggest no real gender differences in attitudes toward Work.

We also noted year, or grade, differences. Twelfth graders participate in Study significantly more than do tenth-graders and in Leisure perhaps less. Although we find high confidence levels for Study, Work, and Leisure, the twelfth graders appear to be higher than the tenth graders on Study and Work but lower on Leisure. Much of this difference results from the large numbers: the means differ by so little, especially in view of the standard deviations, that the apparent differences are not of practical importance, save perhaps in the case of reported Participation in Study.

Table 14.3 contains information on the ranking of the life roles for the three major South African language groups.

The Participation scale shows that the time and energy spent on Leisure and Study tend to be greater than what South Africans spend on Home, Work, and Community. A comparison of role Participation in the subgroups reveals that the Student role has the highest ranking in the African language–speaking sample, where the same role has the third ranking for the English-speaking and for the Afrikaans-speaking students. The Leisure

Table 14.3. Relative Rankings of the Five Life Roles in South Africa.

Salience Measure	Total	English	Afrikaans	African Languages
Participation	1. Leisurite	Leisurite	Leisurite	Student
	2. Student	Homemaker	Homemaker	Homemaker
	3. Homemaker	Student	Student	Leisurite
	4. Worker	Worker	Worker	Worker
	5. Citizen	Citizen	Citizen	Citizen
Commitment	1. Homemaker	Homemaker/ Leisurite	Homemaker	Student
	2. Worker		Leisurite	Homemaker
	3. Student	Worker	Worker	Worker
	4. Leisurite	Student	Student	Citizen
	5. Citizen	Citizen	Citizen	Leisurite
Value Expectations	1. Homemaker	Leisurite	Leisurite	Student
	2. Worker	Homemaker	Homemaker/ Worker	Homemaker
	3. Leisurite	Worker		Worker
	4. Student	Student	Student	Citizen
	5. Citizen	Citizen	Citizen	Leisurite

role has the highest rank for the English-speaking as well as for the Afrikaans-speaking respondents, but is ranked third by the African languages respondents. All three subgroups rank Home and Family in second place. The results suggest there may be cultural differences in time and energy spent on such activities as Study and Leisure in South Africa. There is similarity in the data for the English-speaking students, the Afrikaans-speaking students, and international data—adolescents generally spend most of their time and energy on Leisure (see Chapters Five to Fifteen and Nineteen). The high Participation in Study is therefore notable in the African language–speaking students: they value academic qualifications.

Just as in the case of other countries, the mean scores for Commitment are higher throughout than are those for Participation. Adolescents are in general more emotionally involved in activities than it appears from their participation in such activities.

Commitment to the Homemaker, Worker, and Student roles is greater than to other roles. Secondary school students in the South African sample are less emotionally involved in roles such as Leisurite and Citizen. The subgroups of the South African study vary in terms of their involvement in life roles. The African language–speaking students again rank their Student roles the highest, whereas the Afrikaans-speaking students are the most involved in the Homemaker role. For the English-speaking secondary school students the roles of Leisurite and Homemaker share the highest ranking. If we compare the South African data with data from other countries, South Africa seems to display a unique and diversified pattern in terms of the affective involvement of secondary school students in their life roles (compare Chapters Five to Fifteen and Nineteen).

When the third dimension of the SI, namely, Value Expectations, is studied, the secondary school students in the total South African sample seem to expect to realize their values best in the roles of Homemaker, Worker, and Leisurite. This is followed by expectations regarding the Student and Citizen roles. The various subgroups in South Africa differ also with regard to Value Expectations. The African language–speaking students again place the Student role highest. As far as the Leisurite role is concerned, both the English-speaking and the Afrikaans-speaking students expect the role to be the most self-fulfilling, whereas it is the role with the lowest Value Expectations in the African language–speaking students. It seems that English-speaking and Afrikaans-speaking adolescents in South Africa have approximately the same expectations as their peers in other countries, whereas the African language–speaking students have unique expectations for the Student role.

Reliability. Reliability indexes of the SI for all groups in the South African sample are not reproduced here, because all are, as in other countries, above 0.80. It is worth noting that the SI is a psychometric instrument with higher reliability than any other such instrument for all the diverse cultures in South Africa.

Potential Correlates of Role Salience

We examined the following variables with the aid of a regression analysis as potential correlates of life roles: gender, language, socioeconomic status, and educational level. Table 14.4 contains a summary of the results for the fifteen scales of the SI with $p < 0.05$.

The female respondents tend to score high on all role salience scales with regard to Study, Community, and Home and Family and on Commitment to the Worker role; the male respondents appear to score high on Leisure and Participation in Work when gender comparisons are made.

The lower socioeconomic status group shows greater Commitment to the Student role, whereas the higher- and middle-income students consider Leisure important.

A strong reflector of role salience is language. The African language–speaking students are consistently high on all three aspects of the Student role. Like the Afrikaans-speaking respondents, they place strong emphasis on the Citizen role. The Afrikaans-speaking students score highest on the Worker and Homemaker roles, whereas the English-speaking and the Afrikaans-speaking students emphasize the importance of Leisure.

Grade-12 students place more emphasis on the Student and the Worker roles, and the grade-10 students participate more in the Leisure role.

Table 14.4. Correlates of Role Importance: A Summary Table ($N = 5,350$).

	Gender Highest Score	SES High to Low (*)	Language High to Low (**)	Educational Level (***) Highest Score
STUDENT				
Participation	Female	L/M/H	C/A/B	12
Commitment	Female	L/M/H	C/A/B	12
Value Expectations	Female	L/M/H	C/A = B	12
WORKER				
Participation	Male	L = M = H	A = C/B	
Commitment	Female	H/M = L	A = B/C	12
Value Expectations		H/M = L	A/B/C	12
CITIZEN				
Participation	Female	L = M = H	C/A/B	
Commitment	Female	L = M = H	A = C/B	
Value Expectations	Female	L = M = H	A = C/B	
HOMEMAKER				
Participation	Female	L = M = H	C = B = A	
Commitment	Female	H/M = L	A/B/C	12
Value Expectations	Female	H = M = L	A/B/C	
LEISURITE				
Participation	Male	H/M/L	B = A/C	10
Commitment	Male	H/M/L	A = B/C	10
Value Expectations	Male	H/M/L	A = B/C	10

*H = High SES (professional and managerial); M = Middle SES (clerical, sales, and skilled); L = Low SES (semi- or unskilled)

**A = Afrikaans; B = English; C = African languages

***12 = Grade 12; 10 = grade 10

Relation of Values, Roles, Career Maturity, and Interests

In the South African WIS we administered two additional instruments with the VS and the SI. These were the South African Career Development Questionnaire, a measure for evaluating the level of career maturity (Langley, 1989a), and the Self-Directed Search (SDS), a version of Holland's 1985 SDS for measuring vocational interests (Bisschoff, 1987). We analyzed the intercorrelations of values, roles, career maturity, and interests for the total sample. There is a significant relationship ($p < 0.001$) between the Citizen role and the values of Altruism ($r = 0.36$) and Spirituality ($r = 0.35$) and the social occupational interest field ($r = 0.32$). The Leisurite role displays a significant relation with the values of Social Interaction ($r = 0.35$) and Social Relations ($r = 0.32$). The values of Ability Utilization ($r = 0.34$), Achievement ($r = 0.30$), and Personal Development ($r = 0.32$) are related to career maturity. The value of Authority correlates significantly with the enterprising interest field ($r = 0.32$).

For both the English-speaking and the Afrikaans-speaking students the Citizen role is related to Altruism ($r = 0.45$ and $r = 0.43$, respectively) and Spirituality ($r = 0.42$ and $r = 0.34$, respectively), whereas the same role also correlates significantly with the social occupational interest field ($r = 0.36$ and $r = 0.38$, respectively). Participation in the Homemaker role correlates with Altruism ($r = 0.32$) and Spirituality ($r = 0.30$) for the English-speaking students, whereas Commitment to the Homemaker role relates only to Altruism for the English-speaking students ($r = 0.30$) and for the Afrikaans-speaking students ($r = 0.31$). In the English-speaking students, commitment to the Student role correlates positively with Ability Utilization ($r = 0.31$) and investigative occupational interests ($r = 0.37$), and Value Expectations of the Student role correlate with investigative interests ($r = 0.32$). The Value Expectations of the Worker role in the English-speaking students have a bearing on Advancement ($r = 0.31$). In the Afrikaans-speaking respondents, Commitment to the Leisure role correlates with valuing Social Interaction ($r = 0.31$). In both the English-speaking and the Afrikaans-speaking students there is a relationship between Altruism ($r = 0.45$) and Social Relations ($r = 0.35$) and the social occupational interest field, whereas Authority has a bearing on enterprising occupational interest ($r = 0.36$). Valuing Physical Prowess correlates with Realistic occupational interest ($r = 0.32$).

For the African language–speaking students only Ability Utilization correlates significantly with career maturity ($r = 0.34$).

National Uses of the WIS Data and Instruments

South Africa lacks standardized psychometric instruments for career development work. The VS and the SI are available in English and in Afrikaans and help to satisfy a need for instruments that can be used for career counseling and career development in all phases of an individual's life, from secondary school to retirement.

Although the WIS investigation involved only secondary school students, the use of the VS and the SI for university students seems promising and is being investigated. It will then be extended to adults. Several postgraduate students have commenced research into the VS and the SI. After we released the data from the WIS study, we received good reactions from various organizations, schools, and universities that indicated their interest in using the VS and SI in their guidance and career development programs.

Another idea is to adapt the SI and the VS as modules for a South African microcomputer program for career guidance, a project planned by the Human Sciences Research Council.

An important feature of the VS and the SI for South Africa lies in the fact that they were developed specifically for use with all the diverse educated cultural groups in South African society. Although the data indicate that culture groups display unique value and role qualities, the instruments were developed psychometrically in such a way that interpretation for all culture groups is possible.

Conclusion

The South Africans we studied generally attach considerable importance to inner-oriented values. Only in the case of the African languages–speaking students did we find that humanitarian-religious values are among the five most important. Such factors as language, socioeconomic status, gender, and educational level are related in the values of secondary school students.

South Africans have diversity in the importance of life roles, which makes it difficult to identify a pattern for the total sample. Four of the five life roles—Homemaker, Leisurite, Worker, and Student—seem important, but the importance attached to life roles seems to be a function of language, socioeconomic status, gender, and educational level.

Language correlates with both values and life roles. There is a clear distinction between the Western and the African language groups. We find small differences in humanitarian-religious and physical values between the Afrikaans-speaking and English-speaking respondents. The Afrikaans-speaking students emphasize the Homemaker and Worker roles.

The significant differences between the genders may stem from the gender-role typing of both values and roles. It seems that traditional male/female stereotyping is stronger in South Africa than in other countries. The female respondents deem typical female values such as humanism, religion, and altruism important, and they rank such roles as Homemaker and Citizen higher than men do. Although not traditionally "female," inner-oriented values and the Student role are also more important to the female respondents. The men in the sample strive for such traditionally male values as materialism, autonomous life-style, and physical values, although the Leisurite role is the most important to them.

Socioeconomic status shows a relationship with only two roles: the lower socioeconomic group is more involved in the Student role and the higher socioeconomic group in the Leisurite role. The relationship between socioeconomic status and values is also revealed by the greater emphasis of the higher-status group on inner orientation, autonomous life-style, and social values, and the lower-status group pursues Altruism and physical values.

Educational level appears to be clearly related to values and role salience. Grade-12 and grade-10 students show a significant difference in terms of their values and roles. The grade-12 students emphasize the Student and Worker roles, whereas the grade-10 students rank the Leisurite role highest. The grade-12 students are more inner oriented, materialistic, and autonomous in their life-styles than the grade-10 students, whereas the latter rate humanistic, religious, and physical values the highest.

The relevance, validity, and reliability of the VS and SI should make them useful in a variety of ways in individual and group counseling and in research in schools, universities, and industry. With due consideration for the effects of such determinants as language, socioeconomic status, gender, and educational level on values and roles, the results of the South African WIS offer a wealth of possibilities for application in South Africa.

References

Biesheuvel, S. (1987). Psychology: Science and politics: Theoretical developments and applications in a plural society. *South African Journal of Psychology, 17,* 1–8.

Bisschoff, R. (1987). *The Self-Directed Search.* Pretoria: Human Sciences Research Council. Adapted by permission of American author J. L. Holland (1985) and Psychological Assessment Resources, Inc., Florida.

Bloom, J. B. (1984). Moderating influences on role perception—Outcome relationships in black South African workers. *South African Journal of Psychology, 14,* 131–136.

Bluen, S. D., & Barling, J. (1983). Work values in white South African males. *Journal of Cross-Cultural Psychology, 14,* 329–335.

Burgess, S. M. (1988, November). *Personal values, consumer behaviour, and branch image perceptions.* Paper presented at the annual conference of the South African Marketing Research Association, Mbabane, Swaziland.

Coldwell, D. A. L. (1979). Role conflict, job satisfaction, and situational anxiety among black industrial workers. *Psychologia Africana, 18,* 81–101.

Fitzsimmons, G., Macnab, D., & Casserly, C. (1984). *Canadian Work Importance Study: National norming of the Life Roles Inventory.* Edmonton, Alberta: Psi-Can Consulting.

Holland, J. L. (1985). *The Self-Directed Search: A guide to educational and vocational planning.* Florida: Psychological Assessment Resources.

Joubert, D. (1986). *Waardes: Navorsing, metodologie en teorie* [Values: Research, methodology, and theory]. Pretoria: Human Sciences Research Council.

Langley, R. (1989a). *The South African Career Development Questionnaire.* Pretoria: Human Sciences Research Council.

Langley, R. (1989b). *The South African Work Importance Study.* Pretoria: Human Sciences Research Council.

Macnab, D., Fitzsimmons, G., & Casserly, C. (1987). Development of the Life Roles Inventory–Values Scale. *Canadian Journal of Counselling, 21,* 86–98.

Munro, D. (1985). A free-format values inventory: Explorations with Zimbabwean student teachers. *South Africa Journal of Psychology, 15,* 33–41.

Munro, D. (1986). Work motivation and values: Problems and possibilities in and out of Africa. *Australian Journal of Psychology, 38,* 285–295.

Nevill, D. D., & Super, D. E. (1986). *The Values Scale: Theory, application, and research.* (Manual). Palo Alto, CA: Consulting Psychologists Press.

Orpen, C., & Bernath, J. (1979). Employee relations to role conflict and ambiguity: A study among black supervisors on the gold mines. *South African Journal of Science, 75,* 231–232.

Raddall, J. (1984). Understanding human values: The key to organizational effectiveness. *South African Journal of Psychology, 15,* 121–127.

Second WIS Planning Conference. (1979, December). *Minutes.* Cambridge, England.

Steenekamp, C. S. (1983). Kulturele identiteite onder blanke Suid-Afrikaners: Waarde orientasies van Afrikaanssprekendes en Engelssprekendes [Cultural identities of white South Africans: Value orientations of Afrikaans-speaking and English-speaking people]. *Humanitas, RSA, 9,* 431–440.

Super, D. E. & Nevill, D. D. (1986). *The Salience Inventory: Tables for secondary school and college data.* Palo Alto: Consulting Psychologists Press.

Super, D. E., & Nevill, D. D. (1988). [The Values Scale: Tables for secondary school and college data]. Unpublished data.

Šverko, B. (1987). The structure of work values: A cross-national comparison. *Acta Instituti Psychologici Universitatis Zagrebiensis, 17,* 23–37.

FIFTEEN

The Work Importance Study in the United States

Dorothy D. Nevill

The Work Importance Study in the United States, as was true of all the other national projects, had its roots in the International Congress of Applied Psychology in Munich in 1978. For several years Dr. Donald E. Super served dual roles as the international coordinator and as the U.S. project director. Although the international project received financial support from the European Research Office of the U.S. Army Research Institute for the Behavioral and Social Sciences, the U.S. project never received specific funding. However, we decided to go ahead, using whatever support our institutions could provide from regular operations and what we could manage from personal funds and from publishers. In addition, helpful colleagues made up for the lack of money. In 1980 Super was a visiting professor at the University of Florida, where Dorothy D. Nevill became an active colleague. She has served as project director since 1981.

The refinement of the two instruments, the Salience Inventory and the Values Scale, took several years and much support from colleagues in trying out the instruments with small samples of adults and getting feedback for revisions; data came from organizations in New York State, New Jersey, Florida, and Illinois. The authors later obtained student feedback and data for test refinement in schools and colleges in Florida, Maryland, and New Jersey and from adults in workshops in New York and Virginia.

The final versions of the American Values Scale (Super & Nevill, 1986b) and the Salience Inventory (Super & Nevill, 1986a) were published in 1986 by Consulting Psychologists Press of Palo Alto, California. Manuals for each followed shortly (Nevill & Super, 1986b, 1986a). National and cross-national norms for all high school grades were available in 1987, for all college levels in 1988, and adult norms for all Holland codes in 1989.

Literature

The literature on work importance in the United States has relied extensively on survey and interview data. Classics include Terkel's popular book of case studies (1972), Rokeach's 1973 volume on theory and methods, and the Task Force on Work in America (1973), which noted some reasons that people work and cited the "compelling evidence about the centrality of work in life" (p. 9). A more contemporary example is the book entitled *The Meaning of Working* (Meaning of Work [MOW], 1987). Before 1975 interest in the area of work importance focused primarily on the economic and societal importance of work. Other recent research at the international level is largely of European origin (e.g., Cooper & Mumford, 1979; Hofstede, 1980) and focuses more on the individual, as do the American studies (MOW, 1987; Ronen, 1979).

Theories of values have been well known in philosophy for many years, and values have been the subject of psychological research in the United States for decades. Several values inventories are available. The oldest values inventory, still a classic, is the Allport-Vernon Study of Values (1931; revised with Lindzey, 1960). It was developed to measure the relative prominence of six basic interests or motives in personality and assesses primarily the intrinsic values. The Work Values Inventory (Super, 1970) combines the advantages of tapping both intrinsic and extrinsic values and was developed to assess the wide range of values that affect the motivation to work. Johansson and Webber's Temperament and Values Inventory (1976) measures individual differences in temperament, work values, and work reinforcement hierarchies related to career decisions. Gordon's Survey of Interpersonal Values (1960) and Survey of Personal Values (1964, 1965) measure, respectively, salient values that involve the individual's relationship with other people and the values that help determine how individuals cope with the problems of everyday living. Another values measure, the Minnesota Importance Questionnaire (Rounds, Henley, Dawis, Lofquist, & Weiss, 1981) is widely used and has the advantages of an easy vocabulary and of tapping extrinsic as well as intrinsic values. It deals directly with work.

Interest has increased in how people can attain their values in many different life roles. Astin (1984) alluded to this interrelatedness when she stated that "people whose jobs are repetitive and routine (e.g., typists or assembly line workers) often manifest a high level of job dissatisfaction and must seek to satisfy their pleasure needs in other pursuits" (p. 120). Different values can be realized in the same role at different stages of life, or a value can be realized in different roles at varying points in a person's life. For example, a woman might satisfy her altruistic values through her homemaker role during her twenties and through her worker role later in life (Nevill & Damico, 1978) and family patterns (Yogev & Brett, 1985).

Theorists and researchers are paying more attention to life-span development. Any one individual plays a variety of roles during the course of a lifetime, adding some in adolescence and young adulthood, dropping some in later adulthood. Life-styles vary considerably from person to person. Not everyone plays all roles. The Life-Career Rainbow was conceptualized by Super (1980; see also Chapter Two) to depict careers in the life span as exemplified by the various roles played at any one time. A career is thus a changing constellation of roles, some sequential and some simultaneous. Roles decrease and increase in importance according to the developmental tasks a person must accomplish, the values that individual is seeking, and the ways that person has chosen to attain them.

Based on his life-span approach to career development, Super (1983) proposed a new model for career guidance, one that involves a developmental career assessment process. The Career Development Assessment and Counseling Model (C-DAC) examines the relative importance of work (Super, 1983), the centrality of values sought in work (Super, 1973), and the level of career maturity (Super & Thompson, 1979), including a sense of autonomy and self-esteem (Korman, 1969). Recent research has shown the relevance of such characteristics (e.g., Super & Nevill, 1984; Nevill & Perrotta, 1985; Nevill & Super, 1988). Super and his colleagues at the Counseling Center at the University of Georgia, at the University of North Carolina at Greensboro, and elsewhere have experimented with the model. The model is described more fully later in this chapter.

Description of Sample

We collected all data for the high school sample in classroom settings in New Jersey, Illinois, California, and Maryland. This was a sample of convenience, designed to represent all grade levels, urban, suburban, and rural populations, various socioeconomic levels, major regions of the country, and both sexes. The total sample for the Values Scale was 2,816, for the Salience Inventory 3,347. Descriptions of all subsamples appear in Tables 15.1 and 15.2.

We also sampled colleges and universities in order to include arts, letters, science, and technical students from the major regions of the country. The universities of Maryland, Missouri at Columbia, Boston, Florida, Georgia, Eastern Washington, California at Los Angeles, Washington, Houston, California State at Fullerton, Illinois at Urbana–Champaign, Texas Tech, and Texas at Austin and the State University of New York (SUNY) at Buffalo participated. The total sample for the Values Scale was 2,140, for the Salience Inventory 2,693.

We selected the adult sample to represent all the Holland-type occupations—realistic, investigative, artistic, social, enterprising, and conventional—and the literate socioeconomic levels. We also designed our sampling to obtain a diversity of regions, ages, and both genders, but again it was a sample of convenience. We collected data in three primary ways. First, we distributed questionnaires during professional workshops and seminars given by Nevill and Super and their colleagues at such sites as off-campus programs sponsored by a major midwestern university, the U.S. Navy Personnel Research and Development Center, the Fielding Institute in California, AT&T, and American Transtech, and at workshops on career counseling held throughout the United States. Second, we made random nationwide mailings from selected divisions within the American Psychological Association

Table 15.1. The Values Scale: Sample Descriptions for the United States.

Secondary School	n		Age		Socioeconomic Status (Parental for Students)			
Grade	Females	Males	Mean	Standard Deviation (SD)	Percentage Professional and Managerial	Percentage Clerical and Sales	Percentage Skilled	Percentage Semiskilled & Unskilled
9	348	348	14.51	0.69				
10	435	314	15.44	0.87				
11	357	358	16.52	0.70				
12	321	335	17.38	0.99				
Overall	1,461	1,355	15.93	1.12				

University Level	Females	Males	Mean	SD	Percentage Professional and Managerial	Percentage Clerical and Sales	Percentage Skilled	Percentage Semiskilled & Unskilled
Year 1	201	124	17.42	2.35	6.36	5.19	2.10	1.54
Year 2	636	418	18.37	1.79	20.56	16.82	6.73	5.14
Year 3	242	167	19.79	2.10	7.99	6.54	2.62	1.96
Year 4	196	156	21.35	3.89	6.87	5.61	2.24	1.73
Overall	1,275	865	20.03	3.99	41.78	34.16	13.69	10.37

Adults	Females	Males	Mean	SD	Percentage Professional and Managerial	Percentage Clerical and Sales	Percentage Skilled	Percentage Semiskilled & Unskilled
Realistic	71	327	26.98	9.46	0.63	1.05	6.26	4.01
Investigative	87	232	42.86	14.71	18.21	0.14	1.69	0.28
Artistic	14	11	27.33	8.02	0.56	0.14	.49	0.14
Social	191	237	42.41	14.43	21.94	0.77	2.67	1.48
Enterprising	147	161	34.55	10.20	13.36	2.95	1.05	0.56
Conventional	262	96	32.41	10.37	5.70	11.81	2.67	1.41
Overall	772	1,064	36.93	13.81	60.41	16.88	14.84	7.88

Table 15.2. The Salience Inventory: Sample Descriptions for the United States.

	n		Age		Socioeconomic Status (Parental for Students)			
High School					Percentage Professional & Managerial	Percentage Clerical & Sales	Percentage Skilled	Percentage Semiskilled & Unskilled
Grade	Females	Males	Mean	SD				
9	408	381	14.51	0.68	9.71	2.27	7.11	1.91
10	496	359	15.47	0.65	11.62	2.63	8.63	4.45
11	426	424	16.37	0.60	12.28	1.68	9.71	2.63
12	421	432	17.40	0.61	10.37	1.85	9.50	3.65
Overall	1,751	1,596	15.96	0.93	43.98	8.43	34.95	12.64
University Level					Percentage Professional and Managerial	Percentage Clerical and Sales	Percentage Skilled	Percentage Semiskilled & Unskilled
	Females	Males	Mean	SD				
Year 1	353	243	17.46	2.35	15.89	5.16	0.74	0.33
Year 2	560	369	18.47	2.10	15.82	10.02	3.04	5.61
Year 3	386	235	19.84	2.48	10.28	8.76	1.67	2.34
Year 4	283	264	21.20	3.65	10.14	6.23	2.86	1.11
Overall	1,582	1,111	19.17	4.18	52.13	30.17	8.31	9.39
Adults					Percentage Professional and Managerial	Percentage Clerical and Sales	Percentage Skilled	Percentage Semiskilled & Unskilled
	Females	Males	Mean	SD				
Realistic	48	103	25.83	9.28	0.98	1.09	8.48	4.02
Investigative	50	152	36.10	11.41	17.50	0.11	2.28	0.22
Artistic	14	10	28.63	8.57	1.52	0.33	0.43	0.11
Social	244	135	41.93	15.67	33.59	1.20	3.15	1.85
Enterprising	44	62	32.13	12.58	6.20	3.04	1.09	0.76
Conventional	90	27	30.32	12.99	0.98	8.26	1.85	0.98
Overall	490	489	34.59	13.59	60.76	14.02	17.28	7.93

to sample counseling, clinical, physiological, and experimental psychologists. Third, we asked students in graduate courses in Missouri, Florida, Virginia, Georgia, New York, and California to administer the VS to employed adults of their acquaintance. We asked the graduate students to find people in employment categories that were underrepresented in the sample we already had collected.

The Values Scale: Structure

The Values Scale developed by the international WIS consortium originally contained ten items for each of twenty-three original scales. In the United States we administered these literature- and workshop-derived scales to convenient samples of high school males and females in the tenth and eleventh grades ($n = 686$) and to university students in their first three years ($n = 1,042$). At their fifth meeting, in Lisbon in October 1981, the various national WIS teams pooled their results and reduced the VS to eighteen scales with five items each; only the first three of the latter were to be used in scoring in cross-national comparisons. In most countries the two economic values scales (Economic Rewards and Economic Security) highly correlate; in the United States their correlation is only 0.66, lower than their alpha coefficients, which range from 0.80 to 0.91, and low enough to permit some respondents to be high on one but not on the other.

Consequently, the U.S. version retained both scales. When we did the cross-national scoring of the U.S. version, we omitted the last scale, Economic Security. We called the Economic Rewards scale Economics and used the two item substitutions, as in other countries. The U.S. version includes two additional scales, Cultural Identity and Physical Prowess, which were optional.

We computed two measures of reliability for the VS: internal consistency (alpha coefficients) for secondary school, higher education, and adult samples, and stability (test-retest during a two- to four-week interval) for the higher education sample. High school students are still forming values, and we expected more variability in their responses; however, the value structure should be more stable in older respondents. We did not use an adult sample for test-retest study because of the difficulty of obtaining such data.

The alpha coefficients in the United States generally are above 0.65 for all three populations; only in relatively few instances do the coefficients fall below that level. We found test-retest correlations of less than 0.70 for several of the five-item scales. Ability Utilization, Life-Style, and Personal Development fail to reach reliabilities of 0.70 on both internal consistency and stability measures. Therefore, these are less coherent scales than the others and should be interpreted with more caution.

Validity has been assured by the methods of development and by the expected gender, educational level, curricular, and socioeconomic status (SES) differences, upon which we elaborate later in the chapter. In addition, close inspection of the factor analyses supports the construct validity of the

Values Scale. Strong similarities appear for the secondary school, university, and adult samples. Seven of the VS scales factor into essentially the same six factors for all three samples. Three of the five factors load heavily on the VS scales for Authority, Creativity, and Prestige. One factor, Material, is a combination of items from Economic Rewards, Economic Security, and Advancement. Another is Ability Utilization, with items from the Ability Utilization, Achievement, and Personal Development factors.

The Values Scale: Research

The U.S. research on the Values Scale has centered around various validation studies that show that the instrument actually measures what it was intended to measure. The values to which people are committed vary greatly from person to person, not only as a function of age and status but also in relation to many other personal and situational variables. Because each subculture defines what is appropriate behavior for its members, individual behavior rests upon a value system. Variables such as sex, age, and socioeconomic status are expected to be major determinants of the values a person holds.

Occupational Differences. An individual's occupation is one variable to which increasing attention has been given since the 1940s. Despite the value overlap, occupations vary in the degree to which workers can find opportunity for realizing their values (Centers, 1949).

Holland (1985) described six types of individuals who seek six kinds of environments that will allow them to "exercise their skills and abilities, express their attitudes and values, and take on agreeable problems and roles" (p. 4). Holland called the six types realistic, investigative, artistic, social, enterprising, and conventional. In a nationwide sample of 383 military personnel, Yates (1985b) found that realistic individuals valued Physical Prowess significantly more than did enterprising types and, perhaps less expectedly, that social types valued Economic Security more than realistic types did.

Nevill (1988) investigated the values espoused by two of the Holland types, investigative and social. The investigative category consisted of experimental and physiological psychologists. The social category consisted of counseling and clinical psychologists. Nevill obtained random listings of members of the appropriate divisions of the American Psychological Association and mailed the Values Scale to the names on the lists. The final sample consisted of 259 social (69 women and 190 men) and 190 investigative (41 women and 149 men). Many of the expected differences appeared. Ability Utilization, Achievement, Creativity, Life-Style, and Prestige were more important to the investigative types than to the social. Altruism, Social Interaction, Social Relations, and Cultural Identity were more important to the social types than to the investigative.

Socialization. Several studies have found the values of men and women to be different in important and measurable ways in this society (Allport &

Vernon, 1931; Walberg, 1969). We expected the same patterns of values to be evident in the WIS Values Scale research.

In his WIS study of military personnel Yates (1985b) finds that adult women place significantly greater importance on the values of Aesthetics, Personal Development, Working Conditions, and Altruism than do men. Men value Risk and Physical Prowess more than do women. However, the genders have almost identical rankings for the seven most important values: Economic Security, Achievement, Ability Utilization, Personal Development, Advancement, Economic Rewards, and Life-style.

In her nationwide study of investigative and social psychologists Nevill (1988) found that women scored higher on Ability Utilization, Achievement, Working Conditions, and Personal Development than did men. However, in contrast to the Yates study, this group of high-achieving and committed women also valued Risk more than men.

Life Stage. Increasing attention is being paid to developmental changes over the life span (Baltes & Brim, 1983; Baltes & Schaie, 1973; Levinson, 1978; Lowenthal, Thurnher, & Chiriboga, 1975; Vondracek, Lerner, & Schulenberg, 1986). It is reasonable to assume that values also vary with life stage, because individuals face changing developmental tasks. The values inherent in an establishment stage would be different from those in a growth stage. The former might stress Economic Security, whereas the latter might value Economic Rewards.

Yates's study (1985b) with the WIS VS is particularly relevant. Yates divides his sample into life stages based on age. Subjects who were 17 to 25 years old are more concerned with the initial challenges of job performance (Achievement, Ability Utilization, and Advancement) than with the external aspects and rewards of work (Economic Security and Rewards, Working Conditions, and Autonomy). This age group also values Physical Activity and Physical Prowess, which would presumably be characteristic of young adults not yet committed to family responsibilities and with more time and energy for active leisure activities. The values of the adults who were 25 to 35 years old are appropriate to individuals entering the establishment period who are trying to match personal traits and needs with job requirements. They value Economic Security, Advancement, Achievement, Ability Utilization, Economic Rewards, and Personal Development, a pattern that suggests that this age group is indeed concerned with self-realization in work but also with material welfare. The subjects who were 36 to 45 years old value primarily Economic Security and Economic Rewards. They do not appear to particularly value personal growth through their work. In this group, during the middle of the establishment period adults begin to question their value systems and the central material importance of work. The oldest group of workers, aged 46 to 62, value Autonomy, Personal Development, Creativity, Aesthetics, Altruism, Authority, Prestige, Social Relations, and Cultural Identity. In this stage the importance of meeting personal goals and values becomes paramount.

The Salience Inventory: Structure

The first version of the Salience Inventory had fourteen items for Participation and Commitment and twenty items from the Values Scale for Value Expectations. Early work on the American version of the Salience Inventory, as in other countries, adjusted the format to make it shorter, less repetitive, and clearer. The current form has a total of 170 items with high reliability (Nevill & Super, 1986a).

Super, Mastie, and Nevill (1984) looked at the role of response set. The Commitment and Value Expectations scales both measure the affective components of role importance, whereas the Participation scale measures the behavioral content. However, the Participation and Commitment scales resemble each other in format more than they resemble the Value Expectations scale. The formal similarities in the Participation and Commitment scales might create a general mental set that would dominate the specific mental set that should be created by the directions for each part.

To test the hypothesis, Super, Mastie, and Nevill produced an experimental version of the Salience Inventory that had three separated parts (Participation, Commitment, and Value Expectations) and administered them to secondary school students in three separate sessions with a time lapse between testings of one to eight days. They compared these results with those found in the regular administration. The rationale was that if format and response set contributed significantly to the correlations between Participation and Commitment, the regular administration (control) would produce higher correlations than the experimental condition. This should be true also of the Value Expectations scales, although they are presumably less contaminated by the superficial similarities than the Participation and Commitment scales.

The results of this study suggested that the Value Expectations scales provide more independent measures of affective commitment than do the Commitment scales. This may be the result of format differences in the sections that were more readily perceived by subjects. When time permits, the use of all three parts (Participation, Commitment, and Value Expectations) appears to be warranted. When time is limited, it may be best to use just the behavioral Participation and the affective Value Expectations parts.

We computed two measures of reliability for the current form of the Salience Inventory: internal consistency (alpha coefficients) for secondary and higher education students, and stability (test-retest) for the higher education population sample. The alphas are quite high (above 0.80) for all three samples. However, we found test-retest reliabilities of less than 0.70 for ten of the fifteen scales. Because the scale reliabilities became increasingly lower as the test progressed, and subjects complained of the repetitiveness of the previous version of the SI, fatigue or boredom might have caused subjects in this study to resort to random guessing.

To test the fatigue hypothesis, we gave the Salience Inventory in either the regular sequence or in reverse order (Nevill & Super, 1986a). Thus, half the subjects took pre- and posttests in the normal sequence of Participation, Commitment, and Value Expectations, and half completed specially designed booklets that had a reverse sequence of Value Expectations, Commitment, and Participation. If the length of the test did indeed cause increasing amounts of random guessing, subjects who took Participation first would get the highest test-retest scores on that scale and the lowest on Value Expectations. The opposite would be true for those subjects taking Value Expectations first. Commitment scores should remain the same. Regardless of whether the Value Expectations scale was given first or last, the reliabilities for this scale were lower than for either Participation or Commitment.

Gender and age differences in Commitment to Home and Family support the validity of the Salience Inventory. In concurrent studies with secondary school and higher education students (Nevill, 1985), Nevill and Super (1988) examined the relationship between gender and Commitment to Home and Work in two ways.

In the high school sample we find a low positive correlation between being female and being Committed to Home and Family ($r = 0.16$, $p < 0.01$). There is a marginally significant difference ($\chi^2 = 6.57$, $p < 0.05$) in the relative Commitment of male and female students to the Work and Home and Family roles, with males relatively more Committed to Work and females to the Home.

We found different results for a sample of higher education students from two large public universities in Florida and Maryland. The point-biserial correlation between gender and Commitment to Home equals only 0.14 ($p > 0.05$), whereas that between gender and Commitment to Work equals 0.30 ($p < 0.01$). Men and women in this subsample do not differ in their relative Commitment to Work as compared to Home and Family. Both genders have a greater Commitment to Home and Family than to Work. However, the women indicate more participation in Home and Family than do the college men.

These findings show an interesting progression from secondary to higher education. In the former sample, male students tend to exceed females in Work motivation, and the reverse is true for Homemaking. More advanced students would presumably include a higher percentage of women interested in a career than would a sample of secondary school students. In the same vein a larger proportion of university men would be expected to be affected by contemporary gender-role changes and be willing to endorse Home and Family as a valued part of their lives. Hawley and Even (1982) found that as educational level increased from below secondary school to graduate school, men and women were more willing to endorse similar career development attitudes and behaviors. The changes in Commitment to Home and Work from the secondary to higher education samples for males and females are logical, agree with other evidence, and thus lend support to the validity of the SI.

The relative rankings of the five roles in comparing the three samples also show the validity of the SI (Nevill & Super, 1986a). Secondary school students rate Leisure as most important, Studying and Community Service as least, and Work and Home and Family in the middle. That Leisure tends to be important to younger students is not surprising, but the finding that Work appears to be more important than Studying is somewhat unexpected. Perhaps the students are in general not involved in their schoolwork, but view it as a means to getting a job or becoming an adult. Secondary school study may be something people do when they have to.

By the years of higher education subjects list Participation in Leisure Activities as important, but the maturing of role values is evident in the greater affect (Commitment and Value Expectations) given to Work and to Home and Family, with only moderate emphasis on Leisure. Participation in Studying tends also to be high, as would be expected because the more serious students go beyond secondary school. Community Service tends again to rank as least important.

The central responsibilities of the adult years, Work and Home, are evident in the high rankings for these roles. Although increasing numbers of people spend more time in the Work setting than at Home, Commitment to and Value Expectations in Home and Family tend to outrank Work. Leisure is of only moderate importance, followed, as might be expected, by Study and Community Service. These trends appear consistent with developmental changes.

Yates (1985a) finds similar results for adults in his WIS study of 321 students enrolled in an off-campus adult-education university-degree program conducted by a major midwestern university. He finds the expected gender-role, marital status, and age differences. Women show a greater Participation in Home and Family Activities, maintain a stronger Commitment to Work, to Community Affairs, and to the Home and Family, and seek greater Satisfaction from activities related to the Community and to the Home and Family than do men. Married respondents indicate a greater Participation in, a stronger Commitment to, and place greater value on Home and Family Activities than do the unmarried respondents. Conversely, unmarried respondents indicate greater Participation in Leisure pursuits, a greater Commitment to Community and Leisure Activities, and seek greater satisfaction from their involvement in Community and Leisure Activities than do married respondents. The youngest age group, 17 to 25, Participates the most in Leisure Activities, is the most Committed to them, and indicates the strongest Leisure-related Value Expectations.

Ellermann and Johnston (1988) also find the expected differences with the WIS scales between female seniors who were in traditional academic majors (special education, nursing, and home economics) and those in nontraditional academic majors (premedicine, engineering, and business). Women in nontraditional majors are significantly less Committed to Home and Family. Richardson (1974), although not using the SI, had previously found similar differences.

The interscale correlations also show the validity of the SI. In the norming sample of 3,347 secondary school students the correlations between the Participation and Commitment scales are 0.76 for Study, 0.53 for Work, 0.76 for Community, 0.63 for Home and Family, and 0.70 for Leisure Activities. The correlations between Participation and the less instrumentally contaminated Value Expectations scales are 0.64, 0.43, and 0.66 for Home and Family and 0.70 for Leisure Activities. The correlations between Participation and the less instrumentally contaminated Value Expectations scales are 0.64, 0.43, 0.66, 0.57, and 0.63, respectively. The correlations between the Commitment and Value Expectations scales are 0.77, 0.72, 0.81, 0.77, and 0.79, respectively. Both the Commitment scale and the Value Expectations scale measure Commitment. Thus they are theoretically similar but use a different format. The Participation scale is theoretically different from the other two scales. The two scales (Commitment and Value Expectations) that are theoretically more similar are more highly intercorrelated than Commitment and Value Expectations are to the third variable, Participation, which is theoretically different. Similar relationships hold for the university and adult samples. The findings are good evidence for both the convergent and the divergent validity of the scales.

The Salience Inventory: Research

One primary use of the Salience Inventory has been to assess the relative importance of various roles and their relationship to other variables. A series of research projects has looked extensively at such variables as career maturity, socioeconomic status, gender, and educational level.

Subjects in these studies were 204 secondary school students drawn from three schools in central New Jersey (Super & Nevill, 1984) and 446 higher education students from two large public universities in Florida and Maryland (Nevill & Super, 1988). Approximately half the subjects were women. The researchers attempted to obtain a diverse socioeconomic representation, but subsequent analyses show that the higher socioeconomic levels were as usual overrepresented in the university group. We used the Career Development Inventory (Super, Thompson, Lindeman, Jordaan, & Myers, 1981) to measure career maturity.

Work Commitment shows a significant relationship to career maturity. However, the developmentally less advanced individual components of career maturity show an interesting progression. In the younger group Work Commitment relates to the attitudinal variables but not to the cognitive variables. For these students the world of work seems remote, especially to those anticipating further education and to those whose careers seem less likely to be determined to a great extent by the opportunity structure.

However, in the secondary education group Work Commitment relates to all the career maturity variables except knowledge of preferred occupation. Job exploration has already begun in this developmentally more advanced group. They have explored in breadth, for they know about the world of work. However, they have not yet begun exploration in depth of specific careers: they do not yet know much about their preferred occupation. Thus when the developmental task is appropriate, work importance is relevant to the cognitive as well as the attitudinal aspects of career maturity.

Gender is only minimally related to career maturity, with female students showing a higher level of career maturity on its cognitive aspects. However, this early cognitive development might not be an advantage: women may make career decisions prematurely without realistic information about the world of work or sufficient knowledge of themselves. Women students may know something about educational requirements (Jordaan & Heyde, 1979) or what is appropriate gender-role or social class occupational behavior (Gottfredson, 1981), but they know little about the occupational structure or the nature of a particular job. For example, they might select an occupation more for its gender-role appropriateness than because they have tested and matched their vocational options with their continually evolving self-concepts. The finding that women have already limited themselves to a narrow vocational field by the time they are freshmen in college (Harmon, 1981) supports this notion.

That the early cognitive development of women might not be an advantage is supported by our subsequent canonical correlations of the data. In the secondary school sample, female students who are career committed are more vocationally mature than other females or than males, regardless of level of career commitment. However, the higher education sample shows no such distinction. Highly committed men and women show similar levels of career maturity.

Gender affects role salience. Secondary school females are more often committed to home than to work, but males show the opposite pattern. They are more committed to work than to home. However, female college students express more commitment to both work and home than do men. The former is an unexpected finding, given prevailing gender-role stereotypes, and may show the effects of the increased role of women in the workplace. However, female higher education students do not expect to realize more values through work than do the men, although they are more committed to work than the men are, which perhaps is a manifestation of realism in their views of opportunities for women.

Hackett and Betz (1981) have proposed a women's career development model that might throw some light on female college students' expectations for work. Using Bandura's 1977 concept of self-efficacy expectations, they proposed that women, as a result of their socialization, "lack strong expectations of personal efficacy in relationship to many career-related behaviors and thus fail to fully realize their capabilities and talents in career pursuits" (p. 326). Although our female sample is more committed to the Work role than the males are, these women do not see work as an outlet for realizing personal values to the same extent that men do. Thus the higher levels of work commitment by women may be more related to meeting personal needs, or they may instead reflect awareness of limited opportunities in non-traditional fields.

Women's tendency to be highly involved and responsible is particularly shown by the variables related to home, but this too may be realism rather than actual preference, acceptance of the traditional division of labor. University women not only participate more in home activities but also are more committed to them and expect to realize more values there than do their male peers.

The finding that work commitment is directly related to career maturity has important implications for career development theorists and practitioners. Knowing how important work is to an individual is essential in assessing readiness for career decision making. If work and career are not important, scores on vocational interest inventories have relatively little permanent meaning; they may be useful for guiding exploration but not for decision making. Career counseling in that situation must aim at either making work more meaningful through exploration of work life (as in biography) as well as occupations or in addressing ways in which such individuals can meet their needs through different life roles. Sundal-Hansen (1985) has called for a more holistic approach to career counseling that focuses on the interrelationship of the Work role and the other roles of life. As proposed by Super's Career Development Assessment and Counseling Model (C-DAC, 1983), role importance is an essential ingredient in truly developmental counseling. However, much additional substantial research on role importance and on its relationship with educational, vocational, and homemaking behavior at various age and social levels is needed.

Conclusion

The most exciting national use for the data obtained in the WIS is career counseling using the C-DAC; Super and his colleagues in the Counseling Center at the University of Georgia and others in a growing list of institutions have experimented with it. The C-DAC is a unique process, because it addresses several areas that have been left untapped in previous models:

1. It asks how mature this client is in attitudes toward work and careers— How much planning does this person do, how inquisitive is this person?
2. It ascertains how much the client knows about the stages of an occupational career, the structure and functioning of the world of work, occupational requirements and opportunities, and career decision making.
3. It asks what value the client places on work and on an occupational career, and what part these play in comparison with leisure, homemaking, and roles in self-realization and self-fulfillment.
4. Given the current picture of the individual's aspirations, interests, values,

and aptitudes, it asks how stable these factors are likely to be during the next three, five, or ten years.

5.   It asks how well clients understand their current life stage, its place in their career development, and the developmental tasks with which they must cope now and will need to cope in the future.

6.   It explores what steps clients might take in coping with current career (vocational, homemaking, study, leisure, civic, etc.) tasks in order best to ensure long-term satisfaction in work and other life activities.

7.   It asks which of the life roles the client might play, how the client might combine them, and how the client might prepare for them in order to have a self-fulfilling life career.

As with many assessment models, the first step is a preview of what is to come. The initial step is to review the client's records, interview the individual, and make a counseling plan based on a preliminary assessment. The next step is an in-depth study of the relative importance of work to the client, the values that the client hopes to realize through the worker role, and the client's readiness to assess her or his abilities and interests and to make self- and occupational matching decisions. Only when the client has obtained and assimilated this information does it appear reasonable to begin looking at the individual's level of abilities and field of interests. In assessment of the data and joint review sessions the emphasis is on helping the client understand the implications of the material and in developing a plan of action. Only when the client has obtained this information does planning begin in terms of the individual's level of abilities or field of interests. In addition to the Salience Inventory and the Values Scale, other instruments, specially developed for answering the questions raised in developmental counseling, are available: the Career Development Inventory (CDI, Super et al., 1979, 1981) and the Adult Career Concerns Inventory (ACCI, Super, Thompson, Lindeman, Myers, & Jordaan, 1986), both of which assess career stages and maturity or adaptability. Super (1990) elaborates further on the developmental assessment model for career counseling.

A typical career-counseling series might begin by sharing with the individual or group an understanding of the normal (but not invariable) sequence and nature of life stages and of the life space, perhaps using the analogy of the Life-Career Rainbow (Super, 1980). Then the counselor could discuss a sample CDI or ACCI profile in group counseling, or the individual's own profile in counseling interviews, and help the client to see where he or she is in the life cycle, in coping with career development tasks. After this, the counselor can consider what the individual seeks in pursuing a career, now and in the future, and use the SI to help the client to focus on life roles and the VS to direct attention to what the individual seeks to attain in those roles. The counselor might encourage the client to consider typical role and value changes that come with increasing age and experience in order to broaden the client's perspectives and to extend the client's horizons. Finally, the counselor can bring these developmental data to bear on the results of interest inventories, aptitude batteries, and discussion of educational, occupational, and familial objectives, to help the client attain them.

The C-DAC model is being taught in many university graduate programs in counseling, at a few counseling centers experimenting with innovative methods, and in workshops and seminars organized at the conventions of professional associations and on various campuses by some of the test authors and their colleagues.

References

Allport, G. W., & Vernon, P. E. (1931). *Study of Values* (1st ed.). Boston: Houghton Mifflin.

Allport, G. W., Vernon, P. E., & Lindzey, G. (1960). *Study of values* (3rd ed.). Chicago: Riverside Press.

Astin, H. S. (1984). The meaning of work in women's lives: A sociopsychological model of career choice and work behavior. *Counseling Psychologist, 12,* 117–126.

Baltes, P. B., & Brim, O. G., Jr. (Eds.). (1983). *Life-span development and behavior* (vol. 5). San Diego, CA: Academic Press.

Baltes, P. B., & Schaie, K. W. (Eds.). (1973). *Life-span developmental psychology: Personality and socialization.* San Diego, CA: Academic Press.

Bandura, A. (1977). Self-efficacy: Toward a unifying theory of behavioral change. *Psychological Review, 84,* 191–215.

Centers, R. (1949). *The psychology of social classes.* Princeton, NJ: Princeton University Press.

Cooper, C. L., & Mumford, E. (1979). *The quality of working life in western and eastern Europe.* London: Associated Business Press.

Ellermann, N. C., & Johnston, J. (1988). Perceived life roles and locus of control differences of women pursuing nontraditional and traditional academic majors. *Journal of College Student Development, 29,* 142–146.

Gordon, L. V. (1960). *Survey of interpersonal values.* Chicago: Science Research Associates.

Gordon, L. V. (1964, 1965). *Survey of personal values.* Chicago: Science Research Associates.

Gottfredson, L. S. (1981). Circumscription and compromise: A developmental theory of occupational aspirations. *Journal of Counseling Psychology, 28,* 545–579.

Hackett, G., & Betz, N. E. (1981). A self-efficacy approach to the career development of women. *Journal of Vocational Behavior, 18,* 326–339.

Harmon, L. W. (1981). The life and career plans of young adult college women: A follow-up study. *Journal of Counseling Psychology, 28,* 416–427.

Hawley, P., & Even, B. (1982). Work and sex-role attitudes in relation to education and other characteristics. *Vocational Guidance Quarterly, 31,* 101–108.

Hofstede, G. H. (1980). *Culture's consequences: International differences in work-related values.* Newbury Park, CA: Sage.

Holland, J. L. (1985). *Making vocational choices: A theory of vocational personalities and work environments* (2nd ed.). Englewood Cliffs, NJ: Prentice-Hall.

Johansson, C. B., & Webber, P. L. (1976). *Temperament and values inventory.* Minneapolis, MN: National Computer Systems.

Jordaan, J. P., & Heyde, M. B. (1979). *Vocational maturity in the high school years.* New York: Teachers College Press.

Korman, A. K. (1969). Self-esteem as a moderator in vocational choice: Replications and extensions. *Journal of Applied Psychology, 53,* 188–192.

Levinson, D. J. (1978). *The seasons of a man's life.* New York: Ballantine.

Lowenthal, M. F., Thurnher, M., & Chiriboga, D. (1975). *Four stages of life: A comparative study of women and men facing transitions.* San Francisco: Jossey-Bass.

Meaning of Work (MOW)—International Research Team (1987). *The meaning of working.* San Diego, CA: Academic Press.

Nevill, D. D. (1985, September). Sex, socioeconomic status, role importance, and career maturity in secondary and higher education students in the USA. In D. E. Super (Chair), *Values, life roles, and vocational choice: Some results and implications of the Work Importance Study.* Symposium conducted at the meeting of the International Association of Educational and Vocational Guidance, Dubrovnik.

Nevill, D. D. (1988, January). Results of the Work Importance Study. In D. E. Super (Chair), *Work and other roles for self-realization.* Talk given at the meetings of the National Career Development Association, Orlando, Florida.

Nevill, D. D., & Damico, S. (1978). The influence of occupational status on role conflict in women. *Journal of Employment Counseling, 15,* 55–61.

Nevill, D. D., & Perrotta, J. M. (1985). Adolescent perceptions of work and home in Australia, Portugal, and the U.S.A. *Journal of Cross-Cultural Psychology, 16,* 483–495.

Nevill, D. D., & Super, D. E. (1986a). *The Salience Inventory: Theory, application, and research* (Manual). Palo Alto, CA: Consulting Psychologists Press.

Nevill, D. D., & Super, D. E. (1986b). *The Values Scale: Research, development, and use* (Manual). Palo Alto, CA: Consulting Psychologists Press.

Nevill, D. D., & Super, D. E. (1988). Career maturity and commitment to work in university students. *Journal of Vocational Behavior, 32,* 139–151.

Richardson, M. S. (1974). The dimensions of career and work orientation in college women. *Journal of Vocational Behavior, 5,* 161–172.

Rokeach, M. (1973). *The Nature of Human Values.* New York: Free Press.

Ronen, S. A. (1979). A cross-national study of employee's work-goals. *International Review of Applied Psychology, 28,* 1–12.

Rounds, J. B., Henley, G. A., Dawis, R. V., Lofquist, L. H., & Weiss, D. J. (1981). *Manual for the Minnesota Importance Questionnaire.* Minneapolis: University of Minnesota, Department of Psychology.

Sundal-Hansen, L. S. (1985). Work-family linkages: Neglected factors in career guidance across cultures. *Vocational Guidance Quarterly, 33,* 202–212.

Super, D. E. (1970). *The Work Values Inventory.* Boston: Houghton Mifflin.

Super, D. E. (1973). The Work Values Inventory. In D. G. Zytowski (Ed.), *Contemporary approaches to interest measurement.* Minneapolis: University of Minneapolis Press.

Super, D. E. (1980). A life-span, life-space approach to career development. *Journal of Vocational Behavior, 16,* 282–298.

Super, D. E. (1983). Assessment in career guidance: Toward truly developmental counseling. *Personnel and Guidance Journal, 61,* 555–562.

Super, D. E. (1990). A life-span, life-space approach to career development. In D. L. Brown, L. Brooks, & Associates (Eds.), *Career choice development: Applying contemporary theories to practice.* (2nd ed.). San Francisco: Jossey-Bass.

Super, D. E., Mastie, M., & Nevill, D. D. (1984). *The effects of separate packaging and time intervals on the intercorrelations of seemingly similar test scales.* Unpublished manuscript.

Super, D. E., & Nevill, D. D. (1984). Work role salience as a determinant of career maturity in high school students. *Journal of Vocational Behavior, 25,* 30–44.

Super, D. E., & Nevill, D. D. (1986a). *The Salience Inventory.* Palo Alto, CA: Consulting Psychologists Press.

Super, D. E., & Nevill, D. D. (1986b). *The Values Scale.* Palo Alto, CA: Consulting Psychologists Press.

Super, D. E., & Thompson, A. S. (1979). A six-scale, two-factor test of vocational maturity. *Vocational Guidance Quarterly, 27,* 6–15.

Super, D. E., & Thompson, A. S., Lindeman, R. H., Jordaan, J. P., & Myers, R. A. (1979, 1981). *The Career Development Inventory, school and college forms.* Palo Alto, CA: Consulting Psychologists Press.

Super, D. E., Thompson, A. S., Lindeman, R. H., Myers, R. A., & Jordaan, J. P. (1986). *Adult Career Concerns Inventory.* Palo Alto, CA: Consulting Psychologists Press.

Task Force on Work in America. (1973). *Work in America.* Cambridge, MA: MIT Press.

Terkel, S. (1972). *Working.* New York: Random House.

Vondracek, R. W., Lerner, R. M., & Schulenberg, J. E. (1986). *Career development: A life-span developmental approach.* Hillsdale, NJ: Erlbaum.

Walberg, H. J. (1969). Physics, femininity, and creativity. *Developmental Psychology, 1,* 47–54.

Yates, L. (1985a). *The Salience Inventory: Assessment of adults involved in career development.* Unpublished manuscript.

Yates, L. (1985b). *The Values Scale: Assessment of adults involved in career development.* Unpublished manuscript.

Yogev, S., & Brett, J. (1985). Patterns of work and family involvement among single- and dual-earner couples. *Journal of Applied Psychology, 70,* 754–768.

PART THREE

Cross-National and Topical Studies

Having described the status of theory and of research on work values and role salience in Part One, and the methods and findings of the WIS projects in eleven countries in Europe, Africa, North America, and Asia in Part Two, we now take up in Part Three the cross-national aspects of the Work Importance Study. This is therefore the heart of our project, the report on the International Work Importance Study.

The studies reported in this part fall into two major categories. The first might be described as macroanalyses. The second group consists of microanalyses. In this first category are studies of the universality or stability of the factor structure of values and roles, of age as contrasted with generational differences, and of the clustering of countries in geocultural regions. In the second category are the topical studies, which take up questions of special interest; the available material limited the analyses to a small number of countries that pooled data for cross-national analysis. Here we deal with such topics as the relationships of values and role commitment, the agreement of diary-recorded time use and Salience Inventory Participation scores, the differences between earlier and more recent immigrants from Cuba to the United States (Why did the latter value work more than the former?), the validity of the WIS model of the importance of life roles, the similarities and differences of Belgian Flemish women and American women from the Deep South, and the complex relationships between participation in and commitment to major life roles in New World and Old World countries.

The findings of these topical studies relate in complex and overlapping ways to those of the major cross-national analyses. We leave to the reader and to future research the task of sorting out and explaining the agreements and paradoxes.

SIXTEEN

The Structure and Hierarchy
of Values Viewed Cross-Nationally

Branimir Šverko

It is widely believed that there are marked national differences in a number of psychological characteristics. This holds in particular for values, because the existence of national value patterns is considered almost self-evident. However, although some studies support this truism (e.g., Engel, 1988; Hofstede, 1980; Peck, 1975), they are rare and not definitive. Because of a number of methodological problems, the exceedingly difficult task of identifying and understanding the national patterns of values remains an uncompleted endeavor that requires more systematic evidence. In an attempt to contribute to such evidence, we undertook a cross-national comparison of the WIS Values Scale data from ten countries. The cross-national comparison includes the factor structure of values, and the importance level of different values, analyzed both in terms of the mean value scores and value hierarchies.

The purpose of the analyses was to determine national differences in values and to identify the specific value patterns, if any, in each of the ten countries. We also studied cross-cultural similarities, using a cluster analysis of the values data to identify and analyze the clusters of countries that share similar patterns of values.

Countries, Samples, and Procedures

The analyses presented here examine and compare the value patterns we find in the samples of the ten countries participating fully in the Work Importance Study: Australia, Belgium (Flanders), Canada, Croatia, Italy, Japan, Poland, Portugal, South Africa, and the United States. Israel was omitted because its WIS study used the preliminary version of the Values Scale, which is not suitable for comparison.

Table 16.1 presents the samples from each country that we included in the analysis. Details concerning the sampling procedures, description of the samples, and other methodological information appear in the corresponding national chapters. We should note that in making the cross-national comparisons we collapsed the different secondary school grades into one secondary school sample from each country.

The cross-national analyses used value scores derived from the three-item, eighteen-value international version of the WIS Values Scale. It is described in Chapter Four and in some of the national chapters. Some of our cross-national analyses used the mean score data computed and distributed by the WIS national teams, whereas others started from the original individual scores. The latter analyses, however, had to be restricted to those countries that provided the original data on tapes or diskettes.

The Structure of Values: A Cross-National Comparison

The basic structure of values is generally assumed to be universal. Although studies have supported this assumption (e.g., Ronen, 1979; Šverko, 1987), proving its general validity requires much more evidence. In addition, the cross-national comparison of factor structure is an important methodological step of every cross-cultural study, because the similarity of factor structures is a prerequisite for cross-national comparison of average levels of characteristics. Unless it can be shown that the basic structure of values does not vary across nations, the cross-national comparison of their value importance (i.e., of average scores or rankings) is not fully justified.

The following questions arise from the cross-national analysis of the factor structure of values:

1. Do similar factors underlie values in different nations?
2. What is the degree of congruence among them?
3. Is the generally assumed universality of the factor structure of values confirmed?

Identification of Value Factors

Before we analyzed factor structures in different countries, we determined a general factor structure for the global, across-the-countries pooled sample. This included all subjects from the samples for which we had the original scores from all eighteen cross-national values scales. The total number of subjects in this pooled sample analysis is 18,318. We intercorrelated their scores from the eighteen values scales and submitted the resulting matrix of product moment correlations to principal components analysis, with ones in the diagonal. Five principal components with eigenvalues in excess of one (which explained 59.4 percent of the total variance) were rotated orthogonally in accordance with the Varimax criterion. Appendix A.2 shows the obtained matrix of rotated factor loadings.

The five factors that appeared in the pooled sample analysis were also found in the detailed sample-by-sample analyses, in which we explore factor

Table 16.1. Countries and Samples Used in the Cross-National Analyses.

Country	*Samples and the Number of Subjects*		
	Secondary School	*Higher Education*	*Adults*
Australia	1,251*	181*	90*
Belgium (Flanders)	313*	148*	643*
Canada			
English-Canadians	2,340	623	5,160
French-Canadians	774		1,222
Italy	2,168*	831*	
Japan	834	371	750
Poland		252	
Portugal	2,357*	580	136
South Africa			
English-speaking	1,652*		
Afrikaans-speaking	1,343*		
African language– speaking	1,230*		
United States	2,816	1,862*	1,686*
Croatia	1,871*	348*	344*

Note: Asterisks denote samples for which original data were available. The displayed *n* may be smaller than the number of subjects tested, because only subjects with a complete record for all variables were used.

The Australian secondary school sample comprised the subjects of the Australian stages III and V.

The Portuguese adult sample is the preliminary study sample. The Canadian higher education sample included both English- and French-Canadians.

structure across the countries. We analyzed nineteen samples from seven countries: nine secondary school samples (Australia, Croatia, Belgian Flanders, Italy, Portugal, the United States, and three South African samples), six higher education samples (Australia, Croatia, Belgian Flanders, Italy, Portugal, and the United States), and four adult samples (Australia, Croatia, Belgian Flanders, and the United States). We used the principal components method followed by Varimax rotation in all analyses, having predetermined the criterion for the number of factors to be extracted: we retained five factors for rotation in each analysis (this in almost all cases corresponds to the number of significant factors according to the "eigenvalue one" criterion). Depending on the sample, the five extracted factors explain 53.8 percent to 65.6 percent of the total variance.

An examination of the nineteen rotated factor matrixes (which for reasons of space we do not give here) reveals the presence of factors more or less similar to the pooled sample factors in all individual samples. This is evident from the data added to the factor matrix in Appendix A.2; the numbers in parentheses represent the frequencies of salient factor loadings, showing a given number of times, in the nineteen analyses, that each value loads saliently (above 0.50) on each factor. With a few exceptions, the salient-loading frequencies for each factor are distributed among several values that also obtain the most salient loadings in the pooled sample analysis.

The five manifested factors may be conceived of as value orientations; some of the national chapters already have attempted to interpret them.

The first factor, Utilitarian Orientation (Ut), is defined by five largely extrinsic values (Economics, Advancement, Prestige, Authority, and Achievement) that stress the importance of economic conditions and material career progress. This factor appears to be quite constant across all samples.

The second factor, Orientation Toward Self-Actualization (sA), is defined primarily by Ability Utilization, Personal Development, and Altruism, although Achievement, Aesthetics, and Creativity also have salient loadings in some samples. All the values are inner-oriented goals important in personal development and self-realization.

The third factor is Individualistic Orientation (In); some national teams preferred the label Independence Orientation. Defined primarily by Life-Style and Autonomy, this factor stresses the importance of an autonomous way of living. Creativity and Variety appear also to be saturated with this factor in a few samples.

The fourth factor, Social Orientation (So), is defined primarily by Social Interaction and Social Relations, the two group-oriented values. In some sample loadings on this factor include Variety and Altruism.

Tentatively labeled Adventurous Orientation (Av), some national teams preferred to call the fifth factor Challenge. It is defined primarily by Risk, although in some samples Physical Activity and Authority have some projections on this factor.

Factor Congruence Across the Samples

A visual inspection of the rotated factor matrixes reveals similar factor structure across the samples. However, although we identified well-matched factors exhibiting similar patterns of loadings in all samples, there were some exceptions. Thus the pattern of loadings characteristic of the sA factor does not appear in the Flemish adult sample, the In pattern does not appear in either the Portuguese or the U.S. higher education sample, and we do not find the Av pattern in the Australian higher education sample. Even where we identified the matched factors, their pattern of loadings shows some differences, indicating that the factor structures are similar but not identical. To determine the degree of similarity, we computed coefficients of congruence among the factors obtained in different samples.

As an index of factorial similarity, the coefficient of congruence has interpretative features similar to the correlation coefficient: it ranges from −1.0 to 1.0 (perfect congruence, indicating identical factors), with zero representing no similarity. Customarily, the values of 0.80 or higher have been required to indicate factorial similarity or invariance.

We computed the coefficients of congruence between all possible pairs of samples for each of the five factors. Because it is not possible to display all the coefficients we obtained, Appendix A.3 gives only the factor congruence summary data. Two indexes of congruence appear in the first two rows for each factor: percentage of coefficients of congruence that are below 0.80, and the mean congruence coefficient computed from all between-sample coefficients for a given factor.

The factor of Utilitarian Orientation (Ut) exhibits a high degree of factorial congruence across the samples: of the 171 between-sample congruence coefficients computed for this factor, *none* is below 0.80, and their mean is 0.93, which indicates a high degree of factorial invariance. Individualistic Orientation (In) also appears to be a highly congruent factor, with only a few between-sample coefficients below 0.80 and with a relatively high mean congruence coefficient too. However, the data we obtained for Social Orientation (So), Self-Actualization (sA), and Adventurous Orientation (Av) indicate a relatively low degree of congruence across the samples.

An examination of the individual between-sample coefficients reveals the samples responsible for the greatest part of factor incongruence. These are the higher education samples from Australia, Belgium (Flanders), Portugal, and the United States, and adult samples from Australia, Croatia, Belgium (Flanders), and the United States, all of which obtained relatively low congruence coefficients. To check for this observation, we attempted a breakdown by type of sample in the analysis of congruence; that is, we calculated congruence coefficients only among samples of the same type. Appendix A.3 also presents the mean congruence coefficients for each of the three groups of samples. Both the higher education and adult samples disclose scanty congruences, acceptable for Ut and In factors but insufficient for the remaining three factors. On the other hand, the secondary school samples evidence sufficient congruence for all factors: their mean congruence coefficients are high, and they had only three (out of thirty-six) coefficients below 0.80 for the Av factor and none (out of 144) for the remaining four factors.

The differences in factor congruence are not easy to understand. It is possible that, for a number of reasons, the youngsters in secondary schools worldwide are more alike in their understanding of the meaning of different values than are older segments of the population. The reasons for this may be the similar preoccupations of young people, their adherence to the same models, and so on. However, before we speculate, we should note some of the methodological difficulties we encountered. Both the higher education and adult samples were more or less samples of convenience in most countries, somewhat lacking in comparability in terms of background demographic factors. Besides, all the samples, with the exception of the American one, were relatively small. Thus it is possible that their low congruence may be partly the result of intergroup differences and sampling errors. The secondary school samples, on the other hand, were methodologically better founded, representative of the respective populations in most countries and large enough to produce a stable factor structure.

This suggests a greater reliability of the secondary school data. With respect to these data it is reasonable to conclude that similar factors underlie values in the national samples compared, with a high degree of mutual congruence. We conclude that the data support the assumed universality of the factor structure of values.

Importance of Values in Different Countries

According to the prevailing conceptualizations of values (e.g., Locke, 1976; Rokeach, 1973; Super, 1970), the dimension of importance is basic to a theory of values. Therefore, one purpose of a study of values is to compare the importance of different values across groups of people. Two approaches may be used in this comparison. One is "ipsative": the mean scores of each group are ranked on a set of values to obtain a hierarchy of values for each group, and the resulting hierarchies are then compared. The other approach is "normative": the mean row scores obtained by different groups, or their standard scores if norms are available, are compared for each value scale. Because the two approaches do not necessarily yield similar results, we used both in our cross-national analysis.

Comparison of Value Hierarchies

The value hierarchy—the rank order of importance of the eighteen values—for each sample appears in Appendix A.4. Each hierarchy was constituted from sample mean scores on eighteen values scales. The arrangement of values in Appendix A.4, from left to right, reflects an overall hierarchy based on the median ranks, as shown in the bottom row.

Notable agreement exists among the value hierarchies: for example, Personality Development, Ability Utilization, and Achievement are ranked high in most samples, whereas Risk and Authority rank lowest in almost all samples. Although the extremely ranked values are scarcely distinguishable among the samples, some other values show marked patterns of difference, as inspecting the rankings by column reveals. For example, Social Relations is the first-ranked value for the Flemish secondary school students, whereas Afrikaans-speaking subjects rank it very low, in sixteenth place. Advancement is ranked third by the U.S. secondary school students, whereas two Japanese samples place the least importance on this value. Such examples show that, despite some general similarity among the national value hierarchies, some specific national patterns of values may exist. We will use normative comparisons to explore them more thoroughly.

Normative Comparisons

For normative comparisons, we first computed the overall means and standard deviations for all values, as shown in the bottom two rows of Appendix A.1. They were computed as weighted means and combined distribution standard deviations from the means and standard deviations of all samples. We then converted the individual sample means to standard scores or z scores; that is, we subtracted a corresponding overall mean from each sample mean and divided the difference by the overall standard deviation. Thus, the resulting z scores, which are given in Appendix A.5, represent the deviations of the sample means from the overall means in standard deviation units.

The z scores are easily interpretable; the presence or absence of a negative sign shows whether a particular sample is low or high on given value. It is important to understand that the z scores do not convey ipsative information—they do not reveal the importance of a value with respect to the importance of other values. Instead, they reveal the relative standing of a sample with respect to the overall sample on each value. This means that the z scores yield normative information, and thus the samples or countries can be analyzed successively, one by one.

As we continue the discussion, we will try to discern the distinctive value pattern of each country by identifying the values standing high and low in each country. We declared as the high or low values characterizing a country's value pattern only those values that obtained above-average (positive z score) or below-average (negative z score) positions in all samples representing that country.

The comparison of the mean z scores reveals quite large differences between the samples from different countries, with the extreme differences for each value being greater than one standard deviation. We have taken into consideration the significance of differences. We performed an analysis of variance followed by Scheffé t-test comparisons for each of the eighteen values. We obtained very high F tests (ranging from 35 to 334; all significant at $p < 0.0001$), indicating that the samples differ significantly on each value. A posteriori t-test comparisons reveal that significant differences exist between most samples; in any case, each sample that is accepted as standing high on a particular value is significantly different from each sample viewed as standing low on that value.

In addition to making comparisons at the individual values level, we compared the samples on the factor scores level. In the latter analyses, we estimated the scores on each of the five factors and then averaged across the subjects of each sample. The resulting mean factor scores appear in Appendix A.6; we use them to summarize the insights into "national" value patterns based primarily on the individual value z scores. (The footnote for Figure 16.1 explains the codes to which we refer in discussing specific subsamples from each country.)

Australia

All Australian samples are above average on Life-style (freedom to live according to personal standards and values) and Autonomy (responsibility for own actions, without undue interference from others). Both values have high projections on the In factor (Individualistic Orientation), and consequently the

Australian samples obtained high scores on that factor, as shown in Appendix A.6. On the other hand, Australians tend to be low on most other values, especially on Aesthetics, Creativity, Authority, Risk, and Working Conditions. The obtained value pattern conforms partly to a stereotypical picture of the independent-minded Aussie.

Belgium (Flanders)

The normative data in Appendix A.5 reveal that the Flemish samples score high on Aesthetics, Social Relations, and Social Interaction. The importance these subjects attach to Social Relations (which refers to friendly relationships and understanding among people) is also very high from the ipsative perspective. As Appendix A.4 shows, the B1 sample ranks this value first, and the other two samples rank it third. On the other hand, all Flemish samples score low on Achievement, Altruism, Authority, Economics, Physical Activity, and Prestige. On the factor score level, the data in Appendix A.6 generally reveal below-average utilitarianism (especially for the B2 sample) and self-actualization (especially for B1 and B3) orientations.

Canada

The two major groups in Canada, identified linguistically as Anglophones and Francophones, are represented in the Canadian WIS with separate samples at the secondary school and adult levels. However, we will ignore the differences in the two cultures and concentrate on the value characteristics that express similarities. All Canadian samples, both Anglophones (CE) and Francophones (CF), score consistently high on Authority, Economics, and Prestige; consequently, Appendix A.6 reveals their high standing on the Utilitarian Orientation factor. In addition, all Canadian samples score high on Social Relations, indicating a strong concern for good relationships and understanding among people. On the other hand, there is no single value on which all Canadian groups consistently score low: Anglophones tend to score low on Aesthetics and Creativity, and older Canadian groups tend to score low on Physical Activity, Risk, and Social Interaction.

Croatia

The Croatian samples score more highly on Altruism than the other national groups. They also score high on Social Relations and Aesthetics. They score low on Autonomy and Life-style, as well as on most utilitarian values, in particular on Authority and Prestige. Such results imply a nonmaterialistic, nonindividualistic, socially conscious value pattern.

Italy

Italy is represented only with the student samples, both of which score positively on Creativity, Personal Development, Autonomy, Life-style, and Social

Interaction. On the other hand, they score extremely low in their valuation of Economics, Advancement, Authority, Prestige, and Aesthetics. Consequently, their average factor scores in Appendix A.6 reveal a pronounced individualistic orientation (In factor) and an extremely low utilitarian orientation (Ut factor). Thus the Italian youth seem to exhibit a great concern for an autonomous life-style, with little interest in prestigious advancement and materialistic ends. We have no data on Italian adults.

Japan

The Japanese samples score above average on three values: Aesthetics, Creativity, and Risk. Their traditional regard for beauty also comes out in the ipsative comparisons: as Appendix A.4 shows, Aesthetics is ranked first by the secondary school sample (J1) and third and fourth by the university students (J2) and adults (J3), respectively. As Appendix A.5 shows, the Japanese samples score low on most of the other values, such as Advancement, Achievement, Economics, Authority, Prestige, Altruism, Social Interaction, Social Relations, Variety, and Working Conditions. They stand lowest of all national samples in their valuation of upward mobility and material values.

Poland

It is not possible to draw any general picture of the Polish value pattern, because Poland is represented here by only one sample, the university student sample. Polish university students place a strong emphasis on individualistic values (especially Life-style), expressing at the same time an extremely low interest in all utilitarian values (especially Advancement and Authority). At this stage we have no data on other segments of the Polish population.

Portugal

All Portuguese samples stand high on most of the self-actualization values (e.g., Ability Utilization, Personality Development, and Creativity). They also tend to be high on Achievement and Advancement. On the negative side, they stand lowest of all national groups on Prestige, and they score low on Authority and Economics. Thus for the Portuguese we may infer that they consider self-expression and personal creativity far more important than they do the external trappings of success.

South Africa

South Africa is represented only by secondary school subjects, divided into three subsamples primarily according to their principal native language: SAE1 represents the English-speaking subjects from European, Asian, and African cultures; SAA1 is the sample of Afrikaans-speaking subjects from both Western and mixed, so-called colored, cultures; and SAN1 represents the native population that speaks different indigenous South African languages but was tested with the English version of the WIS instruments. Although the value patterns of the three samples disclose some differences, they have many features in common. Thus, all samples express an above-average concern for all the utilitarian values (Achievement, Advancement, Authority, Economics, Prestige, and Working Conditions), resulting in very high scores on the Ut factor, as shown in Appendix A.6. All samples also score high on Aesthetics and Physical Activity. On the other hand, none of the South African samples attach much importance to Social Relations; they score lowest of all the countries on that value.

United States

The U.S. (American) samples score above the average on Advancement, Prestige, Authority, Life-style, and Autonomy. On the other hand, they tend to score low on Creativity and Aesthetics. On the factor level they are above average on the Utilitarian, Individualistic, and Adventurous orientations and below average on the Orientation Toward Self-Actualization. Taking them all together, the U.S. subjects seem to demonstrate a tendency toward a self-advancing pragmatic individualism, attaching little importance to the self-actualizing expression of aesthetic or intellectual originality.

The Hierarchical Clustering of Countries

The "national" value features we have summarized indicate that each country tends to create a pattern of values with a somewhat unique emphasis on what is important in life. At the same time, there are also notable cross-cultural similarities, especially in the hierarchies of values shown in Appendix A.4. The degree of similarity between any two national samples apparently varies, which raises the question of whether it is possible to cluster countries. Can we identify relatively homogeneous clusters of national samples that share similar patterns of values?

In order to study the agglomeration of national samples in relatively homogeneous groups according to their values, we performed a hierarchical cluster analysis with the Statistical Package for the Social Sciences (SPSS)/PC+ CLUSTER procedure (Norusis/SPSS, 1988) on the matrix of mean Values Scale scores. We considered the cluster solutions according to differing measures of sample similarity and differing methods of cluster formation. Differing solutions provide similar groupings of samples: in only a few cases are there shifts between clusters under different solutions. Therefore, we present only one solution here, that which uses Ward's method of cluster formation with squared Euclidean distances (the sum of the squared differences over all variables) as a measure of sample similarity. Figure 16.1 uses a dendrogram to present the resulting process of the agglomerative hierarchical clustering.

Figure 16.1 Dendrogram Showing the Hierarchical Clustering of Countries According to Their Values Scale Mean Scores.

Rescaled Distance Cluster Combine

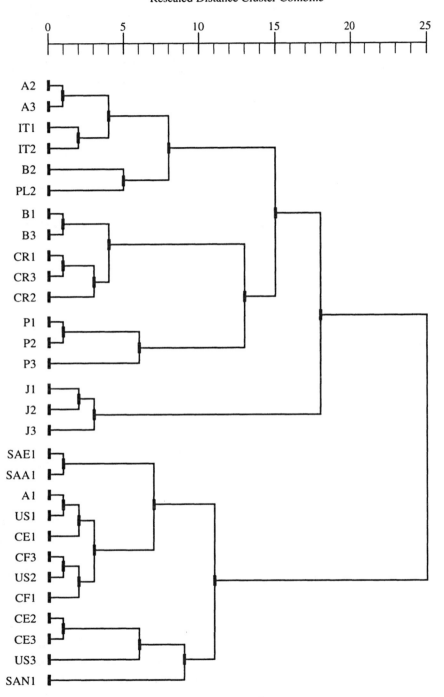

Note: A = Australia; B = Belgium; CE = English-Canadians; CF = French-Canadians; CR = Croatia; IT = Italy; J = Japan; P = Portugal; PL = Poland; SA = South Africa (SAE = English speaking, SAA = Afrikaans, SAN = Native South African languages); US = United States. Numbers 1, 2, and 3 denote secondary school, higher education, and adult samples. For example: A3 = Australian adult sample.

The dendrogram, which is to be read from left to right, shows the clusters being combined and the distances at which the elements combine, rescaled to values between 0 and 25. The distances indicate the similarity of the samples combined in the clusters: the samples that join earlier (i.e., at shorter distances) are more similar than the samples that combine later (at greater distances). Consequently, the clusters formed early are relatively more homogeneous than those that merge later, at a "higher" level of integration.

As our dendrogram reveals, the principal determinant of cluster formation is ethnic kinship: almost all clusters formed at lesser distances (under five) are of the same national origin. Thus, youths and adults from the same countries seem to be more alike than either age group is across different countries. Such an outcome supports our previously reported attempts to identify national patterns of values by treating all samples from a given country as one homogeneous group.

At a "higher" level of integration, all clusters agglomerate in three interpretable higher-order clusters of countries. Although the distances at which two clusters combine are fairly great, indicating that the clusters may not be very homogeneous, we nevertheless retained the three-cluster solution for our final interpretation, because it seems to correspond to three meaningful geocultural regions.

The first of the three higher-order clusters aggregates 14 samples: all of the Belgian (3), Croatian (3), Italian (2), Polish (1), and Portuguese (3) samples, as well as 2 Australian samples. Thus, with the exception of the last two samples, the clusters include all of the European samples we compared plus two of the predominantly European—Australian—samples.

The second of the three clusters combines 12 samples: all of the Canadian (5), U.S. (3), and South African (3) samples, as well as 1 Australian sample. They are all samples from the continents and countries originally settled by European immigrants in or after the sixteenth century. Because the North American (i.e., Canadian and U.S.) samples are preponderant in this cluster, we tentatively label it the New World Cluster.

The third cluster combines only the three Japanese samples. They merged early, at the low distance value, and remained an independent, nationally homogeneous cluster until the last stages of agglomerative clustering.

The results of agglomerative hierarchical clustering show that, with the exception of the Australian samples (which split and joined two different clusters), all national samples group logically and consistently in one of three meaningful geocultural agglomerations. Let us now examine their value scores to establish the characteristics they share, as well as those in which they differ.

To compare the clusters, we computed their unweighted mean scores on each value scale from the means of the samples composing each cluster. Figure 16.2 presents the cluster means obtained. Such a display makes it possible to compare the clusters in terms of their value hierarchies, as well as in terms of the mean importance assigned to each value. To facilitate later comparison we have drawn lines connecting the values and the clusters.

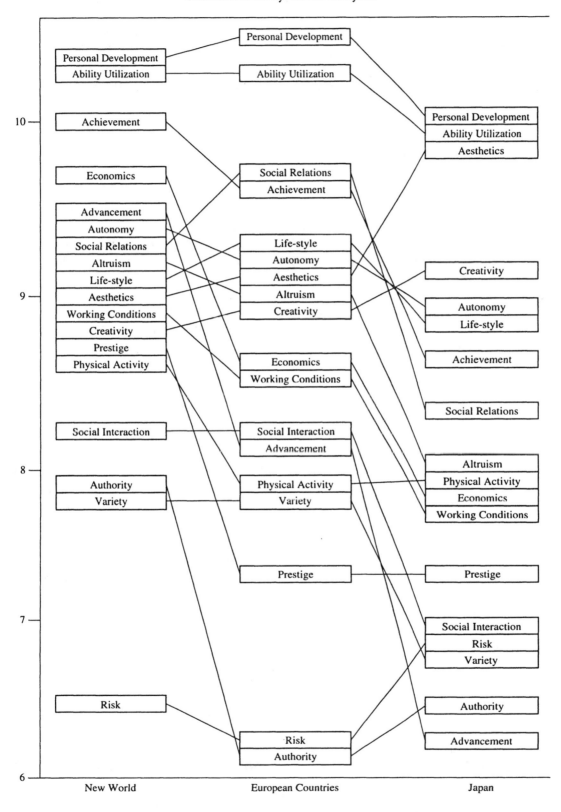

Figure 16.2. Value Hierarchies in the Three Geocultural
Units Identified by Cluster Analysis.

As Figure 16.2 indicates, the values of the three clusters exhibit some similarities but also a number of differences. The similarities are particularly marked in the value hierarchies: the top-ranked values (Personal Development and Ability Utilization) and low-ranked values (Authority, Risk, Variety, Prestige) occupy identical or similar positions in all three hierarchies. On the other hand, most values show more or less pronounced differences in importance ratings. They are easily recognized by the slopes of the lines connecting the values and the clusters: the higher the inclination, the greater the difference in value importance between members of the clusters connected by a line. A comparison of cluster values and an examination of the observed differences among them suggest several observations about their value patterns.

The New World hierarchy of values is characterized by a very high placement of Achievement, Economics, and Advancement. The three values, as well as the other two utilitarian values—Prestige and Authority—are considered much more important in New World countries than in the European countries or in Japan. The opposite is true of Creativity and Aesthetics: the New World countries give these two values relatively less importance. Thus the New World value pattern seems to imply a drive for upward mobility, material success, and prestige, with less emphasis on the less worldly aspects of life.

The European pattern of values emphasizes the importance of Social Relations: this value holds the third position in the European hierarchy, next to Personal Development and Ability Utilization, and it is rated as more important than in either of the remaining two clusters of samples. The Europeans also give relatively more importance to Life-style and Autonomy. On the lower end of the scale, the salient feature of the European pattern is the very low standing of Authority, the last value in the European hierarchy. Thus the distinguishing characteristics of the Europeans seem to be a high valuation of relationships and understanding among people, a tendency toward autonomous life-styles, and rejection of authority.

We described the Japanese pattern of values earlier. It is distinguished from the other two patterns primarily by a high valuation of Aesthetics and Creativity, the values that occupy the third and fourth ranks in the Japanese hierarchy. Another feature of the Japanese assessments is the underrating of most values, especially the utilitarian. As we already have noted, the Japanese samples stand lowest of all national samples in their valuation of upward mobility and material success.

Conclusion

Our attempt to identify and describe national patterns of values by analyzing national hierarchies and z-score data has been largely supported by the results of the cluster analysis. It has clearly shown that nationality, or country membership, is the primary factor in cluster formation, because most of the clusters that formed early are nationally homogeneous—they aggregate different groups (e.g., both students and adults) from the same country. Thus the results of our analyses seem to corroborate Peck's argument (1975) for the existence of distinctive national patterns of values that "confirm the assumption that each culture tends to create and perpetuate its own, partially unique emphases on what is important in life." (p. 132). However, our evidence for this assertion is more suggestive than conclusive, because of the limitations that characterize most cross-cultural studies.

The first limitation concerns the representativeness of the samples: a study of national characteristics should be based on the analysis of truly representative samples. Otherwise, what appear to be differences between two nations may be spurious findings that are the result of sample bias. The respective national chapters have described the methods of drawing the WIS samples. A review of the methods reveals that although some samples (largely of adults) in most countries could hardly be considered representative, other samples (chiefly secondary school samples) may be accepted as adequate for most countries. Besides, most countries are represented by three different samples, and we have declared as national characteristics only the value features that pertain to all: this is a substantial safeguard against any limitations of sample unrepresentativeness.

The second limitation concerns the equivalence of the Values Scale scores across the national groups we studied. Although its development in or adaptation to different countries was done with all necessary care, subtle semantic or syntactic differences may be responsible for the appearance of "national" differences. Is it perhaps possible that the clustering of the countries is simply an outcome of the linguistic similarity or dissimilarity of the inventory versions? Some results of the cluster analysis speak against this possibility: samples from the same geocultural regions join the same clusters despite the fact that respondents took the inventory versions in different languages (e.g., French- and English-Canadians, Afrikaans- and English-speaking South Africans). Also, as an indication of the equivalence of the VS scores across national groups, we tried to provide evidence for what has been termed the *dimensional identity* (Frijda & Jahoda, 1966) or *comparative dimensionality* (Eysenck & Eysenck, 1983) of the value scores. We examined the factor structure of the Values Scale cross-nationally to see whether congruent factors are identified in all countries. This proved to be the case, at least for the technically best (the secondary school) samples, which is an indication that the meaning of the VS scores tends to be similar in different cultures.

The third limitation concerns the stability of the value patterns. Some critics have noted that nations change and that their characteristics established in one period may not necessarily persist. In his analysis of "national" value patterns, Peck (1975) examined samples of urban children from seven countries taken twice, in 1965 and 1969. He found that most national patterns of values were stable across the samples taken four years apart. However, if we compare Peck's results with the findings of our study, we see little stability for each of the countries represented in both studies (i.e., Italy, Japan, and the United States): the values that received above- or below-average rank in the two studies (conducted about fifteen years apart) appear to be more different than similar. The disagreements might be the result of sampling bias, especially because we know that each of Peck's national samples consisted of urban children from only one town in each country. But we cannot rule out as a complementary explanation changes in value patterns over the observed period of time.

As this discussion implies, it is difficult to arrive at firm conclusions about national differences in values. But it is even more difficult to discount the national differences observed in the well-coordinated WIS studies. An attempt to account for the differences we find appears in Chapter Twenty-six.

References

Engel, J. W. (1988). Work values of American and Japanese men. *Journal of Social Behavior and Personality, 3,* 191–200.

Eysenck, H. J., & Eysenck, S. B. G. (1983). Recent advances in the cross-cultural study of personality. In J. N. Butcher & C. D. Spielberger (Eds.), *Advances in personality assessment* (Vol. 2). Hillsdale, NJ: Erlbaum.

Frijda, N., & Jahoda, G. (1966).On the scope and methods of cross-cultural research. *International Journal of Psychology, 1,* 109–127.

Hofstede, G. (1980). *Culture's consequences: International differences in work-related values.* Newbury Park, CA: Sage.

Locke, E. A. (1976). The nature and causes of job satisfaction. In M. D. Dunnette (Ed.), *Handbook of industrial and organizational psychology.* Skokie, IL: Rand McNally.

Norusis, M. J./Statistical Package for the Social Sciences (SPSS). (1988). *SPSS/PC+ Advanced Statistics V2.0 for the IBM PC/XT/AT and PC/2.* Chicago: SPSS.

Peck, F. R. (1975). Distinctive national patterns of career motivation. *International Journal of Psychology, 10,* 125–134.

Rokeach, M.(1973). *The nature of human values.* New York: Free Press.

Ronen, S. (1979). Cross-national study of employee's work goals. *International Review of Applied Psychology, 28,* 1–12.

Super, D. E. (1970). *The Work Values Inventory.* Boston: Houghton Mifflin.

Šverko, B. (1987). The structure of work values: A cross-national comparison. *Acta Instituti Psychologici Universitatis Zagrabiensis, 17,* 23–29.

SEVENTEEN

Values in a Cross-Cultural Perspective: A Further Analysis

Giancarlo Trentini
Giovanni Battista Muzio

That countries differ in many ways is simply a matter of everyday observation. To be more precise, these differences seem to explain the existence of the entities known as countries. This is particularly true of the "mentality" of their respective peoples, a complex of beliefs, habits, attitudes, values, norms, and specific behavior patterns attributed to them. For certain aspects at least, the issues with which we are confronted here are those of basic personality. The differences have been and continue to be explored in countless cross-cultural studies, particularly from the psychological, sociological, and anthropological standpoints.

The Work Importance Study (WIS) has made it possible to gather comparable data on the strength of value orientations in the following ten countries: Australia, Belgium (Flanders), Canada, Croatia, Italy, Japan, Poland, Portugal, South Africa, and the United States. Each country, considered as a whole, may present serious problems (the countries with a "federal" structure in particular) with regard to an unqualified acceptance of their unitary nature and sociocultural identity. However, having said this with heuristic intent, the use of *country* as a unit may be considered useful and acceptable here.

The comparability of the data gathered in the ten countries, with a measure of eighteen values, is based on three elements: the psychometric characteristics of the testing tool used, the comparability of the samples achieved in each country participating in the project, and the standardization of procedures used for processing the data.

Some doubt may remain regarding the possibility of studying "the same thing" in cultural contexts that are different from each other in important ways. We cannot ignore the semantic and conceptual problems in a study

The chapter authors acknowledge the collaboration of Massimo Bellotto, Maria Cristina Bolla, and Marisa Sangiorgi. All research work has been sponsored by SINTAGMA—Gruppo di Studio sulla Comunicazione, Ricerche e Interventi Psico-Sociali, Milan.

such as this, which is based on key terms that are complex both denotatively and connotatively. As described in Chapter Four, we were aware of these limits and worked within the framework of an operationalist perspective that was based on linguistic and methodological conventions accepted by the teams from the countries involved: that values can be defined in terms of the eighteen scales nationally or cross-nationally (identified in the first stages of the study) and that the most suitable method of measurement and analysis is a psychometric one.

The cluster analysis presented in Chapter Sixteen shows that nationality is the primary factor in value similarity: almost all of the clusters that formed early are of the same national origin. But because we analyzed the global samples, we may have missed some other important factors, for example, gender. Here we present results of a more detailed cluster analysis, based on the sample data broken down by gender and education.

Methodological Considerations

We used techniques of cluster and profile analyses in the data analysis. The cluster analysis, applying hierarchical agglomerative criteria, allowed us to observe how the various countries and/or strata group together on the basis of the value data. The profile analysis, based on analysis-of-variance techniques, provides estimates of the effects on mean value scores of country and subgroup (i.e., gender, age, and educational level), as well as possible country-by-country interactions.

The data we processed are the nine national samples of secondary students (Australia, Belgian Flanders, Canada, Croatia, Italy, Japan, Portugal, South Africa, and the United States), eight national samples of higher education students (Belgian Flanders, Canada, Croatia, Italy, Japan, Poland, Portugal, and the United States), and four national samples of adults (Belgian Flanders, Canada, Croatia, and Japan), for a total of ten countries. These analyses use the three-item version of the eighteen values scales. (The Australia data lacked the Personal Development scale; we used multiple regression of the other seventeen scales to estimate this for our purposes here.)

We constructed aggregates that correspond to each of the education, age, or gender categories within each country and assigned the same weight to each elementary set. From these values we defined the nine national "units" for secondary students, the eight for higher education students, and the four for adults.

We carried out the cluster analysis by applying a hierarchical method (Aldenderfer & Blashfield, 1984) to the various sets of elementary units we were examining. In forming clusters we adopted the aggregation method, putting together step by step units that exhibited the minimum distance. We present the results in dendrograms that represent the successive aggregations; the length of various branches is proportional to the distance between the units aggregated.

Our profile analysis is based on a classical additive model (Morrison, 1967; Greenhouse & Greisser, 1959). This is a classical analysis-of-variance model with two classification criteria, which allowed us to examine both the differences between nations (or subgroups) and the interactions between countries and items (profile differences). The Greenhouse and Greisser (1959) method also makes it possible to determine the level of statistical significance of the various effects, even if they are considered not particularly important for the purposes at hand.

We performed each processing operation for secondary students, university students, adults, and for the overall sample. However, for the sake of conciseness we present only the profile analyses and the clustering trees based on them. The profile analysis allows us to examine the particular values that characterize the individual countries, whereas the clustering trees allow us to capture more effectively the correspondences among countries.

Results

Geocultural Identities

In our search for geocultural identities we first attempted a hierarchical cluster analysis of all seventy-six sample units, into which the total international sample had been broken down. The analysis we performed on their mean values scales scores resulted in a linkage dendrogram that is too large to show here (it may be obtained by contacting the authors).

The dendrogram corroborates the analysis presented in Chapter Sixteen, showing that the seventy-six units primarily join along the lines of national and/or geocultural similarity rather than on the basis of other such elements as gender, educational level, or ethnic or linguistic identity. This phenomenon appears most evident for Japan, Italy, and Portugal but may also be observed for Australia and Poland. The United States and Canada seem to be characterized by "national" features that may be regarded as North American. Belgium and Croatia form a single grouping. Finally, in South Africa two groups seem to appear: speakers of European languages (English and Afrikaans) and native speakers of African languages.

Having noted that the groupings relate more to geocultural criteria than any other, it appears prudent to abstain for the time being from further interpretation of the dendrogram. Other points will emerge from the separate cluster analyses of the three subgroups (i.e., secondary students, higher education students, and adults).

Secondary School Students

The two dendrograms in Figure 17.1 present the outcomes of the analysis of the secondary school samples. Dendrogram A shows the aggregation of the nine samples in three sets, obtained by cluster analysis of their general means.

Set A consists of the Canadian, Portuguese, and South African samples (with a general mean of 9.06); set B consists of the Australian, Belgian, Croatian, Italian, and the American samples ($m = 8.68$); and set C includes only the Japanese sample ($m = 8.27$). The mean of all the means thus considered is 8.8, with a range of 8.3 for Japan to 9.1 for Canada and Portugal. The range of variability for the individual values goes from 10.3 for Personal Development to 6.7 for Risk. Thus the national differences emerge in the context that in all countries all the values are considered important or very important.

Let us now examine the results of the cluster analysis based on the differences between the eighteen observed values and their general mean for each country. The resulting dendrogram B, shown in Figure 17.1, reveals three main groupings, denoted as sets A, B, and C. The value characteristics of each set are given in Table 17.1, which contains the means of the profiles calculated for each set. The figure of 1.50, indicated for Ability Utilization of set B, for example, indicates that in Italy and Portugal (set B) the score for Ability Utilization is 1.5 points higher than the general mean for all eighteen values in that set.

Set A consists initially of the Canadian and American samples, to which the Australian, Belgian, Croatian, and South African samples may be linked. Analysis of their values reveal that these samples attach particular relative importance to Advancement and Economics, whereas their scores for Autonomy, Creativity, and Life-style tend to be lower. Set B consists of the Italian and Portuguese samples; they attach greater importance to Achievement and Social Relations, whereas their scores for Authority and Risk are low. Set C consists solely of the sample from Japan, where great importance is attached to Aesthetics and Risk and little to Achievement and Social Relations. In terms of deviation from the mean, the Japanese students exhibit the most differences from the others, followed by the Italians and Portuguese, who are paired. In relation to value positioning, however, all three groupings consider Ability Utilization and Personal Development particularly important, whereas those considered less important are Risk, Prestige, and Authority.

A closer look at the data in Table 17.1 reveals that each country has its idiosyncrasies: the Australian secondary students attach particular importance to Economics and limited importance to Risk and Aesthetics, the Canadian students attach particular importance to Authority and Prestige and limited importance to Creativity, the Italian secondary students attach particular importance to Autonomy, Life-style, and Personal Development and limited importance to Advancement, Economics, and Aesthetics. The Portuguese secondary students attach considerable importance to Creativity and less importance to Prestige, Risk, Economics, and Physical Activity; the Croatian students consider Working Conditions to be important and attach little importance to Autonomy, Authority, Prestige, and Life-style. The American secondary students consider Advancement, Economics, and Prestige particularly important, whereas they attach relatively less importance to Aesthetics and Altruism. The Belgian secondary students attach importance to Social

Figure 17.1. Secondary School Students.

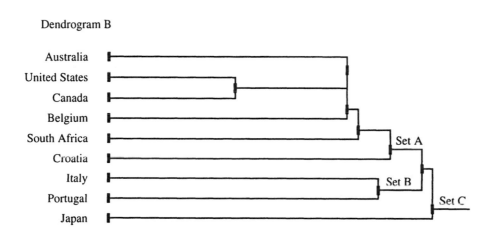

Note: Dendrogram A is based on the general mean of the eighteen observed values and dendrogram B on the differences between the eighteen observed values and their general mean (profiles).

Relations and Aesthetics, on the one hand, and give less importance to Altruism, Authority, and Achievement, on the other. The South African secondary students stand out for the importance they attach to Advancement, Authority, and Prestige and the limited importance they place on Social Relations. The Japanese secondary students are characterized by the great importance they give to Aesthetics, Risk, and Creativity and the limited importance they attach to Advancement, Social Relations, Economics, and Achievement.

Higher Education Students

Figure 17.2 presents dendrograms for higher education students. Dendrogram A indicates the existence of two groupings of the national samples: set

Table 17.1. Results of the Cluster Analysis Based on the Differences Between the Eighteen Observed Values and Their General Mean: The Average Differences for Different Clusters (Sets) of Countries.

Scales	Secondary Students			Higher Education Students			Adults				10 Countries		
	A	B	C	A	B1	B2	A	B	C	D	A1	A2	B
1. Ability Utilization	1.20	1.50	1.71	1.46	1.82	1.99	1.46	1.38	1.23	1.73	1.34	1.67	1.94
2. Achievement	0.98	1.27	0.22	0.78	1.27	0.49	0.93	1.37	0.59	0.87	1.00	1.27	0.50
3. Advancement	0.57	-0.26	-1.52	0.30	-0.64	-1.84	-0.10	-0.33	-0.15	-1.92	0.30	-0.42	-2.16
4. Aesthetics	0.31	0.04	1.86	-0.17	0.40	1.42	-0.12	0.56	1.26	1.38	0.30	0.10	1.41
5. Altruism	0.08	0.57	0.43	0.41	0.49	0.35	0.44	0.74	0.05	-0.63	0.25	0.46	0.24
6. Authority	-1.86	-2.39	-1.71	-0.43	-2.61	-2.66	-0.48	-2.47	-2.17	-1.34	-1.69	-2.43	-2.56
7. Autonomy	0.03	0.74	0.60	0.84	0.79	1.11	0.77	0.15	0.24	0.92	0.27	0.91	0.96
8. Creativity	-0.35	0.70	0.77	-0.22	0.85	0.88	0.15	-0.22	0.12	1.27	-0.16	0.90	1.07
9. Economics	0.78	-0.46	-0.38	0.24	-0.57	-0.20	0.62	0.90	0.30	0.24	-0.58	-0.66	0.18
10. Life-style	0.02	0.77	0.39	0.05	0.97	1.44	0.20	-0.32	0.38	0.84	0.10	1.06	1.49
11. Personal Development	1.44	1.87	1.67	1.60	2.19	2.28	1.72	1.60	1.44	1.79	1.58	2.00	2.16
12. Physical Activity	0.01	-0.12	-0.00	-0.69	-0.60	-0.99	-0.93	-0.89	-0.73	-0.42	-0.27	-0.38	-0.81
13. Prestige	-0.62	-1.60	-0.97	-0.08	-1.73	-1.00	-0.13	-0.96	-0.66	-0.62	-0.57	-1.78	-1.05
14. Risk	-2.10	-2.60	-0.88	-2.46	-2.57	-1.62	-2.96	-1.91	-2.21	-1.37	-2.32	-2.65	-1.33
15. Social Interaction	-0.38	-0.43	-0.82	-0.64	-0.53	-0.84	-1.39	-0.82	-0.29	-1.28	-0.41	-0.47	-1.24
16. Social Relations	0.85	1.01	-0.07	0.63	1.10	0.79	0.93	1.26	1.19	0.03	0.75	1.02	0.43
17. Variety	-0.95	-0.73	-1.14	-1.29	-0.70	-0.68	-1.05	-1.06	-0.91	-1.28	-0.99	-0.64	-0.64
18. Working Conditions	-0.02	0.13	-0.10	-0.31	0.07	-0.92	-0.08	0.98	0.31	-0.27	-0.04	0.06	-0.60

A consisting of the Portuguese, American, and Canadian samples (with a general mean of 8.95), and set B consisting of the Polish, Croatian, Italian, Belgian, and Japanese samples ($m = 8.35$). For the eight units of higher education students considered as a whole, the general mean of the scores assigned to the eighteen values is 8.6, with a range from 8.1 for Japan to 9.0 for Portugal and the United States. The range among individual values is from 10.6 for Personal Development to 6.4 for Risk. Again the national differences occur over and above the high level of importance universally attached to all the values.

Dendrogram B in Figure 17.2 shows the results of the cluster analysis based on the differences in the eighteen values observed and their general mean for each country. There are two groupings. Set A consists of the American and Canadian samples. This set attaches particular importance to Advancement, Authority, Economics, and Prestige and limited importance to Creativity, Life-style, Personal Development, and Variety. An extensive set B combines two subsets: B1, consisting of the Croatian, Italian, and Portuguese samples, and B2 of the Japanese, Belgian, and Polish samples. Subset B1 is characterized by the greater importance attached to Achievement, Social Relations, and Working Conditions and limited importance attached to Prestige; subset B2, compared with the others, considers Aesthetics and Risk more important and Advancement and Working Conditions relatively less important. The three groups of higher education students are similar in regard to the two values at the top of the list: Personal Development and Ability Utilization. The values considered less important are Authority and Risk. This is similar to the results obtained for the secondary school students.

Considering each national sample in more detail, the following "national" characteristics of higher education students stand out (see Table 17.1): the Canadians are characterized by the great importance they attach to Authority, Prestige, Advancement, and Economics, whereas they rate Aesthetics, Life-style, Social Relations, and Risk as less important. The Italians have a higher score for Physical Activity and Social Interaction and a lower score for Aesthetics, Economics, Advancement, and Prestige. The Portuguese attach particular importance to Advancement, Creativity, and Working Conditions, whereas they attach limited importance to Prestige and Risk. The Croatian sample is characterized by the particular attention respondents pay to Working Conditions, whereas they obtain lower scores for Authority, Autonomy, and Life-style. The Americans attach considerable importance to Advancement, Authority, Social Interaction, and Prestige and feel Creativity and Life-style are less important. The Belgian sample attaches considerable importance to Social Interaction and a limited one to Working Conditions. The Japanese attach particular importance to Aesthetics, Risk, and Creativity and limited importance to Advancement and Social Relations. Last, the Poles consider Life-style, Economics, Variety, and Risk to be more important, whereas they attach less importance to Advancement, Authority, Social Interaction, and Physical Activity.

Figure 17.2 Higher Education Students.

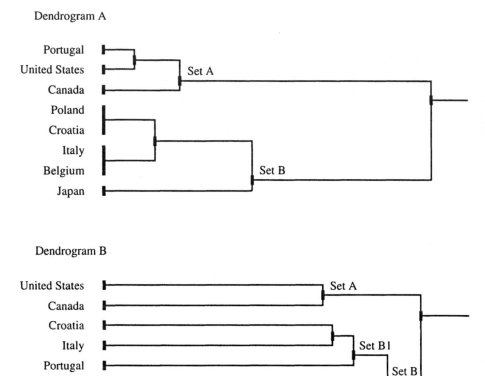

Note: Dendrogram A is based on the general mean of the eighteen observed values and dendrogram B on the differences between the eighteen observed values and their general mean (profiles).

Adults

We applied the same statistical procedures to the adult data, but because there were only four adult samples, the groupings are less useful. In general the Belgian and Croatian samples are most similar. For these adults the most important values are Personal Development, Ability Utilization, and Achievement and the least important ones tend to be Risk, Authority, and Variety.

The particulars for each sample can be formulated from the data in Table 17.1. The Belgian adults are characterized by the importance they attach to Social Interaction and by the low importance they give to Achievement. The Croatian adults consider most important such values as Social Relations, Working Conditions, and Altruism and assign a low score to Authority and Life-style. The Canadian adults attach more importance to Authority and less importance to Aesthetics and Risk. Finally, the Japanese adults prefer Creativity, Risk, Aesthetics, and Life-style, and Advancement, Social Relations, and Altruism have lower scores.

Conclusion

In an attempt to summarize our findings, we performed an additional analysis on the global means of the countries, regardless of variations in age and/or education level. The results of such an analysis provide a distorted picture, of course, because of the diverse composition of the various national samples (e.g., the Canadian sample is dominated by adult workers, whereas the Polish sample consists only of the university students). Nevertheless, the results are instructive.

The cluster analysis based on the differences in the eighteen observed values and their general mean for each country indicates three groupings of countries: set A1, consisting of the United States and Canada, with Belgium, Australia, South Africa, and Croatia joining later; set A2, consisting of Italy and Portugal; and set B, consisting of Japan and Poland. The last three columns of Table 17.1 give their respective value profiles. It is important to note that the three patterns are generally similar. In particular, Personal Development, Ability Utilization, and Achievement emerge with high scores, whereas Prestige, Authority, and Risk have scores much lower than the mean. However, the profiles also show differences among the countries.

In an attempt to summarize some aspects of the value pattern in different countries, we have adopted a theoretical classification scheme that uses two dimensions, or axes (Figure 17.3), based on our analysis of factor correspondence. Labels marking the extreme poles of the two axes are adapted from previous research.

The vertical axis is derived from the affective code theory (Fornari, 1977, 1981, 1985) and the studies on the "maternal" and "paternal" codes (Trentini, 1987; Bellotto & Trentini, 1989). According to this view, the countries close to the paternal code pole show a common "culture of ability," which values differences in aptitude and merit, roles, and responsibilities. Such cultures support, promote, and reward personal and professional growth. On the other hand, countries close to the maternal code pole show a common "culture of security," which values equality of peoples, roles, responsibilities, and status. Such cultures pay particular attention to care and defense of the weakest, to protection, help, and assistance.

We operationalized this maternal-paternal contrast as a dimension by using the scores for Authority, Prestige, and Risk to define the paternal affective code. To define the opposite pole of this dimension, the maternal affective code, we used the scores on Social Relations, Social Interaction, and Working Conditions.

The horizontal axis has at one extreme an expressive value orientation, defined by importance to Life-style and Personal Development and at

Figure 17.3. Position of the Ten National Samples in Relation to Two Theoretically Derived Axes (Expressive-Instrumental and Paternal-Maternal).

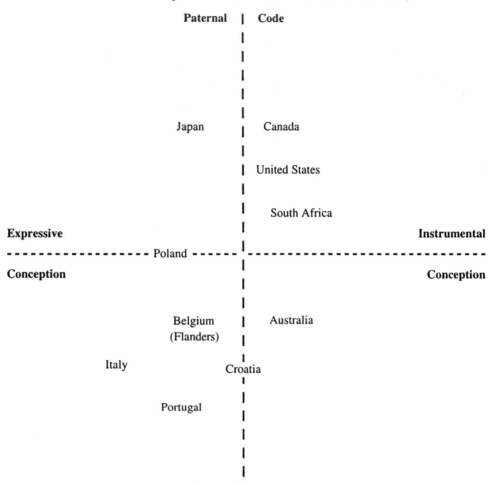

the opposite extreme an instrumental orientation, defined by such values as Advancement and Economics.

Figure 17.3 shows the relative positions of the ten countries on the two axes. In the upper-right quadrant are the two North American and the South African samples, which, according to this model, show a tendency toward the paternal code and instrumental orientation. In the opposite quadrant, representing a combination of the maternal code and expressive orientation, are all the European countries. The remaining two quadrants are mostly less full. The Australian sample is located in the lower-right quadrant, showing a tendency toward an instrumental orientation (like the North American countries) and the maternal code (like the European countries). Finally, the Japanese sample is located in the upper-left quadrant, the only national sample with the tendency toward a paternal-expressive pattern. Such a constellation corroborates and illustrates the findings of Chapter Sixteen, obtained by a somewhat different data-processing approach.

References

Aldenderfer, M. S., & Blashfield, R. K. (1984). *Cluster analysis.* Newbury Park, CA: Sage.

Bellotto, M., & Trentini, G. (1989). *Culture organizzative e formazione* [Organizational culture and development]. Milan: Franco Angeli.

Fornari, F. (1977). *Il minotauro* [The Minotaur]. Milan: Rizzoli.

Fornari, F. (1981). *Il collettivo e le strutture affettive del* Principe *di Macchiavelli* [The collective and affective structure of Machiavelli's *The Prince*] Milan: Unicopli.

Fornari, F. (1985). *Psicoanalisi in ospedale* [Psychoanalysis in the hospital] Milan: R. Cortina.

Greenhouse, S. W., & Greisser, S. (1959). On methods in the analysis of profile data. *Psychometrika, 24,* 95–112.

Morrison, D. F. (1967). *Multivariate statistical analysis.* New York: McGraw-Hill.

Trentini, G. (1987). *Il cerchio magico* [The magic circle]. Milan: Franco Angeli.

EIGHTEEN

The Five Major Life Roles Viewed Cross-Nationally

Alija Kulenović
Donald E. Super

It has been widely assumed that each culture sets a value on each of the major life roles and that the valuations vary from one era to another and from one culture to another (Chapter Two). Tilgher's (1930) and Weber's (1930) historical works on work represented one way to address these theories; dealt with by Gouws in Chapter Two, we need not review them here. What we should note here—what takes up this rather complex but important chapter—is the quantitative approach to these topics that has emerged with the development and use of psychometric methods. The movements of peoples (Chapter Twenty-one), unemployment (Chapter Twenty-two), and other economic, political, and social forces have commanded greater interest than ever in objective studies of the relative importance of education, work, homemaking, and other life roles. For example, Triandis (1972) pointed out that comparative studies are conclusive only if they adduce evidence of the equivalence of experimental manipulation, sampling, and measurement and familiarity with the methods of inquiry. The authors of the Work Importance Study (WIS) believe that, despite some shortcomings, we have made important steps in these directions.

Here we should mention one study to point up a major unique feature of the WIS and its findings. The Meaning of Work study (MOW, 1987) obtained rankings of the relative importance of five major life roles in a sample of countries not unlike that of the WIS: they were all industrialized. MOW researchers looked at almost the same roles, omitting study but adding religion. However, the MOW study compared work with a combination of the other four roles, then combined that ranking with another global rating of work in order to assess its centrality (*importance,* or *salience* in our terminology). The WIS considers each role in its own right in assessing and comparing the importance of five major life roles: Study, Work, Homemaking (Home and Family), Community Service (Citizenship), and Leisure. In its focus on these specific roles and in its objective measurement of each, the Work Importance Study has been unique.

The Salience Inventory (SI) is the result of several years of literature review, inventory design and item writing, and psychometric refinement in each WIS member country and in semiannual meetings; as a result, it has functioned well in the eleven countries on five continents. The study measures three aspects of the importance or salience of each role: Participation in, Commitment to, and Value Expectations from, a role. Thus the WIS uses one behavioral and two technically quite different but empirically related affective measures that, with the five roles, make for fifteen scales or scores.

Here we present and discuss the results of the statistical analyses done by Kulenović:

1. The factor structure of the salience measures in each culture and subculture identified in our sampling
2. Cross-cultural and cross-national similarities and differences in Participation in and Attachment to each role, together with the general (composite) salience of each role
3. The empirical clustering and characterization of each subculture and culture according to its role-salience profile, that is, salient role characteristics

Instruments, Data, and Methodological Considerations

The instrument the WIS used is the Salience Inventory; the international version is used for research only, whereas the national versions are suited both to research and to counseling. The SI assesses the five roles of Student, Worker (potential or actual), Homemaker, Citizen, and Leisurite. The SI defines each role, as well as the three scales for each role—Participation, Commitment, and Value Expectations—clearly and concretely. See Chapter Two for more discussion of the anthropological, psychological, and sociological constructions, Chapter Four for more psychometric data, and Chapters Five to Fifteen for national data.

Table 18.1 reports the data supplied by ten of the eleven countries for intensive cross-national analysis.

We did not use all of the data for all of the analyses. We carried out cluster analyses on all samples but we analyzed the factor structure and the congruence of the factor solutions only for samples noted with asterisks in Table 18.1, because they provided us with the raw scores we needed: Australia, samples from all three levels (secondary schools, higher education, and adults); Belgian Flanders, all three levels; Canada, all three levels for each major language group (Anglophones and Francophones); Italy, secondary and higher education (the WIS covenant was to collect data from at least the secondary level, others according to interest and resources); Japan, all levels; Poland, university students only, because of personnel and support changes; Portugal, secondary and higher education (and adults but no raw scores for this analysis); South Africa, secondary school samples from each major language group (Afrikaans, English, and major African tribal lan-

Table 18.1. Countries and Samples Used in the Cross-National Analyses of Role Salience.

Country	Secondary Education		Higher Education		Adults	
			Samples and the Number of Subjects			
Australia	A1	276*	A2	155*	A3	81*
Belgium (Flanders)	B1	235*	B2	113*	B3	512*
Canada						
English-Canadians	CE1	1,228	CE2	623	CE3	5,160
French-Canadians	CF1	406			CF3	1,222
Croatia	CR1	1,871*	CR2	348*	CR3	344*
Italy	IT1	1,869*	IT2	753*		
Japan	J1	834	J2	371	J3	883
Poland			PL2	252		
Portugal	P1	2,388*	P2	580		
South Africa						
English-speaking	SAE1	1,802*				
African language– speaking	SAN1	1,607*				
Afrikaans-speaking	SAA1	1,694*				
United States	US1	1,937*	US2	1,978*	US3	379

Note: Asterisks denote samples for which original data were available.

A = Australia; B = Belgium; CE = English-Canadians; CF = French-Canadians; CR = Croatia; IT = Italy; J = Japan; P = Portugal; PL = Poland; SA = South Africa (SAE = English speaking, SAA = Afrikaans, SAN = Native South African languages); US = United States. Numbers 1, 2, and 3 denote secondary school, higher education, and adult samples, respec-

guages used in the home); the United States, all three levels; and Croatia, all three levels. In these analyses we used only individuals for whom we had complete data, which means that some data reported here may not coincide exactly with data in the national chapters. Thus for this first analysis we had seven national samples, seventeen specific samples, and a total of 16,750 subjects (male and female).

We would have preferred to control all factors that might cause differences in role salience, but we could not equate national samples with confidence, because field conditions and limited resources required different sampling methods. Similarly, we could not equate the samples statistically because of unsuitable recording or reporting methods and lack of some data (e.g., ethnicity in the United States, Belgian Flanders, and others). Given these considerations, the sampling in the secondary schools is probably the best cross-nationally, but even here we must note that North American schools admit a much higher percentage of the age cohort than is true in European countries and certain others. The higher education samples are no doubt even less comparable for the same reason, and the adult samples, which were samples of convenience (as is generally the case in work with adults) are of uncertain comparability, although the national teams tried to obtain subjects from all fields of work (Holland's 1985 RIASEC model) and all literate occupational levels (necessitated by the use of paper-and-pencil tests and the lack of resources for their oral administration). The national chapters (Chapters Five to Fifteen) describe the various samples; readers should refer to them for clarification of the comparability of the data.

Role Salience in the WIS Countries

Factor Structure

Factor analysis makes it possible to test hunches or hypotheses about the relationships of the three aspects of salience in the WIS model of salience, because we can expect convergence within roles and divergence between roles from the behavioral and affective measures in the SI, and convergence of knowledge when such is included, as in the several national versions of career maturity tests. This was how Graen (1969) and Mitchell (1982) determined the boundary conditions that expectancy theory requires for prediction. Briefly, if a particular behavior or action is part of a person's repertoire, if this behavior is under the subject's control (as in making a choice), and if rewards are contingent upon certain specific behaviors, we can expect convergence. Thus measures of Participation, Commitment, and Value Expectations in the role of Worker should relate moderately well in mature people, whereas these measures should relate less highly, or even negatively, to measures of the salience of the Leisure or Community Service roles. This is the convergence-divergence model of Campbell and Fiske (1957).

In factor analysis terms this means that hypothetically the SI's fifteen role-salience measures could be reduced to five factors that correspond to the five roles that the WIS assessed. Thus a factor analysis of the SI is a multivariate empirical test of the WIS model of role salience. It is also a test of the model's cross-national and cross-cultural generality.

This factor analytic study is also interesting because it may explain the origins of cross-cultural differences we observed in the various behavioral and affective aspects of role salience as well as role salience in general. Such comparisons are legitimate if the variables have the same psychological meanings in all samples, a goal for which the WIS teams strove in developing the SI. Similar factor structures in different samples indicate similarity of meaning in ostensibly similar variables (scales) in different cultures.

To test the similarity of the factor structures of the SI scales in each of the seventeen samples (marked with asterisks in Table 18.1), we took the following steps:

1. We carried out seventeen principal components analyses with "ones" in the main diagonal of the correlation matrix. We retained factors according to the Guttman-Kaiser criterion of eigenvalues that exceeding one and rotated them orthogonally according to the Kaiser Varimax criteria, which yields identical results for the number of dimensions. In each of the seventeen samples five significant components explain 72.4 percent (SAN1, South African blacks) to 83.9 percent (B3, Belgian adults) of the

total variance. All rotated factor matrixes had simple structure, as defined by Thurstone. The factors are therefore easily interpreted as indicators of the *general* importance of each of the five roles: the measures embody well the behavioral and affective components of salience.

2. We calculated the Burt-Tucker coefficients of congruence of all the rotated factors. The factor obtained in a given sample is identical to the greatest congruence in any other sample. Thus factors extracted from any one sample are located in the other samples.

3. We calculated average coefficients for each of the five factors with each of the equivalent five factors, which yields mostly high coefficients (about 0.95). Average congruence for the factors, calculated on the basis of 17 × 16:2 = 136, yields the following coefficients: the Leisurite role, 0.978; Citizen, 0.969; Homemaker, 0.964; and Student, 0.956. These four analyses identify essentially the same factors as the four roles similarly named. This does not, however, hold true so clearly for the fifth role, that of Worker.

The Worker role yields a mean congruence coefficient of 0.923 for Participation, Commitment, and Value Expectations, a very high relationship. However, some deviations from this mean are worthy of comment: in four of the seventeen samples these coefficients are somewhat lower—the Australian is 0.886 for adults, the Italian 0.866 for students, the Portuguese 0.714 for students, and the Croatian 0.887 for adults. These coefficients suggest that the salience of Work in these samples has a slightly different structure.

The main Work salience representatives in the Australian adults are Work Value Expectations (0.91) and Commitment (0.86). This expected structure is, however, upset by a modest correlation with Work Participation (0.47) and unexpected correlations with the Homemaker (0.51) and Citizen (0.33) roles. Among the Italian students Work salience is appropriately defined by Work Participation (0.91) and Commitment (0.72), whereas Value Expectations in the Work role are highly saturated with Study—not surprising in students. In Portuguese students Participation in Work has little commonality and is somewhat related to Homemaking and Community Service (recall that the WIS operational definitions of *Work Participation* include reading and talking about work, *Homemaking* includes being tidy, and *Community Service* relates to being a scout, thus permitting participation at low age levels and what might be called marginal activities, compared to adult participation, but including such adult activities as having a job). The Work salience factor in the Portuguese students includes all other role Value Expectations, suggesting that they fail to make some common semantic distinctions or have an optimistic future orientation: is this perhaps a factor that our analyses do not identify? In Croatian adults the only hypothesis or hunch that is not sustained is their very moderate to low Value Expectations of Work (0.44), as in Australia. It is tempting to speculate that these findings may be a function in Croatia of lack of opportunity in a controlled and depressed economy and in Australia of a leisure orientation that some Australian sociologists call a "shirk ethic," valuing work only because it supports a leisurely life-style.

The deviations from the expected structure of the Work salience factor presumably indicate the existence of some within- and between-country differences in the psychological meaning of work. These differences lie primarily in Participation and Value Expectations, in current behavior in and hopes for work. However, these unexpected relationships are not large enough to contradict our theoretical postulates, and the structure we hypothesized may be considered confirmed. Table 18.2 reports our main findings.

The factor structure matrix appears to be practically identical to that shown in the analysis of subsamples. Five significant factors have been identified, meet the requirements of simple structure, and make possible the reproduction of 78.1 percent of the total variance. Because we find high intercorrelations only among measures that assess the same role—and, for the most part, only with those measures—the factors we identify may confidently be taken as indicators of the importance of distinct roles.

Generational Differences

Before we examine cross-national differences in detail, it would be helpful to consider other general characteristics of our data that describe the role structure of the three main age samples: secondary school pupils, higher education students, and adults, regardless of country, and also the characteristics of the aggregate samples (national and age). Bear in mind that the adult samples are aggregations of people of various ages and varying amounts of education, including not only secondary and higher but also an unknown (in these analyses) percentage of former elementary and middle school dropouts and recent graduates. Table 18.3 presents the results of our analyses.

The two student samples Participate most in Study and in Leisure, which is not surprising because they generally have fewer responsibilities than adults. They report little activity in Work and Home and Family and least in Community Service. In adults the Work role dominates, as we anticipated, followed by Homemaking and Leisure, with Study and Community Service less salient.

Affectively, role structure differs considerably from its behavioral structure. In Commitment, Community Service has a lowly place, whereas the remaining four roles are, in the case of the younger samples, rather uniform in their importance, despite the greater differences in Participation. The hierarchy is as follows: Leisure, Work, and Home and Family are about equal, in first place, among secondary school students; Work, Leisure, Home and Family, and Study lead among university students. In the adult samples Home and Family and Work are notably higher than Leisure, Study, and Community Service.

The hierarchy for Value Expectations is, appropriately, almost identical to that for Commitment: both scales are affective and measure aspects of com-

Table 18.2. Rotated Factor Structure Matrix of the Salience
Measures (N = 16,730, PCA, Varimax).

Role	Factors				
Participation	F1	F2	F3	F4	F5
1. Student	−0.064	**0.859**	0.115	0.052	0.014
2. Worker	−0.098	−0.108	0.150	0.225	**0.718**
3. Citizen	−0.054	0.040	**0.889**	0.102	0.021
4. Homemaker	−0.024	0.055	0.182	**0.843**	0.084
5. Leisurite	**0.852**	−0.024	0.029	0.050	0.002
Commitment					
1. Student	−0.056	**0.895**	0.116	0.121	0.109
2. Worker	0.062	0.152	0.021	0.190	**0.867**
3. Citizen	0.000	0.159	**0.901**	0.156	0.082
4. Homemaker	0.059	0.069	0.082	**0.895**	0.190
5. Leisurite	**0.901**	−0.029	−0.007	0.089	0.055
Value Expectations					
1. Student	0.101	**0.855**	0.152	0.061	0.137
2. Worker	0.252	0.270	0.038	0.061	**0.763**
3. Citizen	0.115	0.212	**0.845**	0.104	0.110
4. Homemaker	0.225	0.128	0.099	**0.778**	0.218
5. Leisurite	**0.895**	0.033	0.021	0.063	0.102
Percentage of total variance	16.7	16.5	16.3	15.3	13.4
Percentage of total factor variance	21.4	21.1	20.8	19.5	17.1

Note: The loadings in excess of 0.30 are in boldface.

mitment. In secondary school and university students this partly future-oriented hierarchy is Worker, Leisurite, and Homemaker, with Study ranking lower and Community Service much lower. In the adult combined samples the principal anticipated sources of satisfaction are Home and Family and Work, followed at a much lower level by Leisure, Study, and Community Service.

In addition to the differences in role salience seen in Table 18.3, there are sizable intergenerational differences and similarities within some roles. Participation in Study is, as we expected, least in adults and greatest in students. This is true also of Commitment and Value Expectations of Study. The differences between the two younger education samples are negligible. The sporadic and limited work participation of secondary school and university students is shown in their markedly lower scores on Work Participation. The Commitment and Value Expectations scores are far smaller.

We may conclude that the psychological picture of Work is quite uniform within age groups. Commitment to Work does show a moderate increase with age as the labor market and labor force get closer and seem more real. Higher education students show somewhat greater Value Expectations from Work than do secondary school students and slightly greater expecta-

Table 18.3. Means (M) and Standard Deviations (SD) of Salience
Variables for Secondary and Higher Education Students and Adults.

Role	Secondary Education		Higher Education		Adults		Total	
	M	SD	M	SD	M	SD	M	SD
Participation								
1. Student	25.6	6.62	27.9	6.31	23.2	7.49	25.3	7.01
2. Worker	21.1	6.89	21.0	6.95	28.8	6.13	23.3	7.56
3. Citizen	18.3	7.07	17.2	6.94	18.0	7.33	18.0	7.14
4. Homemaker	23.9	6.46	23.2	6.66	26.8	6.71	24.6	6.72
5. Leisurite	29.4	6.46	28.4	6.36	26.1	6.54	28.3	6.62
Commitment								
1. Student	27.9	7.16	29.3	6.64	25.5	7.87	27.5	7.41
2. Worker	29.8	6.61	31.1	6.37	33.0	6.09	30.9	6.57
3. Citizen	23.6	7.84	23.3	8.05	22.0	8.05	23.1	7.97
4. Homemaker	29.1	7.32	30.4	8.13	33.2	7.32	30.5	7.65
5. Leisurite	30.8	6.72	30.5	6.52	28.4	6.94	30.0	6.83
Value Expectations								
1. Student	37.5	9.49	37.9	8.83	33.8	10.62	36.5	9.87
2. Worker	42.1	8.80	43.1	8.02	42.9	8.82	42.5	8.69
3. Citizen	33.0	10.84	32.0	10.98	30.1	11.18	32.0	11.04
4. Homemaker	39.9	9.17	40.8	9.46	43.5	9.26	41.1	9.38
5. Leisurite	41.8	9.01	41.4	8.56	38.9	9.45	40.9	9.15
Number of subjects	16,147		5,173		8,581		29,901	

tions than do adults: with higher education they have hopes of better careers, and they may still be somewhat lacking in realism.

Community Service is about equally unimportant to all WIS subjects. The least Participation is reported by students: the technical institute, college, or university may be their community sociologically. Positive attitudes toward Community Service decrease somewhat with age level as sampled in the WIS, because all adults are treated as one group.

Home and Family increase in importance with age in the WIS groupings. But again, higher education students are an exception, perhaps because they are more detached from their homes than are secondary school students and working adults.

Leisure activities are of about equal importance in the younger two samples and are more important to them than to adults.

A Cross-National Comparison of Role Salience

We did the analysis of cross-national differences in two ways. In the first we focused on potential role structure differences within specific samples, what might be called an "ipsative interpretation" of role importance that disregards differences within the roles themselves. Then we examined the differences in the importance that subjects attributed to specific roles cross-nationally, regardless of the roles' relative positions within the samples, what might be called a "normative view."

Role Structure

To simplify our presentation of role structure, we ordered the roles hierarchically according to their importance as determined by the three aspects of salience: Participation, Commitment, and Value Expectations. Bear in mind that these hierarchies are designed by mathematical rather than statistical methods, which would take the significance of differences into account. We made the procedural simplification in order to produce a general preliminary picture. The data are shown in Table 18.4.

Table 18.4 shows great apparent differences in the relative importance of the five roles and some similarities. Participation in the Citizen role occupies the last place in the hierarchy in most samples. Study is a dominant role in higher education students, less so in secondary education students; as expected, adults rank lowest. Exceptions are the high place of Study in American adults and its rather low place in the behavior of Afrikaans- and English-speaking secondary school pupils in South Africa and higher education students in Poland. Its especially low place in Anglophonic Canadian and American secondary school students is notable and may be related to both the high percentage of underprivileged adolescents in American schools and to the steady decline in test scores reported by American school authorities.

As we anticipated, the major difference between the younger subjects and adults is evident in the Work role. Work tends to occupy the highest place in the adult hierarchy in general, but it has the lowest place in all three Flemish samples. Croatian higher education students place Work equally low in the hierarchy.

Participation in Home and Family, viewed relative to other roles, is important to Polish students and South African secondary school pupils; it is, perhaps surprisingly, the least important of the roles of French-Canadian secondary school students. In all other samples Home and Family occupies the second or third place, particularly in the secondary schools.

Participation in the Leisure role appears to be generally the most important consumer of time and energy: is this indeed the postindustrial era? In twenty-four of the twenty-eight samples suitable for this analysis, Leisure occupies first or second place. Only among American adults, and to a lesser degree among Flemish and French-Canadian adults and South African blacks (all pupils) does it have a low place.

Table 18.5 shows the lack of Commitment to Community Service that is almost universal in our samples, which bodes ill for the British and North American tradition of volunteerism. Is the lack of Commitment to Commu-

Table 18.4. Relative Role Salience Within Samples: Participation.

Rank of Role	Student	Worker	Citizen	Homemaker	Leisurite
1	B2 IT2 P2 SAN1 CR2 CE2	A3 B3 US3 CR3 CE3 CF3		PL2	A1 A2 IT1 B1 P1 SAA1 SAE1 US1 US2 CR1 CE1 CF1 J1 J2 J3
2	A1 A2 B1 IT1 P1 US2 US3 CR1 CF1 J1 J2	J3		B3 SAA1 SAE1 SAN1 US1 CE1 CE3	A3 B2 IT2 P2 CR2 CR3 CE2 CF3 PL2
3	SAA1 SAE1 PL2	US1 CE1 CF1		A1 A2 A3 B1 B2 IT1 IT2 P1 P2 US2 US3 CR1 CR2 CR3 CE2 CF3 J1 J2 J3	B3 SAN1 CF3
4	A3 B3 US1 CR3 CE1 CE3 CF3 J3	A1 A2 IT1 IT2 P1 P2 SAA1 SAE1 SAN1 US2 CR1 CE2 J1 J2 J3	CR2 B1 B2	CF1	US3
5		B1 B2 CR2	A1 A2 A3 B3 IT1 IT2 P1 P2 SAA1 SAE1 SAN1 US1 US2 US3 CR1 CR3 CE1 CE2 CE3 CF1 CF3 J1 J2 J3 PL2		
Mean rank	2.5	3.3	4.9	2.7	1.6

Note: For identification of symbols see Table 18.1.

nity Service perhaps a reflection of a greater influence by other cultures (stemming from greater immigration), pressures from dual careers, and the desire for leisure, or was that tradition of volunteerism a myth? Only the Portuguese and South African blacks score higher on the Citizen role; these groups also are at the *bottom* of the hierarchy in Commitment to the Home and Family role. Commitment is different from the Participation hierarchy in that the role differences for Commitment are somewhat greater for all roles but Student, which varies little across the samples.

Commitment—that is, positive attitudes toward the Work role relative to other roles—characterizes all adult samples and the younger samples in Canada, Portugal, and Italy. The younger samples tend to view Leisure most positively relative to other roles; the exception is the sample of South African black students, who value Leisure less than all other roles. This finding is not

Table 18.5. Relative Role Salience Within Samples: Commitment.

Rank of Role	Student	Worker	Citizen	Homemaker	Leisurite
1	B2 IT2 SAN1	P1 P2 CR3 CE1 CE3 CF3 J3		A3 B3 SAA1 SAE1 US2 US3 CE2 PL2	A1 A2 B1 IT1 US1 CR1 CR2 CF1 J1 J2
2	P1 P2 CR2 J2	A3 B2 B3 IT1 IT2 US2 US3 CF1 CE2 PL2		A1 A2 B1 SAN1 US1 CR1 CR3 CE3 J1	SAA1 SAE1 CE1 CF3 J3
3	A2 US3 CF1 J1	A1 B1 SAA1 SAE1 SAN1 US1 CR1 CR2 J2		B2 IR1 CE1 CF3 J3	A3 B3 IT2 P1 P2 US2 CR3 CE2 CE3 PL2
4	A1 A3 B1 B3 IT1 SAA1 SAE1 US1 US2 CR1 CR3 CE3 CF3 CE1 CE2 J3 PL2	A2 J1	P1 P2 SAN1	IT2 CR2 CF1 J2	B2 US3
5			A1 A2 A3 B1 B2 B3 IT1 IT2 SAA1 SAE1 US1 US2 US3 CR1 CR2 CR3 CE1 CE2 CE3 CF1 CF3 J1 J2 J3 PL2	P1 P2	SAN1
Mean rank	3.2	2.2	4.9	2.4	2.2

Note: For identification of symbols see Table 18.1.

unexpected, given the small number of South African blacks who expected to reach secondary school when the sample was taken and the role that qualifications or training have traditionally played in their occupational status in that culture. Table 18.6 presents the data regarding the relative importance of Leisure.

The role hierarchy as determined by Value Expectations is quite similar to that for Commitment. This too is an affective measure but one with more focus on the future. With the exception of the Citizen role, which constantly occupies last place in the hierarchy, Study is about the least important source of anticipated satisfaction. Work is a major source of satisfaction in most groups. The influence of age or generation is evident in the Homemaker and Leisurite roles, for Home and Family rank relatively high among adults, whereas Leisure dominates in the school and higher education samples.

Table 18.6. Relative Role Salience Within Samples: Value Expectations.

Rank of Role	Student	Worker	Citizen	Homemaker	Leisurite
1	SAN1	B2 IT1 IT2 P1 P2 US2 US3 CR3 CE1 CF1 CE2 CF3 J3		A3 B3 CE3 PL2	A1 A2 B1 SAA1 SAE1 US1 CR1 CR2 J1 J2
2	P2	A1 A2 A3 B1 B3 SAA1 US1 CR1 CR2 CE3 J1 J2		B2 SAE1 SAN1 US2 US3 CR3 CE2 CF3	IT1 IT2 P1 CE1 CF1 PL2
3	P1 US3 CR2 CF1	SAE1 SAN1 PL2		A1 A2 B1 IT1 IT2 SA1 US1 CR1 CE1 J1 J2 J3	A3 B2 B3 P2 US2 CR3 CE2 CE3 CF3 J3
4	A1 A2 A3 B1 B2 IT1 IT2 J2 J3 PL2 SAA1 SAE1 US1 CE2 CF2 CE3 CF3 J1 US2 CR2 CR1 CE1		B3	P1 P2 CR2 CF1	SAN1 US3
5	B3		A1 A2 A3 B1 B2 IT1 IT2 SAA1 SAE1 SAN1 US1 US2 US3 CR1 CR2 CR3 CE1 CE2 CE3 CF1 CF3 J1 J2 J3		
Mean rank	3.8	1.6	5.0	2.6	2.1

Note: For identification of symbols see Table 18.1.

Summary: Role Structure

Role structure is connected with generation (in this study, operationally the educational level of the subject or membership in the labor force). National culture partly determines the relative importance of each role. For example, although Study is of major importance to South African black pupils for whom reaching secondary school was a hard to attain and valued prize, it is in last place among American secondary school students—its ready availability to Americans makes it no longer the key to advancement. The determinants of the several roles do not appear to be the same cross-nationally, not even in the several behavioral and affective aspects of the importance of a given role. Neither generational nor national factors appear to affect the relative importance or unimportance of Community Service; their relationship to the importance of other roles is both significant and diverse. Although the relative degree of Participation is largely set by age or generation, nationality seems to be of greater significance in determining the affective aspects of role differentiation. It is therefore necessary to examine the differences between samples, not only for each role but also for each of the two major aspects (behavioral and affective) of their salience.

Normative Comparison

Thus far we have examined the nature and significance of cross-national differences in role salience by means of one-way analysis of variance. Our dependent variables are one behavioral and two affective measures of all five life roles (fifteen variables); in another process we derived factor scores on the basis of the overall factor analysis results, which yield five factors constituting global measures of salience. These analyses include only the seventeen samples for which the original raw data had been made available (asterisked in Table 18.1). To obtain as detailed a description of cross-national differences as possible, we supplemented these data with relevant indexes from the national reports. We used the transformed arithmetic means (z scores) to approximate the mean factor scores for the samples for which the original raw data were not available, and the overall factor analysis produced a matrix of factor coefficients. All the analyses, both those based on raw data and on factor scores, reveal significant differences between samples in all twenty ANOVAs ($p < 0.0001$). Post hoc analysis of the significance of the differences between all pairs of samples (Scheffé test) reveals a number of statistically and practically significant large differences, both between groups in the same country and between nominally similar samples in various countries. The significance data are not included here for space reasons, but the differences reported in the text are all statistically significant at a high level of confidence.

We developed a z score for each variable in order to simplify the presentation and interpretation of cross-national differences while controlling the effects of generational differences by separate transformations for each generation group. We divided the difference between the mean of each sample and its unweighted mean by the corresponding overall standard deviation (Table 18.7). Such a handling results in each arithmetic mean being treated as having the same standard error and makes clear by how many standard deviations each sample mean exceeds or falls short of the mean value of the reference group. These data are not intended to and do not contain information on the relative importance of the various roles within a country or on absolute generational differences.

The presentation of factor scores is somewhat different. Here the generational differences are not held constant, so that comparisons may be made between the various generational groups. Again, these data do not lend them-

selves to establishing hierarchies of role importance, as we did in the preceding section. Tables 18.7 and 18.8 provide the results of the cross-national
analyses of differences in role salience.

The data confirm earlier observations: the cross-national differences
are statistically significant and quite large. Systematically greater differences
are evident in the Study, Work, and Home and Family domains; they are
smaller in those of Community Service and Leisure (the sample ranges are,
respectively, 1.5 SD and 1 SD). This also applies to the factors (Table 18.8),
although the generational differences greatly extend the range. Table 18.8
presents not only the cross-national differences but also the generational differences between the means of the composite role scores: Study and Leisure
are evidently the principal roles for the younger subjects, Work and Home
and Family for the adults.

Some of the role salience profiles reveal interesting national characteristics, which we describe country by country as portraits of ten nations.

Australia

The role profiles of the three Australian samples are rather similar, at about
the mean level. The importance of Leisure and of Home and Family appears
more pronounced here than in other countries when judged by Participation and Commitment, but not by Value Expectations in the higher education students. This not only justifies the use of the two affective scales but
suggests that students anticipate changes in roles and role salience once they
leave the shelter of the educational institution. The distinctive importance
of these two roles and of Work in Australia is, however, supported by their
high places in the hierarchy of roles and by their mean factor scores, which
treat salience as a unity rather than as a triad.

Belgian Flanders

A general feature of the Flemish-speaking Belgian samples is the relatively
low importance of almost all major roles, particularly in secondary school
students and adults. Compared to the other WIS countries, the Belgians Participate less in Work and Leisure, they are less Committed to them, and they
have lower Value Expectations from them. They expect less from Study and
slightly less from Home and Family. Is the Protestant work ethic dead in the
Flemish culture? Are they disillusioned, suffering from weltschmerz as the
Japanese appear to be? There are, however, some differences between Belgian higher education students and their compatriots, primarily in the
importance of Study and Community Service. Participation and Commitment to these roles are higher than they are in the students in some of the
other WIS countries.

The generally lesser importance of Study and Community Service is
also evident in their factor scores. In our WIS data, Belgians tend to occupy

Table 18.7. Role Salience (Z Scores) for Secondary (1) and Higher Education (2) Students and Adults (3) in Participating Countries.

	Participation					Commitment					Value Expectations				
	Student	Worker	Citizen	Home-maker	Leisurite	Student	Worker	Citizen	Home-maker	Leisurite	Student	Worker	Citizen	Home-maker	Leisurite
A1	-0.10	0.05	-0.24	0.03	0.28	-0.06	0.09	-0.21	0.16	0.29	-0.08	0.09	-0.11	0.16	0.18
A2	0.00	0.02	-0.11	0.12	0.14	0.05	-0.24	0.04	0.18	0.19	-0.14	-0.28	0.00	-0.08	-0.11
A3	0.29	0.24	0.07	0.14	0.32	0.01	0.05	0.05	0.20	0.20	0.04	0.03	0.13	0.07	0.13
B1	-0.21	-0.68	-0.04	-0.33	-0.14	-0.17	-0.27	-0.03	0.09	-0.05	-0.27	-0.15	-0.14	-0.04	-0.12
B2	0.15	-0.34	0.26	-0.11	-0.19	0.17	-0.08	0.19	0.00	-0.17	-0.14	-0.19	-0.05	-0.07	-0.25
B3	-0.52	-0.66	-0.12	0.00	-0.27	-0.50	-0.32	-0.13	0.09	-0.23	-0.71	-0.47	-0.28	-0.11	-0.37
CE1	-0.53	0.66	-0.11	0.31	0.28	-0.48	0.43	-0.27	0.29	0.15	-0.32	0.39	-0.18	0.36	0.28
CE2	0.15	0.70	0.02	0.51	0.00	0.11	0.55	0.09	0.65	0.07	0.26	0.55	0.23	0.63	0.19
CE3	0.14	0.14	0.17	0.45	0.22	0.09	0.32	0.20	0.50	0.09	0.17	0.31	0.21	0.50	0.23
CF1	0.18	0.51	0.09	-0.10	0.08	0.15	0.24	-0.06	-0.28	0.01	0.35	0.33	0.08	-0.09	0.24
CF3	0.10	0.08	-0.05	-0.16	0.12	0.10	0.14	-0.13	-0.51	0.00	0.29	0.43	0.09	-0.04	0.26
CR1	0.08	-0.10	0.21	-0.02	0.15	-0.11	-0.20	0.06	-0.12	0.26	0.13	-0.15	0.06	0.00	0.07
CR2	0.43	-0.44	-0.07	-0.18	0.25	0.11	-0.17	-0.26	-0.33	0.35	0.12	0.00	-0.23	-0.24	0.45
CR3	-0.26	0.29	0.29	0.05	0.08	-0.05	0.22	0.14	-0.05	0.20	0.03	0.05	0.03	-0.09	0.12
IT1	0.44	-0.31	0.09	-0.16	0.08	0.16	0.08	-0.01	0.01	-0.03	0.34	0.49	0.34	0.27	0.35
IT2	0.42	-0.02	0.25	-0.17	0.00	0.23	0.16	-0.05	-0.12	-0.19	0.40	0.49	0.23	0.21	0.32
J1	-0.95	-1.04	-0.65	-0.81	0.01	-0.77	-1.38	-0.59	-0.94	-0.14	-0.85	-1.03	-0.62	-1.04	-0.65
J2	-0.93	-0.29	-0.27	-0.45	0.30	-0.65	-0.85	-0.27	-0.62	0.01	-0.58	-0.72	-0.31	-0.60	-0.52
J3	-0.36	-0.56	-0.37	-0.46	-0.01	-0.23	-0.75	-0.36	-0.74	-0.14	-0.41	-0.81	-0.39	-0.74	-0.42
P1	0.47	-0.44	-0.15	-0.62	-0.17	0.35	0.18	0.34	-0.66	-0.21	0.28	0.08	0.22	-0.53	-0.10
P2	0.45	-0.34	-0.28	-0.70	-0.39	0.36	0.42	0.18	-0.83	-0.17	0.27	0.06	0.03	-0.70	-0.25
PL2	-0.52	0.14	0.10	0.49	-0.39	-0.39	-0.27	-0.23	0.38	-0.46	-0.23	-0.31	-0.23	0.29	-0.14
SAA1	0.08	0.35	0.34	0.38	0.03	0.18	0.32	0.40	0.50	0.21	0.00	0.08	0.24	0.31	0.15
SAE1	-0.06	0.15	0.02	0.45	0.09	0.09	0.27	0.06	0.40	0.13	-0.02	0.01	-0.04	0.25	0.09
SAN1	0.89	0.37	0.55	0.54	-0.82	0.88	-0.13	0.43	0.13	-0.84	0.60	-0.34	0.27	-0.01	-0.75
US1	-0.31	0.47	-0.10	0.32	0.14	-0.23	0.36	-0.11	0.43	0.22	-0.17	0.20	-0.13	0.36	0.25
US2	-0.14	0.57	0.07	0.51	0.28	0.02	0.49	0.32	0.69	0.38	0.05	0.41	0.34	0.57	0.31
US3	0.61	0.48	0.02	-0.01	-0.46	0.59	0.35	0.23	0.50	-0.12	0.59	0.47	0.21	0.41	0.05

Notes: Data are centered within secondary, higher education, and adult overall sample. For identification of symbols see Table 18.1.

Table 18.8. Mean Factor Scores (Hierarchies of Samples) for Role Salience.

					Role					
Rank	*Student*		*Worker*		*Citizen*		*Homemaker*		*Leisurite*	
1.	P2	0.69	US3	1.04	SAN1	0.33	CE3	0.77	A1	0.31
2.	SAN1	0.66	CF3	0.93	SAA1	0.25	US3	0.44	IT1	0.27
3.	IT2	0.59	CR3	0.85	P1	0.11	B3	0.43	CE1	0.24
4.	CR2	0.53	CE3	0.79	CR1	0.10	US2	0.40	CR2	0.24
5.	P1	0.40	A3	0.64	IT1	0.02	CE2	0.40	CR1	0.23
6.	IT1	0.31	CE1	0.53	CF1	−0.01	A3	0.39	US1	0.20
7.	B2	0.28	CE2	0.44	CR3	−0.04	PL2	0.38	CF1	0.13
8.	CE3	0.26	CF1	0.37	US2	−0.06	SAE1	0.29	SAA1	0.10
9.	A2	0.15	US1	0.30	B2	−0.08	SAA1	0.26	US2	0.10
10.	CF1	0.08	US2	0.29	SAE1	−0.10	US1	0.26	SAE1	0.09
11.	US2	0.04	B3	0.13	B1	−0.11	CE1	0.17	B1	0.01
12.	US3	0.02	SAA1	0.10	IT2	−0.13	CR3	0.16	P1	−0.06
13.	CR1	−0.10	P2	0.07	CE3	−0.14	SAN1	0.14	IT2	−0.08
14.	SAA1	−0.14	IT2	0.05	A3	−0.19	A1	−0.03	J1	−0.11
15.	SAE1	−0.17	SAE1	−0.01	P2	−0.21	A2	−0.09	A2	−0.13
16.	A1	−0.20	A1	−0.03	US1	−0.22	CF3	−0.18	CE2	−0.16
17.	PL2	−0.25	IT1	−0.04	CE2	−0.24	B1	−0.21	J2	−0.20
18.	B1	−0.26	P1	−0.07	A2	−0.25	CR1	−0.23	B2	−0.39
19.	CF3	−0.45	J3	−0.09	US3	−0.25	IT1	−0.26	P2	−0.41
20.	US1	−0.47	SAN1	−0.31	CE1	−0.26	B2	−0.30	A3	−0.46
21.	CE3	−0.58	CR1	−0.34	A1	−0.29	J3	−0.34	CF3	−0.47
22.	J2	−0.50	PL2	−0.38	CF3	−0.29	IT2	−0.44	CE3	−0.48
23.	A3	−0.60	B2	−0.43	J2	−0.31	CF1	−0.49	CR3	−0.54
24.	CE1	−0.72	A2	−0.44	PL2	−0.35	CR2	−0.59	PL2	−0.58
25.	J1	−0.86	CR2	−0.46	B3	−0.37	J2	−0.79	J3	−0.84
26.	CR3	−0.89	B1	−0.52	C1	−0.54	J1	−0.96	US3	−0.88
27.	J3	−0.99	J2	−0.78	CR2	−0.44	P1	−1.02	B3	−0.96
28.	B3	−1.34	J1	−1.34	J3	−0.50	P2	−1.32	SAN1	−0.96

Note: For indentification of symbols see Table 18.1.

the bottom positions in the cross-national hierarchies of Study, Community Service (except for students, as noted), Work, and Leisure.

Canada

For Canada we have five samples, possibly the best sampling in the Work Importance Study, which, like other studies relying on questionnaires and inventories, is biased toward the professional, managerial, and clerical end of the occupational scale. The five samples used in this analysis are all three levels of Anglophones and two levels (secondary education students and adults) of Francophones. It is also worth noting that Canada and South Africa are the only two countries that took ethnicity into account in the WIS, although they are not alone in having significant minorities and minority problems.

Anglophones and Francophones (their terminology) are similar in the importance they attach to Work and Leisure in each of the three aspects we assessed (Participation, Commitment, and Value Expectations). Despite this, the two language and culture groups do differ in some ways, for the Anglophones attach more importance to Home and Family than do Francophones when compared with other countries, as Table 18.8 shows. All Canadian samples occupy one of the eight places (out of twenty-eight) in the national list of Work salience. The secondary school students rank high in Leisure. There is clear Anglo-Franco differentiation in the Homemaker role: it appears more esteemed by the Anglophones than by the Francophones. (Could this be a result of the greater social and occupational mobility and lessened inter-province mobility brought about by the "quiet revolution"?)

We did note some special group characteristics. Study is ranked below-average by secondary school students, but it occupies a more important place in the hierarchy in other Canadian groups than it does in other countries. Within language groups, Work, Home and Family, and Leisure occupy first place among the Anglophones, Study, Work, and Leisure among the Francophones. (Note that not all Francophones are of French origin nor all Anglophones of British descent, for both official language groups include varying numbers and percentages of ancient or recent citizens of Inuit, Italian, German, Polish, Russian, West Indian, and other ethnic group descent).

Croatia

In comparison with other countries, all three Croatian samples are distinguished only by the importance they attach to Leisure, especially the higher education sample. Study, Community Service, and Home and Family stand out among students; adult Participation in Study is of course lower, and adults are generally more active in Work and Community Service. Students are consistent in their role means, but Work does tend to be consistently lower than the other roles in their sample.

Italy

The Italian WIS includes the secondary and higher education levels. For Italian students Study is the most important life role, as shown by very high Participation, Commitment, and Value Expectations scores. Although the Italian students are average in other roles, they expect more from the Study, Citizen, and Leisure roles than do their peers in other countries (Table 18.4). When factor scores that include all three aspects of salience are considered (Table 18.7), the Italian educational sample considers Community Service and Leisure more important than Home and Family.

Japan

The Japanese data present us with a surprise: all three Japanese samples rank low on almost all salience measures. The mean factor scores (Table 18.8) show that all roles, even those for the traditionally valued roles of Student,

Worker, and Homemaker, rank considerably lower than in other WIS countries. Inspection of the several components of salience reveals that some deviation from this trend in Participation and Commitment to Leisure and to Study but not in Value Expectations: by and large, Japanese Value Expectations are lower than in other countries. Is this another case of disillusionment? Systematically low scores raise several questions, including the validity of the measures. Although Japanese team members did a careful and skilled job of adapting the WIS measures, they joined the WIS when it was well underway and made their adaptations of the SI and VS at that point. In order to catch up, they did not develop what in the other countries are both indigenous and cross-national instruments. It is important to note, however, that during the WIS symposium at the International Congress of Applied Psychology at Kyoto, in July 1990, Professor Nobuo Nakanishi presented empirical evidence of the suitability of the SI and the VS for use with Japanese subjects.

Poland

Poland's study was interrupted by the premature death of its leader (see Chapter Twelve); Poland studied only a sample of students in higher education (one university). In the cross-national role profile, all roles except Homemaker (the Home and Family) have negative scores. However, Homemaker is near the top of the hierarchy on all three salience measures—Participation, Commitment, and Value Expectations. (Is this a reflection of Poland's post–Warsaw Pact economic problems?) Work and Community Service indexes are inconsistent: Participation is higher than in other countries (people do what they can?), whereas Commitment and Value Expectations are well below the international average.

Portugal

The Portuguese subjects for whom we had relevant data were all students in secondary or higher education. Their Worker and Citizen profiles are similar to those of their counterparts in the other countries studied. A distinctive feature in the mean factor scores is the importance the Portuguese attach to Study and the relative unimportance of Home and Family and Leisure. In other roles the lack of congruence of behavior and affect presents a less uniform picture: average or lower student Participation in Work and Community Service (perhaps inherent in national social class traditions and practices) is accompanied by a very positive Commitment to these roles.

South Africa

The South African samples are from secondary education, perhaps the best technically in the WIS. They include an important variety of ethnic and language groups. Three samples are linguistic: those attending English-language schools (SAE1), those enrolled in Afrikaans-language schools (SAE2), and the black students who attend segregated English-language schools (SAE3; see Chapter Fourteen). Although the profiles of these groups are somewhat similar to each other, some important differences are manifested between those most exposed to Western cultures (English and Afrikaaner) and those growing up in various African tribes. All South African subjects report Participation in Work, Community Service, and Home and Family more than do other national samples of the same educational level; they are also more Committed to Study, Community Service, and Home and Family. But in Value Expectations the native and transplanted cultures split: specific to the blacks are high scores on the importance of Study (the road to advancement), the second highest in the cross-national samples. The blacks report more Participation in, are Committed to, and have high Value Expectations of Study. With the Leisure role the obverse is true: black students rank low on Leisure. There is interesting inconsistency in the Work role, for blacks rank high on Participation in Work but are not Committed to it and expect little of it, presumably reflecting their then-limited opportunities in the employment system. In the two white samples the picture is quite different, for high Participation in Work is accompanied by a high degree of Commitment to it, although the factor score (Table 18.8) is in the middle of the distribution.

United States

All American samples are characterized by very high Work salience. The Work role is more important in the United States than in most other countries in both behavioral and affective measures. The second most important role is in Home and Family, with rather more youth than adult Participation, however. Higher education students and adults rank rather high on Community Service, although their Participation in this role is not significantly above average. Study Participation again shows a difference between the youngest and the oldest subjects, as in the Canadian Anglophones: Study in the secondary education sample has a negative z score; it is one of the three most important roles for adults (it should be noted, however, that many U.S. adults were reached in continuing education courses).

The Clustering of Countries

We have shown that role salience is related to nationality and have identified some distinctive role configurations for each country. There also are some similarities between some countries, for example, Americans and Canadian Anglophones. At the same time, Japan—Asian but industrialized—is a distinctive homogeneous country, although not found in this study to match its stereotype. It is therefore reasonable to ask whether it is possible to organize our twenty-eight samples in relatively homogeneous role salience clusters, with each cluster having a distinctive role structure that unites its member countries.

Such clustering is not a simple task. Generational differences could lead to the formation of international generational groups; if generation and country combine, the outcome could be undefinable clusters. The choice of statistical method also presents problems. For these reasons we carried out a series of hierarchical cluster analyses in which we tried dissimilarity profile measures as methods of cluster formation (Norusis/SPSS, 1988). All analyses were made of two data groups independently. In the first, we standardized the arithmetic means by using the overall mean and standard deviation; these data include generational and international differences. In the second, we partialed out the generational differences; the results appear in Table 18.7.

Given that several analyses yielded essentially the same results, we chose two solutions, which are shown in Figures 18.1 and 18.2. In both cases the distance measures are the sum of the squared differences of the corresponding elements (squared Euclidean distance), and we used Ward's method of clustering.

The two figures show two solutions to the classification problem. The first dendrogram, Figure 18.1, gives a rough picture of the agglomeration process, using the data on generational and national differences. Starting with clusters at the lowest level on the distance scale—that is, with the smallest distances between groups—the first cluster is that of the American and English-Canadian educational samples and the two South African samples of European origin.

The second cluster is made up of the adult Australian, Croatian, and Canadian Anglophones; the Canadian Francophones appear at a slightly greater distance, and the U.S. adults join these other adults at a slightly greater but still relatively small distance. This cluster links up with the first—the younger samples of this cluster plus what might be called the Euro–South African secondary school students. (We should note here that for clarity and brevity the clusters that appear at about level 1 on the distance scale are called *miniclusters,* as are those at the not very distant levels of 2, 3, and 4; clusters at points 5 to 9 are here called *clusters* for lack of enough such modifiers, those from 10–14 *megaclusters,* and those at 15 and above *maxiclusters*).

The third cluster contains five samples of students. One combines the two Portuguese samples, already identified as similar to each other. Combining with these groups from a greater distance is a megacluster dominated by the younger "ex-European" Australian, Canadian Francophone, and younger European samples. Especially striking here are the South African black pupils, with a distinctive role profile but one that is nevertheless akin to those of the others in this cluster and, less closely, to the "Western" South African and North American profile at the maxicluster level.

Each of the last two clusters has only two members, the younger Japanese in one and the unexpected combination of Flemish and Japanese adults in the other, both of which clustered moderately early in the analytical process.

Figure 18.1. Dendrogram A Showing the Hierarchical Clustering of Countries According to Their Salience Inventory Mean Scores.

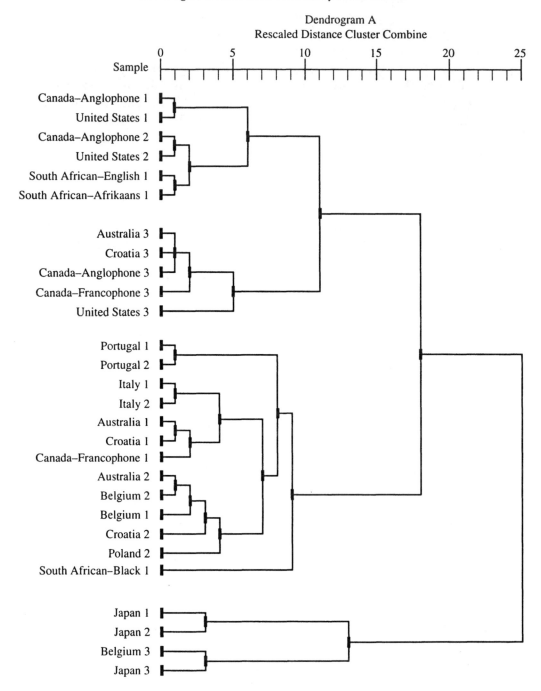

Figure 18.2. Dendrogram B Showing the Hierarchical Clustering of Countries According to Their Salience Inventory Mean Scores.

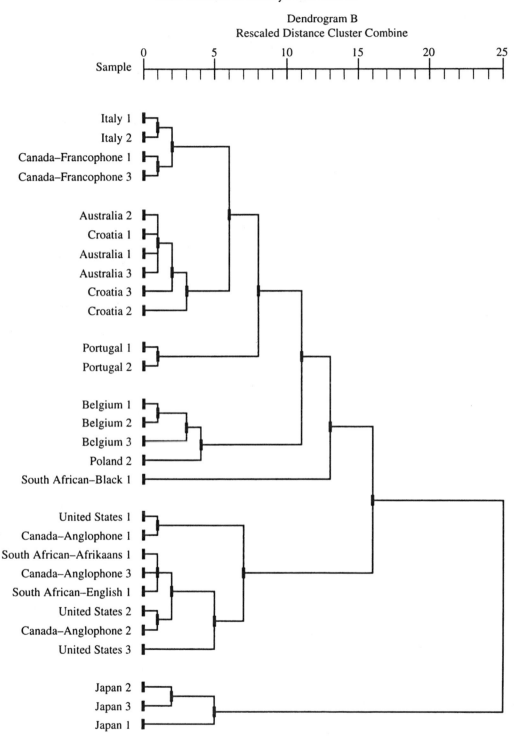

The similarity of the latter two samples may be a statistical artifact, the result of their both having very low profiles. They come together only at the mega-cluster level and join the other megaclusters only at the maxicluster level.

It is clear from these results that groups are formed largely on the gen-erational principle and to a much lesser extent on the national. This is not an unexpected result, because generation has already been seen to play a part in role cluster formation.

Figure 18.2 shows the effects of controlling generational differences. Here we see the samples organized in a dendrogram based on national cri-teria. The first cluster (first fifth of the distance scale) is occupied by seven miniclusters that coalesce into larger and more heterogeneous clusters be-fore becoming a cluster. First comes a Romance-language group formed by two Italian and two Canadian Francophonic samples. Another homogeneous cluster is formed by all the samples from Australia and Croatia, perhaps because they have generally homogeneous profiles and a distinctive empha-sis on Leisure. (Could this be because one is a relatively recently evolved and the other an evolving culture?) The two Portuguese samples continue to retain their separate status at this level. They are followed by a three-gener-ation Belgian Flemish cluster and the Polish students. Finally, and very dis-tant from the others, come the South African black students. This final megacluster of this maxicluster is made up largely of European and "neo-European" countries, a function of invitation and self-nomination (see Chap-ter Four).

In the next part of this dendrogram two miniclusters are formed. The first contains the very similar American and Canadian Anglophonic sec-ondary school students. The second cluster, the remaining American, Cana-dian Anglophonic, and South African whites, forms a cluster that may perhaps be called *Teutonophonic,* using the modifier in its historical and lin-guistic sense, which includes Dutch, English, the Nordic languages, German, and Afrikaans.

The last part of this dendrogram is the simplest, consisting of all the Japanese—and only the Japanese—groups. (It is noteworthy that in this analy-sis the Flemish adults do not combine with the Japanese but cluster with their compatriots at distance scale levels 2 and 3.) It would have been good to have another good sample or two of industrialized Asians, such as South Koreans or Taiwanese, to know whether an Asian megacluster would have formed.

To try to describe the typical role structure in these three major clus-ters, we calculated their unweighted means for all aspects of role salience, as shown in Table 18.9.

The role salience profile of the European megacluster is quite homo-geneous, with only slight deviations from the means observed in this table. The other two megaclusters are distinguished by greater Participation in Study and slightly above-average Participation in Home and Family, together with an incongruent lack of Commitment to the Homemaking role and low Value Expectations of it. The American–English-Canadian profile is clear and

Table 18.9. Mean Role Salience in European (E), North American (A), and Japanese (J) Clusters.

	Participation					Commitment					Value Expectations				
	Student	Worker	Citizen	Home-maker	Leisurite	Student	Worker	Citizen	Home-maker	Leisurite	Student	Worker	Citizen	Home-maker	Leisurite
E	0.13	−0.10	0.05	0.07	−0.05	0.08	−0.01	0.02	−0.10	−0.05	0.08	0.01	0.03	−0.06	0.00
A	−0.01	0.44	0.05	0.36	0.07	0.05	0.38	0.11	0.49	0.14	0.07	0.30	0.11	0.42 —	0.19
J	−0.75	−0.63	−0.43	−0.57	0.16	−0.55	−0.99	−0.99	−0.77	−0.09	−0.61	−0.85	−0.44	−0.79	−0.53

consistent: role salience there is greater than in the Europeans and the Japanese, but Study is an exception to this generalization. Compared to the other megaclusters, the Japanese Participated slightly more in Leisure activities, but their other roles are shown to be less important to them than to the other major clusters.

Conclusion

It would have been informative if the demands on testing time, and the development in all WIS countries of a measure of career information, had permitted us to include such an instrument in the WIS battery. The Career Development Inventory (CDI) in Francophonic Canada and in Portugal and the United States and the Career Development Questionnaire in South Africa contain such measures. It may perhaps be worth reporting here, without going into detail, that the complete salience model (Super, 1972) of behavioral, affective, and cognitive components has been tested with the American CDI's World of Work Information Test, demonstrating their near independence in first- and second-year American university students and their significantly higher intercorrelations at higher age levels and at the higher occupational levels in adults.

Our findings challenge many stereotypes that may have been valid in the 1960s or 1970s (e.g., the French-Canadian and Japanese "public images") and confirm some other existing concepts, such as that of the adolescent focus on Leisure. Herein lie challenges to further research, in which the multicultural Salience Inventory, available in seven languages and used in more than eleven countries, should be very useful.

References

Campbell, D. T., & Fiske, D. W. (1957). Convergent and discriminant validation by the multitrait-multimethod matrix. *Psychological Bulletin, 56,* 81–105.

Graen, G. (1969). Instrumentality theory of work motivation: Some experimental results and suggested modifications. *Journal of Applied Psychology Monograph, 53,* 1–25.

Meaning of Work (MOW) International Research Team (1987). *The meaning of working.* San Diego, CA: Academic Press.

Mitchell, T. (1982). Expectancy-value models in organizational psychology. In N. T. Feather (Ed.), *Expectations and actions: Expectancy-value models in psychology.* Hillsdale, NJ: Erlbaum.

Norusis, M. J./Statistical Package for the Social Sciences. (1988). *SPSS/PC+ advanced statistics V2.0 for the IBM PC/XT/AT and PC/2.* Chicago: Statistical Package for the Social Sciences.

Super, D. E. (1972). The relative importance of work: Models and measures for meaningful data. *Counseling Psychologist, 10*(4), 95–103.

Tilgher, A. (1930). *Work: What it has meant to men through the ages.* San Diego,

CA: Harcourt Brace.

Triandis, H. (1972). *The analysis of subjective culture.* New York: Wiley.

Weber, M. (1930). *The Protestant ethic and the spirit of capitalism.* London: Allen & Unwin.

NINETEEN

Role Commitment and Values Among Adolescents from Four Countries

Janice J. Lokan

Earlier chapters describe the major objectives of the Work Importance Study—to clarify the construct of work salience, to investigate the relative importance of work in relation to other life roles for groups both within and across countries, and to investigate relationships between work values and work salience both nationally and cross-nationally. They also detail how the underlying structures of the domains of role salience and human values, as measured by the Salience Inventory (Chapter Eighteen) and Values Scale (Chapter Sixteen and Seventeen), scarcely vary across many countries. Further, at least from midadolescence on, the structures do not seem to depend on the age level or life stage of the sample in which the domains are measured. Here we address the third of the WIS project's main objectives by examining relationships between the domains of role salience and values. We explore the extent of cross-national similarity in the relationships through a series of discriminant analyses that use data from four countries.

On a theoretical level both commitment to and participation in life roles and the values a person seeks to attain are aspects of personality. Individual differences are expected. All aspects are expected to change somewhat over time, although value patterns tend to emerge earlier and to be relatively stable by late adolescence. Most societies expect that individuals will play a variety of roles during the course of their lives and that they will attribute different meanings to the roles, although the actual number of roles may be quite small. Super (1980) conceptualized the Life-Career Rainbow (see Chapter Two) to show the "changing constellations of roles," some sequential and some concurrent, in which people in contemporary societies typically engage. Not all individuals play all roles, and the roles played increase and decrease in importance according to a person's life stage, the satisfactions the person seeks to attain, and the activities the person chooses or feels obliged to undertake.

Participation in a role can mean merely the amount of time spent in carrying it out—that is, it can be defined as a behavioral variable, as the WIS project has done, but the WIS also uses the term *commitment* to denote the affective connotation. The Life-Career Rainbow allows for illustration of both components; the area shaded or colored denotes time spent in a role, and the intensity of shading or color denotes the degree of feeling of commitment. The Work Importance Study clearly makes the distinction between the behavioral and affective aspects of involvement, which are operationalized as the Participation and Commitment scales of the Salience Inventory (Nevill & Super, 1986b; see also Chapter Four).

Whereas people's values are likely to be reasonably stable by late adolescence, the priorities for attaining those values are likely to show variations in relation to life stage. Patterns of values, or the "objectives sought in behavior" (Nevill & Super, 1986a; see also Chapter Three), are a function of personality and context. Considerable research (for example, Pryor, 1983; Holland, 1985) has substantiated the idea that patterns of values vary in predictable ways when people are grouped by occupation. Of interest here is whether the same is true for people grouped according to the degree of salience they reveal in regard to the major life roles. Just as an individual may attain more than one value through activities in a given role, that person may satisfy a given value in more than one role. The questions we are investigating here are whether people (defined in terms of their role commitment levels) tend to seek to attain a value in one role rather than another and whether any such tendencies are similar from country to country.

Data Sources and Variables

We analyzed data from four countries: Australia, Belgium, Portugal, and the United States. We used the common WIS versions of the SI and the VS and only the cross-national items to compute the values scores. Because we needed common versions of the instruments, we had to base the analyses for Australia on the stage III sample (see Chapter Four). To exercise some control over any effects stemming from life stage, we used data for only one cohort, the tenth-grade students. However, the "control" probably was not strong, because Australian students in year 10 are a year or more younger than students at the same grade level in the other countries. Further, the school retention rate at the tenth year in Australia and the United States is almost 100 percent, and the students are largely in comprehensive high schools where they receive a broad education appropriate to that stage of their schooling. Other studies have shown that the Australian and U.S. respondents in this study are probably somewhat more representative of the population as a whole than are the respondents from the more selective schools of Belgium and Portugal.

Given the existence of the Value Expectations section, we could have conducted the investigation using responses to the SI only. However, the Value Expectations section contains items for only fourteen of the eighteen cross-national values assessed in the VS, and each value within a role is assessed by only one item. Thus we decided to use scores from the longer, and therefore more reliable, scales in the VS. Given the life stage of the respondents under study—in the middle period of secondary education, when participation in study and leisure appears to dominate their lives—we used the Commitment rather than the Participation scales as indicators of the importance of the various roles. Because all the national studies found gender differences in some VS scores, we included "sex of respondent" as a variable in all our analyzes.

Research Questions

Our goal was to examine value patterns in relation to commitment to each of the five life roles of Study, Work, Homemaking, Community Activities, and Leisure Activities and to see whether values associated with commitment to each role vary from country to country. The research is exploratory and descriptive in nature; it was not intended as a definitive exercise in hypothesis testing. Nevertheless, we made some predictions based on general expectations and research knowledge about the values patterns more likely to be associated with commitment to specific roles. Table 19.1 shows these predictions. Given that students in midadolescence have not yet reached the life stages in which Work, Community Activities, and Homemaking become prominent, and that research on values patterns associated with roles has been done more commonly with older students or workers, we regarded the predictions as very tentative. They do, however, guide our reporting and discussion of results.

Analyses

As an initial step, we computed zero-order correlation coefficients between the VS scores and the SI Commitment scores together with gender of respondent. An interpretation based on the correlations would be simplistic and misleading, though, because they say nothing about patterns of values—that is, about how the values variables behave as a multivariate set. They are useful mostly as a gauge of the degree of relationship that is likely between the values variables as a set and each Commitment variable and as a preliminary indication of the likely correspondence of results across countries.

The main technique we used was discriminant analysis (via the SPSS-X program). Using the SI Commitment scale scores, we divided the respondents from the four countries that had data—Australia, Belgium, Portugal, and the United States—into groups with high and low levels of Commitment for each of the five roles. We usually used a median split to constitute the groups, but sometimes we omitted respondents scoring at the median in order to make the high and low groups more nearly equal in size. The reliability of the SI Commitment scales is high, commonly exceeding 0.9, hence

Table 19.1. Roles and Predictions of Associated Variables.

Role	Expected Associated Variables
Study	Ability Utilization, Achievement, Advancement, Personal Development
Work	Ability Utilization, Achievement, Advancement, Authority, Economics, Prestige
Community	Aesthetics, Altruism, Social Interaction, Gender
Home	Ability Utilization, Achievement, Altruism, Personal Development, Social Relations, Gender
Leisure	Aesthetics, Creativity, Life-style, Physical Activity, Social Relations

the standard error of measurement is low and the likelihood of being assigned to the "correct" group correspondingly high. We divided the Portuguese sample, the largest, into two subsamples. We used one for the main discriminant analysis, the other as a cross-validation group in which to corroborate the initial group separation findings (Huberty, 1984, p. 171).

Our primary goal was to describe relationships between the role salience and values domains, so we used discriminant analysis of each country's data initially in a descriptive sense. To achieve the additional aim of examining the correspondence of results from country to country, we used discriminant analysis in a predictive sense. We applied the classification coefficients derived from the primary analyses for each country to the data from each other country to classify the respondents in Commitment groups for each role, and we compared the results of the classifications with the subjects' known group membership in each case. Klecka (1980) and Huberty (1989) clearly describe the distinction between the two purposes of discriminant analysis.

Results

Table 19.2 shows by country the means and standard deviations on the SI Commitment scales, used as grouping variables. This table includes the cutoff scores used to establish the groups. We can legitimately compare these data, because all four countries used the same version of the truly cross-national SI, albeit in three different languages. The results show some probable differences by country:

- Australian, Belgian, and U.S. secondary school students were about equally (moderately) committed to Studying, with the Portuguese students rather higher.
- Australian, Portuguese, and U.S. students had about the same level of commitment to the Worker role, with the Belgian students somewhat less committed.

Table 19.2. Mean and SD on Salience Inventory Commitment Scales and
Cut-Off Scores for Commitment Groups by Country.

Role	Australia	Belgium	Portugal	United States
Study				
Mean	26.48	26.42	29.33	24.91
SD	7.31	6.81	6.17	8.07
High cut-off	> 27	> 26	> 30	> 26
Low cut-off	< 27	≤ 26	< 30	< 26
Work				
Mean	29.71	26.50	29.80	29.62
SD	6.24	6.12	5.47	8.24
High cut-off	> 30	> 26	> 30	> 31
Low cut-off	< 30	≤ 26	< 30	≤ 31
Community				
Mean	19.60	22.83	25.61	20.93
SD	7.81	7.97	7.11	8.08
High cut-off	> 19	> 23	> 25	> 21
Low cut-off	< 19	< 23	< 25	≤ 21
Home				
Mean	30.05	28.85	24.37	29.87
SD	7.42	5.85	6.69	8.82
High cut-off	> 31	> 29	> 24	> 32
Low cut-off	< 31	< 29	< 23	≤ 32
Leisure				
Mean	33.20	31.70	30.10	30.72
SD	5.80	5.78	6.73	8.71
High cut-off	> 34	> 32	> 31	> 33
Low cut-off	< 34	≤ 32	< 30	≤ 33
n males	134	74	584	272
n females	142	103	614	377

- Portuguese students were relatively high in their commitment to Community Activities, and the Australians were relatively low, with the Belgian and U.S. students in between.
- Australian, Belgian, and U.S. students had similar levels of commitment to Homemaking, whereas the Portuguese students were lower in commitment to this role.
- Australians were somewhat more committed to Leisure Activities than were the students from the other three countries.

Our main purpose here is to examine relationships between the values and role commitment domains, not to identify cultural differences as such. However, if the respondents are at different levels of maturity in their general development, despite all being in the tenth year of school in their respective countries, this factor could well contribute to differences between countries in the patterns or relationships we find. The results in Table 19.2 suggest that the Portuguese students in the tenth year may have a more adaptive orientation toward their future than their counterparts from the other three countries, at least in terms of taking the Student role seriously and being more interested in helping their communities.

The zero-order correlations between the values scales and the commitment scales vary considerably in magnitude from country to country, although most are quite low. For the Flemish sample several exceed 0.4 for each of the Study, Work, and Homemaking roles; in the U.S. sample several exceed 0.3 for each role except Leisure; for the Australian and Portuguese samples few exceed 0.3. The highest correlation for both the Australian and Portuguese groups is 0.42 between Altruism and Community Commitment, the highest for the Belgian group is 0.47 between Ability Utilization and Study Commitment, and the highest for the U.S. group, 0.38, occurred between Ability Utilization and Study Commitment and between Achievement and Work Commitment. The highest correlation between gender of respondent and any commitment scale is 0.34, 0.29, and 0.26 for Home Commitment in the Australian, Belgian, and Portuguese samples, respectively. The only other correlations greater than 0.2 for this variable and a commitment scale are for Study Commitment in each of these countries. In Australia and Portugal the relationship is positive, indicating a tendency for females to be more committed to study, whereas in Belgium it was negative.

A general expectation would be that the values variable correlating most highly with a commitment variable would contribute significantly to any multivariate relationship, but in discriminant analysis the "best" subset of variables of a given size is not necessarily selected by the analysis procedures—the variable's "effect" may be suppressed by its interrelationships with other independent variables (Huberty, 1984, p. 162). Hence we did not assume that the above values variables would necessarily be among those discriminating most between groups formed on the basis of their role commitment. We expected the Altruism/Community relationships would carry through, because few other values scales correlated noticeably with Altruism. We expected the picture for Ability Utilization and Achievement would be less clear, because these two scales correlated moderately highly (0.5 or higher) in each sample. Other values scale pairs that correlate moderately highly in all samples are Autonomy/Life-style, Economics/Advancement, and Achievement/Prestige.

Tables 19.3a and 193b summarize the results of the twenty primary discriminant analyses in each country, one for each role. Most of the linear discriminant functions significantly separate the role commitment groups. Separation for the Work role in Australia and Belgium is marginal, and the function for the Leisure role in Belgium does not significantly separate the commitment groups. As could be expected from the moderately low magnitude of the zero-order correlations, the canonical correlation results also tend to be quite low, as shown in the tables. On the recommendation of

Klecka (1980, p. 34), we used the total "structure coefficients," or correlations between each variable and the relevant discriminant function in each case, as a guide to the meaning of the function. These coefficients, where they exceed 0.4 in absolute value, appear in Tables 19.3a and 19.3b. The coefficients for other variables that we expected would contribute to the group separation are also given, as are those for gender of respondent. Where gender of respondent has already been listed among the highest four structure coefficients, the variable name is enclosed in brackets on the line where gender is normally shown. For each analysis the lowest structure coefficient is also shown in the relevant table. Finally, the largest four standardized discriminant function coefficients, provided that they exceed 0.3 in absolute value, are included in the tables for those who prefer to base interpretation of the functions on these coefficients.

Clearly, the high and low Study Commitment groups in all countries can be separated by their degree of valuing the use of their abilities. In three of the four countries (although not always the same three) they value Achievement, Personal Development, and to a lesser extent Advancement. The Belgian groups are distinct in that they cannot be separated by their level of valuing Advancement or Personal Development. Gender of respondent contributes to the group separation in each sample except that from the United States. Not expected was the presence of Altruism among the discriminating variables, which occurs for the U.S.

Ability Utilization is also among the most discriminating variables between the high and low Work Commitment groups in all countries, although less so for the Australian and Portuguese samples. Achievement and Advancement are highly valued by the high commitment group in three countries, less so in the Australian sample. Prestige contributes to the group separation in three countries' samples, but not in Australia's, whereas Economics has one of the highest structure coefficients in all countries except Portugal. Other variables we had expected to contribute to the worker group separation were Personal Development, relevant only in the Australian and U.S. samples, and Authority, moderately relevant in all countries' samples but that of the United States. Unexpected results are the contributions of valuing Creativity and Risk as sources of satisfaction in work to the separation of Work Commitment groups in the United States and Australia, respectively. In terms of the structure coefficients, gender of respondent does not contribute to the discrimination between groups with high and low Work Commitment.

For the groups with high and low Community Commitment, most of the group separation can be accounted for by the respondents' degree of valuing Altruism. Aesthetics contributes to the group separation in all countries' samples, whereas Social Interaction is relevant in all countries but the United States. Gender of respondent is relevant only in the Australian sample, whereas in the U.S. sample both Creativity and Personal Development appear among the variables with the highest structure coefficients.

For the Home Commitment groups, the most useful variable in sep-

Table 19.3a. Results of Primary Discriminant Analyses for Each Role by Country: Study and Work.

	Study Role				Work Role			
	Australia	Belgium	Portugal	United States	Australia	Belgium	Portugal	United States
R_c	0.44	0.54	0.45	0.43	0.34	0.44	0.38	0.39
χ^2	48.4	46.5	82.1	90.9	28.0	27.8	56.5	79.8
$p<$	0.0002	0.0004	0.0001	0.0001	0.08	0.08	0.0001	0.0001
Structure Coefficients (First Four, if > 0.40), and Gender								
	AbU 0.49 Gender 0.47 PDv 0.47	AbU 0.58	Ach 0.64 AbU 0.48 Adv 0.44	AbU 0.77 Ach 0.63 Alt 0.54 PDv 0.51	Eco 0.60 Risk 0.46 PDv 0.42	Ach 0.70 Eco 0.69 Adv 0.57 Pres 0.50	Ach 0.60 Adv 0.57 Aes 0.53 Cre 0.53	Ach 0.73 Eco 0.70 PDv 0.65 AbU 0.58
	(Gender) 0.47	(Gender) 0.28	(Gender) 0.35	(Gender) 0.13	(Gender) 0.15	(Gender) 0.00	(Gender) 0.24	(Gender) 0.15
Other Predicted Variables								
	Adv 0.34 Ach 0.31	Ach 0.25 Adv 0.15 PDv 0.02	PDv 0.38	Adv 0.36	Adv 0.36 Ach 0.31 AbU 0.30 Auth 0.24	AbU 0.49 Auth 0.44	Pres 0.40 Auth 0.36 AbU 0.35 Eco 0.22	Pres 0.56 Adv 0.56
Variable with Lowest Coefficient								
	Var −0.01	Auth 0.00	Var 0.02	Risk −0.01	Autn 0.00	Gender 0.00	LSt 0.00	Risk 0.04
Standardized Discriminant Function Coefficients (First Four, $Lf. \geq 0.30$)								
	Gender 0.48 Auth 0.44 PDv 0.41 AbU 0.39	AbU 0.85 Autn −0.49 Eco 0.45 Gender 0.43	Gender 0.44 Ach 0.35 Cre 0.30 Pres 0.30	AbU 0.57 Alt 0.38 Autn 0.38 LSt −0.32	Eco 0.81 Risk 0.54 LSt −0.41 Pres −0.34	Eco 0.39 Ach 0.38 Alt 0.36 LSt 0.31	Cre 0.45 Adv 0.41 Gender 0.34 Autn −0.33	Eco 0.48 Autn −0.35 PDv 0.33

Note: AbU = Ability Utilization; Ach = Achievement; Adv = Advancement; Aes = Aesthetics; Alt = Altruism; Auth = Authority; Autn = Autonomy; Cre = Creativity; Eco = Economics; Lst = Life-style; PAc = Physical Activity; PDv = Personal Development; Pres = Prestige; SInt = Social Interest; Srel = Social Relations; Var = Variety; WkC = Working Conditions.

Table 19.3b. Results of Primary Discriminant Analyses for Each Role by Country: Community, Home, and Leisure.

	Community Role				Home Role				Leisure Role			
	Australia	Belgium	Portugal	United States	Australia	Belgium	Portugal	United States	Australia	Belgium	Portugal	United States
R_c	0.44	0.46	0.39	0.36	0.51	0.53	0.36	0.44	0.46	0.39	0.37	0.38
χ^2	50.8	30.2	63.2	66.3	68.8	41.1	50.2	105.2	53.3	22.3	49.9	73.7
$p<$	0.0001	0.05	0.0001	0.0001	0.0001	0.002	0.0001	0.0001	0.0001	0.27	0.0001	0.0001

Structure Coefficients (First Four, If > 0.40), and Gender

Australia	Belgium	Portugal	United States	Australia	Belgium	Portugal	United States	Australia	Belgium	Portugal	United States
Alt 0.77	Alt 0.77 Slot 0.45	Alt 0.78 Aes 0.45	Alt 0.77 Cre 0.46 Aes 0.46 PDv 0.44	Alt 0.63 Gender 0.62 PDv 0.49 Aes 0.44	Alt 0.48 AbU 0.46	Gender 0.65 Alt 0.47	PDv 0.71 Alt 0.67 Ach 0.60 Aes 0.56	PAc 0.73 SRel 0.45 LSt 0.44	PAc 0.73 WkC 0.45	PAc 0.62 Pres 0.46 WkC 0.46 SInt 0.46	SRol 0.60 PDv 0.59 PAc 0.57 Aes 0.47
Gender 0.32	Gender 0.13	Gender 0.15	Gender 0.20	(Gender) 0.62	Gender 0.33	(Gender) 0.65	Gender 0.15	Gender –0.07	Gender –0.36	Gender –0.35	Gender –0.04

Other "Predicted" Variables

Australia	Belgium	Portugal	United States	Australia	Belgium	Portugal	United States	Australia	Belgium	Portugal	United States
SInt 0.30 Aes 0.29	Aes 0.33	SInt 0.39		Ach 0.41 AbU 0.27 SRel 0.16	PDv 0.38 SRel 0.34	SRel 0.27 PDv 0.13 Ach 0.10	AbU 0.52 SRel 0.29	Aes 0.34 Cre 0.09	Cre 0.22 Aes 0.15 SRel 0.13 LSt 0.07	SRel 0.41 Cre 0.37 Aes 0.36 LSt 0.25	Cre 0.34 LSt 0.33

Variable with Lowest Coefficient

Australia	Belgium	Portugal	United States	Australia	Belgium	Portugal	United States	Australia	Belgium	Portugal	United States
Auth 0.00	PAc –0.01	Var 0.03	LSt 0.00	Risk 0.02	Autn 0.01	Var 0.04	Var 0.09	Auth 0.07	Alt 0.06	Alt 0.00	Gender –0.04

Standardized Discriminant Function Coefficients (First Four, If ≥ 0.30)

Australia	Belgium	Portugal	United States	Australia	Belgium	Portugal	United States	Australia	Belgium	Portugal	United States
Alt 0.97 SRel 0.48 LSt –0.47 WkC –0.45	Alt 0.69 Auth 0.43 Aes 0.36	Alt 0.59 Adv 0.48 Eco –0.33	Alt 0.57 SRel –0.45 Achv 0.39 Auth 0.37	Gender 0.56 Alt 0.52 Eco 0.39 Ach 0.32	Auth –0.58 LSt –0.50 Rsk 0.39 Var –0.39	Gender 0.75 Aes 0.36 LSt –0.34 WkC 0.33	Alt 0.41 PDv 0.35 Ach 0.32 Autn –0.30	PAc 0.71 LSt 0.34 Alt 0.34	PAc 0.55 Autn –0.41 Advt 0.36 PDv 0.33	PAc 0.44 Alt –0.43 SInt 0.30	Autn –0.59 SRel 0.40 Auth 0.38 PDv 0.36

Note: See Table 19.3a for abbreviations.

arating the groups across all countries is Altruism, as it is for the Community Commitment groups. Gender of respondent is also useful in the Australian and Portuguese samples, whereas Personal Development contributes substantially to the group separation in the Australian and U.S. samples, less so in the Belgian sample. Ability Utilization is relevant only in the Flemish and U.S. samples, whereas Social Relations, which we had expected to be among the discriminating variables across the board, has structure coefficients of the order of 0.3 only, even lower in the Australian sample. Aesthetics appears on the list for the Australian and U.S. samples, and Achievement is one of the most discriminating variables in the U.S. sample, is moderately discriminating in the Australian sample, and is not relevant in the remaining samples.

Finally, Physical Activity is among the variables contributing most to the separation of the Leisure Commitment groups for the three countries with significant discriminant functions, as we expected. Social Relations is relevant in two countries but is replaced by Social Interaction in the Portuguese sample. Aesthetics, as expected, is among the discriminating variables in each of the three countries but at a moderate level of contribution only. Life-style is most relevant in the Australian sample. Creativity, which we had speculated would be useful in separating the Leisure Commitment groups, is of some use in the Portuguese and U.S. samples, not in the Australian sample. Gender of respondent is relevant only in the Portuguese sample, showing as a negative coefficient—that is, males are more likely than females to be associated with higher Commitment to the Leisure role in that country.

These findings reveal some commonalities among the values–role salience relationships across the four countries. However, as is the case also for multiple regression, the ordering of variables in terms of their contribution to discrimination among groups is necessarily sample specific and needs to be cross-validated in one or more external samples before the results can have meaning beyond the initial sample (Huberty, 1984, p. 162). As a first step in cross-validation, then, we applied the linear classification function coefficients (the "Fisher" discriminant function coefficients) from the primary discriminant analysis for each role carried out with part of the Portuguese sample to the scores of respondents in the remainder of the sample. The results of these analyses serve two purposes, one as a cross-validation of the initial findings, the other as a benchmark against which to assess the results of the further cross-validation steps we undertook.

Following the analyses with the Portuguese "hold-out" sample, we applied the discriminant function weights from each country for each role (except the Leisure role for the Belgian sample for which the discriminant function is not significant), to that role for each of the other countries. We assessed whether the initial results can be said to have "meaning" beyond the initial sample in each case through the "hit rate" of respondents correctly classified by applying the weights from the initial analysis.

A feature of most discriminant analysis programs is that they allow for the classification function weights to be applied back to the scores from which they were derived, to do what Huberty (1989, p. 161) calls an *internal* classification. The proportion of cases correctly classified into their known group, or "hit rate," can then be assessed against the probability that they would be correctly classified by chance. In these analyses the hit rates range from 62 percent (Work Commitment in Australia) to 77 percent (Study Commitment in Belgium). Six of twenty hit rates are greater than 70 percent and only two are below 65 percent—all substantially higher than the 50 percent that would be expected by chance alone. Generally it is more useful to consider hit rates from an *external* classification, however, where the classification function weights are applied to data from a sample other than the one in which they were derived. We did one such analysis, using half of the large Portuguese data set as a "hold-out" sample. The hit rates in the hold-out sample are generally lower than those from the primary sample, ranging from 57 percent (Work) to 66 percent (Community). These results are useful both in comparison with those from the internal classification and as an indication of an upper limit to what might be expected when weights derived in samples from other countries are applied.

In the latter situation our hit rates range from 56 percent (Work in both Australian and U.S. data with Portuguese coefficients) to 69 percent (Home in the Australian data with U.S. coefficients). On average, though, the hit rate is about three percentage points lower than it is for the Portuguese hold-out data. Also on average, Work Commitment groups are a little less likely to be classified accurately by the classification function weights (59 percent) than are the other role groups. The Study and Home Commitment groups are a little more likely to be classified correctly (62 percent). All but one of the χ^2 statistics for these classification analyses is significant, a few at the 0.05 level but most at a more stringent level. However, as Huberty (1984, p. 167) reminds us, a significant statistic is a necessary but not a sufficient basis on which to conclude that the classification result is better than chance; it is more informative to look at the diagonal entries in a classification table. Frequently, it turns out that the accuracy of classification is not balanced—that is, one group is frequently more accurately classified than another.

This was certainly true in our study. For example, the low Study, Home, and Leisure Commitment groups are usually much more accurately classified than the high ones. The picture is less uniform for the Work and Community groups. For example, only 45 percent of the low Community Commitment group is correctly classified when the U.S. coefficients are applied to the Australian data, but the hit rate is 83 percent when the same coefficients are applied to the Belgian data. Indeed, the U.S. coefficients used in the Belgian data classify all the low role commitment groups with accuracy greater than 80 percent. By contrast, the accuracy for the high role commitment groups for the same analysis combination varies from 33 percent to 42 percent.

Conclusion

What are all these statistics telling us? Obviously, a great many complex interactions among the variables are going on that ask for further investigation and clarification. Given the somewhat notorious vagaries of the results of regression and discriminant analysis, both of which techniques are sensitive to small differences in the magnitude of zero-order correlations, the amount of overlap in the variables with the highest structure coefficients from country to country reported here (Tables 19.3a and 19.3b) is not unrespectable. The hit rates we obtain when we use classification coefficients from one country's data in another's data are significantly better than chance in all but one of the sixty classifications we examined. Thus it is justifiable to conclude that there is some consistency, when all the values variables and gender are considered as a multivariate set, in the patterns of relationships between the values domain and the construct of role commitment among adolescents in each of several role contexts.

The data in this work have limitations in that the assumption of equal population covariance matrixes was violated, according to Box's criterion, in about half of the primary analyses. However, the Box M statistic is highly significant in only one analysis (Home Commitment in the United States), and the sample sizes are mostly "large" according to Huberty's definition (1989, p. 161) of the smallest group size being at least five times the number of predictor variables. In large samples the violation of assumptions is usually less relevant to the outcomes of the analyses. We referred earlier to the probable differences in general maturity levels of the samples, although all were in tenth grade. Values and role concepts are complex domains, and multivariate statistics are capricious. Perhaps it is even more remarkable that we find as much commonality as is indicated by the results, and as many of the hypothesized patterns indicated in Table 19.1.

References

Holland, J. L. (1985). *Making vocational choices* (2nd ed.). Englewood Cliffs, NJ: Prentice-Hall.

Huberty, C. J. (1984). Issues in the use and interpretation of discriminant analysis. *Psychological Bulletin, 95,* 156–171.

Huberty, C. J. (1989). An introduction to discriminant analysis. *Measurement and Evaluation in Counseling and Development, 22,* 158–168.

Klecka, W. R. (1980). *Discriminant analysis.* Series: Quantitative applications in the social sciences, No. 19. Newbury Park, CA: Sage.

Nevill, D. D., & Super, D. E. (1986a). *The Salience Inventory: Theory, application, and research* (Manual). (Research ed.) Palo Alto, CA: Consulting Psychologists Press.

Nevill, D. D., & Super, D. E. (1986b). *The Values Scale: Theory, application, and research* (Manual). (Research ed.) Palo Alto, CA: Consulting Psychologists Press.

Pryor, R.G.L. (1983). *Work Aspect Preference Scale* (Manual). Hawthorn, Victoria: Australian Council for Educational Research.

Super, D. E. (1980). A life-span, life-space approach to career development. *Journal of Vocational Behavior, 16,* 282–298.

TWENTY

Role Salience and
Time Use in Canada

Catherine Casserly
Andrew S. Harvey

In any one day people have twenty-four hours to accomplish all that they must or want to do. For some this is more than enough time; others, research has shown, cram so much into their days that the total time spent in concurrent activities often adds up to thirty or forty hours. Perhaps when a person is committed to a variety of roles, the only way to participate in them is to carry out several activities at the same time. Here we compare how Canadians use their time and their various life roles' salience. The research results support the proposition that Canadians are acting in keeping with the importance they attach to each life role.

The use of time is basically a twentieth-century topic and probably reflects the increasing importance of time allocation in people's lives. It gives an accurate and meaningful reading of what individuals do with their lives. Time imposes serious constraints on the options that people perceive as feasible and has a ripple effect on life roles. As people move through the life cycle, they assume new roles, either in addition to or instead of roles they already play. The concept of role provides an integrating perspective that depicts the most significant aspects of life, placing people in the context of their lives. Canadian researchers in the use of time (Harvey, 1983; Clark, Elliot, & Harvey, 1982; Conger & Casserly, 1983) have pointed out the significance of the concept of role in determining the time allocation of individuals. From this perspective individuals occupy a number of statuses in which the expectations of other people, their own expectations, and opportunities interact with their skills and personalities in such a way as to result in behavior that constitutes the playing of a role.

Note: Home and family care in this chapter refers to actual work to maintain the house and family, such as housework, cooking, and child care. Therefore, we consider it a form of working. This is in contrast to the term *family life*, which conveys spending time with family in recreational activities as well as any related work that might be undertaken.

Use of Time

Recorded Time

The Canadian Time Use Study (cf. Casserly & Kinsley, 1983–1984) used a time-budget approach and provided a systematic recording of an individual's use of time during a given twenty-four-hour period. Time budgets are constituted from diaries in which subjects record sequentially all activities in which they engage during the reporting period, along with the start and end times of each activity. The approach has a number of advantages for measuring people's behavior. It can be used to examine events or episodes with respect to when, where, with whom, and for how long they occur. It reveals the scheduling of events. The study was done during the same period as the Canadian Work Importance Study.

The Canadian Time Use Study had about twenty-seven hundred subjects, with an equal split between men and women. All were aged 15 or older, with about two-thirds aged 15 to 44. Demographically, they were typical of Canadians and comparable to those who completed the Canadian Life Roles Inventory (Values Scale and Salience Inventory).

Table 20.1 shows how adult Canadians use their time on any given day. We should note that the results are highly compressed for purposes of this chapter. They are based on total time per week, averaged over seven days to arrive at daily figures. The general adult population spends just under one-half of its time (47 percent, or 78 hours) on personal care, including sleeping. People use almost one-quarter of their available time (45 hours a week) for leisure activities. The third-largest expenditure of time (about 14 percent or 24 hours) is on paid work. Close behind is the percentage of time—12 percent (21 hours)—spent on home and family care. Canadians spend only a small amount of time (2 percent) on study-related activities and minimal time (1 percent) on community service. These findings hold for both men and women. A difference between the genders is reflected in the mix of work time: each gender devotes approximately 26 percent of the week to work activities; however, men allocate their time primarily to paid or labor market work, whereas women primarily allocate their time to home and family care.

There are certain differences between the paid workday and the non-work day, which is traditionally the weekend. Men are more likely to take part in a study activity or participate in an organized activity than are women, and in their leisure time men are more likely to be involved in an active leisure activity outside the home. Even so, men's participation in home and family care increases by 70 percent on the weekend as compared to a normal work-day. Women, on the other hand, tend to do far more work on the weekend. Their total work, including paid work, home and family care, and study, increases by 200 percent compared to the normal weekday. If women have any leisure time, they tend to spend it in passive activities, such as watching television or reading. They may simply be too tired to do much else.

Table 20.1. Average Use of Time per Day During a Seven-Day Week.

	Gender					
	Men		Women		Total	
Activity	Minutes	Percentage	Minutes	Percentage	Minutes	Percentage
Personal care (includes sleeping)	658.6	45.7	678.6	48.1	669.4	46.4
Leisure activities	348.5	24.2	335.9	23.3	341.7	23.7
Paid work	267.5	18.6	148.4	10.3	203.3	14.1
Home and family care	119.1	8.3	230.0	16.0	179.1	12.4
Study-related activities	34.4	2.4	33.7	2.3	34.4	2.4
Community service	11.1	0.8	13.5	0.9	12.4	0.9

Students devote little time to work-related activities or home and family care. However, if we include study as a part of the work time of students, their allocation of time to work is comparable to that of employed workers. A distinguishing feature of the time use pattern of students is their low allocation of time to home and family care or community service work. This undoubtedly reflects the fact that they live at home or are otherwise housed in a manner that demands relatively little from them in terms of household or family care. As in the case of employed female workers, female students have somewhat less free time than do males.

In essence, the Canadian results, which include measurements from a ten-year period, suggest two realities. First, there appears to be a balance of 27 percent of time for work (both paid and home and family care) and 27 percent for leisure. People appear to achieve that balance over an extended period and as a consequence of membership in a variety of economy-based subpopulations. Second, students clearly resemble employed workers in terms of their time allocation patterns when study is considered the equivalent of paid work.

Measured Importance of Life Roles

Given the self-reported behavioral measure of participation, what is the inventory-measured participation rate? We used data on role salience from the Canadian Work Importance Study (Fitzsimmons, Macnab, & Casserly, 1986) to find out. As reported in Chapter Seven, the total Canadian sample that completed the Salience Inventory was 10,120 and represented all geographical regions, major demographic variables, major occupational categories, and age groupings for members of the labor force (ages 14 to 65). It consists of three subsamples: postsecondary students, secondary students in grades 10 and 12, and adults. In the adult sample the role scored highest for

Participation by both English- and French-speaking respondents is Working. The lowest-ranked role in all cases is Community Service. This also holds true for each occupational group. Although there are no differences between genders in the French-speaking sample, women in the English-speaking sample rate their Participation in the Home and Family role higher than do the men.

The scores of postsecondary students show characteristics similar to those of the adult sample for Commitment and Value Expectations, but they show Studying as the major Participation role. Again, women are more likely to score high on Commitment and Value Expectations for Home and Family, higher than are the male students.

All secondary school samples score highest on Participation in Leisure Activities and lowest on Community Service. All female high school samples are higher on Participation in, Commitment to, and Value Expectations for Home and Family and Community Service than are the corresponding male samples.

Conclusions

By and large, the Canadian Time Use Study and WIS agree in identifying the major Participation roles as Work and Home and Family. However, perhaps because Leisure involves so many discrete activities—ranging from watching television to talking to friends to skating—respondents are not aware that it constitutes (after personal career needs) the major role in which they participate. They not only participate in but are also committed to both Work and Home and Family. Again, the detailed results of the time use data indicate that Leisure Activities most often involve Home and Family locations, so the commitment to these roles is consistent with the actual use of time. In Canada people spend most of their nonpersonal care time in the roles that are most important to them.

The results of the Canadian Work Importance Study and the Canadian Time Use Study thus confirm the congruence of what people do and what they hold to be important. Furthermore, they lead to the conclusion that the Salience Inventory, which is simpler and more time-saving than the Canadian Time Use Study, is a valid measure of role Participation.

References

Casserly, C., & Kinsley, B. (Eds.). (1983–1984). *Explorations in time use series* (A series of 8 reports). Ottawa: Employment and Immigration Canada.

Clark, S., Elliott, D. H., & Harvey, A. S. (1982). Hypercodes and composite variables: Simple techniques for the reduction and analysis of time budget data. In Z. Staikov (Ed.), *It's about time.* Sofia, Bulgaria: Institute of Sociology at the Bulgarian Academy of Sciences–Bulgarian Sociological Association.

Conger, D. S., & Casserly, C. (1983). The time of our lives: Factors in career counseling. *NATCON, 3,* 63–70.

Fitzsimmons, G. W., Macnab, D., & Casserly, C. (1986). *The life roles inventory: Values and salience* (Technical manual). Edmonton: PsiCan Consulting.

Harvey, A. S. (1983). How Canadians use their time: Implications for career counseling. *NATCON, 6,* 25–42.

TWENTY-ONE

The Importance of Work in Two Waves of Cuban Immigrants to the United States

Dorothy D. Nevill
Andres Nazario, Jr.

Work forms a central core in the life experience of most adults. However, a person's work role, as well as the other roles played in a life career, may increase or decrease in importance, depending upon the life stage of the individual (Super, 1980). Entine (1976) proposed two sets of factors to account for changes in the vocational behavior of the individual: internal versus external, and anticipated versus unanticipated. Most psychological studies have dealt with the effect of internal anticipated factors on vocational behavior, such as job change because of changes in an individual's self-concept (e.g., Murphy & Burk, 1976).

The immigrant population offers an opportunity to study a group of people for whom vocational change is often neither anticipated nor caused by internal factors. The research literature is replete with the effects of migration upon the individual, from the implication of desocialization suggested by Eisenstadt (1954) through the "culture shock" first mentioned by Oberg (1960) to the later discussions of resocialization and enculturation (e.g., Taft, 1977). Smither and Rodriguez-Giegling (1979) found higher marginality and state and trait anxiety in Indochinese refugees to the United States than in a random sample of Americans. Horowitz (1979) found feelings of powerlessness and alienation in immigrants to Israel. In his pioneering work with skill acquisition by immigrants to Israel, Krau (1981) demonstrated that involvement and attitudes play a central role in the coping strategy of immigrants, that immigrants follow expected career stages but do so at an accelerated pace (Krau, 1982), and that vocational interest and involvement are

This chapter is based on a paper presented at the International Congress of Applied Psychology, Edinburgh, Scotland, August 1982. The authors are indebted to Donald E. Super, University of Florida, on whose suggestion the research was based; to F. J. Romeo Martínez de Lecea of the National Institute of Employment, Madrid, Spain, for authorizing the adaptation of the Spanish version of the Salience Inventory; and to Terry M. LaDue, University of Florida, for carrying out the statistical analysis.

more important at the beginning of training but become less so as time in the country increases (Krau, 1984).

An immigration situation of particular interest to the United States is that of Cuban immigrants to this country. Before 1980, Cuban immigration to the United States fluctuated according to the political relations between the two countries. When diplomatic relations were good, airlifts brought regulated numbers of immigrants from Cuba to the United States. At other times flights between Cuba and the United States were suspended, and immigration decreased.

Several factors made the 1980 wave different from previous migration. First was the sheer volume of the flow. More than 125,000 refugees came in a period of six months (Azicri, 1981–1982). In fact, more immigrants arrived in the month of May alone than in any previous single year. A second factor was the negative image that accompanied this wave. Before, immigrants had been welcomed in the United States as political refugees. However, this time Cuban president Fidel Castro labeled those who were departing as "scum" and declared that all people with criminal or delinquent records could register to leave. Many immigrants labeled themselves as such in order to leave (Clark, Lasaga, & Reque, 1981). The U.S. media picked up the theme of "social undesirables" and focused attention on those people—prisoners and mental patients—who were a minority. Finally, the United States was in the middle of a recession, and people feared that conditions would worsen with the new influx. A CBS–*New York Times* poll found that almost half of those sampled nationwide opposed admitting more Cubans (Bach, 1980). Thus, Americans saw the Mariel boatlift as containing a large core of undesirable, criminal, and unemployable individuals who would be a severe economic drain on the U.S. economy.

Bach, Bach, and Triplett (1981–1982) have shown that this negative view was not warranted. Although the economic status of the 1980 immigrants was modest when compared to that of the exiled professionals of the 1960s, their economic profile was similar to that at the end of the aerial bridge in 1973. We speculated that a more convincing case could be made if the attitudes and values held by the recent immigrants were known. One aim of our study was to compare a sample of the post–1980 immigrants with a sample of the pre–1980 ones on the dimensions of commitment to work and values realization through work. If, as Krau (1984) suggested, involvement in work is more important at the beginning of entry than later, work would be particularly important to the newly arrived Cuban immigrants who not only underwent the normal stress of migration but also encountered an especially negative climate. Work would be one avenue by which they could prove their worth.

A second aim of our study was to investigate the effect of external factors on vocational behavior. If, as Entine (1976) hypothesized, both external and internal factors contribute to vocational change, commitment to work and values realization through work are predictable by using characteristics of the migration condition itself.

Therefore, we investigated the following four hypotheses:

- Recent immigrants will demonstrate a higher level of commitment to work than will earlier immigrants.
- Recent immigrants will expect to realize more values through their work than will earlier immigrants.
- A set of external factors can predict commitment to work.
- A set of external factors can predict values realization through work.

Method

Subjects

Our subjects were 122 (66 male and 56 female) immigrants from Cuba to the United States who resided in the Miami area. We classified 45 (34 male and 11 female) as recent arrivals because they arrived after April 1980. We chose Miami as a data-collection center because approximately one-half of the Cubans in the United States live in this area (Azicri, 1981–1982). The representativeness of our sample is hard to determine because of a paucity of reliable and basic data, particularly those concerning education and economic status (Jorge & Moncarz, 1980).

The gender distribution of our sample appears adequate. Our sample includes a higher percentage of women (52 percent) than men for the early arrivals, with the reverse holding for the current arrivals, the majority of whom are male (76 percent). These ratios agree with those of Clark et al. (1981), who found that 58 percent of early arrivals were women but 70 percent of the Mariel boatlift were men. However, our sample is somewhat older: 56 percent of the recent immigrants were younger than thirty-six at entry, compared to 68 percent found by Clark and colleagues' survey. Our recent and previous arrivals were primarily whites; this is true also of immigrants who registered in Miami, but not for recent immigrants placed in resettlement camps, where there was a greater proportion of blacks and mulattoes (Bach et al., 1981–1982).

The vast majority of our sample came with at least one family member (64 percent currently, 70 percent earlier) and had relatives already residing in the United States (74 percent currently, 81 percent previously). These family patterns are similar to those found by Bach (1982), Clark et al. (1981), and Portes, Clark, and Bach (1977).

Occupational comparisons are somewhat more difficult to make but can be seen in Table 21.1. Previous arrivals in this study appear to be similar to exiles who arrived between 1959 and 1974, but recent arrivals in this study have a higher occupational status than those who were registered in Miami or were sent to resettlement camps.

Educational data are similarly difficult to compare. The highest education obtained in Cuba in our study was primary 11 percent, secondary and

Table 21.1. Principal Occupation in Cuba for Employed Cuban Entrants.

	Before April 1980[a] n = 77 %	After April 1980[a] n = 45 %	Exiles 1959–1974[b] n = 732 %	Miami May 1980[c] n = 641 %	Resettlement Camps[d] n = 4,393 %
Professional and managerial	21.3	26.0	22.2	12.2	11.5
Clerical and sales	12.0	26.0	27.8	8.4	6.3
Skilled	33.3	18.0	50.0	30.7	25.3
Semiskilled	21.3	30.0	included in Skilled	24.8	26.4
Unskilled	12.1	0.0	included in Skilled	23.9	30.5

Sources:
[a]Current study
[b]Clark et al., 1981
[c]Bach, 1980
[d]Bach et al., 1981–1982

pre-university 50 percent, high school 14 percent, and university 25 percent. Clark et al. (1981) and Bach (1980) reported the average level of education of the 1980 refugees as the ninth grade, lower than that of those arriving in the 1960s but similar to that of those arriving in the 1970s. Immigrants in our study appear to have been better educated than average upon arrival in the United States.

In our study, 62 percent of the earlier immigrants knew no English upon arrival in the United States, 25 percent knew some, and 13 percent had sufficient command of English. This proportion is similar to the 62 percent who knew no English, 24 percent who knew some, and 14 percent who could speak English well in Portes and colleagues' survey of immigrants arriving in 1973 and 1974 (1977). In our study, 69 percent of the recent immigrants knew no English upon arrival in the United States, 24 percent knew some, and 7 percent had sufficient English. These figures can be compared with Clark and colleagues' 1981 estimate that 2 percent to 5 percent of the new exiles could communicate in English upon arrival. Thus, when compared to other sources, the immigrants in our study had obtained a higher level of education in Cuba, but their knowledge of English upon arrival was no greater.

Our sample contains 25 percent (51 percent recent, 9 percent earlier) who acknowledged having been in jail in Cuba. This compares with the 16 percent found by Bach (1980) for recent arrivals. However, our group does not necessarily contain more criminals, for Bach's data were taken from U.S. Immigration and Naturalization Service files from two processing centers in Miami and from Eglin Air Force Base, whereas our data were collected by individuals in the Miami Cuban community, and names were not required. Under the latter conditions respondents would be more likely to acknowledge behavior that might be labeled undesirable. Furthermore, a prisoner in Cuba is not necessarily a criminal. Most had been in prison for deeds that would not be considered criminal in the United States: for political causes or for such simple offenses as slaughtering their own animals for food or for buying coffee on the black market (Nazario, 1981).

Our population appears to be representative of Cubans who are settled in Miami, although those who are better educated and from higher socioeconomic levels might be disproportionately represented. Such a finding is not unexpected. The nature of the information requested requires a minimum level of reading ability and might have discouraged the less educated from participating. The government sources with which we compared our sample required everyone to register.

Instruments

We used a Cuban-Spanish version of the Salience Inventory. Rather than translate the U.S. version of the SI (Super & Nevill, 1986), we obtained the Spanish version (Instituto Nacional de Empleo, 1981), and Nazario adapted it for a Cuban-American population. Three independent bilingual judges read the modified version for accuracy and understandability. The judges were all of Cuban origin and had maintained their ties with the Cuban community in Miami; they included a University of Florida graduate student, a University of Miami graduate student, and a Miami housewife. They read the modified Spanish version to assure a clear understanding by Cuban readers, and then they translated the inventory back to English to compare it with the original and verify the accuracy of the Cuban-Spanish version. The three judges agreed that the final modified Spanish version was appropriate for Spanish readers of Cuban origin, and their translations to the English language proved it was addressing the same questions as the original inventory. Because the emphasis in our study was on attitudes and values and not behavior, our final version omitted the Participation scale. Thus the Cuban-Spanish version of the SI contains two scales: Commitment to the roles of Student, Worker, Citizen, Homemaker, and Leisurite, and Value Expectations in each role.

In addition to the SI, each respondent answered questions deemed by us and shown by the literature to be relevant. The questions relate both to demographic characteristics and to events of migration, such as "Did you come from Cuba via Mariel?"

Procedure

We collected data by distributing the inventories in the Miami area among several personal contacts established by Nazario. The contacts then distributed the inventories in the following places: two garment industries, one university class, one junior college class, one anti-Castro organization, two service stations, and door-to-door in one neighborhood. All were places habituated by both recently and previously arrived Cuban immigrants. We distributed a total of 150 inventories; 142 were returned. Of those, we had to eliminate 20 from the data analysis because they were incomplete.

Results

Table 21.2 shows a consistent occupational adjustment pattern in the comparison of occupational level in Cuba, first job in the United States, and current employment. The professional and managerial classes were initially unable to find jobs at their level but were eventually able to upgrade. However, skilled workers were about as marketable in the United States upon arrival as they had been in Cuba and as they were during our study. Both homemakers and students went to work outside the home and stayed employed. The ranks of the clerical, semiskilled, and unskilled initially swelled. Interestingly enough, the earlier immigrants took longer to find a job ($t = 2.50$, $p < 0.01$) than did more recent arrivals, who found an already established Spanish-speaking community awaiting them in Miami. Earlier arrivals had been handicapped by having to learn a new language before being readily employed.

Several other characteristics distinguish the recent and earlier arrivals. Of course, earlier arrivals were now older ($\overline{X} = 42$ years) than recent arrivals ($\overline{X} = 34$ years) ($t = 3.02$, $p < 0.01$). The recent arrivals were older ($\overline{X} = 33$ years) when leaving Cuba than were the earlier arrivals ($\overline{X} = 25$ years) ($t = 2.62$, $p < 0.01$), but the difference in age could be caused by the passage of years—we did not sample children in the recent arrivals. However, the earlier arrivals who were now adults and responded to our questions could have been children when they left Cuba. Their presence would have lowered the mean. As would be expected, the recent arrivals spoke less English than did their earlier counterparts ($t = 3.93$, $p < 0.01$) because the latter have had more opportunity to learn the language. Recent arrivals were more likely to have been political prisoners ($\chi^2 = 19.18$, $p < 0.01$) and to have spent a longer time in prison ($t = 2.01$, $p < 0.05$).

Recent arrivals rank Work as their most important commitment, followed by Home and Family, Community Service, Study, and Leisure. In contrast, earlier arrivals rank Home and Family first, followed by Work, Study, Community Service, and Leisure.

The most important findings of this study are that recent immigrants are significantly ($t = 2.47$, $p < 0.01$) more committed to work than were earlier immigrants and that recent immigrants are more optimistic about realizing their values through their work than were members of the earlier wave (see Table 21.3). Of the twenty-one values measured, recent immigrants score higher on all but two of the values (Variety and Physical Activity). The difference becomes significant on a majority of the remaining values: Ability Utilization ($p < 0.05$), Advancement ($p < 0.05$), Aesthetics ($p < 0.01$), Economic Rewards ($p < 0.01$), Economic Security ($p < 0.05$), Environment

Table 21.2. Occupational Adjustment Patterns of Cuban Immigrants
to the United States ($N = 122$).

	Occupation in Cuba %	First Job in U.S. %	Current Occupation %
Professional and managerial	14	3	13
Clerical and sales	11	19	28
Skilled	17	11	19
Semiskilled	15	38	24
Unskilled	4	26	10
Student	26	2	4
Homemaker	13	1	2

($p < 0.05$), Intellectual Stimulation ($p < 0.05$), Participation in Organizational Decisions ($p < 0.05$), and Supervisory Relations ($p < 0.01$).

A correlation between number of years in the United States and Commitment to Work shows that the shorter the time in the United States, the higher the Commitment to Work ($r = -0.24$, $p < 0.01$). This same correlational relationship holds for twenty of the twenty-one values measured, with only the value of Physical Activity being realized more through work by individuals who had been in the United States longer. The finding that shorter length of time in the United States correlates with higher levels of value realization reaches significance on six of the remaining twenty values: Aesthetics ($p < 0.01$), Economic Rewards ($p < 0.05$), Economic Security ($p < 0.01$), Environment ($p < 0.01$), Responsibility ($p < 0.05$), and Supervisory Relations ($p < 0.01$). Despite newspaper headlines to the contrary, recent immigrants from Cuba to the United States hold a high regard for work, are committed to it, and expect to realize a large proportion of their life's values through their occupations.

Two stepwise regressions, one on commitment to work and another on value realization through work, highlight the variables that influence recent immigrants to value work highly. Table 21.4 shows that the best model for predicting commitment to work consists of three variables: having come from Cuba via Mariel ($F = 6.02$, $p < 0.01$), not having had a blue-collar job in Cuba ($F = 3.98$, $p < 0.01$), and having been more highly educated in Cuba ($F = 3.97$, $p < 0.01$). Table 21.4 also shows the results of the stepwise regression to predict value realization through work. The best predictor model has six variables: shorter time before landing a job in the United States ($F = 8.38$, $p < 0.01$), not having had a blue-collar job in Cuba ($F = 7.93$, $p < 0.01$), having spent less time as a prisoner ($F = 6.93$, $p < 0.01$), not having relatives already in the United States ($F = 4.82$, $p < 0.05$), having spent fewer years in the United States ($F = 4.24$, $p < 0.05$), and having migrated without family ($F = 4.02$, $p < 0.01$).

Table 21.3. Comparison of Recent ($n = 45$) and Earlier ($n = 77$) Cuban Immigrants to the United States on Commitment to Work and Values Realization Through Work.

	Recent Arrivals Scored Higer than Earlier Arrivals	t	p	Shorter the Time in United States the Higher the Score	t	r
Commitment to Work	yes	2.47	0.01	yes	−0.24	0.01
Values RealizationThrough Work						
1. Ability Utilization	yes	2.34	0.05	yes	−0.17	
2. Advancement	yes	2.01	0.05	yes	−0.15	
3. Aesthetics	yes	3.47	0.01	yes	−0.24	0.01
4. Altruism	yes	1.78		yes	−0.13	
5. Associates	yes	1.22		yes	−0.08	
6. Authority	yes	1.34		yes	−0.14	
7. Autonomy	yes	1.46		yes	−0.14	
8. Creativity	yes	1.04		yes	−0.14	
9. Economic Rewards	yes	2.88	0.01	yes	−0.18	0.05
10. Economic Security	yes	2.14	0.05	yes	−0.26	0.01
11. Environment	yes	2.43	0.05	yes	−0.28	0.01
12. Intellectual Stimulation	yes	2.33	0.05	yes	−0.14	
13. Life-style	yes	1.90		yes	−0.09	
14. Participation in Organizational Decisions	yes	2.05	0.05	yes	−0.12	
15. Prestige	yes	1.49		yes	−0.08	
16. Responsibility	yes	1.93		yes	−0.20	0.05
17. Risk Taking	yes	1.53		yes	−0.11	
18. Supervisory Relations	yes	2.80	0.01	yes	−0.25	0.01
19. Variety	no	−0.24		yes	−0.08	
20. Cultural Identity	yes	0.05		yes	−0.02	
21. Physical Activity	no	−0.24		no	0.01	

Conclusion

Our study shows a clear occupational adjustment pattern for immigrants. After a period of time in the United States, immigrants regain the types of positions they lost; the disruption is the least for skilled workers and the greatest for the professional and managerial classes. The professional workers are especially prone to initial underemployment, perhaps because of language barriers and such professional requirements as licensing (Jorge & Moncarz, 1980). Other studies have found similar results. Portes, Clark, and Lopez (1981–1982) found that after six years, the proportion of their sample in professional and managerial positions was greater than the figure in Cuba, with a fifth owning their own businesses. Bach (1980) found that after three years in the United States, most exiles had regained positions comparable to those they had abandoned in Cuba, and 40 percent of the workers were employed by companies owned and operated by other Cubans. The existence of an economic enclave as an employment source is of particular importance in the successful incorporation of this particular group of immigrants.

Table 21.4. Stepwise Regression Models for Predicting Commitment to Work and Values Realization Through Work in Cuban Immigrants to the United States ($N = 122$).

Commitment to Work   ($s^2 = 0.13$)

    Coming from Cuba via Mariel
        ($F = 6.02$, $p < 0.01$)

    Not having a blue-collar job in Cuba
        ($F = 3.98$, $p < 0.05$)

    Being more highly educated in Cuba
        ($F = 3.97$, $p < 0.05$)

Values Realization Through Work ($s^2 = 0.22$)

    Shorter time before finding a job in U.S.
        ($F = 8.38$, $p < 0.01$)

    Not having a blue-collar job in Cuba
        ($F = 7.93$, $p < 0.01$)

    Having spent less time as a prisoner
        ($F = 6.93$, $p < 0.01$)

    Not having relatives already in the U.S.
        ($F = 4.82$, $p < .05$)

    Having spent fewer years in the U.S.
        ($F = 4.24$, $p < 0.05$)

    Having migrated without a family
        ($F = 4.02$, $p < 0.05$)

The study supports our first two hypotheses. Not only do the recent immigrants rank work as the most important role in their lives, but they are more committed to it and expect to realize more values through work than did earlier arrivals. New immigrants need to establish their identity and worth through their work and only later are able to turn their attention to other aspects of life. Immigrants who have been in this country a longer period of time value home and family above work, are less committed to work, and expect to achieve fewer values through it than do the more recent arrivals. Therefore, the migration condition itself affects the individual's attitudes toward the various roles in life.

But what particular factors are relevant? Our third and fourth hypotheses dealt with the external factors affecting work commitment and values realization through work. The model that best predicts work commitment consists of three elements: having come from Cuba via Mariel, not having had a blue-collar job in Cuba, and having been more highly educated in Cuba. Obviously, those people who came through Mariel were the more recent arrivals, and those who were more highly educated and did not hold blue-collar jobs in Cuba were more likely to be at the professional and managerial levels. Thus high levels of Commitment to Work are more likely to be found among the more recent arrivals and at higher occupational levels. Certainly we are not surprised to find that the well educated and well placed have a high Commitment to Work. However, why does the fact of more recent arrival from Cuba, particularly through Mariel, so affect Commitment to Work? Again, we need to remember the negative and chaotic climate that greeted these people upon their arrival in the United States. Much maligned, labeled as undesirable, these individuals were forced to prove their worth as honorable citizens. Certainly one of the quickest ways to demonstrate value in a hostile environment is by demonstrating commitment to the work ethic. Earlier arrivals are already established and are not under the same kind of stress to prove themselves.

We can gain further understanding of the influence of external factors on vocational behavior from the results of the stepwise regression to predict values realization through work. The best predictor model has six variables: shorter time before finding a job in the United States, not having had a blue-collar job in Cuba, having spent less time as a prisoner, not having relatives already in the United States, having spent fewer years in the United States, and having migrated without family. Several variables are consistent with those found in the model to predict Commitment to Work, and thus much the same logic applies in this case. For example, we would expect that the managerial and professional classes would have more opportunity to seek values realization through their work than blue-collar workers. Also in agreement with the model, recent arrivals to the United States would seek to realize more of life's values through their work because work is the arena in which they can reasonably begin to find affirmation of their worth.

A particularly important variable that emerges in this model is the length of time that elapses before the first job in the United States. The shorter the length of time here, the more important work is as an outlet for values realization. Thus, having placed much emphasis on work, recent immigrants who find jobs quickly have their expectations validated and do not become disillusioned. However, those immigrants who take longer to find employment find less values realization through work because they have to find other outlets for these needs while waiting for a job. Two other predictor variables—not having relatives in the United States and not coming with family—paint the portrait of an unattached immigrant who because of circumstances cannot rely upon home and family as a support and thus turns to work as an outlet for values realization. This picture is more typical of the recent arrivals, who were more likely to have been forced to leave their families in Cuba: more than a fifth had to leave their spouses behind (Clark et al., 1981).

The last variable that emerges, less time as a prisoner, is perhaps the most interesting of all. A superficial rationale for the importance of this variable might be that of course criminals find less value in work than noncriminals. However, a prisoner in Cuba was not necessarily a criminal; most were in prison for deeds that would not be considered criminal in the United States. In particular, recent arrivals were more likely to have been political prisoners and to have spent a longer time in prison than earlier immigrants. Thus this group of people is the most politically active of the recent arrivals and values Commitment to Community Service over Work. Anecdotal evidence we obtained while collecting the data indicates that to those who had served time in prison in Cuba, Community Service meant participating in activities designed to overthrow the Castro government. Thus to this group of people, Community Service, as defined by them, offers a greater outlet for values realization than does Work. Consequently, the less time a person spent in prison, the more that person sees Work as an arena for value realization.

A clear pattern related to work emerges to distinguish the more recent Cuban immigrants to the United States from earlier immigrants. The more recent arrivals see work as of utmost importance as a way of establishing worth and as a compensation for not having close family ties. The awaiting environment, particularly the opportunity of immediate employment, plays an important role. So too do such individual variables as educational level, occupation, and degree of political activism.

References

Azicri, M. (1981–1982). The politics of exile: Trends and dynamics of political change among Cuban-Americans. *Estudios Cubanos, 11*(2) / *12*(11), 55–73.

Bach, R. L. (1980). The new Cuban immigrants: Their background and prospects. *Monthly Labor Review, 103*(10), 39–46.

Bach, R. L. (1982). The new Cuban exodus: Political and economic motivations. *Caribbean Review, 11*(1), 22–25, 58–60.

Bach, R. L., Bach, J. B., & Triplett, T. (1981–1982). The flotilla "entrants": Latest and most controversial. *Estudios Cubanos, 11*(2) / *12*(11), 29–48.

Clark, J. M., Lasaga, J. I., & Reque, R. S. (1981). *The 1980 Mariel exodus: An assessment and prospect* (A special report). Washington, DC: Council for Inter-American Security.

Eisenstadt, S. (1954). *The absorption of immigrants.* New York: Routledge & Kegan Paul.

Entine, A. (1976). The mid-career counseling process. *Industrial Gerontology, 3*(2), 105–111.

Horowitz, R. T. (1979). Jewish immigrants to Israel: Self-reported powerlessness and alienation among immigrants from the Soviet Union and North America. *Journal of Cross-Cultural Psychology, 10*, 366–374.

Instituto Nacional de Empleo. (1981). *Inventario de la relevencia* [The Salience Inventory]. Madrid: Ministerio de Trabajo.

Jorge, A., & Moncarz, R. (1980). Cubans in South Florida: A social science approach. *Metas, 1*(3), 37–87.

Krau, E. (1981). Immigrants preparing for their second career: The behavioral strategies adopted. *Journal of Vocational Behavior, 18*, 289–303.

Krau, E. (1982). The vocational side of a new start in life: A career model of immigrants. *Journal of Vocational Behavior, 20*, 313–330.

Krau, E. (1984). Commitment to work in immigrants: Its functions and peculiarities. *Journal of Vocational Behavior, 24*, 329–339.

Murphy, P. P., & Burk, D. H. (1976). Career development of men at mid-life. *Journal of Vocational Behavior, 9,* 337–343.

Nazario, A., Jr. (1981, March). Counseling with Cuban refugees: Counseling techniques. In T. Landsman (Chair), *Counseling with the Cuban refugees,* Symposium conducted at the meeting of the Southeastern Psychological Association, Atlanta.

Oberg, K. (1960). Cultural shock: Adjustment to new cultural environments. *Practical Anthropology, 7,* 177–182.

Portes, A., Clark, J. M., & Bach, R. L. (1977). The new wave: A statistical profile of recent Cuban exiles to the United States. *Estudios Cubanos, 7,* 1–32.

Portes, A., Clark, J. M., & Lopez, M. M. (1981–1982). Six years later: The process of incorporation of Cuban exiles in the United States. *Estudios Cubanos, 11*(2)/*12*(1), 1–24.

Smither, R., & Rodriguez-Giegling, M. (1979). Marginality, modernity, and anxiety in Indochinese refugees. *Journal of Cross-Cultural Psychology, 10,* 469–478.

Super, D. E. (1980). A life-span, life-space approach to career development. *Journal of Vocational Behavior, 16,* 282–298.

Super, D. E., & Nevill, D. D. (1986). *The Salience Inventory.* Palo Alto, CA: Consulting Psychologists Press.

Taft, R. (1977). Coping with unfamiliar cultures. In N. Warren (Ed.), *Studies in cross-cultural psychology* (Vol. 1, pp. 121–153). San Diego, CA: Academic Press.

TWENTY-TWO

Role Salience in Employment and Unemployment: A Cross-National Comparison of Canada, Belgian Flanders, and Italy

Rita Claes
Massimo Bellotto
Catherine Casserly
Pol Coetsier
Donald Macnab
Marisa Sangiorgi

The psychological effects of unemployment have been investigated by a number of researchers. In an eight-country cross-sectional study, the Meaning of Work International Research Team (1987) found that the meaning-of-work pattern in unemployed people resembled that in the employed. O'Brien (1986) reviewed both cross-sectional and longitudinal studies on adult and youth unemployment. From his review of *cross-sectional* studies of adult unemployment O'Brien concluded that "unemployed people do not differ greatly from the employed on work values and personality" and that "unemployment is associated with immediate dissatisfaction, which is, in turn, partly related to work orientation, feelings of personal control, economic resources and prior job activities" (1986, p. 220). From his analysis of *longitudinal* studies of adult unemployment, he formulated some tentative generalizations on the psychological effects of unemployment: depression, dissatisfaction with financial deprivation and social support, and changes in finances and activities, but with relatively slight long-term effect. Kirsh (1983) looked at the effect of unemployment in Canada, as did Borgen and Amundson (1984) Amundson and Borgen (1987). They concluded that the experience of unemployment is a traumatic one, characterized by dramatic shifts in economic power, personal support, and self-esteem.

In Flanders, Rosseel (1982), Elchardus and associates (1984), and Spoelders-Claes and Lybaert (1982) have researched adult unemployment. In Italy, research has been conducted on attitudes toward work (Trentini, 1981), the psychological effects of unemployment (De Polo & Sarchielli, 1987), economic problems (Vinci, 1981; Valli, 1988; Frey et al., 1989), the sociological effect (Pugliese, 1981; Accornero, 1986; Cavalli & De Lillo, 1988), and concerns in the political and legislative domain (De Michelis, 1986; Varesi, 1986).

The definitions of unemployment vary across countries and must be understood for purposes of cross-national comparisons. The official

Canadian government definition of an unemployed person is one who is actually without work, has actively looked for work in the past four weeks and is available for work, or has not actively looked for work in the past four weeks but has been on layoff for twenty-six weeks or less and is available for work, or has not actively looked for work in the past four weeks but has a new job to start in four weeks or less and is still available for work. This legal definition may be condensed into a psychological definition: the unemployed are all those who do not have a job but would like to have one. Canadian workers who have a sufficient record of paid work are eligible to collect unemployment insurance for periods as long as fifty-two weeks. The long-term unemployed are also eligible for government-sponsored training programs and for geographical relocation grants for identified job openings. Both the federal and provincial governments provide job training and job search services.

In the European Community (EC) an unemployed person is someone who is without an employment contract, looking for paid work, and immediately available in the labor market. In Belgian Flanders each person meeting the EC definition is registered as unemployed with the State Employment Service. A person who loses a job can receive an unemployment allowance immediately for an unrestricted time period; a person who has never had paid work (such as a recent graduate or dropout) must qualify through a waiting period and then is eligible for an unemployment allowance. The registered unemployed must confirm their status every day. The State Employment Service provides career guidance, sets up training programs, and cooperates in a large number of initiatives to fight unemployment.

Italy has no national employment service, but there are regulations for different types of unemployment. Most of the Italian unemployed receive about 80 percent of their former total wage. Some legislative and administrative measures promote the creation of cooperatives run by the unemployed, whereas other recent laws deal with opportunities for part-time employment and trainee contracts for unemployed youth.

All three countries experienced serious employment problems from the mid-1970s to the mid-1980s. Canada experienced a period of high unemployment despite a record number of new jobs in the early 1980s. This was caused in part by the number of late baby boomers entering the market for the first time as well as by an increase in labor-force participation by women (from 28 percent to 59 percent). The country continues to experience great regional disparities in unemployment. In the industrial areas of central Canada, the unemployment rate can be 3 percent, although in geographical areas with traditional primary-resource industries, such as fishing and forestry, unemployment is closer to 30 percent, with wide seasonal variations.

In Belgian Flanders unemployment exploded from 1980 until 1984. For those insured against unemployment, the unemployment rate moved from 6.3 percent to 12.9 percent. The unemployment figures for women, youth, less skilled workers, and the public and nonprofit sectors were even worse. After 1985 the increase in unemployment slowed and began to decrease; economic revival started. The major efforts of the government to deal with unemployment are financial support programs to create jobs, legalization of longer compulsory training, alternative training, early retirement, flexible work schedules, and leaves of absence.

In Italy permanent job loss in industry has become a major problem in the economy since the mid-1970s. Unemployment increased from 5 percent or 6 percent to 11.2 percent in the mid-1970s and remained high (9.8 percent in 1990). The unemployment rate in the south of Italy was more than twice that of northern and central Italy in the late 1980s. The growing unemployment resulted from the technological restructuring of manufacturing, which was not adequately counterbalanced by the growth of jobs in the tertiary sector; it also resulted from the growing presence of women in the labor market and the increase of youth and young adult unemployment by 50 percent. The rate continued to increase because of the institutional rigidity of the Italian labor market and the inadequacy of the educational system.

The short-term economic future was somewhat brighter for Canada and Belgian Flanders than for Italy, although the labor market in the late 1980s was changing in all industrialized countries. Researchers and observers (Blyton, 1985; Robertson, 1985; Super, 1981) have predicted that many people will no longer be directly involved in the production process. In the future, people may find it more difficult to achieve self-actualization and social identification through the work role. If career counseling is to be successful, it must be based on an adequate knowledge of the values and of the means of attaining them that may be available to both employed and unemployed people. This requires knowing the importance that people attach not only to work but also to other life roles. It also means gaining more insight into the values people might attain in nonpaid work, the home, and leisure.

Our study examines the work-related values and the importance of major life roles for groups of unemployed people as compared to employed people in three countries: Canada, Belgian Flanders, and Italy. We used the cross-national version of the Salience Inventory (SI) to measure role salience (see Chapters Two and Three). In Canada, the SI was administrated in English and French (Chapter Seven), in Belgian Flanders (Chapter Six) it was administered in Dutch, and in Italy (Chapter Ten) it was administered in Italian.

Research Methods

Samples

In Canada the unemployed and the employed samples of 505 each were drawn from the national norming data of the Life Roles Inventory (Salience Inventory and Values Scale) collected in the summer and the fall of 1984 (Chapter Seven; Fitzsimmons, Macnab, & Casserly, 1985, 1986). The employed sample was designed to match the unemployed sample in gender distribution, age, proportion of people in professional, clerical, skilled, and

Table 22.1. Characteristics of Samples of Employed and Unemployed Groups.

	Canada		Flanders		Italy	
	Employed	*Unemployed*	*Employed*	*Unemployed*	*Employed*	*Unemployed*
Age						
Median	29	28	32	25	29	28
Mean	32	32	32	27	29	29
Gender (%)						
Male	64%	64%	52%	51%	54%	47%
Female	36%	36%	48%	49%	46%	53%
Educational Level						
Median years of education	12–13	12–13	12	12	12–13	12–13
Marital Status (%)						
Single	47%	46%	8%	49%	55%	68%
Married/Living with partner	38%	38%	89%	45%	42%	28%
Separated/ Divorced	15%	16%	3%	6%	3%	4%
Employment Status (%)						
Employed	100%	0%	76%	0%	100%	0%
Unemployed	0%	100%	6%	100%	0%	100%
Homemaker	0%	0%	18%	0%	0%	0%
Occupational Level (%)						
Professional and managerial	35%	34%	6%	5%	11%	16%
Clerical and sales	15%	15%	21%	27%	42%	45%
Skilled	29%	31%	33%	37%	29%	25%
Semiskilled or unskilled	20%	20%	40%	31%	18%	14%

unskilled groups, average years of education, regional-provincial distribution and urban-rural residence (Table 22.1). The employed include 14 percent immigrants and 10 percent Inuit and Amerindian, whereas in the unemployed sample the respective percentages were 17 and 12. Employed persons completed the SI and VS at work in both public and private sector organizations. The unemployed respondents completed the inventory as part of their registration with government agencies for unemployment insurance, employment counseling, and assistance in their job search.

In Belgian Flanders the employed sample ($n = 150$) is representative of the labor force for ages 30 to 34. It is representative for gender, educational level, marital status, employment status, geographical region, urban-rural residence, and employment level. This sample was collected with the help of personnel managers and through the files of city administrations.

One interviewer conducted the interviews between September 1987 and March 1988 at homes or workplaces, the average interview lasting about two hours. The sample of unemployed ($n = 28$) was one of convenience, gathered in cooperation with the State Employment Service by one interviewer between November 1987 and May 1988. The WIS instruments were administered in small groups during training programs in centers for the unemployed in the province of East Flanders. As Table 22.1 shows, the two samples are comparable for gender, educational level, and occupational level but vary in marital status and age.

In Italy the employed sample ($n = 192$) is representative of the employed population between the ages of 24 and 35 in gender, educational level, marital status, geographical region, and urban-rural residence. The employed were sampled with the help of the management of public and private business organizations. With the help of the State Employment Agency, trade unions, and private associations, interviewers contacted 145 unemployed as a presumably random sample of the unemployed population aged 24 to 35. All interviews were done at the individual's home or workplace for the employed and at the individual's home or training center for the unemployed. All interviews took place from September through November 1988. Interviews lasted about two hours. As Table 22.1 shows, employed and unemployed groups are comparable for gender, age, and occupational level but vary in marital status. Canadian, Flemish, and Italian samples are acceptable for cross-national comparisons, if the distributions of gender, marital status, and occupational level are indeed representative of each country. However, the Flemish unemployed are younger than their Canadian and Italian counterparts, perhaps because of sampling method.

Statistical Analyses

The respective national research teams did all analyses for each country. In addition to descriptive statistics (means, standard deviations, alpha coefficients), they carried out a number of analyses to examine the differences in role salience between the employed and the unemployed samples.

At the scale level for role salience, the teams used discriminant analysis to test the overall differences between the two groups (Klecka, 1980; Huberty, 1975). For descriptive purposes we also present univariate F tests and t tests between means. The canonical structure matrix (Bray & Maxwell, 1982), including the correlation of each variable with a discriminant function, yields both a measure of how well each variable independently relates to the discriminant function and a way to interpret the substantive nature of the discriminant functions.

To identify which values people expected to realize in which roles, we examined the mean item score of the Value Expectations part of the SI. (We should note here the salience scores are highly reliable—see Chapters Six, Seven, and Ten).

Results

The Hierarchy of Life Roles for Employed and Unemployed People. Table 22.2 gives the relative rankings by country and group of the fifteen SI scales, based on the means.

In the Canadian employed and unemployed groups the hierarchy of roles is identical for the three sets of scales (Participation, Commitment, and Value Expectations). Both groups say Participation in Work and Leisure Activities takes most of their time. In Canada, looking for work is considered a work-related activity because it is a condition for receiving unemployment insurance. However, Work and Home and Family are the two central areas for both groups, as far as emotional involvement (Commitment) is concerned. Congruently, the primary areas in which both the employed and the unemployed expect to achieve their values are in Work and Home and Family. The most striking difference between the Flemish employed and unemployed groups is in the behavioral aspect of role salience (Participation). The unemployed report spending significantly more time and energy in Study than do the employed. For the affective component of role salience (Commitment and Value Expectations) the employed and unemployed have the same hierarchy of relative importance of life roles. Both groups consider the two most important roles to be Home and Family and Work.

The Italian unemployed and employed share the same relative order of life roles for the affective components (Commitment and Value Expectations) of role salience. The Work role is the most important for both groups; surprisingly, it is higher in the importance hierarchy than is Home and Family. However, as in Belgium, the unemployed report significantly more time and energy spent in Study. The relative importance of Participation in life roles differs between the two Italian groups as in the Flemish groups.

Comparisons within and between countries point to the similarity in relative rankings of life roles for employed and unemployed in regard to the affective component of role salience or, more specifically, Commitment and Value Expectations of Work and Home and Family. Because of the high level of Participation of Flemish and the Italian unemployed in Study, Canada differs in this respect.

Differences in Role Salience Between Employed and Unemployed Groups. Table 22.3 provides the results of the discriminant analysis in the three countries for both groups.

In Canada the significant discriminant function (canonical correlation = 0.26; Wilks's lambda = 0.93; χ^2 = 68.29; 15 degrees of freedom) indicates significant differences between the unemployed sample and the employed sample. The group centroids indicate the location of the two groups on the discriminant function; that for the unemployed was 0.26, and for the employed group it was –0.26. Cooley and Lohnes (1971) have suggested that only canonical correlations above 0.30 are worth discussion. However, for

Table 22.2. Relative Rankings of the Five Life Roles.

	Canada		Flanders		Italy	
	Employed	Unemployed	Employed	Unemployed	Employed	Unemployed
Participation						
1.	Work	Work	Home and Family	Leisure	Leisure	Study
2.	Leisure	Home and Family	Leisure	Study	Work	Leisure
3.	Home and Family	Leisure	Work	Home and Family	Home and Family	Home and Family
4.	Study	Study	Community	Work	Study	Work
5.	Community	Community	Study	Community	Community	Community
Commitment						
1.	Work	Work	Home and Family	Work	Work	Work
2.	Home and Family	Home and Family	Work	Home and Family	Home and Family	Home and Family
3.	Leisure	Leisure	Leisure	Leisure	Leisure	Study
4.	Study	Study	Community	Study	Study	Leisure
5.	Community	Community	Study	Community	Community	Community
Value Expectations						
1.	Home and Family	Work	Home and Family	Work	Work	Work
2.	Work	Home and Family	Work	Home and Family	Home and Family	Home and Family
3.	Leisure	Leisure	Leisure	Leisure	Leisure	Leisure
4.	Study	Study	Community	Study	Study	Study
5.	Community	Community	Study	Community	Community	Community

Table 22.3. Discriminative Power of the Salience Inventory (SI).

| | | Canonical Variate Correlation | |
	Canada	Flanders	Italy
Participation			
Study	0.06	0.63	0.73
Work	0.01	−0.03	−0.25
Community	0.41	−0.01	0.29
Home and Family	0.19	−0.17	0.17
Leisure	0.03	0.29	−0.13
Commitment			
Study	0.12	0.44	0.50
Work	0.50	0.42	0.08
Community	0.37	−0.02	0.29
Home and Family	−0.06	−0.08	0.04
Leisure	−0.06	0.22	−0.04
Value Expectations			
Study	0.16	0.47	0.56
Work	0.18	0.39	0.22
Community	0.39	0.02	0.44
Home and Family	0.07	−0.12	0.01
Leisure	−0.03	0.24	0.05

purposes of exploration, it is perhaps useful to indicate some of the substantive differences possible. The correlations in Table 22.3 indicate that the discriminant function that separates the two groups in Canada and Flanders is best described by Commitment to Work and in Flanders and Italy by Commitment to Study. Other variables that correlate highly in Canada and Italy are the three measures of Community Service (Participation, Commitment, and Value Expectations). The unemployed score significantly higher on Commitment to Work than do those who are working. Further, the unemployed are significantly more likely to indicate that they spend time in Community Service than are the employed, and they also report a significantly higher degree of Commitment to and Value Expectations of Community Service than do the employed.

In Belgian Flanders the significant discriminant function (canonical correlation = 0.76; Wilks's lambda = 0.42; χ^2 = 165.78; 15 degrees of freedom) indicates significant differences between the unemployed sample and the employed sample. The group centroid for the unemployed group is 1.16 and for the employed group −1.16. The correlations in Table 22.3 indicate that the discriminant function that separates the two groups is best described by the three measures of Study (Participation, Commitment, and Value Expectations) and by the two affective measures of Work (Commitment and Value Expectations). The unemployed score significantly higher on the overall salience of Study and on Commitment to and Values sought in Work than do the employed.

In Italy the significant discriminant function (canonical correlation = 0.51; Wilks's lambda = 0.74; χ^2 = 88.29; 15 degrees of freedom) indicates significant differences between the unemployed sample and the employed one. The group centroid for the unemployed is 0.51 and for the employed group –0.51. The correlations in Table 22.3 indicate that the discriminant function that separates the two groups is best described by the three measures of Study (Participation, Commitment, and Value Expectations) and the Value Expectations of Community Service. The unemployed score significantly higher on Participation, on Values sought, and on Commitment to Study than the employed. The unemployed also report a significantly higher degree of Value Expectations in Community Service.

Commitment to Work discriminates best between employed and unemployed in Canada and Belgian Flanders. In both countries the unemployed score significantly higher on Commitment to Work than do the employed. On the other hand, Value Expectations in Community Service discriminates best between employed and unemployed in Canada and Italy. In both countries the unemployed score significantly higher than the employed. Three of the SI scales discriminate best between employed and unemployed in Flanders and Italy: Participation, Commitment, and Value Expectations in Study. In both countries the unemployed score significantly higher on Study than the employed.

The country-specific discriminative power of the SI for Flanders lies in the Value Expectations in Work, whereas for Canada it is the Participation and Commitment to Community Service.

Values Sought in Life Roles by the Employed and Unemployed. The four values (included in the Value Expectations part of the SI) Canadians seek most are Ability Utilization, Achievement, Economics, and Variety, which are the same for job seekers and for the employed. Examination of the mean item score of the Value Expectations part of the SI (see Table 22.4) shows that both samples expect to realize the values of Ability Utilization, Achievement, and Economics in the Work role and in the Home and Family role. Unemployed and employed seek to find Variety in three life roles: Work, Home and Family, and Leisure.

The Flemish data show that the three most important values (Ability Utilization, Achievement, and Aesthetics) are in the same rank order for both the unemployed and employed (as was the case in Canada). Unemployed Belgians place Economics fourth in importance, whereas employed Belgians place Working Conditions fourth. The Value Expectations part of the SI (Table 22.4) shows that the employed expect to realize their important values mainly in the Home and Family role, which is quite surprising for the value of Working Conditions. The unemployed expect to realize Ability Utilization and Achievement in two life roles, Work and Home and Family. Further, they seek Aesthetics mainly in the Home and Family role and Economics mainly in Work.

In Italy, of the values included in the Value Expectations part of the SI, the three the unemployed and the employed seek most are Aesthetics,

Table 22.4. Mean Item Scores on Most Important Values Within the Value Expectations Scale.

Canada

	Employed					Unemployed				
	Study	Work	Community	Home	Leisure	Study	Work	Community	Home	Leisure
Ability Utilization	2.76	3.44	2.20	3.23	2.85	2.70	3.43	2.26	3.22	2.82
Achievement	2.77	3.55	2.24	3.37	2.96	2.82	3.51	2.37	3.31	2.90
Economics	2.73	3.33	2.30	3.24	3.03	2.69	3.51	2.37	3.18	2.96
Variety	2.48	3.09	2.10	2.94	3.03	2.54	3.05	2.31	3.00	2.98

Belgian Flanders

	Employed					Unemployed				
	Study	Work	Community	Home	Leisure	Study	Work	Community	Home	Leisure
Ability Utilization	1.62	2.72	1.94	3.28	2.61	2.53	3.19	1.84	3.03	2.76
Achievement	1.57	2.62	1.80	3.19	2.51	2.47	3.16	1.81	3.04	2.77
Aesthetics	1.60	2.41	1.92	3.22	2.65	2.10	2.99	1.99	3.15	2.89
Economics	—	—	—	—	—	2.22	3.06	1.58	2.50	2.19
Working Conditions	1.58	2.62	1.84	3.17	2.55	—	—	—	—	—

Italy

	Employed					Unemployed				
	Study	Work	Community	Home	Leisure	Study	Work	Community	Home	Leisure
Aesthetics	2.56	2.62	2.40	3.24	3.26	2.85	3.11	2.77	3.23	3.10
Social Interaction	2.26	3.07	2.43	3.04	3.19	2.74	3.18	2.79	3.09	3.21
Life-Style	2.36	3.22	2.34	3.20	2.91	2.85	3.35	2.66	3.01	2.91
Altruism	—	—	—	—	—	2.79	3.26	2.88	3.06	2.73
Ability Utilization	2.41	3.34	2.23	3.09	2.76	—	—	—	—	—

Life-style, and Social Interaction. The unemployed seek Altruism fourth; the employed, Ability Utilization. Examination of the mean item score of the Value Expectations part of the SI (Table 22.4) shows that both samples expect to realize Aesthetic values especially in the Home and Family and Leisure roles (the unemployed also mention the Work role), Social Interaction from three roles (Leisure, Work, and Home and Family), and Life-style from the Work and the Home and Family roles. The unemployed expect to realize the value of Altruism in both Work and Home and Family. The employed expect to achieve Ability Utilization in Work and in the Home and Family.

Similarities between Flanders and Canada lie in the Values sought by the employed and the unemployed: Ability Utilization and Achievement. However, only the unemployed in these two countries seek these values in the same two roles, Home and Family and Work. Country-specific findings include the seeking of Variety in Canada and of good Working Conditions in Flanders.

In Italy the country-specific values are Social Interaction and Life-Style, sought equally in Home and Family, Work, and Leisure.

Conclusion

Although the employed and the unemployed groups within and between countries show highly intriguing similarities, there are also differences.

The rank-orders of the three most important roles, Work, Leisure, and Home and Family, for both employed and unemployed groups in Canada, Belgian Flanders, and Italy, are affectively the same (Commitment and Value Expectations). Moreover, the employed from the three countries and the unemployed from Canada and Flanders are highly committed to Work, Home and Family, and Leisure. This finding is in line with previous research, which suggests that most people who are unemployed want to work and that when asked to choose among work and other resources as a means of attaining life's most important goals, the majority of unemployed people choose work (Kirsh, 1983; MOW, 1987). The values the two samples in Canada and Flanders seek in life roles are quite similar: Ability Utilization and Achievement, mainly in Work and Home and Family roles. However, Italy is different: Italians seek other values (Social Interaction and Life-style) more in Work, Home and Family, and Leisure roles.

The discriminant function analysis suggests significant differences between the groups within countries. But there is similarity in difference, because the variables that contribute highly to the differences are identical in *pairs* of countries: Commitment to Work in Canada and Flanders, Value Expectations of Community Service in Canada and Italy, and the overall salience of Study in Flanders and Italy.

The differences in role salience between unemployed and employed suggest that the Salience Inventory would be a useful tool in counseling unemployed persons and helping them to better understand the various roles and theaters in which they can find ways to attain their values. In fact, the inventory is being used with large numbers of adults going through the vocational rehabilitation process in Canada. In Flanders the State Employment Service is interested in trying out the Salience Inventory in so-called job clubs in which unemployed people, in small groups and under the guidance of a psychologist, meet to gain better insight into themselves with the goal of retraining or reorientation. So far, the inventory has not been used in practice in Italy.

However, there is still a need for more research, as well as practical use. For example, it would be good to distinguish in further studies between those who have lost a job and those who never had a job. In Canada and Flanders the number of dropouts and recent graduates who have never had a job has increased. The psychological situation of these teenagers, to whom the ordinary transition to adulthood is denied, is largely unexplored. Work by Borgen and Amundson (1984) in Canada suggests that much more trauma is associated with increasing age and unemployment. The Flemish WIS manual (Coetsier & Claes, 1989) presents some basic SI data for graduates and dropouts, but it would be useful to study those who have just lost a job in contrast with those who have been unemployed for a longer period of time. Researchers have proposed that unemployed persons seem to pass through a number of stages (e.g., Amundson & Borgen, 1987; Powell & Driscoll, 1973; Hopson & Adams, 1976). It would seem reasonable that role salience and work-related values might change during a period of unemployment. Again, this is a largely unexplored area. Certainly, with more knowledge about role salience, life roles, and goals of these groups, more adequate steps could be taken to produce effective counseling interventions.

References

Accornero, A. (1986). *I paradossi della disoccupazione.* Bologna: Il Mulino.

Amundson, N., & Borgen, W. (1987). *At the controls: Charting your course through unemployment.* Toronto: Nelson Canada.

Blyton, P. (1985). *Changes in working time: An international review.* London: Croom Helm.

Borgen, W. A., & Amundson, N. E. (1984). *The experience of unemployment.* Toronto: Nelson Canada.

Bray, J. H., & Maxwell, S. E. (1982). Analyzing and interpreting the significance of MANOVAs. *Review of Educational Research, 2,* 340–367.

Cavalli, A., & De Lillo, A. (1988). *A Giovanni anni '80.* Bologna: Il Mulino.

Coetsier, P., & Claes, R. (1989). *Belang van levensrollen en waarden* [Salience of life roles and values]. Ostende: Infoservice.

Cooley, W. W., & Lohnes, P. R. (1971). *Multivariate data analysis.* New York: Wiley.

De Michelis, G. (1986). *Piano di lavoro: La politica occupazionale in Italia.* Rome: Laterza.

De Polo, M., & Sarchielli, G. (1987). *Psicologia della disoccupazione*. Bologna: Il Mulino.

Elchardus, M., et al. (1984). *Tijdsbesteding en maatschappelijkeintegratie van werklozen*. [Time budget and societal integration of the unemployed]. Brussels: Vrije Universiteit, Centrum voor Sociologie.

Fitzsimmons, G. W., Macnab, D., & Casserly, C. (1985). *Administrator's manual for the Life Roles Values and Salience*. Edmonton: PsiCan Consulting.

Fitzsimmons, G. W., Macnab, D., & Casserly, C. (1986). *Technical manual for the Life Roles Values and Salience*. Edmonton: PsiCan Consulting.

Frey, L., et al. (1989). *L'articolazione delle professioni verso glianni 90*. Milan: Franco Angeli.

Hopson, B., & Adams, J. (1976). Toward an understanding of transition: Defining same boundaries of transition dynamics. In J. Adams, J. Hayes, & B. Hopson (Eds.), *Transition*. London: Martin Robinson.

Huberty, C. J. (1975). Discriminant analysis. *Review of Educational Research, 45,* 543–598.

Kirsh, S. (1983). *Unemployment: Its impact on body and soul*. Toronto: Canadian Mental Health Association.

Klecka, W. R. (1980). *Discriminant analysis*. Newbury Park, CA: Sage.

Meaning of Work International Research Team (MOW). (1987). *Meaning of working: An international view*. San Diego, CA: Academic Press.

O'Brien, G. (1986). *Psychology of work and unemployment*. New York: Wiley.

Powell, D., & Driscoll, P. (1973). Middle-class professionals face unemployment. *Society, 10,* 18–26.

Pugliese, E. (1981). *I giovani tra scuola e lavora nel Meridione*. Milan: Franco Angeli.

Robertson, J. (1985). *Future work: Jobs, self-employment, and leisure after the industrial age*. Aldershot: Gower.

Rosseel, E. (1982). Werkloosheidsbeleving: resultaten en bemerkingen bij een onderzoek bij een representatieve steekproef van Belgische werklozen [Experiencing unemployment: Results of and remarks on a study with a representative sample of the Belgian unemployed]. *Tijdschrift voor Sociologie, 3,* 117–136.

Spoelders-Claes, R., & Lybaert, P. (1982). Waarde en betekenis van werken voor werklozen [Value and meaning of working for the unemployed]. *Tijdschrift voor Sociale Wetenschappen, 4,* 378–388.

Super, D. (1981). Perspectives on the meaning and value of work. In N. Gysbers and Associates (eds.), *Designing careers: Counseling to enhance education, work, and leisure*. San Francisco: Jossey-Bass.

Trentini, G. (1981). *Gli atteggiamenti dei laureandi e dei neo laureati neiconfronti del loro inserimento nel mondo del lavoro*. Milan: IBM.

Valli, V. (1988). Tempo di lavoro e occupazione. *La nuova Italia Scientifica*.

Varesi, P. A. (1986). *Regioni e mercato del lavoro: Il quadroistituzionale e normativo*. Milan: Franco Angeli.

Vinci, S. (1981). *Il mercato del lavoro in Italia*. Milan: Franco Angeli.

TWENTY-THREE

Tests of the Work Importance
Study Model of Role Salience

Donald E. Super

One unique and valuable product of the Work Importance Study is the Salience Inventory. This is, to date, the only instrument of its kind, highly reliable, available in several major languages, and standardized and validated in eleven countries. Its uniqueness lies in its assessment of the relative importance of each of five major life roles or activities: Study, Work, Home and Family, Leisure, and Community Activities or Service. Other methods have compared the importance of Work with that of all other roles combined (e.g., Dubin & Champoux, 1977; MOW, 1987), or the importance of Work and Homemaking, but the Salience Inventory looks at each of the five major roles and yields scores that make it possible to see how participation in, commitment to, and value expectations in *each* role compare with every other role.

The source of this model is the Life-Career Rainbow (Super, 1980), which is a graphic portrayal of the roles played by an individual throughout his or her lifetime. The rainbow is colorful and dramatic but not precise, and it takes considerable interviewing time to draw the rainbow of an individual. The Salience Inventory, on the other hand, is quickly administered and scored, precise, and reliable, and it helps subjects to see themselves, their use of time, and their commitment to its use with new and sometimes surprising clarity. So much for the measure. But what of the model on which it is based?

The model was developed by Kidd and Knasel (1979), and by Knasel, Super, and Kidd (1981), the Anglo-American WIS team based in Cambridge, England. After reviewing the relevant literature, the national project directors discussed the model in working conferences and provided the specifications for the Salience Inventory. Tests of the model have been run by Šverko (1989) and Super (reported here for the first time in print).

Šverko's study (1989) especially deserves summarizing here because of its hypothesis testing and the number of subjects (923 tenth graders, 949 twelfth graders, 348 university students, and 344 adults). His instruments are the Values Scale and the Salience Inventory's Value Expectations scale, which enable him to relate what the secondary school and higher education students and adult subjects value and which values they think they might realize in work. The SI's Participation and Commitment scales assessed the importance of work. Several specific hypothesized relationships are indeed found: people seek in work that which they value in life.

The hitherto unreported study in the United States was much more modest in scale, having as subjects 126 first- and second-year students at the University of Florida, a fairly typical group of American university students.

Figure 23.1 presents the correlations between measures of Commitment to Work, Value Expectations from Work, Participation in Work, and Knowledge of Work. Thus we have two affective measures of work salience: Commitment and Value Expectations, which have a correlation of 0.58 ($p < 0.01$) satisfactory for two operationally different measures. There is one measure of Participation in Work. And there are two measures of Knowledge of Work: the Career Development Inventory's (CDI) World of Work Information scale (WW) and its Knowledge of the Preferred Occupational Group scale (PO), which have an intercorrelation of –0.23 ($p < 0.05$) (for more information on the CDI, see Thompson & Lindeman, 1984). Incidentally, the low negative relationship suggests that perhaps relatively inexperienced American university students (first and second year) who know something about their preferred type of work may have foreclosed their occupational choices and thus neglected to learn what other outlets the world of work might offer them. As noted in the Salience Inventory manual (Nevill & Super, 1986) the Commitment (C) and Participation (P) scales are sufficiently similar in format that there may be some instrumental contamination in their correlation, whereas this is highly unlikely in the Value Expectations scale (VE) with its utterly different format. This may explain the difference between the correlations of 0.46 (C with P) and 0.26 (VE with P). In any case, this sample of young American university students appears to show only a moderate or slight relationship between being committed to work and doing anything about it during the first two years of higher education.

None of the four intercorrelations (0.02, 0.02, 0.00, 0.14) is significant in regard to the relationships between Commitment to and Knowledge of Work: no matter how we assess Commitment to Work or Knowledge of Work, we find no relationship. The gap between the university and the world of work at this early level is so great as to be almost shocking, although university faculty and staff members often have observed that entry into the labor force plays little part in students' thinking until graduation approaches. The student years have been well labeled as a period of moratorium and of removal from the realities and pressures of the world of work. For some, data such as these are a call for action, a sign of the need to close the gap between the groves of academe and the droves jamming the trains or the roads to office or factory. For others they are a comforting sign that campus and class-

**Figure 23.1. Correlations Between Salience Inventory Scales and
Career Development Inventory Scales.**

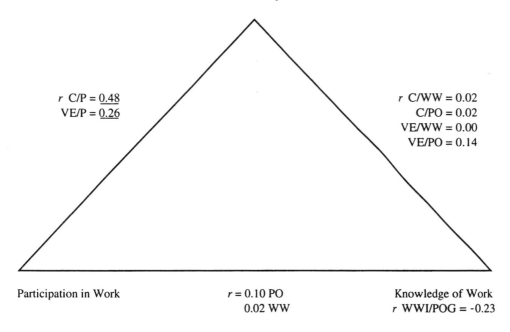

r Commitment/Value Expectations = 0.58

r C/P = <u>0.48</u>
VE/P = <u>0.26</u>

r C/WW = 0.02
C/PO = 0.02
VE/WW = 0.00
VE/PO = 0.14

Participation in Work

r = 0.10 PO
0.02 WW

Knowledge of Work
r WWI/POG = -0.23

Note: Underlined coefficients of correlation are significant at better than the 0.01 level. Note that Commitment to Work is more highly correlated with Participation in Work than are Value Expectations from Work. This may be a function of the fact that most student employment is chosen for income production rather than for its vocation's preparatory value; the VE scale involves both current and future perspectives.

C = Commitment scale from the Salience Inventory; P – Participation scale from the Salience Inventory; PO = Knowledge of the Preferred Occupational Group from the Career Development Inventory; VE = Value Expectations scale from the Salience Inventory; WW = World of Work Information from the Career Development Inventory.

room may indeed still be the preserve of learning . . . although shared by athletics with its role in preparation for an early-entry, early-leaving career.

The low intercorrelations reported here for university students can be expected to increase in size in what Havighurst (1973) called "self-expressive" occupations but not to increase much in "society-maintaining" occupations. In the former, job satisfaction is greater (e.g., Centers, 1948, and many studies since), for these are higher-level occupations in which individuals usually have more control over their work activities, behavior, and schedules. In the latter, as for example in an assembly line, the system predetermines the pace and the task. Commitment and Knowledge scores, especially the former, are those most affected, except that in the higher-level managerial and professional fields work often carries over into evenings and weekends and affects Participation scores. It should not be assumed, however, that the lower-level occupations are always lacking in satisfactions: see, for example,

Hoppock's now forgotten but classic study (1935): pride in craftsmanship and in public service are found even in such humble occupations as street cleaner, crossing guard, and information-desk clerk.

Figure 23.1 makes it clear that the three components hypothesized in the model of role salience are indeed relatively distinct in "naïve" subjects and are thus identifiable. That they are likely to prove less distinct in older, more experienced, and better informed subjects does not necessarily negate the validity of the model or its measures; rather, it may reflect their validity as measures of developing human characteristics.

References

Centers, R. (1948). Motivational aspects of occupational stratification. *Journal of Social Psychology, 28,* 187–217.

Dubin, R., & Champoux, J. E. (1977). Central life interests and job satisfaction. *Organizational Behavior and Human Performance, 18,* 366–377.

Havighurst, R. J. (1973). Social roles, work, leisure, and education. In C. Eisdorfer & M. P. Lawton (Eds.), *The psychology of adult development and aging.* Washington, DC: American Psychological Association.

Hoppock, R. (1935). *Job satisfaction.* New York: HarperCollins.

Kidd, J. M., & Knasel, E. G. (1979, December). *Work values and work salience: A review of research.* Paper presented at Second Work Importance Study (WIS) Conference, Cambridge, England (Mimeo).

Knasel, E. G., Super, D. E., & Kidd, J. M. (1981). *Work salience and work values: Their dimensions, assessment, and significance.* Cambridge, England: National Institute for Careers Education and Counselling (Mimeo).

Meaning of Work (MOW) International Research Team. (1987). *The meaning of working.* San Diego, CA: Academic Press.

Nevill, D. D. & Super, D. E. (1986). *The Salience Inventory: Theory, application, and research* (Manual). Palo Alto, CA: Consulting Psychologists Press.

Super, D. E. (1980). A life-span, life-space approach to career development. *Journal of Vocational Behavior, 16,* 282–298.

Šverko, B. (1989). Origin of individual differences in importance attached to work: A model and a contribution to its evaluation. *Journal of Vocational Behavior, 34,* 28–39.

TWENTY-FOUR

Homemakers and Employed Women in Belgian Flanders and the Southeast United States

Rita Claes
Grace Martin
Pol Coetsier
Donald E. Super

At the beginning of this century female workers were mostly single people who stopped working when they married or gave birth to their first child. Man was the breadwinner; woman was the wife. Women who worked for a substantial portion of their married lives were usually at one end of the socioeconomic continuum—for example, physicians and scientists, or domestics and agricultural workers. When other women did work, or returned to work at a later date, society assumed that their purpose was to provide supplementary income for the family. In such circumstances it was expected that commitment to career would be rather low. Rambo (1982) suggested that under this model it would be extremely difficult to measure commitment to work and even more difficult to offer definitive answers to questions about its long-range consequences in women's lives.

By mid-century, dramatic changes were taking place. Women were becoming increasingly attracted to work outside the home. The evolution had various interacting causes: the growth of a service sector that employed large numbers of women, the decline in the birth rate, an increase in part-time working opportunities, the increased educational level among women, changed attitudes toward gender-role stereotypes, increased numbers of single and divorced women who had to work for financial reasons, and the development of life-styles that required two incomes, making it difficult for many women to give up their jobs. Super (1957) called attention to the growing number of women in the work force and the valuable studies of women's occupations conducted by the Women's Bureau of the U.S. Department of Labor. At the same time, he recognized that women's careers could be studied in exactly the same way that men's careers had been viewed. He proposed career patterns for women that include stable homemaking (no significant work experience), along with six variations on the theme of work for pay outside the home, all of which recognize that the female role of child bearer makes many women the focus of the home, which occupies a central point in their lives.

The last quarter of the twentieth century has seen an increased awareness among behavioral scientists of the role of work in women's lives, focusing on factors other than economic necessity. In this, the postindustrial era,
even the definition of family has changed: families are smaller, more women
divorce and remarry, and single parents are more common. Mishler (1975)
reported a burgeoning list of surveys suggesting that women wanted to participate in both work and family and did not believe that a strong commitment to one precluded a strong commitment to the other. One survey by
Gannon and Hendrickson (1973) found that, despite the traditional view,
working women with strong commitment to the family were just as likely to
be heavily invested in their jobs as those with low commitment to the family.
Findings of this nature suggested the need to measure and compare the levels of dual commitments. Note that this is in sharp contrast to earlier researchers, such as Sobol (1983), who maintained that a woman's commitment to
work is a function of the perceived adequacy of the family income, and specifically that commitment is strongest when the woman's income is sufficient to
raise the family to the desired standard of living.

A recent sociological study by Pauwels and Deschamps (1988a, 1988b)
revealed that in Belgium from 1960 to 1985 homemakers decreased in number from 1.9 million to 1.3 million, whereas employed women increased
in the same time period from 900,000 to 1.2 million. In the United States,
McDaniels (1989) quoted statistics adapted from Johnson (1987) that indicated that women in the work force had increased from 23.2 million in 1960
to a projected 57.2 million in 1990. According to Pauwels and his Flemish colleague, homemakers were homemakers because they wanted to raise their
children themselves, their husbands wanted them to remain at home, and
they believed in principle that a married woman's place is at home. Employed
women wanted to work for intrinsic reasons, for economic reasons, and to
have social contact outside the home. The same women reported that the bulk
of homemaking tasks was assigned to them. Thus they were fulfilling two phys-
ically and socially different roles, worker and homemaker. At the same time,
approximately one-third of the homemakers declared that they wanted to
return to work, mostly for financial reasons and to have social contact, whereas
about the same percentage of working women expressed the wish to work
fewer hours in order to spend more time with their children.

Thus the 1990s see more and more women wanting to combine the
roles of homemaker and worker, either sequentially or simultaneously. To
some investigators the eventual interrole conflict between the roles of worker
and homemaker is obvious. To others the issue is not so clear. At the outset
of this project we were divided in our views. Each of us could point to substantial literature to support either position. For example, Greenhaus and
Beutell (1985) defined work-family conflict as a form of interrole conflict
wherein pressures from one domain, work or family, make it incompatible
with the other. They suggested that participation in work is made difficult by
virtue of participation in the family role. Their model of work-family role

incompatibility proposed that role conflicts are more intensive when both roles are important central life roles and when strong negative sanctions for noncompliance with roles exist. It included time-based and behavior-based conflicts that are similar to participation and commitment.

An informal literature review on dual roles and psychological well-being of working women and homemakers by the Belgian authors (all of whom are cited in the reference list at the end of this chapter) pointed to the presence of children, the role of the husband, working conditions, and the educational level of the worker as potential determinants of interrole conflicts and built further evidence for positive as well as negative consequences of employment for women. For example, Hulbert (1988) found that male norms of commitment clearly influenced the personal lives of women. In her study of young professional women, which she suggested does not generalize well to all working women, Hulbert found "no indication that any husband compromised his career plans or significantly altered his work commitments in the interest of his wife's career or their children."

However, nowhere is there a definitive body of research that allows it to be said that working women who are also homemakers will experience interrole conflict, or that women who are homemakers only will not experience interrole conflict. Indeed, the issue is surely more complex, as popular commentary has noted.

Behavior clearly is influenced by roles. A role is "the functions a person performs when occupying a particular [position] within a social context" (Shaw & Constanzo, 1982, p. 296). It is an expected pattern of behavior that is more specific than a generalized norm: "Role conflict results when a person holds several positions that make incompatible demands (interrole conflict) or when a single role involves expectations that are incompatible (intrarole conflict)" (Deaux & Wrightsman, 1988, p. 13). People play a variety of roles. What is appropriate behavior in one setting is not necessarily acceptable in another. To recognize that changing contexts require that individuals draw upon different behavioral modes is not to accept the notion that multiple roles always result in conflict.

Nevill (1984) stated that occupying multiple roles does not necessarily lead to conflicts. "In fact, one viable definition of mental health would be based on two factors: (1) the availability to the individual of a wide range of roles from which to choose, and (2) the ability and freedom to move between those roles" (p. 132). Her hypothesis, like Super's (1980), was that satisfaction is a function of the degree to which an individual's needs are met through a wide range of activities, suggesting that success in one role can facilitate success in others and difficulties in one can have a like effect in others.

Given the large, although decreasing, number of women primarily involved in the role of homemaker and the increasing number of women dealing with the dual roles of worker and homemaker, along with many unanswered questions about role conflicts, it seems relevant to study the importance of life roles and values of women. The WIS instruments allow the determination of the most salient life roles for homemakers as compared with employed women, the identification of important values that the two groups want to realize in the most salient roles, and the career concerns that are found in each group. The SI in particular offers the possibility of analyzing eventual interrole conflicts for both categories.

This project is a two-country comparative portrait of homemakers and employed women in terms of their perceived life roles. Here we describe the project's design and focus on the following research questions:

1. What are women's important life roles?
2. Do certain key roles appear equally important?
3. What are women's important values?
4. In which roles do women realize the values that are important to them?
5. What are women's important career concerns?
6. How satisfied with their life roles are homemakers and working women?
7. What is the potential for role conflict?

Subjects and Procedure

In the Belgian Flemish study, the samples of homemakers and working women are restricted to 40-year-old respondents. In general, adult women have two major transition periods. The first psychosocial transition period takes place between the ages of 27 and 30. "For many women this time of life was characterized by disruption of one's seeking something for self, and finally the emergence of increased feelings of personal competence and confidence," according to Reinke, Holmes, and Harris (1985, p. 1355). The second major transition period concerns the menopause, occurring at about the age of 50 (Notman, 1979) and characterized by neurological and psychosocial symptoms (Stevens-Long, 1979). To compare homemakers and working women, the Belgian authors preferred a life period without critical transitions. At age 40, women are usually installed in home, work, or both. The 40-year-old woman has completed her career exploration (Gill, Coppard, & Lawther, 1983) and is no longer confronted with the problems of very young children (Person, 1982). The participation of 40-year-old women in the Belgian labor force is about 52 percent (Belgian Ministry for Emancipation, 1984).

The homemaker group in the Belgian WIS study is a completely random sample, whereas the sample of working women is stratified according to educational level and random for all other personal determinants. The two samples show variability for educational level, employment status, occupational level, number of children, and husband's occupational level but not for marital status. The majority of the women, more than 90 percent in each sample, are married. The modal woman has more than a secondary school education and, in the case of working women, is employed full-time in a skilled position requiring postsecondary education.

Through personal acquaintances, two interviewers sampled 161 home-makers randomly from October 1987 to May 1988. They administered the WIS instruments to small groups at one respondent's home. An interviewer was present and the procedure took about two hours. Most interviews were conducted in the evenings or during weekends.

With the help of personnel managers, an advertisement in a well-known women's magazine, and the files of the city administration, the Belgian WIS team sampled 120 working women. One interviewer conducted the inter-views, usually in the evenings, from September 1987 through February 1988. All interviews were conducted in the respondents' homes and lasted about two hours. Each subject in the two groups completed the Salience Inventory and the Values Scale.

In the Southeast United States sample from the American WIS, the respondents were not restricted to any particular age group. The mean age for both groups is 37 years, ranging from 27 to 54. As part of a larger project, twenty-nine homemakers were recruited between January 1987 and May 1988 by nontraditional mature female students enrolled in a four-year college in Georgia. Students enrolled in organizational psychology and work behavior classes recruited twenty-nine working women. Each interview was conducted individually, either in the home or office, and lasted about two hours. No data on time of day are available. Each subject in the two groups completed the Salience Inventory and the Adult Career Concerns Inventory (ACCI) (Super, Thompson, and Lindeman, 1988).

Despite the differences in sampling techniques, the U.S. women are very similar to those in Belgium. More than 90 percent are married. Again, the modal women has more than a secondary education, and the working women were employed in skilled positions requiring postsecondary education.

Findings

We subjected the data from the four samples and three instruments to a wide range of statistical analyses, including alpha coefficients for internal consis-tency, factor analysis, multiple classification analysis, multiple discriminant analysis, and correlations. Space precludes inclusion of all data in this chap-ter. Additional data on the Salience Inventory are found in Chapters Four and Fifteen and are available from the authors. This chapter focuses on only those results that are specific to the research questions and discussion. Table 24.1 gives the per-country and per-group means, standard deviations, rela-tive rankings, and critical comparisons for the three scales of the Salience Inventory.

Homemakers in Belgium and the United States rank Home Participa-tion first and Leisure second. Similarly, both groups of homemakers rank Commitment to Home first and Leisure second. For Value Expectations, the Belgian homemakers rank Home first and Leisure second. The U.S. home-makers rank Home first for Value Expectations and Community second.

Thus homemakers in both countries are the same in that they rank Home first on all three scales and rank Leisure second on Participation and Commitment. They are different in that the Belgian homemakers rank Leisure second on Value Expectations and the U.S. sample ranks Community second on this scale.

Working women in both countries rank Home first in terms of Commitment and Value Expectations. For Belgian working women, Work is tied with Home for first place in Participation. The U.S. women rank Work Participation first and Home second. The groups are the same in that they rank Work second for Commitment and second for Value Expectations. Thus the working women in both countries place Home first and Work second on two scales. The exception is the behavioral component of the Participation scale: Home and Work are tied for first place among the Belgian working women, and Work and Home rank first and second, respectively, in the U.S. sample. But the difference between Work and Home Participation is not significant: in both countries, working women and homemakers rank Home at the top of each scale.

It is not surprising that individual t tests indicate that working women in both samples participate significantly more in Work than homemakers do. Working women are significantly more committed to Work and expect value realization through Work more than do homemakers. The working women and homemakers in both samples differ significantly in Participation in the Home but not in Commitment to the Home. The mean for Home Value Expectations for Belgian homemakers is significantly different from that for working women; in the United States, it is not.

The mean scores for Community, Study, and Leisure do not differ within countries, with the exception of Value Expectations for Community Activities between U.S. homemakers and working women: homemakers' mean for Community is significantly greater than that of working women. For purposes of clarity, the insignificant comparisons for Leisure, Study, and Community, along with the one exception, are not included in Table 24.1.

Within-group comparisons indicate that in Belgium working women have significantly more Commitment to Home than to Work, and their Value Expectations for the Home are significantly greater than are those for Work. This is not the case for the U.S. working women, whose Commitment to Home versus Work, and Value Expectations for them, are not significantly different.

The Values Scale was administered only to the Flemish subjects in this study. The worker and homemaker groups are quite similar in their relative rankings of the eighteen VS scales. The mean importance rating of values ranges from 10.07 for Personal Development in working women (highest in both groups) through 5.41 for Risk in homemakers (lowest in both groups), covering almost the entire range (minimum 4 to maximum 12).

The four most important values for both homemakers and working women are Ability Utilization, Aesthetics, Personal Development, and Social

Table 24.1. The Salience of Life Roles.

	RANK	MEAN	SD	RANK	MEAN	SD	T	P
		Flanders						
		Homemakers $n = 165$			*Working women* $n = 120$			
Participation								
Study	(5)	16.37	6.07	(3)	16.24	5.94		
Work	(4)	16.52	6.19	(1)	26.95	4.42	−16.07	< 0.01
Community	(3)	18.46	7.19	(4)	15.34	6.26		
Home	(1)	29.86	4.85	(1)	26.95	5.30	4.67	< 0.01
Leisure	(2)	23.47	5.95	(2)	20.00	5.96		
Commitment								
Study	(5)	19.56	7.10	(4)	20.07	7.28		
Work	(4)	20.55	8.15	(2)	32.16	5.08	−14.28	< 0.01
Community	(3)	22.25	7.72	(5)	20.01	7.66		
Home	(1)	35.05	4.98	(1)	34.38	5.54	1.03	ns
Leisure	(2)	26.59	7.49	(3)	23.94	7.33		
Value Expectations								
Study	(5)	22.34	8.54	(5)	21.78	8.44		
Work	(4)	25.57	10.81	(2)	37.98	8.40	−10.45	< 0.01
Community	(3)	27.63	9.65	(4)	24.60	9.72		
Home	(1)	42.78	8.16	(1)	40.78	8.07	1.99	< 0.01
Leisure	(2)	34.71	9.27	(3)	29.81	10.04		
Working women: Commitment, Home versus Work							4.21	< 0.01
Value Expectations, Home versus Work							3.33	< 0.01
		Southeast United States						
		Homemakers $n = 29$			*Working women* $n = 29$			
Participation								
Study	(4)	19.32	9.42	(4)	21.11	6.49		
Work	(5)	17.64	5.95	(1)	29.43	5.15	−7.66	≤ 0.01
Community	(3)	21.16	1.20	(5)	19.89	8.55		
Home	(1)	32.48	5.69	(2)	28.75	7.17	2.07	≤ 0.05
Leisure	(2)	23.12	5.97	(3)	26.07	6.54		
Commitment								
Study	(5)	22.64	9.40	(5)	23.00	7.34		
Work	(4)	25.40	8.01	(2)	33.75	6.20	−4.20	< 0.01
Community	(3)	25.56	7.68	(4)	24.04	7.92		
Home	(1)	37.36	5.05	(1)	36.18	6.02	0.82	ns
Leisure	(2)	26.76	7.46	(3)	29.50	7.97		
Value Expectations								
Study	(5)	29.20	11.98	(5)	30.79	10.22		
Work	(3)	33.92	11.19	(2)	43.07	9.70	−3.14	< 0.01
Community	(2)	42.84	9.08	(4)	32.85	10.92		
Home	(1)	47.28	6.52	(1)	45.54	8.73	0.81	ns
Leisure	(4)	33.68	8.38	(3)	38.42	10.05		
Working women: Participation, Home versus Work							0.41	ns
Commitment, Home versus Work							1.43	ns
Value Expectations, Home versus Work							0.96	ns

Relations. The values that best discriminate among the two groups are Economics, Physical Activity, Advancement, Ability Utilization, and Autonomy. Homemakers attach more importance to Physical Activity, whereas working women value Ability Utilization, Advancement, Autonomy, and Economics more highly.

To find out which important values women expected to realize in which roles, we combined the means of the Belgian VS scales with the mean item scores of the Value Expectations part of the SI, which includes fourteen of the eighteen VS scales. Two findings resulted:

1. Flemish homemakers expect to realize their most important values (Aesthetics, Ability Utilization, Working Conditions, Life-style, Altruism, and Autonomy) in the role of homemaker.
2. Career women also expect to realize their most important values (Aesthetics, Ability Utilization, Autonomy, and Life-style) in the role of homemaker. Only Working Conditions is a value that they expect to realize in both Work and Home and Family.

We assessed the effect of some personal and some situational determinants of the salience of life roles and values through a series of analyses of variance, combined with multiple classification analyses. In the case of working women, participation in the role of homemaker is related to the number of children: the more children she has, the more time and energy a woman spends on the homemaker role. Occupational level is related to the value women attach to Working Conditions: the lower the level, the higher the importance of good working conditions.

Because they share to a large extent the most salient life role of homemaker and the most important values, we combined the two Belgian samples. Educational level and husband's occupational level were used as predictors. Participation in and Value Expectations of the role of homemaker are related to the women's educational level: respondents with a university education score extremely low on homemaker role salience, whereas women who attended teacher-training institutions of less than university level tend to score high. The husband's occupational level is related to the importance women attach to Personal Development and Aesthetics, although not in a consistent way. Women with semiskilled or unskilled husbands score lowest on these values, whereas women with husbands working at the clerical or sales level score highest.

The U.S. women completed the Adult Career Concerns Inventory instead of the Values Scale. The two groups, although similar in age, are not in similar career stages: the working women tend to be concerned with Maintenance tasks, homemakers with those of Disengagement.

The mean Maintenance stage score of the working women is 3.42, SD 1.13, which places them at the sixty-second percentile for this career stage, according to the American norms for women (Super et al., 1988). This mean is higher than the average Maintenance stage score for women in the 35–44 age cohort, and there is more variability. Closer inspection indicates that 38 percent of these women have Establishment stage scores that are equal to or greater than their individual Maintenance scores. Thus the majority of the working women are in the Maintenance stage, and a smaller group is in Establishment. To women involved in the Maintenance stage, the concerns of considerable importance are updating their knowledge and skills, followed by innovating and holding their own. (Note that these are not substages but developmental tasks, and that they do not follow any sequential pattern.)

For homemakers, the highest mean score, 3.36, SD 1.39, indicates that as a group they are in the Disengagement stage. This score, according to the published norms, places them in the seventy-seventh percentile. Again, there is much variability. Of these women, 52 percent have individual scores in Exploration that are greater than or equal to their Disengagement scores. The mean Exploration score for the homemaker subgroup is 3.9, SD 0.84, and the mean Disengagement score is 3.24, SD 1.05. Thus, roughly half the homemakers are concerned with Disengagement and the other half with Exploration, followed by Disengagement. For the combined group, Disengagement issues that are of great or considerable concern are, in rank order, Retirement Living, Retirement Planning, and Deceleration. The other half is more concerned with Exploration. Their concerns of considerable or great interest are Specification, Crystallization, and Implementation. The homemakers in the Exploration stage are thinking about choosing an occupation, wondering what they really want to do, and perhaps getting started, while looking toward retirement.

Finally, women in all four groups were asked how they felt about their current life roles. The questions were phrased somewhat differently in the two countries. Belgian working women were asked about the roles of Worker, Homemaker, and Leisurite; Belgian homemakers were asked about Homemaker and Leisurite. U.S. women were asked about occupation (respectively, homemaker or worker) and the roles of Leisurite and Citizen. The response choices in Belgium were, respectively, "enthusiastic," "satisfied," and "not satisfied"; in the United States, "enthusiastic," "satisfied," and "dissatisfied." Table 24.2 lists the results.

The majority of women in both Flemish samples are quite satisfied with their most important roles. Homemakers are only somewhat more satisfied with Home and Family and clearly more satisfied with Leisure. However, Leisure ranks third in all three SI categories for working women in this sample.

The majority of women in both U.S. samples are also satisfied with their most important roles. However, approximately one-fourth are dissatisfied with them. For homemakers, the dissatisfaction is as Homemaker and Leisurite, the roles they rank first and second in Participation and Commitment. For working women, the dissatisfaction is in Leisure and Community, neither of which is an important role for them. Only 7 percent of the working women report they are dissatisfied with their occupational role.

Table 24.2. Satisfaction with Life Roles (in Percentages).

Flanders

	Homemakers			*Working Women*		
	Enthusiastic	*Satisfied*	*Not Satisfied*	*Enthusiastic*	*Satisfied*	*Not Satisfied*
Worker	NA	NA	NA	22	69	9
Homemaker	34	65	1	25	73	3
Leisurite	16	72	8	13	55	23

Southeast United States

	Homemakers			*Working Women*		
	Enthusiastic	*Satisfied*	*Dissatisfied*	*Enthusiastic*	*Satisfied*	*Dissatisfied*
Occupation	25	50	25	34	59	7
Leisurite	15	65	20	23	50	27
Citizen	9	82	9	20	50	30

Conclusion

The striking aspect of this study is the similarity between the women in Flanders and in the Southeast United States. Although they are all products of Western culture, conventional wisdom would suggest that dramatic differences might be present. This is not the case. The role of Homemaker is very important for all groups in terms of Participation, Commitment, and Value Expectations. The role of Worker is also very important for working women.

Are some roles equally important? Yes and no. For women who do not work outside the home, the choice is straightforward: Homemaker is the most salient role. Homemakers in both countries view that role as most important. Leisurite, and Citizen in the case of Value Expectations for the U.S. sample, are a distant second. For women who do work outside the home, the answer is mixed. Flemish working women spend equal amounts of time participating in Home and Family and in Work. However, they are significantly more committed to Home and Family, and they expect to realize important values in the Homemaker role more than in the Worker role. U.S. working women spend the same amount of time in Home and Family and in Work. They are equally committed to the roles of Worker and Homemaker and expect to realize important values equally in these roles. In other words, for Flemish working women, Homemaker is more important than Worker; for U.S. women, they are of equal importance.

In Flanders, working women and homemakers (the only ones for whom VS data are available) share the same four most important values: Personal Development, Aesthetics, Social Relations, and Ability Utilization. Both groups value Self-Realization and Autonomy, and both expect to achieve them in their current roles. The women seem very comfortable with their lives.

The U.S. working women are, on the whole, in the Maintenance stage of their work lives. They seem interested in improving their skills and using their creative abilities but show little concern with Exploration of new job possibilities or Disengagement. A smaller number are concerned with Establishment, seeming to be in a chosen field but at the same time not feeling the sense of permanence that might be associated with Maintenance. In any event, they have made the choice to work and display no strong propensity to quit the labor force.

The American homemakers as a group are somewhat mixed. Half of these women are clearly in the Disengagement stage, focusing on retirement planning. The other half seem to be in Exploration and Disengagement, an interesting combination. Martin, a member of our research team, has had considerable contact with reentry women, people who return to higher education after a period of interruption in their schooling. In her experience, women who return to school differ from those who do not in their perspective on life. Reentry students express the desire to expand their horizons: they have a strong career orientation but are interested in exploring all possibilities (Martin, Super, & Crosby, 1988). With the exception of those who enroll in nursing or teacher-education programs, they seldom specify a particular type of job as their ultimate goal. Women who remain primarily homemakers and do not continue formal education often express the desire to do so but preface their remarks with something like "I'd like to go to school, but I don't know what I want to do." In other words, before they begin any type of reentry, they feel that they must focus on a specific occupation. They do not actively gather information about options available to them. This observation provides some insight to the homemakers in the combined stages of Exploration and Disengagement. Their greatest concerns are in specifying what field to enter. It may be that these homemakers are interested in doing something, but until they can identify exactly what, they are doing nothing. Also concerned about retirement planning, it could be that this group, more than all others in this study, would benefit most from career development counseling. The problem, of course, is how to make such counseling available to them, and how to get them to seek it.

Are the women in this study satisfied with their most important roles? The answer is yes. In Belgium fewer than 10 percent report dissatisfaction; in the United States 25 percent of the homemakers report dissatisfaction with their occupations, whereas only 7 percent of the working women are dissatisfied. In fact, not only are the majority satisfied but approximately one-fourth of all the women are enthusiastic. All the women are actively fulfilling the roles that, to them, are most salient. They expect to realize important values in their roles, and their career concerns generally seem to fit with their current status. There is no strong suggestion that any are experiencing interrole conflict.

The question, then, becomes not whether interrole conflict exists for them now but what the likelihood is of conflict in the future. In the case of working women, conflict does not appear likely. Despite a strong media emphasis on "Superwoman," there is little evidence that today's woman can realistically anticipate attaining all her needs in *each* of her two roles, homemaker and worker (Gerson, 1987). The women in this study are not trying to achieve that; they are attempting to attain different values in two different roles. They are cognitively, conatively, and affectively committed to both. In those instances in which circumstances might require that one role be temporarily minimized in favor of the other, the working women will probably experience little conflict. Theirs seems to be a balanced state in which their dual commitments allow for a healthy ebb and flow between roles. Should participation in either role be denied them, these women might then experience intrarole conflict. They are accustomed to having their needs met through more than one major role, and the curtailment of one would result in situations wherein all their needs and expectations could not be fully realized. In their current situations working women, as contrasted to homemakers, seem to have the potential for greater satisfaction.

If anything, the prediction for some type of conflict is strongest for homemakers. They are totally committed to the role of Homemaker, seeking to have all their important needs met in one major role. Denied full participation in that role, they would have little to replace it. Leisurite ranks as the second most important role for homemakers, but it is a distant second. Because they report current satisfaction with the Leisurite role, there is little reason to believe that they wish to enhance its importance. At the same time, the lack of a prominent secondary role may be related to the observation that homemakers, despite their young age, are similar to many people planning retirement. They may simply lack options.

To suggest that the potential for interrole conflict is not great among working women is not to deny that it exists. Many studies suggest that it does. However, the issue probably cannot be addressed by simply looking at the *number* of roles to which women are committed.

It is important to understand what variables other than number of roles may contribute to role conflict. Obviously, participation, commitment, and value expectations are involved. Earlier in the chapter we suggested that husbands, children, and working conditions influence the roles and satisfactions of women. Little research has examined the correlations between relationship variables, personnel policies, and family life (Voydanoff, 1987). Much of what does exist looks at flextime, showing that it has little benefit in reducing stress in families with children and two working parents (Bohen & Viceros-Long, 1981). Much needs to be investigated, but, in general, work and family research lacks an integrated theoretical grounding.

Research should examine the content and contextual aspects of the Homemaker and Worker roles that may relate to conflict. Health and stress issues may be affected by the way in which women are able to integrate the Worker, Homemaker, and Leisurite roles. Of interest are not only the health and stress of the women but those of the entire family unit. Included in the studies might be an examination of the interaction between woman's role as primary or supplementary provider and the balance of economics and self-realization.

Investigators should look at homemakers in two-person careers, defined here as the situation in which a woman does not work outside the home but acts in a nonwork supporting role to her husband's career. Such supporting roles include volunteering, acting as host, social functioning, and making contacts. It would be interesting to see whether these women perceive that role as work and how salient that role is for them.

Finally, the issue of leisure must be addressed, particularly for homemakers. In today's world, families are smaller and likely to be separated by geography as children mature. It is unlikely that many women will be able to devote an entire adult lifetime to family concerns. Because women can anticipate extended life spans, it is similarly unrealistic to think that they will work all their lives. Leisure will become increasingly important. Leisure includes physical as well as creative, social, and intellectual activities (McDaniels, 1989). Women need preparation for the role of Leisurite. Who will be the counselors? What will be their approach? Will they promote only passive (spectator) and active (physical) pursuits, or will they provide guidance in intellectual growth and expanded social interactions? Will communities respond by providing greater opportunities for women so that they can continue to live fulfilling lives?

References

Belgian Ministry for Emancipation. (1984). *Eurostat.* Brussels: Belgian Ministry for Emancipation.

Bohen, H., & Viceros-Long, A. (1981). *Balancing jobs and family life.* Philadelphia: Temple University Press.

Deaux, K., & Wrightsman, L. S. (1988). *Social psychology* (5th ed.). Pacific Grove, CA: Brooks/Cole.

Gannon, M. J., & Hendrickson, D. H. (1973). Career orientation and job satisfaction among working wives. *Journal of Applied Psychology, 57,* 339–340.

Gerson, K. (1987). How women choose between employment and family: A developmental perspective. In N. Gerstel & H. E. Gross (Eds.), *Families and work.* Philadelphia: Temple University Press.

Gill, S., Coppard, L., & Lawther, M. (1983). Mid-life career development. Theory and research: Implications for work and education. *Aging and Work, 1*(6), 15–29.

Greenhaus, J., & Beutell, N. (1985). Sources of conflict between work and family roles. *Academy of Management Review, 10,* 76–88.

Hulbert, K. (1988, August). *Having it all: The impossible dream for young professional women.* Paper presented at the annual meeting of the American Psychological Association, Atlanta.

Johnson, W. B. (1987). *Workforce 2000.* Indianapolis: Hudson Institute.

McDaniels, C. (1989). *The changing workplace: Career counseling strategies for the 1990s and beyond.* San Francisco: Jossey-Bass.

Martin, G. B., Super, D. E., & Crosby, D. A. (1988, April). *Reentry women: A comparison of nontraditional students and full-time homemakers.* Paper presented at the annual meeting of the Southeastern Psychological Association, New Orleans.

Mishler, S. A. (1975). Barriers to the career development of women. In S. H. Osipow (Ed.), *Emerging women: Career analysis and outlooks*. Columbus, OH: Merrill.

Nevill, D. (1984). The meaning of work in women's life: Role conflict, preparation, and change. *Counseling Psychologist, 12*(4), 131–133.

Notman, M. (1979). Midlife concerns of women: Implications of the menopause. *American Journal of Psychiatry, 136*(10), 1270–1274.

Pauwels, K., & Deschamps, D. (1988a). *De arbeidsverdeleing van de thuiswerkende, de buitenshuiswerkende en de werkzoekende vrouwen in Vlaanderen, een dynamisch perspectief* [Women of Flanders: Homemakers, employees, unemployed. A dynamic perspective]. (Werkdocument, nr. 53). Brussels: Centrum voor Bevolkings-en Gezinsstudiën (CBGS).

Pauwels, K., & Deschamps, D. (1988b). *Sociaal-psychologisch en cultureel profiel van de thuiswerkende, de buitenshuiswerkende en de werkzoekende vrouw in Vlaanderen* [Social-psychological and cultural profile of women of Flanders: Homemakers, employees, unemployed]. (Werkdocument, nr. 54). Brussels: Centrum voor Bevolkings-en Gezinsstudiën (CBGS).

Person, E. (1982). Working women: Fears of failure, deviance, and success. *American Academy of Psychoanalysis, 10*(1), 67–84.

Rambo, W. W. (1982). *Work and organizational behavior.* Troy, MO: Holt, Rinehart & Winston.

Reinke, B., Holmes, D. S., & Harris, R. L. (1985). The timing of psychological changes in women's lives: The years 25 to 45. *Journal of Personality and Social Psychology, 48*(5), 1353–1364.

Shaw, M. E., & Constanzo, P. R. (1982). *Theories of social psychology* (2d ed.). New York: McGraw-Hill.

Sobol, M. G. (1983). Commitment to work. In F. I. Nye & L. W. Hoffman (Eds.), *The employed mother in America*. Skokie, IL: Rand McNally.

Stevens-Long, J. (1979). *Adult life developmental processes*. Mountain View, CA: Mayfield.

Super, D. E. (1957). *The psychology of careers*. New York: HarperCollins.

Super, D. E. (1980). A life-span, life-space approach to career development. *Journal of Vocational Behavior, 16*, 282–298.

Super, D. E., Thompson, A. S., & Lindeman, R. H. (1988). *Adult Career Concerns Inventory: Manual for research and exploratory use in counseling*. Palo Alto, CA: Consulting Psychologists Press.

Voydanoff, P. (1987). *Work and family life*. Newbury Park, CA: Sage.

TWENTY-FIVE

Perceptions and Expectations of the Worker and Homemaker Roles in Australia, Portugal, and the United States

Dorothy D. Nevill

One of the first tasks of the Work Importance Study was to review the relevant literature in each country. In a summary of these papers Super, Kidd, and Knasel (1980) concluded that two predominant situational determinants were influencing role change: the effect of automation on economic conditions, and the increased involvement of women in the workplace.

The Australian team (Shears, Stevens, & Lokan, 1979) found an additional theme in Australia. Although Australians had a strong belief in the right to work for all citizens, they did not necessarily associate this attitude with the practice of working hard (Bardow, 1977). Musgrave (1979) suggested that the Australian worked hard in order to consume hard. Subsequently, Dwyer (1981) noted that automation and the resultant structural change in the Australian economy had decreased employment opportunities for young working-class people. Rowland (1980) found that many attitudes regarding gender roles and work remained strongly entrenched.

A survey of the Portuguese literature produced two relevant articles. Ferreira-Marques (1983) studied work values and attitudes toward work in a sample of U.S. and Portuguese high school students. He found greater gender differences in the Portuguese sample. One source of the greater gender differences found in Portugal might have been the high illiteracy rate among women, as well as a governmental and religious emphasis on the importance of women to the home (Barbosa, 1981).

The Anglo-American team (Kidd & Knasel, 1979) found that most research focused on the economic and societal importance of work. Little attention had been paid to the meanings of work to the individual. Two more

An earlier version of this chapter was presented at the meetings of the American Educational Research Association in Montreal in 1983 and in the December 1985 issue of the *Journal of Cross-Cultural Psychology*. The author is indebted to Professor J. Ferreira-Marques of the University of Lisbon, Portugal, and Dr. Jan Lokan of the Australian Council for Educational Research for supervising the collection of data in their respective countries.

recent studies investigated the relative importance of the work and home role to high school students (Farmer, 1983; Super & Nevill, 1984). Farmer found that female students scored higher than male students on both commitment to home and commitment to work. Later work by Nevill and Super (1988) found that university women were more committed to work and to home than were university men but expected to realize fewer values through the work role than men did. A common theme found in the U.S. literature was the endorsement of changing female roles (Young, 1977) and of similar career development attitudes and behaviors for the genders (Hawley & Even, 1982).

Using Super's 1980 model, the study of life roles provides valuable information regarding a young person's perceptions and expectations. In a time when automation is changing the economic structure, and the involvement of women in the work force is changing the social structure, further research looking at role importance would be an important contribution to our understanding of young adults. The study we describe here investigates the perceptions and expectations of two life-career roles (worker and homemaker) among female and male adolescents in three nations: Australia, Portugal, and the United States. Although the countries possess many similarities (i.e., Western, capitalistic, Christian, etc.), the differences we found should be reflected in differing perceptions of role importance. Trained examiners native to the country administered the appropriate national version of the Salience Inventory (Super & Nevill, 1985; Australian Council for Education Research, 1982; Ferreira-Marques, 1982) in the three countries during regular class periods. Samples came from technical and academic secondary schools with a variety of socioeconomic levels. The schools were mainly in urban and suburban locations. A single site could have been used so long as the selected institution was not atypical. Here we compare each national sample with national norms (International Labour Office, 1983). Because the countries used different classification methods, we sometimes combined levels in order to make comparisons.

The Australian data sampled tenth-year students at four schools (two coed schools in Melbourne, a boys' private school in Melbourne, and a coed church school in Brisbane). Subjects number 132 (51 percent male and 49 percent female). Parental occupation is coded into five socioeconomic categories (Broom, Duncan-Jones, Lancaster-Jones, & McDonnell, 1977), with 42 percent professional, 20 percent managerial and farmers, 15 percent clerical, armed service, and police, 5 percent skilled, and 18 percent semi- and unskilled. The top level is overrepresented and the two lowest levels are underrepresented when compared to national norms of 15 percent professional, 18 percent clerical, armed service, and police, 9 percent skilled, and 40 percent semi- and unskilled.

The Portuguese sample consists of 149 (46 percent male and 54 percent female) eleventh-year students from one secondary school in Lisbon. Lisbon schools contain half the secondary school population in Portugal. Parental occupation is coded into five categories, with 19 percent professional, 5 percent managerial, 21 percent clerical and sales, 7 percent skilled, and 48 percent semi- and unskilled. The professional level is overrepresented and the semi- and unskilled underrepresented when compared to national norms of 6 percent professional, 3 percent managerial, 18 percent clerical and sales, 10 percent skilled, and 63 percent semi- and unskilled.

The U.S. sample was drawn from tenth- and eleventh-year students of three socioeconomically different schools in central New Jersey. Subjects number 312 (42 percent male and 58 percent female). Parental occupation is coded according to the Hamburger Revision of the Warner Scale (Warner, Meeker, & Eells, 1949), with 42 percent professional, 16 percent managerial, 20 percent clerical, 17 percent sales and service, and 5 percent related to agriculture and production. Again, the top level is overrepresented and the lowest underrepresented when compared to national norms of 16 percent professional, 11 percent managerial, 18 percent clerical, 20 percent sales and service, and 35 percent related to agriculture and production.

Samples in all three countries are skewed to the upper socioeconomic levels. Because the samples were not truly representative, generalizations from the data should be made with care. However, the samples are comparable. In each country there are approximately three times as many subjects from upper socioeconomic levels as would be predicted from national norms. The middle levels are about as would be expected. The lowest levels are correspondingly underrepresented.

To determine the effect of nation and gender, we performed a 3×2 multivariate analysis of variance. The main effects were nation (Portugal, Australia, and United States) and gender. There were four dependent variables: participation in work, commitment to work, commitment to home and family, and value expectations through work. We chose the Phillai-Barlett V as the most appropriate MANOVA statistic. To further examine the effects of the two between-subjects variables, we conducted separate 3×2 univariate analyses of variance for each dependent measure to determine which were affected. We are reporting results that were significant. Because the cell means were unequal, we used the Tukey method to test for simple effects. And we used the Statistical Analysis System (SAS Institute, 1982) in all analyses.

The multivariate analysis yields a significant main effect of nation, $F(8, 1,170) = 112.93$, $p < 0.0001$; a main effect for gender, $F(4, 584) = 10.77$, $p < 0.0001$; and an interaction for nation by gender, $F(8, 1,170) = 5.33$, $p < 0.0001$. The mean scores of the four dependent variables for each nation appear in Table 25.1; those for gender appear in Table 25.2.

A series of univariate analyses shows significant differences between countries on participation in work $F(2, 587) = 159.11$, $p < 0.0001$. Students in Australia report more work experience than do those in the United States, who in turn report more work experience than their peers in Portugal. Post hoc inspection of the means shows that this relationship holds for each gender across countries, although differences do not reach significance when comparing male high school students in Australia with those in the United States.

Table 25.1. Mean Role Salience Scores by Nation.

Nation	n	PW	CW	CH	VW
Australia	132	30.16[a]	–22.55[a]	24.31[a]	43.45[a]
United States	312	25.01[b]	31.02[b]	30.42[b]	41.05[b]
Portugal	149	17.25[c]	31.55[b]	23.65[a]	43.48[a]

Note: Means not sharing a common subscript within columns differ significantly; $p < 0.05$. PW = participation in work; CW = commitment to work; CH = commitment to home and family; VW = value expectations through work.

Table 25.2. Mean Role Salience Scores by Gender.

Gender	n	PW	CW	CH	VW
Male	261	24.45[a]	28.27[a]	25.08[a]	42.09[a]
Female	332	23.94[a]	30.02[b]	29.15[b]	42.22[a]

Note: Means not sharing a common subscript within columns differ significantly; $p < 0.05$. PW = participation in work; CW = commitment to work; CH = commitment to home and family; VW = value expectations through work.

The nation-by-gender interaction for participation in work is significant, $F(2, 587) = 10.12$, p < 0.0001. Post hoc analysis indicates that Australian female students report more work experience than do Australian males, but the reverse is true in the United States. We find no differences between the genders in Portugal. The reverse gender patterns in Australia and the United States might explain why we find no significant gender main effects.

Secondary school students in Australia are significantly less committed to work than are students in either Portugal or the United States but the Americans do not differ from each other: univariate analysis yields a significant main effect for nation, $F(2, 587) = 105.19$, $p < 0.0001$. We find a significant effect for gender, $F(1, 587) = 41.95$, $p < 0.0001$. Female students are significantly more committed to home than are males. The nation-by-gender interaction is not significant.

In both Portugal and Australia, students expect to realize significantly more values through their work than students in the United States: univariate analysis yields a significant effect for nation, $F(2, 587) = 5.34$, $p < 0.005$. We find no significant gender effect. Although we find a significant nation-by-gender interaction, $F(2, 587) = 4.45$, $p < 0.01$, post hoc analyses show few significant differences. Female students in Australia score higher than males in Australia. Females in Australia score higher than females in the United States.

Thus we find significant differences among adolescent perceptions of work and home in Australia, Portugal, and the United States. The differences hold for all four dependent variables: participation in work, commitment to work, commitment to home, and value expectations through work.

Portuguese students report the least work participation, although the sample came from the eleventh year rather than from the eleventh and tenth years, and the tenth in Australia. However, Portugal is a more traditional European developing country, with a high unemployment rate (Barbosa, 1981), so it is not surprising to find less work experience for teenagers in Portugal as compared to Australia and the United States, with their highly developed and similar economic structures (Ray, 1982).

The high participation in work even by secondary school students shows the strong commitment in Australia to the right to work for every citizen. However, we should mention one potential source of contamination: Australian students in the tenth year take a vocational course that includes a work experience unit, so the scores on this variable may be artificially high. Nonetheless, the insistence that all students take the course underscores the importance of participation in work in Australia.

However, Australian students do endorse significantly lower levels of commitment to work than do students in Portugal and the United States. Adolescents mimic the Australian adult pattern (Shears et al., 1979) of working diligently, not for the sake of work itself but in order to play. Of the three nationalities, the Australian students participate the most in work but are the least committed to it. Although the other two countries do have individuals for whom work is merely a means to another end, this attitude appears more predominant in Australia. This less committed attitude toward work is an issue that could be addressed in the vocational course that Australian students take.

Both male and female secondary school students in the United States show higher levels of commitment to the home and expect to achieve fewer values through their work than do their counterparts in Australia and Portugal. The Anglo-American literature (Kidd & Knasel, 1979) showed the endorsement of changing female roles, which is partly the result of women's entry into the work force. In the United States in particular this has resulted in the development of similar attitudes and behavior in the genders. Our study suggests that men and women in the United States are similar in their willingness to be involved in the home and to realize important values through channels other than work.

Female students express more commitment to both work and home than do male students. This is an unexpected finding, given prevailing gender-role stereotypes, and shows the effects of the increased role of women in the workplace. However, female secondary school students do not expect to realize more values through work than do males. Hackett and Betz (1981) have proposed an explanatory model of women's career development: using Bandura's concept of self-efficacy expectations, they proposed that women, as a result of their socialization, "lack strong expectations of personal efficacy in relationship to many career-related behaviors and thus fail to fully realize their capabilities and talents in career pursuits" (p. 326). Although they might be more committed to the work role, women might not see work as an outlet for personal value realization. Thus women's higher levels of commitment relate more to feelings of responsibility or tendencies to persevere than to meeting personal needs.

Continued research on relative role importance would improve our understanding of adolescent career motivation and role self-concepts. As we learn more about the way in which different needs can be met through different life roles, we may better help our young people to make self-fulfilling life-role choices in this time of economic and social change.

References

Australian Council for Educational Research. (1982). *The Salience Inventory.* Hawthorn: Australian Council for Educational Research.

Barbosa, M. (1981). Women in Portugal. *Women's Studies International Quarterly, 4,* 477–480.

Bardow, A. (Ed.). (1977). *The worker in Australia.* St. Lucia, Australia: University of Queensland Press.

Broom, L., Duncan-Jones, P., Lancaster-Jones, F., & McDonnell, P. (1977). *Investigating social mobility.* Canberra: Australian National University.

Dwyer, P. J. (1981). Structural change, job prospects, and working-class responses. *Australian and New Zealand Journal of Sociology, 17,* 31–40.

Farmer, H. S. (1983). Career and homemaking plans for high school youth. *Journal of Counseling Psychology, 30,* 40–45.

Ferreira-Marques J. (1982). *Inventario sobre a saliencia das actividades* [The Salience Inventory]. Lisbon: Faculty of Psychology and Education, Work Importance Study.

Ferreira-Marques, J. (1983, April). Values and role salience in Portugal and the USA. In D. E. Super (Chair), *Values and roles in diverse modern societies.* Symposium at the meeting of the American Educational Research Association, Montreal.

Hackett, G., & Betz, N. E. (1981). A self-efficacy approach to the career development of women. *Journal of Vocational Behavior, 18,* 326–339.

Hawley, P., & Even, B. (1982). Work and sex-role attitudes in relation to education and other characteristics. *Vocational Guidance Quarterly, 31,* 101–108.

International Labour Office. (1983). *Year book of labour statistics.* Geneva: International Labour Office.

Kidd, J. M., & Knasel, E. G. (1979). *Work values and work salience: A review of research.* Unpublished manuscript, National Institute for Careers Education and Counselling, Hertford, England.

Musgrave, P. W. (1979). *Contemporary schooling, competence, and commitment to work.* Paper presented at the 20th Annual Conference of the Australian College of Education, Perth.

Nevill, D. D., & Super, D. E. (1988). Career maturity and commitment to work in university students. *Journal of Vocational Behavior, 32,* 139–151.

Ray, J. J. (1982). The Protestant ethic in Australia. *Journal of Social Psychology, 116,* 127–138.

Rowland, R. (1980). Attitudes to sex roles: A discussion of Australian data and of methodology. *Australian and New Zealand Journal of Sociology, 16,* 85–90.

SAS Institute. (1982). *SAS User's guide: Statistics.* Cary, NC: Statistical Analysis Institute.

Shears, M., Stevens, S., & Lokan, J. (1979). *Work Importance Study: Review of literature—Australia and New Zealand.* Unpublished manuscript. Australian Council for Educational Research, Hawthorn.

Super, D. E. (1980). A life-span, life-space approach to career development. *Journal of Vocational Behavior, 16,* 282–298.

Super, D. E., Kidd, J. M., & Knasel, E. G. (1980). *Work values and work salience: A survey of literature in fourteen countries.* Unpublished manuscript, National Institute for Careers Education and Counselling, Hertford, England.

Super, D. E., & Nevill, D. D. (1984). Work role salience as a determinant of career maturity in high school students. *Journal of Vocational Behavior, 25,* 30–44.

Super, D. E., & Nevill, D. D. (1985). *The Salience Inventory.* Palo Alto, CA: Consulting Psychologists Press.

Warner, W. L., Meeker, M., & Eells, K. (1949). *Social class in America.* Chicago: Science Research Associates.

Young, R. F. (1977). Current sex-role attitudes of male and female students. *Sociological Focus, 10,* 309–323.

PART FOUR

Conclusion

Research teams from eleven countries, ranging from moderately developed to some of the world's richest and industrially most advanced nations, have been involved in a series of coordinated projects in the Work Importance Study (WIS). This large-scale, cross-cultural project is concerned with values (the rewards that people seek from life) and with the importance assigned to work and to each of several other important life roles or activities. This combined study of specific life values and roles in cross-cultural perspective is the Work Importance Study's distinctive approach to the study of the meanings of work, study, homemaking, leisure, and community service in the lives of individuals.

A vast amount of data, comprising responses of more than thirty thousand respondents from eleven countries to two psychometrically sound inventories and personal data sheets, has been collected and analyzed both within and across participating countries in this study. The outcomes of the analyses have been presented in the preceding chapters of this volume; this concluding section—a single chapter—summarizes and comments on only some of the findings that seem to be of great moment and interest.

TWENTY-SIX

The Findings of the
Work Importance Study

Branimir Šverko
Donald E. Super

The purpose of the Work Importance Study (WIS) was twofold: to develop an integrated series of measures for the systematic assessment of values and the relative importance of major life roles, and to advance the cross-cultural study of value priorities and life-role salience. We see the first goal as not only the prerequisite for achieving the second but also as important in its own right: truly cross-national measures of values and life-role importance are needed in both research and practice. Therefore, throughout the study, much effort has been devoted to the development and evaluation of WIS instruments, from establishing the conceptually adequate models of values and role salience that guided the writing of items through the psychometric analysis and selection of the items to the careful analysis of both the metric and logical properties of the final forms. Most national teams actively participated in this endeavor; only two, which joined the project after it was well advanced, omitted the early creative steps for the sake of comparability. As a result, we have developed two truly international, logically and psychometrically sound, inventories—the Values Scale (VS) and Salience Inventory (SI).

The national chapters examine the data on the metric properties of the VS and SI; more detailed analyses are presented in the national manuals published in several countries, particularly in the Australian and Croatian manuals (Coetsier & Claes, 1990; Fitzsimmons, Macnab, & Casserly, 1986; Nevill & Super, 1986a & 1986b; Šverko, 1987). The levels of reliability proved satisfactory for their principal intended use: for the Values Scale, the alpha coefficients are generally good for research purposes but barely sufficient for use with individuals; for the Salience Inventory, they are remarkably reliable for both research and individual assessment. The WIS project examined the validity of the two inventories cross-nationally and in several countries; indicative of their construct validity are the meaningful factor structures of their scales, their power to discriminate among groups of individuals known to differ in various ways, and the theoretically predicted correlations with certain other measures. The validation of an instrument is of course a continuing and complex process, requiring the integration of the results of different studies that slowly accumulate the information needed. For the WIS instruments, this process is not yet complete, but all the analyses thus far speak in favor of their validity and utility.

The two WIS inventories are not only adequate for the cross-national analyses but also are promising diagnostic tools that should prove valuable for other purposes, especially in career counseling and human resource development applications. The initial developments of such applications in some countries (see, for example, the Belgian and U.S. national chapters) seem to be promising.

Stability of the Factor Structure: Evidence of Cross-National Universality

The factor structure of the variables we measured was an early issue for consideration in our cross-national study. Each national team analyzed the factor structure of its respective national versions of the WIS instruments, with congruent outcomes: visually matched factors emerge across most analyses of both values and roles. In the values domain, the WIS labeled, with minor terminological variations, the five factors identified in most of the national analyses: Utilitarian, Self-Actualizing, Individualistic (or Independent), Social, and Adventurous. In the role salience domain, the WIS found a simple universal structure, with the five factors corresponding to the five scales for the life roles identified in all eleven countries on all five continents.

We then undertook a more formal cross-national comparison of the factor structure, using identical factor procedures followed by an analysis of congruence coefficients, for values assessments (Chapter Sixteen) and role salience measures (Chapter Eighteen). These analyses confirmed the existence of a remarkable degree of factorial similarity or invariance across the eleven countries, in both values and role salience. This is particularly true for the secondary school subjects, who are both more numerous and better sampled than are the other groups. Therefore, we concluded that the data support the universality and stability of the factor structure of values and roles, despite widespread expectations to the contrary.

Such a finding is important for two reasons. First, it contributes to a better understanding of the domains of values and roles and of the generality of the interrelations of their components. "Since most social-psychological studies are done within the framework of western European culture, one can never be certain whether they are an artifact of some limitation or special circumstance of the culture in which they have been discovered" (Whiting, 1968, p. 694). The findings of our study support the view that the structures of human values and roles are not those of a single culture; rather, they pertain more broadly to human behavior in the modern industrial world.

The second reason is heuristic: the demonstration of factor invariance is an important methodological step that should precede any comparison of importance levels. Such comparisons are justified only if the variables examined share the same meaning across the groups studied. This is indicated by the similarity of their factor structures. Because our analyses tend to support the postulate of factor similarity across national groups, for both values and roles the comparisons seem warranted.

The Important Values: Self-Fulfillment

We analyzed the cross-national importance of values both in terms of their rankings and of their standard scores. The comparison of samples from different countries reveals both similarities and differences in national value priorities.

We first observed cross-cultural similarities in the hierarchy of values. In all our countries the fulfillment of personal potential, self-realization, is clearly an extremely important life goal for the majority of our subjects: the self-realization values (Personal Development, Ability Utilization, and Achievement) are among the highest ranked in all countries. At the lower extreme, the willingness to take risks, as well as the desire for authority and prestige, are of little importance everywhere.

It is important to keep in mind that all subjects in this study, whether in Africa, North America, Asia, Australia, or Europe, could read and write: the data-collection instruments required literacy because limited funding made it essential to rely on questionnaires and inventories. The younger adolescents were in secondary schools, the older adolescents were in postsecondary or higher education, and the adults could complete objective tests. Many subjects—blacks, whites, rural and inner-city residents of North America and South Africa, Amerindians, Inuits, Belgians, and Croatians—were in school or in higher education because they sought self-realization in cultures of increasing complexity or because their parents encouraged them to prepare for an industrial or postindustrial economy. We therefore must limit our generalizations to the literate members of the societies we studied.

The prevalence of the inner-oriented values, indicating the importance of self-fulfillment, is a not unfamiliar finding, although perhaps better established in this empirical study than in most earlier works. Studies in the Western world, largely Anglo-American, have empirically supported the assertion of humanistic psychologists (e.g., Maslow, 1970) that most people want to use their abilities, to express themselves creatively, and to achieve self-realization. A review of such studies led Yankelovich (1981) to suggest that searching for self-fulfillment may be the dominant principle of American culture. Our study demonstrates, subject to the cautions we have noted, the generality of this principle by showing the striking pervasiveness of the self-fulfillment orientation: we found Personal Development and Ability Utilization to be the most important life values both for students and for adults from all the countries we studied.

Two cautions, however, need to be kept in mind. One concerns the possibility that the value priorities revealed by our subjects are somewhat influenced by a tendency to give socially desirable answers. Although we cannot entirely exclude the social desirability bias, the Croatian team carried out a study that indicates that an indirectly obtained hierarchy of values, in which there was no possibility for faking, agrees with the WIS value priorities.

The second caution concerns the masking of individual differences in the averaging of value assessments. The dominance of values indicative of self-fulfillment is a general finding, based on the analysis of average scores. Such a procedure masks individual differences. To some groups of subjects self-fulfillment is not as important as the general finding would imply: the breakdown of adult samples by occupational level, attempted in some of the national studies, gives clear evidence that the majority of unskilled and semi-skilled workers tend to place more emphasis on utilitarian and social values (see also Centers, 1948). But here we should stand by our findings for our subjects; although we found a number of significant group differences, generally consistent across the nations, the prevalence of the self-actualizing orientation seems to characterize both men and women of various ages.

Role Salience: Pronounced Age Differences

Unlike the values data, the analysis of role salience data revealed pronounced differences between the students and adults. At a very general level of analysis, disregarding some differences between national groups and integrating data from the three salience measures, we found substantial consistency across countries in the pattern of these differences.

The secondary school students consider Leisure their most important activity. Next in the role importance hierarchy are three kinds of activities with similar average importance scores: Work, Home and Family, and Study. Community Service ranks last, with little importance. The higher education students attach slightly less importance to Leisure and rather more to Study, Work, and Home and Family. But their general role salience pattern is essentially like that of the secondary students.

However, adults show quite a different pattern of role salience. The most important activity in their life is Work, closely followed by the Home and Family: the Worker and Homemaker roles have clear priority. Much less importance attaches to Leisure, with Study next. Community Service is again the lowest-ranked activity. Based on average scores, these findings of course play down individual differences.

The term *age differences* refers to one kind of difference we observed. But of course the groups do not differ in age only; they also differ in employment status. But we should note that we also observed age-related differences in employed adults. And the differences between younger and older workers are like those we found between students and adults. Younger workers attach relatively greater importance to leisure, whereas older workers consider Work and Homemaking their most important life activities. As Chapter Twenty-two demonstrates, this last finding holds also for unemployed adults.

That the place of work and of other life activities changes greatly with age is a truism stated in theoretical treatises and supported by controlled observation. "Roles wax and wane in importance . . . with the life stage in which a person finds himself, according to the developmental tasks which are encountered with increasing age" (Super, 1980, p. 288). Our study's cross-sectional comparisons clearly show this to be a contemporary reality for all roles in each of the eleven countries we studied.

There is a widespread belief that life-role salience has changed dramatically since the end of World War II. The changes are reflected primarily in a decline of the work ethic, which is believed to be yielding primarily to competing social values, especially leisure. Indeed, many scholars claim that leisure is growing in importance in contemporary industrialized (postindustrial) societies and that the traditional view of work as a central role in most people's lives may no longer be valid (e.g., Dumazedier, 1974; Roberts, 1970). However, the adult data in our study do not support such assertions, although we found that our young subjects in all countries clearly prefer leisure to work. All too often, the supposed decline in work ethic has been evidenced by differences in the work attitudes of younger and older people. However, the differences are not necessarily indicative of a *social* change in values: they may more parsimoniously be considered a result of a normal maturational, developmental process that takes place in each generation.

Observations made in the 1970s also showed that young people prefer leisure to work. Today, these people resemble our adult subjects in age, and to them work and homemaking are now the most important activities, whereas leisure is far less important. Maturation affects role salience.

The Clustering of Countries: Geocultural Entities

Along with the cross-national similarities there are substantial and reliable differences both in value importance and in role salience. We have explored these thoroughly in an attempt to identify what may be unique emphases in each country. Chapters Sixteen, Seventeen, and Eighteen describe the patterns of value and role importance peculiar to each country. The differences we observed between national samples support the view that each country tends to have its own pattern of identical values and roles.

But because we found that the degree of similarity between any two national samples varies, we tried to group countries in relatively homogeneous clusters, both according to value importance and role salience. The cluster analysis of the value similarities among different samples from different countries (Chapters Sixteen and Seventeen) shows that ethnic kinship is a primary determinant of clustering: all clusters formed early in the process are nationally homogeneous. This supports the existence of distinctive national patterns of *values* that are consistent across different samples of subjects from a given country. On the other hand, in the cluster analyses of the *role salience* data (Chapter Eighteen), most clusters that formed early are based on similarity in regard to age and status—most adult groups tend to cluster, regardless of nationality.

On a higher level of integration, however, all the primary role salience–based clusters tend to agglomerate in three groupings of countries that are virtually identical to the three values-based clusters identified in Chapter Sixteen. The three higher-order clusters of countries correspond well to three meaningful geocultural regions: North America (also called New World), Europe, and Japan. All the North American, European, and Japanese samples tend to join their respective clusters, whereas the Australian and South African samples tend, respectively, to join the European and New World clusters. A comparison of the three clusters in terms of their value priorities and role salience reveals several distinguishing characteristics. They are summarized in Table 26.1.

The cluster characteristics we describe are their distinguishing features: they differentiate among the clusters. They thus show in what respect the clusters differ, but not necessarily their dominant features. For example, self-fulfillment (e.g., Personality Development and Ability Utilization) is of utmost importance to the members of *all* clusters; these characteristics are therefore value universals, not distinguishing cluster characteristics. Our analyses have not identified many distinguishing features of cluster differences: our clusters appear more similar than different. We should note, however, that the three final clusters are higher-order groupings that agglomerate different national samples that merged late (at fairly large distances in the cluster analysis). This means that the three agglomerations are not very homogeneous units, and consequently their value and role salience means mask more pronounced national differences. It is worth asking where differences originate.

Any attempt to account for the differences we observed is of course laden with various limitations typical of cross-cultural methodology. These limitations concern primarily the representativeness of the samples and equivalence of the inventory measures. We believe that the methodological features of our study surpass those of typical cross-cultural studies, for we have used multiple and relatively large samples, as well as carefully developed measures suitable for cross-national use. They were developed cross-nationally, not merely adapted for cross-national use. But the sampling methods differ somewhat from country to country, and the levels of semantic and conceptual equivalence achieved among the versions of the instruments adopted in various languages may not be identical. Our findings should therefore be considered tentative rather than conclusive.

If proving the existence of national differences is difficult, it is even more difficult to account for their origin. What the different cultural groups value may be related to such differences as their growth, industrialization, urbanization, political climate, religious beliefs, and historical circumstances.

**Table 26.1. Groupings of Countries According to Values and Role Salience:
A Cluster Analysis Summary.**

Cluster Name	National Samples Making Up Cluster	Distinguishing Characteristics
New World	All U.S. All Canadian* All South African* One Australian	A value pattern implying a drive for upward mobility, material success and prestige, with less emphasis on the less worldly aspects of life. Role salience characterized by the importance attached to Work and Homemaking: both are considered important, as shown by Participation, Commitment, and Value Expectations.
Europe	All Belgian Both Italian One Polish All Portuguese All Croatian Two Australian	High valuation of relationships and understanding among people, a tendency toward an autonomous life-style, and strong rejection of authority. A "flat" salience profile, with relatively more emphasis attached to studying than in the other two geocultural units.
Japan	All Japanese	High valuation of Aesthetics and Creativity; relatively low rating of all other values, especially of values indicative of upward mobility and material success. Low ratings of all life-role activities.

*In the values-based clusters, all the Canadian and South African samples joined the New World cluster, whereas in the role salience–based clusters, one Canadian (Francophone secondary school students) and one South African (African-languages respondents) merged with the European cluster.

We can speculate as to which factors may have been influential in our findings by looking at how they relate to the clustering of countries. Thus we may infer that the degree of economic development and industrialization does not seem to be a decisive factor, because the most highly developed and industrialized countries (Belgium, Canada, Italy, Japan, and the United States) are dispersed in all three clusters. We can reach a similar conclusion about the degree of urbanization. Nor does the political system seem to play an important role: Poland and Croatia, the only two postsocialist countries, fall in the same higher-order cluster as other European countries but do not show any tendency to cluster at lower distances that would suggest special similarity. What seems to be common to all countries within a cluster and to be different across the clusters is *geocultural* similarity, which includes both geographical proximity and similar cultural traditions. Thus one cluster includes mostly North American or New World countries, with a predominantly Protestant tradition; the next, European countries, with mainly Roman Catholic traditions; and the third, only the samples from Japan, a country with Shintoist-Buddhist traditions. The different cultural traditions appear to account for at least part of the value and role salience variations we observed.

Findings from the Topical Studies of More Limited Focus

The findings we have discussed thus far derive from analyses of agglomerated data, from macroanalyses. But in Part Three we reported a number of more limited and more focused studies. In this section we review their major findings, to round out the picture of our work.

As Chapter Nineteen reports, some consistency appears in the relationships between values and role commitment when gender is held constant. In Australia, Belgian Flanders, Portugal, and the United States, we find that values do appear to contribute to commitment, if not participation, in such roles as Study, Work, Home and Family, and Leisure.

As reported in Chapter Twenty, the Canadian project studied the validity of the Salience Inventory as a measure of participation in major life roles. Detailed logs kept in an independent study of a large sample of adults show substantial agreement with Salience Inventory scores for role participation, which establishes the construct validity of the much shorter and simpler measure. Work and home and family consume about one-fourth of the Canadian adults' time, and they devote an equal amount to leisure.

Work serves rather different purposes in groups of adults with differing recent life experiences. The differences disappear as the adults' statuses and experiences become more similar. Chapter Twenty-one reports that recent immigrants from Cuba value the Work role most; for them it is a way to prove their social worth in a new setting, and a way to compensate for the lack of family ties, because work provides opportunities for social interaction and linkage.

No differences appear in Commitment to Work, Leisure, and Home and Family between unemployed and employed in Belgian Flanders, Canada, and Italy (Chapter Twenty-two). But in Flanders and in Canada, people seek Ability Utilization and Achievement in Work and Home and Family, whereas in Italy people seek Social Interaction and Life-style in Work, Home and Family, and Leisure.

The model of role salience or importance developed by the Anglo-American team (Knasel, Super, & Kidd, 1981) was independently tested in two different studies, as Chapter Twenty-three reports. One study, which considered only commitment to and participation in a given life role, supports the distinction made by the Salience Inventory; the second investigation, which used the two knowledge measures of the Career Development Inventory, shows further support for the model. What is more, the second study demonstrates that, at least in university students and a small sample of adult workers in America, there is little relationship between commitment to, participation in, and knowledge of occupations. As in other adult studies with larger numbers and better samples, this study does show that the relationship is nonexistent at the less skilled, less self-expressive occupational levels, whereas the higher-level occupations show more agreement in commitment, participation, and knowledge.

Another cross-national topical study compared Flemish (Belgian) women with women of comparable ages from the Deep South of the United States and concluded, as it were, that there were no real differences in their role commitments: the granddaughters of Scarlett O'Hara closely resemble those of nineteenth-century Flemish burghers (Chapter Twenty-four).

Chapter Twenty-five compares American, Australian, and Portuguese secondary school students for role Commitment and Value Expectations in their current and future life roles. The comparisons need to be made with caution because a much higher percentage of the age cohort attends school in Australia and the United States than in Portugal. Australian tenth-year pupils are less committed to Work than are Portuguese and American but expect more from Work than do the Americans. Australian pupils participate most in Work but are the least committed to it. Women tend to be more committed to both Home and Family and Work than are men, but the women's Value Expectations from these roles are not proportionately high: is it the security of a home and a job that appeals to them, more than the content or activity? The analyses do not address that question, although the WIS instruments provide the data for more probing in this area.

It is worth noting that the limited-focus, topical studies have served their intended purpose: to examine significant questions not covered by the major studies. They have raised and answered, although in some cases in a tentative way, questions of general interest. The WIS instruments are now available to those who wish to pursue these and other questions in a psychometrically rigorous manner.

References

Centers, R. (1948). Motivational aspects of occupational stratification. *Journal of Social Psychology, 28,* 187–217.

Coetsier, P., & Claes, R. (1990). *Belang van Levensrollen en Waarden* [Salience of life roles and values]. Ostende: Infoservice.

Dumazedier, J. (1974). *Sociology of leisure.* Amsterdam: Elsevier.

Fitzsimmons, G. W., Macnab, D., & Casserly, C. (1986). *Technical manual for the Life Roles Inventory: Values and salience.* Edmonton: PsiCan Consulting Ltd.

Knasel, E., Super, D. E., and Kidd, J. M. (1981). *Work salience and work values: Their dimensions, assessment, and significance.* Cambridge, England: National Institute for Careers Education and Counselling.

Maslow, A. H. (1970). *Motivation and personality* (2nd ed.). New York: Harper-Collins.

Nevill, D. D., & Super, D. E. (1986a). *The Salience Inventory: Theory, application, and research* (Manual). Palo Alto, CA: Consulting Psychologists Press.

Nevill, D. D., & Super, D. E. (1986b). *The Values Scale: Theory, application, and research* (Manual). Palo Alto, CA: Consulting Psychologists Press.

Roberts, K. (1970). *Leisure.* White Plains, NY: Longman.

Super, D. E. (1980). A life-span, life-space approach to career development. *Journal of Vocational Behavior, 16,* 282–298.

Šverko, B. (1987). Priručnik za upitnik vrijednosti (V-upitnik) [Manual for the Values Scale]. Zagreb: Savez samoupravnih zajednica za zapošlajavanje Hrvatske.

Whiting, J.W.M. (1968). Methods and problems in cross-cultural research. In G. Lindzey and E. Aronson (Eds.), *The handbook of social psychology* (Vol. 2, pp. 693–728). Reading, MA: Addison-Wesley.

Yankelovich, D. (1981, April). *New rules in American life: Searching for self-fulfillment in a world turned upside down.* New York: Random House.

APPENDIX A

Tables of the
Values Scale Data

Appendix A.1. Values Scale Data from Different Countries: Mean Scores (First Row) and Standard Deviations (Second Row) in Secondary Education (SeEd), Higher Education (HrEd), and Adult Samples.

	AbUt	Ach	Adv	Aes	Alt	Ath	Atn	Cre	Ecn	LfSt	PeDv	PhAc	Pre	Ris	SoIn	SoRe	Var	WoCo	Clld	EcSe	PaDe	PhPr	Spi
Australia																							
SeEd	10.1 / 1.6	10.2 / 1.5	9.2 / 1.9	8.5 / 2.1	8.6 / 2.1	6.9 / 2.1	9.3 / 1.8	8.7 / 2.1	9.8 / 1.8	9.3 / 1.8	10.3 / 1.7	8.8 / 2.3	8.2 / 2.2	6.3 / 2.2	8.7 / 1.9	9.7 / 1.8	8.0 / 2.0	8.1 / 2.1					
HrEd	9.9 / 1.6	9.5 / 1.8	8.2 / 2.2	8.4 / 1.9	9.0 / 2.3	6.5 / 2.2	9.5 / 1.6	8.7 / 2.0	8.7 / 1.9	9.6 / 1.8	10.3 / 1.4	8.1 / 2.5	7.5 / 2.1	5.4 / 2.3	8.3 / 2.0	9.5 / 1.7	7.9 / 1.9	8.2 / 2.0					
Adult	10.3 / 1.4	9.6 / 1.5	8.0 / 2.3	8.3 / 2.2	9.1 / 2.0	6.7 / 2.0	9.7 / 1.6	8.7 / 2.1	8.9 / 2.0	9.5 / 1.9	10.4 / 1.2	8.0 / 2.6	7.7 / 2.1	5.1 / 2.1	8.0 / 2.0	8.9 / 1.9	7.8 / 2.1	8.4 / 1.9					
Belgium (Flanders)																							
SeEd	10.0 / 1.4	9.1 / 1.6	9.1 / 2.0	9.8 / 1.4	8.4 / 2.0	5.9 / 2.1	9.1 / 1.8	8.6 / 1.9	9.0 / 1.9	9.0 / 1.9	10.1 / 1.4	8.4 / 2.3	7.8 / 1.9	7.0 / 2.2	8.6 / 2.2	10.2 / 1.4	7.9 / 1.7	8.5 / 1.9					
HrEd	10.2 / 1.5	8.8 / 1.5	7.5 / 1.7	9.5 / 1.6	9.0 / 1.8	5.7 / 1.8	9.6 / 1.5	8.7 / 1.8	7.8 / 1.8	9.4 / 1.6	10.6 / 1.2	7.0 / 1.8	7.6 / 2.0	6.2 / 2.1	8.5 / 1.8	9.8 / 1.4	7.6 / 1.6	7.1 / 1.8					
Adult	9.6 / 1.8	9.0 / 1.8	8.3 / 2.3	9.7 / 1.5	8.5 / 2.1	6.2 / 2.2	8.7 / 2.0	8.6 / 2.1	8.7 / 1.9	8.8 / 1.9	9.9 / 1.6	7.7 / 2.1	7.8 / 2.1	6.2 / 2.2	8.2 / 2.1	9.6 / 1.6	7.5 / 1.7	8.7 / 2.1					
Canada																							
Yr10 English	10.2 / 1.4	9.8 / 1.5	9.3 / 1.8	8.5 / 1.9	8.8 / 2.2	8.5 / 1.8	9.4 / 1.6	8.1 / 2.0	10.0 / 1.7	9.0 / 1.8	10.2 / 1.4	8.7 / 2.2	9.0 / 1.9	7.1 / 2.4	8.3 / 2.0	10.2 / 1.7	7.6 / 1.8	8.6 / 2.0	7.8 / 2.2		7.2 / 2.3	
Yr10 French	10.0 / 1.5	9.9 / 1.5	9.8 / 1.5	9.5 / 1.6	9.4 / 1.9	7.9 / 1.8	9.0 / 1.7	8.4 / 1.9	9.4 / 1.6	8.6 / 1.8	10.4 / 1.4	9.4 / 2.0	9.1 / 1.9	7.6 / 2.2	8.6 / 1.9	10.3 / 1.7	8.1 / 1.9	8.7 / 1.9	8.2 / 2.0		7.7 / 2.2	
Yr12 English	10.1 / 1.4	9.8 / 1.6	9.2 / 1.7	8.5 / 2.0	8.8 / 2.2	8.6 / 1.8	9.4 / 1.6	8.2 / 2.1	10.1 / 1.6	9.3 / 1.7	10.3 / 1.4	8.6 / 2.1	8.9 / 1.9	6.9 / 2.4	8.1 / 2.0	10.2 / 1.6	7.7 / 1.8	8.5 / 1.9	7.7 / 2.0		7.0 / 2.4	
Yr12 French	10.6 / 1.3	10.1 / 1.4	9.9 / 1.4	9.8 / 1.6	9.7 / 2.0	7.8 / 1.8	9.2 / 1.6	8.6 / 1.8	9.7 / 1.5	8.9 / 1.6	10.7 / 1.3	9.2 / 1.9	9.2 / 1.8	7.1 / 2.0	8.6 / 1.9	10.5 / 1.6	8.4 / 1.8	8.7 / 1.7	8.3 / 1.8		6.9 / 2.4	
HrEd English	10.4 / 1.4	10.0 / 1.5	8.7 / 2.1	8.6 / 2.1	9.4 / 2.2	8.8 / 1.8	9.6 / 1.6	8.8 / 2.0	9.4 / 1.8	9.0 / 1.7	10.7 / 1.3	8.3 / 2.2	9.1 / 1.8	5.9 / 2.1	7.6 / 2.0	10.0 / 1.6	7.8 / 1.9	8.4 / 2.0	7.5 / 2.1		5.6 / 2.1	
Adult English	10.2 / 1.4	10.0 / 1.5	8.3 / 2.2	8.2 / 2.2	9.4 / 2.0	9.0 / 1.9	9.7 / 1.6	8.8 / 2.0	9.5 / 1.7	8.9 / 1.7	10.6 / 1.3	7.7 / 2.1	9.0 / 1.8	5.5 / 2.1	7.2 / 2.0	9.8 / 1.7	7.6 / 2.0	8.7 / 2.0	7.6 / 2.2		5.2 / 2.0	
Adult French	10.6 / 1.3	9.8 / 1.6	9.3 / 1.8	9.6 / 1.7	9.6 / 1.9	7.9 / 2.1	9.7 / 1.7	9.3 / 1.9	9.7 / 1.5	9.4 / 1.6	10.9 / 1.1	8.3 / 2.2	8.6 / 2.0	6.3 / 2.2	8.0 / 2.2	10.2 / 1.8	8.3 / 2.0	9.2 / 2.1	7.3 / 2.1		4.6 / 1.8	

Appendix A.1. Values Scale Data from Different Countries: Mean Scores (First Row) and Standard Deviations (Second Row) in Secondary Education (SeEd), Higher Education (HrEd), and Adult Samples.

	AbUt	Ach	Adv	Aes	Alt	Ath	Atn	Cre	Ecn	LfSt	PeDv	PhAc	Pre	Ris	SoIn	SoRe	Var	WoCo	Clld	EcSe	PaDe	PhPr	Spi
Croatia																							
Yr8	10.0	9.9	9.7	9.8	9.6	7.4	8.3	8.8	9.7	8.5	9.9	9.4	8.3	8.0	8.9	9.9	8.0	9.5			8.9		
	1.5	1.5	1.5	1.6	1.7	1.9	1.9	1.8	1.6	1.8	1.5	1.8	2.1	1.8	1.9	1.6	1.9	1.8			1.7		
Yr10	10.0	9.7	9.0	9.5	9.5	5.9	7.8	8.2	9.5	8.2	9.4	8.7	7.2	7.0	8.3	10.0	7.6	9.5	7.8		9.3		
	1.4	1.5	1.7	1.6	1.7	1.8	2.0	2.0	1.7	2.0	1.4	2.2	2.1	2.0	2.1	1.6	2.1	1.8	2.5		1.8		
Yr12	10.0	9.6	8.7	9.4	9.3	5.9	8.1	8.3	9.3	8.3	10.4	8.6	7.1	7.0	8.3	9.9	7.9	9.4	7.6		9.2		
	1.5	1.5	1.7	1.7	1.8	1.8	2.0	1.9	1.8	1.8	1.5	2.2	2.0	1.9	2.1	1.6	2.1	1.8	2.5		1.8		
HrEd	10.3	9.8	7.7	9.4	9.4	5.5	8.7	8.8	8.4	8.7	10.8	7.8	7.2	6.1	7.9	9.8	7.6	8.7	6.4		8.9		
	1.3	1.4	2.0	1.7	1.8	1.7	1.9	1.8	1.9	1.9	1.3	2.4	2.0	1.9	2.1	1.7	2.2	2.1	2.3		1.8		
Adult	10.1	10.1	8.4	9.3	9.4	6.3	8.9	8.5	9.6	8.4	10.3	7.9	7.7	6.8	7.9	9.9	7.6	9.6	7.1		9.2		
	1.5	1.4	2.1	1.7	1.8	2.0	2.1	2.0	1.7	1.9	1.5	2.2	2.2	2.2	2.2	1.7	2.2	2.0	2.7		2.0		
Italy																							
SeEd	10.0	9.8	7.4	8.0	9.1	6.3	9.4	9.1	7.9	9.3	10.7	8.9	7.3	6.2	8.6	9.5	7.7	8.5	2.2				
	1.8	1.7	2.3	1.7	2.2	2.2	1.9	2.1	2.3	1.8	1.4		1.9	2.6	2.5	2.3	1.8	2.2					
HrEd	10.0	9.5	6.6	8.0	8.9	5.8	9.5	9.4	7.0	9.6	10.8	8.1	6.6	5.8	8.2	9.4	7.8	8.0					
	1.6	1.8	2.3	1.7	2.3	2.2	1.9	1.9	2.2	1.7	1.4	2.0	2.6	2.3	2.4	1.7	2.2	2.2					
Japan																							
SeEd	10.0	8.5	6.7	10.1	8.7	6.6	8.9	9.0	7.9	8.6	9.9	8.3	7.3	7.4	7.5	8.7	7.1	8.2		7.2			
	1.6	1.8	2.3	1.6	1.9	1.7	1.5	1.9	2.0	1.7	1.7	2.0	2.2	2.0	2.1	1.9	2.0	1.9		1.8			
HrEd	10.3	8.8	6.0	10.2	8.1	6.1	9.2	9.3	7.4	9.1	10.3	7.8	7.1	6.8	6.9	8.4	6.8	7.5		6.7			
	1.6	1.8	2.1	1.7	2.2	1.8	1.6	1.9	1.9	1.6	1.5	2.1	2.0	2.2	2.0	1.9	2.0	2.3		2.1			
Adult	9.5	8.5	6.2	9.2	7.4	6.8	8.9	9.3	8.2	8.5	9.5	7.4	7.1	6.2	6.6	7.6	6.3	7.4		6.3			
	1.7	1.6	2.0	1.6	1.7	1.7	1.7	1.6	1.8	1.7	1.5	1.9	1.9	1.9	1.7	1.7	1.8	2.0		1.8			
Poland																							
HrEd	10.5	8.9	6.0	9.5	9.1	5.0	9.5	9.5	9.1	10.7	10.9	7.0	7.3	7.0	7.2	9.3	8.4	7.6	6.9	7.3			
	1.3	1.6	2.1	1.9	2.1	1.9	1.5	1.8	1.9	1.2	1.2	2.0	1.9	2.1	2.1	1.6	1.6	2.1	2.1	2.3			

	AbUt	Ach	Adv	Aes	Alt	Ath	Atn	Clld	Cre	Ecn	EcSe	LfSt	PaDe	PeDv	PhAc	PhPr	Pre	Ris	SoIn	SoRe	Spi	Var	WoCo
Portugal																							
Yr10	10.4	10.3	9.8	9.6	9.6	6.7	9.6	9.8	8.9	9.7	10.5	8.7	7.2	6.4	8.2	10.1	8.3	9.6					
	1.4	1.4	1.6	1.8	1.7	2.0	1.7	1.6	1.9	1.8	1.3	2.3	2.0	2.2	1.9	1.5	1.9	1.8					
Yr12	10.8	10.5	9.7	9.8	9.7	6.5	9.8	10.0	8.7	9.9	10.8	8.4	7.1	6.1	8.2	10.1	8.7	9.3					
	1.5	1.6	1.7	1.9	1.8	2.1	1.8	1.7	2.0	1.8	1.4	2.3	2.0	2.2	2.1	1.6	2.0	2.1					
HrEd	11.0	10.3	9.4	9.7	9.1	6.5	10.0	10.2	8.5	10.4	10.9	7.8	6.7	6.2	8.1	10.1	8.5	9.3					
	1.4	1.5	1.9	1.9	2.1	2.2	1.8	1.6	2.1	1.6	1.3	2.3	2.2	2.3	2.2								
	1.6																						
South Africa																							
Yr10 English	10.7	10.6	9.8	9.4	9.2	7.7	9.4	9.0	9.7	9.3	10.5	9.1	8.8	6.9	9.3	8.4	7.9	9.1	8.3	10.4		7.1	8.8
	1.4	1.5	1.8	1.7	2.0	2.0	1.9	2.0	1.9	1.8	1.4	2.1	2.2	2.3	1.9	2.1	1.9	1.9	2.1	1.5		2.1	2.0
Yr12 English	10.7	10.6	10.1	9.3	8.9	8.0	9.7	9.0	9.5	8.7	10.7	8.7	8.9	6.5	9.3	8.2	8.0	9.1	8.2	10.7		6.4	8.5
	1.4	1.4	1.8	1.9	2.2	2.0	1.8	2.1	1.8	2.2	1.4	2.2	2.3	2.3	1.8	2.1	1.9	1.9	2.2	1.5		2.1	2.2
Yr10 African Language	9.5	9.6	8.9	9.2	9.7	7.9	7.5	8.8	9.2	8.6	9.5	7.6	8.6	5.9	7.6	7.7	7.5	8.6	7.7	8.5		7.6	9.5
	2.0	1.6	2.2	1.6	1.9	1.9	1.8	1.9	2.1	1.6	1.3	2.0	2.1	2.2	2.2	1.9	2.0	1.9	1.7				
Yr12 African Language	10.4	10.1	9.7	9.0	10.0	7.8	7.7	9.2	9.4	8.0	10.0	9.4	8.8	5.6	7.5	8.0	7.5	8.9	8.1	9.3		7.1	9.6
	2.0	1.3	1.4	1.6	1.9	2.0	1.9	1.9	1.6	1.9	1.4	2.0	2.1	2.2	2.0	2.0	1.7	1.6	1.7				
Yr10 Afrikaans	10.5	10.2	10.4	9.5	9.7	7.7	8.9	9.3	9.5	8.8	10.4	9.1	8.6	7.1	8.3	8.3	8.6	9.5	9.7	10.4		7.7	10.1
	1.4	1.4	1.5	1.7	1.8	2.0	2.0	1.9	1.7	1.8	1.5	2.2	2.1	2.2	2.0	2.2	1.8	1.7	1.7	1.5		2.1	1.7
Yr12 Afrikaans	10.8	10.4	10.6	9.4	9.6	7.8	9.2	9.0	9.6	8.9	10.7	9.3	8.6	6.7	9.2	8.3	8.8	9.6	9.8	10.7		7.1	9.9
	1.3	1.3	1.4	1.6	1.8	2.0	1.9	2.1	1.6	1.9	1.4	2.0	2.1	2.2	2.2	2.0	1.9	1.8	1.7	1.4		2.0	1.7
United States																							
SeEd	9.6	9.9	9.7	8.8	8.7	7.5	9.2	8.5	9.7	8.6	10.1	8.1	8.7	6.7	9.5	8.1	7.8	8.6	7.3			6.8	
	1.8	1.7	1.9	2.0	2.1	2.2	1.9	2.1	2.1	2.2	1.7	2.1	2.1	2.4	2.0	2.1	2.0	2.1	2.7			2.2	
HrEd	10.4	9.9	9.6	9.0	9.4	7.9	9.8	8.5	9.8	8.7	10.6	8.8	8.7	6.5	9.8	8.2	7.7	8.8	8.0			6.2	
	1.4	1.8	1.9	2.0	2.0	2.1	1.8	2.0	1.8	2.1	1.4	2.0	2.1	2.4	1.9	2.1	1.9	2.0	2.4			2.2	
Adult	10.3	9.9	8.8	8.4	9.1	7.5	9.6	8.7	9.6	8.6	10.3	7.7	8.6	6.0	9.0	7.7	7.3	8.5	7.2			5.6	
	1.5	1.7	2.2	2.2	2.2	2.3	1.8	2.1	1.8	2.2	1.6	2.4	2.2	2.6	1.9	2.4	2.0	2.2	2.7			2.3	
Overall	10.2	9.9	8.8	8.9	9.2	7.4	9.3	8.9	9.2	8.4	10.4	8.1	8.2	6.4	9.4	8.1	7.8	8.8					8.8
	1.6	1.7	2.3	2.1	2.2	2.3	1.9	2.1	2.1	2.3	1.6	2.2	2.3	2.4	2.1	2.2	2.1	2.1					2.1

Note: AbUt = Ability Utilization; Ach = Achievement; Adv = Advancement; Aes = Aesthetics; Alt = Altruism; Ath = Authority; Atn = Autonomy; Clld = Cultural Identity; Cre = Creativity; Ecn = Economics; EcSe = Economic Security; LfSt = Life-Style; PaDe = Participation in Decisions; PeDv = Personal Development; PhAc = Physical Activity; PhPr = Physical Prowess; Pre = Prestige; Ris = Risk; SoIn = Social Interaction; SoRe = Social Relations; Spi = Spirituality; Var = Variety; WoCo = Working Conditions.

**Appendix A.2. Values Structure: Rotated Factor Matrix for a
Global Pooled Sample (N = 18,218).**

Values Scale	Factor				
	1	2	3	4	5
	(Ut)	(sA)	(In)	(So)	(Av)
Ability Utilization	0.27 (2)	0.71 (16)	0.21	−0.03	−0.03
Achievement	0.56 (15)	0.49 (8)	0.21	0.06	−0.15
Advancement	0.80 (18)	0.18	0.06	0.07	0.16
Aesthetics	0.21	0.52 (11)	0.05	0.32 (3)	0.14
Altruism	−0.13	0.66 (12)	−0.22	0.26 (5)	0.27 (1)
Authority	0.59 (15)	0.07	0.15	−0.09	0.51 (6)
Autonomy	0.16	0.13 (1)	0.80 (17)	−0.03	0.14
Creativity	0.05 (1)	0.49 (7)	0.48 (4)	0.03	0.29
Economics	0.83 (19)	−0.05	0.07	0.17 (1)	−0.04
Life-style	0.11	0.04	0.82 (17)	0.16	−0.02
Personal Development	0.09	0.60 (15)	0.40 (2)	0.21	−0.19
Physical Activity	0.17	0.25 (2)	−0.11	0.35 (4)	0.33 (6)
Prestige	0.72 (19)	0.13	0.13	0.00	0.21
Risk	0.12	0.01	0.16	0.14	0.77 (18)
Social Interaction	0.05	0.10 (1)	−0.04 (1)	0.65 (18)	0.28 (1)
Social Relations	−0.03	0.08	0.16	0.79 (19)	−0.13
Variety	0.07	0.15 (4)	0.39 (4)	0.50 (5)	0.25 (3)
Working Conditions	0.44	0.16	0.02	0.49 (3)	−0.09
Percentage total variance	16.3	12.4	11.7	11.0	8.1

Note: The numbers in parentheses are the additional results of nineteen individual sample factor analyses: they represent the frequencies of salient factor loadings (above 0.50) on each of the factors.

Av = Adventurous Orientation; In = Individualistic Orientation; sA = Orientation Toward Self-Actualization; So = Social Orientation; Ut = Utilitarian Orientation.

**Appendix A.3. Similarity of Value Factors Across the Countries:
Factor Congruence Summary Table.**

Indicator of Congruence	Ut	sA	Factor		
			In	So	Av
Mean congruence for all between-sample comparisons	0.93	0.82	0.90	0.86	0.82
Percentage of congruence coefficients below 0.80	0	35.4	0.4	17	34.6
Congruence Within Same Sort of Samples					
Mean congruence among secondary school samples	0.95	0.91	0.92	0.93	0.87
Mean congruence among higher education samples	0.96	0.69	0.92	0.79	0.84
Mean congruence among adult samples	0.89	0.81	0.94	0.82	0.70

Note: For abbreviations of factors, see note in Appendix A.2.

Appendix A.4. Value Hierarchies of National Samples.

(The rankings of values for each sample were inferred from the sample's mean scores on the eighteen values scales.)

	PeDv	AbUt	Ach	SoRe	Atn	LfSt	Alt	Ecn	Aes	Cre	Adv	WoCo	PhAc	Soln	Pre	Var	Ath	Ris
A1	1	3	2	5	6	7	14	4	14	11	8	12	9	10	15	16	17	18
A2	1	2	4	5	6	3	7	9	10	8	12	13	14	11	16	15	17	18
A3	1	2	4	7	3	5	6	8	11	9	14	10	13	12	16	15	17	18
B1	2	3	7	1	5	8	13	9	4	11	6	12	14	10	16	15	18	17
B2	1	2	8	3	4	6	7	11	5	9	14	15	16	10	12	13	18	17
B3	1	3.5	5	3.5	9	6	11	8	2	10	12	7	15	13	14	16	17	18
CF1	1	3	4	2	11	12	7	8	6	15	5	13	9	14	10	16	17	18
CE1	1	3	5	2	6	8	10	4	14	16	7	13	11	15	9	17	12	18
CE2	1	2	4	3	5	9	7	6	13	11	12	14	15	17	8	16	10	18
CF3	1	2	4	3	6	9	8	5	7	11	10	12	14.5	16	13	14.5	17	18
CE3	1	2	3	4	5	10	7	6	14	11	13	12	15	17	8	16	9	18
CR1	1	2	4	3	14	12	7	8	5.5	13	9	5.5	10	11	16	15	18	17
CR2	1	2	3.5	3.3	9.5	9.5	6	11	5	7	14	8	13	12	16	15	18	17
CR3	1	2	3	4	9	11.5	7	6	8	10	11.5	5	13	14	15	16	18	17
IT1	1	2	3	4	5	6	7	13	12	8	15	11	9	10	16	14	17	18
IT2	1	2	3.5	6	4.5	3	8	14	11	7	15	12	19	9	16	13	17	18
J1	3	2	9	6.5	5	8	6.5	12	1	4	17	11	10	13	15	16	18	14
J2	1	2	7	8	5	6	9	12	3	4	18	11	10	14	13	15	17	16
J3	2	1	7	9	5	6	12	8	4	3	18	11	10	15	13	16	14	17
P1	1	2	3	4	7	6	10	12	9	5	8	11	13	15	16	14	17	18
P2	2	1	4	6	7	3	11	13	8	5	9	10	15	14	16	12	17	18
P3	2	1	3	7	10	11	6	13	8	4	5	12	15	9	17	14	16	18
PL2	1	3	10	7	5	2	8	9	4	6	17	12	15	14	13	11	18	16
SAE1	2	1	3	15	6	7	11	5	8	12	4	10	13	9	14	16	17	18
SAA1	2	1	4	16	12	13	8	5	6	10	3	7	9	11	15	14	17	18
SAN1	4	1	3	12	15	14	2	5	8	9	7	10	6	16	11	17	13	18
US1	1	5	2	6	8	7	10	3	9	14	3	13	12	15	11	16	17	18
US2	1	2	3	5	4	9	7	8	10	14	6	12	15	11	13	17	16	18
US3	2	1	3	14	4	7	6	5	12	9	8	11	17	13	10	16	15	18
Median rank	1	2	3	4	6	6	7.5	8	8	9	9	12	13	13	14	15	17	18

Note: A = Australia; B = Belgium; CE = English-Canadians; CF = French Canadians; CR = Croatia; IT = Italy; J = Japan; P = Portugal; PL = Poland; SA = South Africa (SAE = English speaking, SAA = Afrikaans, SAN = Native South African languages); US = United States. Numbers 1, 2, and 3 denote secondary school, higher education, and adult samples, respectively: A3 = Australian adult sample. For abbreviations of values see note in Appendix A.1.

Appendix A.5. Values Scale Mean Z Scores for Secondary Education (1), Higher Education (2), and Adult Samples (3) in Different Countries.

	AbUt	Ach	Adv	Aes	Alt	Ath	Atm	Cre	Ecn	LfSt	PeDv	PhAc	Pre	Risk	Soin	SoRe	Var	WoC
A1	-0.05	0.21	0.17	-0.21	-0.27	-0.30	0.02	-0.08	0.31	0.11	-0.05	0.19	-0.02	0.00	0.28	0.17	0.08	-0.07
A2	-0.22	-0.21	-0.26	-0.24	-0.09	-0.45	0.10	-0.08	-0.24	0.25	-0.08	-0.13	-0.34	-0.39	0.07	0.04	0.04	-0.28
A3	0.03	-0.12	-0.38	-0.31	-0.04	-0.39	0.22	-0.08	-0.14	0.21	0.02	-0.17	-0.25	-0.54	-0.04	-0.23	0.01	-0.18
B1	-0.11	-0.46	0.09	0.43	-0.34	-0.71	-0.09	-0.15	-0.10	-0.03	-0.19	0.01	-0.18	0.28	0.22	0.42	0.04	-0.14
B2	-0.03	-0.63	-0.59	0.28	-0.09	-0.79	0.15	-0.08	-0.66	0.19	0.12	-0.59	-0.27	-0.08	0.16	0.19	-0.10	-0.79
B3	-0.36	-0.49	-0.25	0.37	-0.30	-0.56	-0.31	-0.15	-0.22	-0.14	-0.36	-0.30	-0.20	-0.06	0.02	0.12	-0.13	0.00
CF1	0.06	0.08	0.45	0.35	0.21	0.12	-0.08	-0.17	0.18	-0.15	0.08	0.41	0.38	0.42	0.21	0.49	0.23	0.00
CE1	-0.04	-0.03	0.17	-0.21	-0.16	0.40	0.07	-0.34	0.43	0.05	-0.10	0.13	0.31	0.28	0.06	0.37	-0.06	-0.11
CE2	0.09	0.08	-0.04	-0.15	0.10	0.52	0.18	-0.03	0.10	-0.05	0.16	-0.04	0.37	-0.18	-0.23	0.29	-0.01	-0.15
CF3	0.25	-0.04	0.21	0.31	0.19	0.12	0.20	0.21	0.23	0.15	0.31	-0.04	0.16	-0.03	-0.07	0.38	0.24	0.23
CE3	0.02	0.11	-0.25	-0.37	0.09	0.58	0.25	-0.03	0.14	-0.07	0.10	-0.29	0.35	-0.36	-0.39	0.18	-0.10	-0.02
CR1	-0.14	-0.11	0.01	0.25	0.13	-0.60	-0.67	-0.30	0.08	-0.42	-0.02	0.11	-0.48	0.27	0.09	0.27	0.01	0.32
CR2	0.05	-0.05	-0.50	0.24	0.10	-0.87	-0.30	-0.02	-0.36	-0.20	0.29	-0.27	-0.44	-0.10	-0.10	0.18	-0.11	-0.03
CR3	-0.06	0.15	-0.19	0.15	0.13	-0.55	-0.18	-0.16	0.19	-0.34	-0.07	-0.21	-0.22	0.21	-0.11	0.26	-0.08	0.42
IT1	-0.13	-0.02	-0.62	-0.44	-0.01	-0.54	0.05	0.10	-0.62	0.14	0.18	0.22	-0.39	-0.06	0.20	0.07	-0.04	-0.14
IT2	-0.15	-0.21	-0.95	-0.46	-0.11	-0.74	0.11	0.23	-1.03	0.29	0.23	-0.11	-0.72	-0.23	0.05	0.00	-0.01	-0.37
J1	-0.15	-0.79	-0.91	0.58	-0.21	-0.43	-0.20	0.08	-0.62	-0.22	-0.30	-0.04	-0.41	0.43	-0.30	-0.34	-0.32	-0.27
J2	0.03	-0.62	-1.25	0.62	-0.49	-0.61	-0.04	0.23	-0.83	0.02	-0.07	-0.25	-0.49	0.20	-0.54	-0.50	-0.45	-0.57
J3	-0.46	-0.72	-1.31	0.15	-0.94	-0.49	-0.31	0.07	-0.57	-0.25	-0.57	-0.46	-0.48	0.01	-0.74	-0.79	-0.64	-0.60
P1	0.23	0.29	0.36	0.36	0.21	-0.43	0.22	0.48	-0.20	0.36	0.16	0.04	-0.49	-0.07	0.04	0.34	0.33	0.30
P2	0.49	0.30	0.25	0.38	-0.04	-0.47	0.39	0.65	-0.33	0.70	0.31	-0.25	-0.65	-0.07	0.00	0.32	0.37	0.24
P3	0.61	0.27	0.27	0.02	0.12	-0.57	-0.22	0.47	-0.53	-0.21	0.23	0.39	-0.90	-0.14	0.38	0.00	-0.40	-0.22
PL2	0.19	-0.55	-1.24	0.29	-0.01	-1.09	0.11	0.29	-0.05	0.83	0.33	-0.58	-0.43	0.25	-0.41	-0.05	0.32	-0.56
SAE1	0.27	0.38	0.49	0.21	-0.04	0.07	0.13	0.05	0.31	0.18	0.10	0.23	0.26	0.16	0.54	-0.54	0.07	0.17
SAA1	0.26	0.27	0.72	0.29	0.15	0.07	-0.12	0.15	0.31	-0.13	0.09	0.45	0.15	0.22	0.46	-0.54	0.42	0.37
SAN1	-0.15	0.00	0.20	0.10	0.33	0.12	-0.87	0.06	0.15	-0.65	-0.44	0.49	0.21	-0.24	-0.25	-0.75	-0.14	0.00
US1	-0.34	0.04	0.39	-0.05	-0.21	-0.05	-0.03	-0.17	0.25	0.09	-0.26	0.12	0.19	0.17	0.01	0.07	0.02	-0.08
US2	0.14	0.02	0.33	0.02	0.14	0.12	0.27	-0.17	0.02	0.07	0.14	-0.08	0.20	0.05	0.33	0.18	-0.05	0.02
US3	0.12	0.07	0.01	-0.27	0.04	0.04	0.23	-0.08	0.08	0.06	-0.07	-0.53	0.17	-0.13	-0.13	-0.82	-0.23	-0.11

Note. For abbreviations of values, see note in Appendix A.1; for abbreviations of countries see note in Appendix A.4.

Appendix A.6. Mean Value Factor Scores for Secondary Education (1), Higher Education (2), and Adult (3) Samples in Different Countries.

	Value Dimension (Factor)				
Sample	Ut	sA	In	So	Av
A1	0.23	−0.40	0.12	0.20	−0.13
A2	−0.33	−0.34	0.28	0.00	−0.24
A3	−0.25	−0.15	0.30	−0.23	−0.36
B1	−0.19	−0.43	0.02	0.40	0.04
B2	−0.84	−0.12	0.39	−0.07	−0.10
B3	−0.24	−0.48	−0.13	0.16	−0.10
CF1	0.35	−0.06	−0.21	0.36	0.38
CE1	0.46	−0.56	0.05	0.09	0.24
CE2	0.27	−0.09	0.14	−0.21	0.04
CF3	0.21	0.10	0.23	0.15	−0.04
CE3	0.28	−0.17	0.20	−0.36	−0.13
CR1	−0.10	−0.11	−0.56	0.49	−0.13
CR2	−0.52	0.23	−0.09	0.09	−0.45
CR3	0.03	−0.09	−0.25	0.24	−0.25
IT1	−0.62	−0.08	0.26	0.07	−0.06
IT2	−1.08	−0.03	0.53	−0.10	−0.19
J1	−0.76	−0.13	−0.07	−0.34	0.51
J2	−0.98	0.06	0.30	−0.70	0.17
J3	−0.72	−0.61	0.11	−0.94	0.10
P1	−0.14	0.29	0.36	0.27	−0.20
P2	−0.28	0.34	0.78	0.14	−0.36
P3	−0.44	0.58	−0.02	−0.14	−0.25
PL2	−0.97	0.00	0.89	−0.15	−0.22
SAE1	0.51	0.04	0.03	−0.13	0.22
SAA1	0.52	0.18	−0.25	0.03	0.40
SAN1	0.36	0.14	−0.93	−0.48	0.34
US1	0.37	−0.56	0.01	0.04	0.16
US2	0.23	−0.10	0.10	0.06	0.09
US3	0.21	−0.08	0.15	−0.77	0.01

Note: For abbreviations of factors, see note in Appendix A.2; for abbreviations of countries see note in Appendix A.4.

APPENDIX B

Tables of the
Salience Inventory Data

Appendix B.1. Role Salience Data from Different Countries: Mean Scores (First Row) and Standard Deviations (Second Row) in Secondary Education (SeEd), Higher Education (HrEd), and Adult Samples.

	Participation					Commitment					Value Expectations				
	Study	Work	Community	Home	Leisure	Study	Work	Community	Home	Leisure	Study	Work	Community	Home	Leisure
Australia															
SeEd	24.3	21.2	16.3	23.8	31.4	27.0	29.9	21.3	30.1	32.9	36.1	42.6	31.1	41.1	43.3
	6.3	5.9	6.9	6.4	5.6	6.9	6.5	8.4	7.6	5.8	9.3	7.8	10.6	8.7	7.9
HrEd	27.8	19.7	16.3	23.1	28.8	29.5	28.1	22.8	30.3	31.0	35.9	39.1	30.4	38.1	39.3
	6.5	6.0	6.4	7.0	6.4	6.3	7.0	8.3	7.4	6.2	7.4	7.5	9.7	9.1	8.0
Adult	25.0	30.1	18.1	26.4	27.2	25.3	32.5	21.8	33.3	29.6	33.3	41.7	30.4	42.0	39.0
	7.8	5.8	6.7	6.8	7.3	8.7	5.6	7.5	7.6	7.5	9.8	7.1	9.8	8.2	9.5
Belgium (Flanders)															
SeEd	23.5	16.5	17.6	21.4	28.7	26.6	27.7	22.7	29.3	31.2	34.8	40.4	30.8	39.3	41.1
	5.2	5.3	7.3	4.8	5.6	6.6	5.7	8.0	6.5	6.0	8.6	7.7	10.8	8.3	8.2
HrEd	28.9	16.9	19.5	21.6	26.6	30.4	29.0	24.9	29.1	28.4	36.4	39.8	30.9	38.1	38.2
	4.9	4.7	7.1	4.6	5.2	5.5	5.4	7.4	6.2	6.1	6.5	6.7	9.7	6.4	7.0
Adult	19.6	24.4	16.7	25.5	24.1	21.7	30.5	20.4	32.4	26.8	25.7	37.5	26.2	40.6	34.6
	7.7	6.8	6.8	6.0	7.0	7.8	7.8	7.7	6.2	7.7	9.9	10.8	9.9	7.9	10.3
Canada															
YR10 English	21.3	25.0	17.2	25.8	31.7	23.8	31.7	20.7	30.9	31.9	33.9	45.1	30.5	42.7	44.2
	6.4	6.1	7.4	6.6	6.5	7.9	6.0	8.5	7.5	6.9	10.9	7.4	12.2	9.7	9.2
YR10 French	25.6	24.8	18.8	23.6	29.9	28.1	30.4	22.6	26.8	30.7	40.0	44.1	33.5	38.6	43.4
	6.6	5.9	7.1	6.6	7.1	7.1	5.9	7.9	7.3	7.2	9.6	7.5	10.9	10.0	9.5
Yr12 English	21.5	25.8	17.1	25.3	31.1	24.1	32.4	20.8	31.1	31.9	33.6	45.2	30.2	42.9	44.2
	7.0	6.0	7.4	6.8	6.4	8.3	5.8	8.7	7.2	6.7	11.2	7.2	12.3	9.2	8.9
Yr12 French	26.9	24.0	18.6	22.8	30.1	29.2	31.4	22.7	27.4	31.2	40.6	45.3	33.2	39.2	44.2
	6.3	6.7	7.0	6.8	6.0	6.4	5.9	8.0	7.7	6.2	9.1	7.8	11.6	10.3	8.2
HrEd English	29.0	24.3	17.5	26.1	28.4	30.1	33.3	23.7	34.4	30.2	39.6	45.8	33.4	45.2	41.8
	6.4	6.5	7.1	6.5	6.3	6.8	5.4	8.2	6.2	6.6	8.9	6.4	11.3	8.2	8.5

Appendix B.1. Role Salience Data from Different Countries: Mean Scores (First Row) and Standard Deviations (Second Row) in Secondary Education (SeEd), Higher Education (HrEd), and Adult Samples.

	Participation					Commitment					Value Expectations				
	Study	Work	Community	Home	Leisure	Study	Work	Community	Home	Leisure	Study	Work	Community	Home	Leisure
Adult English	23.9	29.4	18.8	28.5	26.8	25.9	34.1	23.0	35.5	28.8	34.7	44.2	31.4	45.6	40.1
	7.3	5.9	7.5	6.3	6.3	7.9	5.3	8.1	5.9	6.9	10.4	7.7	11.2	8.0	9.0
Adult French	23.6	29.1	17.2	24.4	26.2	26.0	33.0	20.4	28.1	28.2	35.9	45.3	30.0	41.0	40.2
	7.2	5.4	6.9	6.9	6.3	7.6	5.6	7.7	8.3	6.8	10.5	7.5	11.3	10.2	9.5
Croatia															
Yr10	25.8	19.7	19.1	23.2	30.7	27.2	28.0	23.7	28.0	32.9	38.4	40.5	33.3	39.5	44.5
	5.5	7.1	7.2	5.8	5.9	5.9	7.0	7.7	6.6	5.8	7.4	9.5	10.2	7.9	7.3
Yr12	25.1	20.7	19.9	23.7	30.5	26.0	28.0	23.1	28.1	32.4	37.7	40.4	32.8	39.7	43.6
	5.9	7.0	7.3	5.8	6.0	6.1	6.9	7.6	6.6	5.7	7.6	9.8	10.2	8.0	7.6
HrEd	30.5	16.5	16.6	21.1	29.5	29.9	28.5	20.4	26.2	31.9	38.2	41.3	27.9	36.6	42.3
	4.9	5.6	6.2	5.5	5.8	5.4	6.6	7.1	6.7	5.2	6.1	7.8	9.2	7.8	6.6
Adult	20.9	30.4	19.7	25.8	25.9	24.8	33.5	22.5	31.5	29.6	33.2	41.9	29.3	40.6	38.9
	7.8	5.0	7.1	6.0	6.7	7.8	5.1	8.0	6.5	6.3	10.0	7.4	10.4	7.9	8.1
Italy															
SeEd	28.0	18.8	18.5	22.6	30.2	28.6	29.8	22.7	29.0	30.7	36.0	44.1	30.4	38.8	41.5
	6.2	6.4	7.8	6.3	6.5	7.0	6.1	8.6	7.2	7.0	11.8	10.3	13.9	11.3	10.8
HrEd	30.2	19.5	18.9	21.3	28.0	30.5	30.6	22.2	27.9	28.6	38.3	43.9	29.5	38.3	40.2
	5.7	6.9	8.3	6.4	6.4	6.5	5.9	9.1	7.6	6.8	9.9	8.8	13.2	10.2	9.9
Japan															
SeEd	18.7	13.7	13.4	18.4	29.7	21.9	20.2	18.3	22.1	30.0	28.8	32.7	25.6	30.1	35.8
	6.2	5.5	5.4	6.3	7.2	6.5	7.0	6.6	7.3	6.9	9.2	11.8	10.6	10.4	10.0
HrEd	21.9	17.5	15.2	19.3	29.8	24.9	24.2	20.3	23.9	29.8	32.0	35.5	27.0	33.2	35.8
	6.5	6.5	6.7	6.2	6.9	6.8	6.6	7.2	7.5	6.6	9.3	10.0	10.3	10.3	9.8
Adult	20.1	25.2	14.9	22.4	25.3	23.4	27.6	18.5	26.4	27.2	28.6	34.3	24.6	34.5	33.8
	6.6	6.4	5.9	6.1	6.9	6.9	7.0	6.4	7.1	6.4	9.1	9.9	9.4	9.4	9.2

Poland															
HrEd	24.5 / 4.6	20.4 / 4.3	17.8 / 6.2	25.6 / 5.0	25.4 / 5.2	26.6 / 6.1	27.9 / 5.2	20.6 / 6.7	31.9 / 5.7	26.7 / 5.7	35.2 / 7.2	38.8 / 6.6	27.9 / 9.9	41.6 / 6.8	39.0 / 7.4
Portugal															
Yr10	27.4 / 5.3	17.9 / 5.7	17.2 / 6.6	19.7 / 5.4	29.3 / 6.8	29.4 / 6.2	29.9 / 5.6	25.6 / 7.1	24.4 / 6.9	30.1 / 6.9	40.1 / 8.5	42.9 / 8.1	35.4 / 10.2	35.2 / 9.1	41.7 / 9.3
Yr12	28.7 / 5.2	17.7 / 5.7	16.7 / 6.3	19.6 / 5.2	27.6 / 6.3	30.4 / 6.5	31.2 / 5.5	25.7 / 7.0	23.8 / 6.7	28.9 / 6.7	39.0 / 8.6	42.1 / 8.1	34.0 / 9.9	34.3 / 8.8	39.9 / 8.8
HrEd	30.6 / 5.3	17.2 / 6.8	15.3 / 6.1	17.7 / 5.4	25.5 / 6.7	31.6 / 6.4	32.3 / 5.7	23.9 / 7.7	22.2 / 7.3	28.6 / 7.0	39.5 / 8.2	41.8 / 8.1	30.7 / 10.1	32.3 / 9.2	38.1 / 8.9
South Africa															
Yr10 English	23.4 / 6.3	21.8 / 6.5	18.0 / 6.7	26.7 / 5.7	30.7 / 5.6	27.6 / 7.0	30.4 / 6.2	23.4 / 7.7	31.7 / 6.2	32.3 / 6.2	36.1 / 9.8	40.7 / 8.8	31.9 / 10.3	41.2 / 8.6	42.5 / 9.0
Yr12 English	25.4 / 6.3	21.5 / 6.2	17.7 / 6.7	26.0 / 5.8	29.5 / 5.8	27.9 / 7.2	30.9 / 6.4	22.9 / 7.7	31.5 / 6.6	30.9 / 6.5	36.0 / 9.3	41.5 / 8.6	30.7 / 10.6	41.3 / 8.3	41.6 / 8.5
Yr10 Afrikaans	24.9 / 5.6	23.1 / 6.4	20.4 / 6.7	26.1 / 6.1	29.6 / 6.1	28.4 / 6.2	30.6 / 6.0	25.9 / 7.2	32.1 / 6.2	32.2 / 6.0	36.6 / 8.7	41.6 / 8.1	34.8 / 9.6	41.9 / 8.3	43.0 / 7.9
Yr12 Afrikaans	25.7 / 6.0	23.0 / 6.0	20.0 / 6.9	25.6 / 6.0	29.6 / 6.0	28.4 / 6.2	31.6 / 5.9	25.8 / 7.5	32.6 / 6.0	31.8 / 6.2	36.5 / 9.1	42.4 / 8.1	34.2 / 9.9	42.1 / 8.0	42.3 / 8.2
Yr10 African language	29.0 / 7.2	22.9 / 6.8	21.4 / 6.4	26.3 / 6.7	23.9 / 7.1	31.6 / 7.7	27.1 / 7.7	24.9 / 7.1	28.5 / 7.5	24.9 / 7.7	39.4 / 11.2	36.3 / 10.5	33.2 / 9.9	37.2 / 10.1	33.8 / 10.9
Yr12 African language	31.5 / 5.3	22.7 / 6.5	21.6 / 6.7	26.7 / 6.2	23.7 / 6.4	34.3 / 5.6	28.2 / 7.2	26.5 / 6.7	30.2 / 6.4	24.6 / 7.0	42.4 / 9.3	37.9 / 10.1	34.4 / 9.8	38.6 / 9.4	33.2 / 9.8
USA															
SeEd	22.7 / 6.3	25.0 / 6.3	18.0 / 7.1	26.0 / 6.0	30.3 / 6.2	25.5 / 7.4	31.4 / 6.1	22.4 / 8.0	31.6 / 6.8	32.0 / 6.7	35.3 / 10.0	43.3 / 8.2	32.0 / 11.3	42.7 / 8.6	43.8 / 9.0
HrEd	26.6 / 6.1	23.2 / 6.4	17.6 / 6.7	25.5 / 6.0	29.4 / 6.2	29.0 / 6.8	32.2 / 6.1	24.9 / 7.7	34.0 / 6.2	31.9 / 6.2	37.1 / 9.0	43.8 / 7.9	33.8 / 10.8	43.6 / 8.2	42.3 / 8.5
Adult	24.5 / 7.3	30.4 / 5.6	18.2 / 6.7	27.0 / 6.2	25.2 / 6.4	27.7 / 8.0	34.2 / 5.6	23.6 / 7.9	35.0 / 6.1	28.2 / 7.0	35.6 / 10.2	43.7 / 7.8	31.3 / 10.7	43.6 / 8.7	37.6 / 9.7

Appendix B.2. Rotated Factor Structure Matrix of the Salience Measures
(N = 16,730, Principal Components Analysis, Varimax).

Role	Factors				
	F1	*F2*	*F3*	*F4*	*F5*
Participation					
1. Student	−0.064	**0.859**	0.115	0.052	0.014
2. Worker	−0.098	−0.108	0.150	0.225	**0.718**
3. Citizen	−0.054	0.040	**0.889**	0.102	0.021
4. Homemaker	−0.024	0.055	0.182	**0.843**	0.084
5. Leisurite	**0.852**	−0.024	0.029	0.050	0.002
Commitment					
1. Student	−0.056	**0.895**	0.116	0.121	0.109
2. Worker	0.062	0.152	0.021	0.190	**0.867**
3. Citizen	0.000	0.159	**0.901**	0.156	0.082
4. Homemaker	0.059	0.069	0.082	**0.895**	0.190
5. Leisurite	**0.901**	−0.029	−0.007	0.089	0.055
Value Expectations					
1. Student	0.101	**0.855**	0.152	0.061	0.137
2. Worker	0.252	0.270	0.038	0.061	**0.763**
3. Citizen	0.115	0.212	**0.845**	0.104	0.110
4. Homemaker	0.225	0.128	0.099	**0.778**	0.218
5. Leisurite	**0.895**	0.033	0.021	0.063	0.102
Percentage of total variance	16.7	16.5	16.3	15.3	13.4
Percentage of total factor variance	21.4	21.1	20.8	19.5	17.1

Note: The loadings in excess of 0.30 are in boldface.

Appendix B.3. Overall Means (M) and Standard Deviations (SD) of Salience Variables for Secondary Education, Higher Education, and Adult Subjects.

Role	Secondary Education		Higher Education		Adults		Total	
	M	SD	M	SD	M	SD	M	SD
Participation								
1. Student	25.6	6.62	27.9	6.31	23.2	7.49	25.3	7.01
2. Worker	21.1	6.89	21.0	6.95	28.8	6.13	23.3	7.56
3. Citizen	18.3	7.07	17.2	6.94	18.0	7.33	18.0	7.14
4. Homemaker	23.9	6.46	23.2	6.66	26.8	6.71	24.6	6.72
5. Leisurite	29.4	6.46	28.4	6.36	26.1	6.54	28.3	6.62
Commitment								
1. Student	27.9	7.16	29.5	6.64	25.5	7.87	27.5	7.41
2. Worker	29.8	6.61	31.1	6.37	33.0	6.09	30.9	6.57
3. Citizen	23.6	7.84	23.3	8.05	22.0	8.05	23.1	7.97
4. Homemaker	29.1	7.32	30.4	8.13	33.2	7.32	30.5	7.65
5. Leisurite	30.8	6.72	30.5	6.52	28.4	6.94	30.0	6.83
Value Expectations								
1. Student	37.5	9.49	37.9	8.83	33.8	10.62	36.5	9.87
2. Worker	42.1	8.80	43.1	8.02	42.9	8.82	42.5	8.69
3. Citizen	33.0	10.84	32.0	10.98	30.1	11.18	32.0	11.04
4. Homemaker	39.9	9.17	40.8	9.46	43.5	9.26	41.1	9.38
5. Leisurite	41.8	9.01	41.4	8.56	38.9	9.45	40.9	9.15
Number of subjects	16,147		5,173		8,581		29,901	

Appendix B.4. Role Salience Z Scores for Secondary Education (1), Higher Education (2), and Adult (3) Samples in Different Countries.

	Participation					Commitment					Value Expectations				
	Study	Work	Community	Home	Leisure	Study	Work	Community	Home	Leisure	Study	Work	Community	Home	Leisure
A1	-0.10	0.05	-0.24	0.03	0.28	-0.06	0.09	-0.21	0.16	0.29	-0.08	0.09	-0.11	0.16	0.18
A2	0.00	0.02	-0.11	0.12	0.14	0.05	-0.24	0.04	0.18	0.19	-0.14	-0.28	0.00	-0.08	-0.11
A3	0.29	0.24	0.07	0.14	0.32	0.01	0.05	0.05	0.20	0.20	0.04	0.03	0.13	0.07	0.13
B1	-0.21	-0.68	-0.04	-0.33	-0.14	-0.17	-0.27	-0.03	0.09	-0.05	-0.27	-0.15	-0.14	-0.04	-0.12
B2	0.15	-0.34	0.26	-0.11	-0.19	0.17	-0.08	0.19	0.00	-0.17	-0.14	-0.19	-0.05	-0.07	-0.25
B3	-0.52	-0.66	-0.12	0.00	-0.27	-0.50	-0.32	-0.13	0.09	-0.23	-0.71	-0.47	-0.28	-0.11	-0.37
CE1	-0.53	0.66	-0.11	0.31	0.28	-0.48	0.43	-0.27	0.29	0.15	-0.32	0.39	-0.18	0.36	0.28
CE2	0.15	0.70	0.02	0.51	0.00	0.11	0.55	0.09	0.65	0.07	0.26	0.55	0.23	0.63	0.19
CE3	0.14	0.14	0.17	0.45	0.22	0.09	0.32	0.20	0.50	0.09	0.17	0.31	0.21	0.50	0.23
CF1	0.18	0.51	0.09	-0.10	0.08	0.15	0.24	-0.06	-0.28	0.01	0.35	0.33	0.08	-0.09	0.24
CF3	0.10	0.08	-0.05	-0.16	0.12	0.10	0.14	-0.13	-0.51	0.00	0.29	0.43	0.09	-0.04	0.26
CR1	0.08	-0.10	0.21	-0.02	0.15	-0.11	-0.20	0.06	-0.12	0.26	0.13	-0.15	0.06	0.00	0.07
CR2	0.43	-0.44	-0.07	-0.18	0.25	0.11	-0.17	-0.26	-0.33	0.35	0.12	0.00	-0.23	-0.24	0.45
CR3	-0.26	0.29	0.29	0.05	0.08	-0.05	0.22	0.14	-0.05	0.20	0.03	0.05	0.03	-0.09	0.12
IT1	0.44	-0.31	0.09	-0.16	0.08	0.16	0.08	-0.01	0.01	-0.03	0.34	0.49	0.34	0.27	0.35
IT2	0.42	-0.02	0.25	-0.17	0.00	0.23	0.16	-0.05	-0.12	-0.19	0.40	0.49	0.23	0.21	0.32
J1	-0.95	-1.04	-0.65	-0.81	0.01	-0.77	-1.38	-0.59	-0.94	-0.14	-0.85	-1.03	-0.62	-1.04	-0.65
J2	-0.93	-0.29	-0.27	-0.45	0.30	-0.65	-0.85	-0.27	-0.62	0.01	-0.58	-0.72	-0.31	-0.60	-0.52
J3	-0.36	-0.56	-0.37	-0.46	-0.01	-0.23	-0.75	-0.36	-0.74	-0.14	-0.41	-0.81	-0.39	-0.74	-0.42
P1	0.47	-0.44	-0.15	-0.62	-0.17	0.35	0.18	0.34	-0.66	-0.21	0.28	0.08	0.22	-0.53	-0.10
P2	0.45	-0.34	-0.28	-0.70	-0.39	0.36	0.42	0.18	-0.83	-0.17	0.27	0.06	0.03	-0.70	-0.25
PL2	-0.52	0.14	0.10	0.49	-0.39	-0.39	-0.27	-0.23	0.38	-0.46	-0.23	-0.31	-0.23	0.29	-0.14
SAA1	0.08	0.35	0.34	0.38	0.03	0.18	0.32	0.40	0.50	0.21	0.00	0.08	0.24	0.31	0.15
SAE1	-0.06	0.15	0.02	0.45	0.09	0.09	0.27	0.06	0.40	0.13	-0.02	0.01	-0.04	0.25	0.09
SAN1	0.89	0.37	0.55	0.54	-0.82	0.88	-0.13	0.43	0.13	-0.84	0.60	-0.34	0.27	-0.01	-0.75
US1	-0.31	0.47	-0.10	0.32	0.14	-0.23	0.36	-0.11	0.43	0.22	-0.17	0.20	-0.13	0.36	0.25
US2	-0.14	0.57	0.07	0.51	0.28	0.02	0.49	0.32	0.69	0.38	0.05	0.41	0.34	0.57	0.31
US3	0.61	0.48	0.02	-0.01	-0.46	0.59	0.35	0.23	0.50	-0.12	0.59	0.47	0.21	0.41	0.05

Note: For abbreviations of countries, see Appendix A.4.

Appendix B.5. Mean Factor Scores (Hierarchies of Samples) for Role Salience.

Rank	Student		Worker		Citizen		Homemaker		Leisurite	
1.	P2	0.69	US3	1.04	SAN1	0.33	CE3	0.77	A1	0.31
2.	SAN1	0.66	CF3	0.93	SAA1	0.25	US3	0.49	IT1	0.27
3.	IT2	0.59	CR3	0.85	P1	0.11	B3	0.43	CE1	0.24
4.	CR2	0.53	CE3	0.79	CR1	0.10	US2	0.40	CR2	0.24
5.	P1	0.40	A3	0.64	IT1	0.02	CE2	0.40	CR1	0.23
6.	IT1	0.31	CE1	0.53	CF1	-0.01	A3	0.39	US1	0.20
7.	B2	0.28	CE2	0.44	CR3	-0.04	PL2	0.38	CF1	0.13
8.	CE2	0.26	CF1	0.37	US2	-0.06	SAE1	0.29	SAA1	0.10
9.	A2	0.15	US1	0.30	B2	-0.08	SAA1	0.26	US2	0.10
10.	CF1	0.08	US2	0.29	SAE1	-0.10	US1	0.26	SAE1	0.09
11.	US2	0.04	B3	0.13	B1	-0.11	CE1	0.17	B1	0.01
12.	US3	0.02	SAA1	0.10	IT2	-0.13	CR3	0.16	P1	-0.06
13.	CR1	-0.10	P2	0.07	CE3	-0.14	SAN1	0.14	IT2	-0.08
14.	SAA1	-0.14	IT2	0.05	A3	-0.19	A1	-0.03	J1	-0.11
15.	SAE1	-0.17	SAE1	-0.01	P2	-0.21	A2	-0.09	A2	-0.13
16.	A1	-0.20	A1	-0.03	US1	-0.22	CF3	-0.18	CE2	-0.16
17.	PL2	-0.25	IT1	-0.04	CE2	-0.24	B1	-0.21	J2	-0.20
18.	B1	-0.26	P1	-0.07	A2	-0.25	CR1	-0.23	B2	-0.39
19.	CF3	-0.45	J3	-0.09	US3	-0.25	IT1	-0.26	P2	-0.41
20.	US1	-0.47	SAN1	-0.31	CE1	-0.26	B2	-0.30	A3	-0.46
21.	CE3	-0.58	CR1	-0.34	A1	-0.29	J3	-0.34	CF3	-0.47
22.	J2	-0.50	PL2	-0.38	CF3	-0.29	IT2	-0.44	CE3	-0.48
23.	A3	-0.60	B2	-0.43	J2	-0.31	CF1	-0.49	CR3	-0.54
24.	CE1	-0.72	A2	-0.44	PL2	-0.35	CR2	-0.59	PL2	-0.58
25.	J1	-0.86	CR2	-0.46	B3	-0.37	J2	-0.79	J3	-0.84
26.	CR3	-0.89	B1	-0.52	J1	-0.54	J1	-0.96	US3	-0.88
27.	J3	-0.99	J2	-0.78	CR2	-0.44	P1	-1.02	B3	-0.96
28.	B3	-1.34	J1	-1.34	J3	-0.50	P2	-1.32	SAN1	-0.96

Note: For abbreviations of countries, see note in Appendix A.4.

Name Index

Subject Index

Printed in the United Kingdom
by Lightning Source UK Ltd.
132689UK00001B/31-32/A